Frieda Lawrence

She is the daughter of Baron von Richthofen, of the ancient and famous house of Richthofen—but she's splendid, she is really. I'll bet you've never met anybody like her, by a long chalk. Oh, but she is the woman of a lifetime.

D. H. Lawrence to Edward Garnett
17 April 1912

Frieda Lawrence

The Story of Frieda von Richthofen and D. H. Lawrence

ROBERT LUCAS, 1904-

Translated from the German by
GEOFFREY SKELTON

Secker & Warburg · London

First published in England 1973 by
Martin Secker & Warburg Limited
14 Carlisle Street, London W1V 6NN

SBN: 436 26910 4

Printed in Great Britain by
Richard Clay (The Chaucer Press) Ltd,
Bungay, Suffolk

To John and David with love

List of Illustrations

Acknowledgments

The author and publishers are grateful to the following for permission to reproduce the illustrations in
this book: Mrs Barbara Barr (3, 4, 6), Dr Marianne
von Eckardt (1), Mr David Garnett (13), Dr Else
Jaffe (7), Tenente Colonnello Angelo Ravagli (21),
Dr Keith Sagar (12, 17, 19, 20, 22, 24), Mr C.
Montague Weekley (2, 5, 8, 9, 10), Camera Press Ltd
(23), and Radio Times Hulton Picture Library (11, 14,
15, 16, 18).

Preface

There may be difficulties in describing the life of Frieda von Richthofen, but lack of material is not one of them. D. H. Lawrence's letters—a source of endless fascination—are strewn with illuminating references to her, usually precise down to the smallest detail. There are her own letters and memoirs—and what a mine of information they are, despite their scrappiness and despite Frieda's disconcerting habit of changing names and camouflaging facts. Lawrence's numerous friends were sufficiently impressed (perhaps not always favourably) to write about her not merely as his wife, but as a very remarkable woman in her own right. Those who are still alive recall her in almost dramatic terms. In a dozen guises, but always recognisable, Frieda continues to live in D.H.L.'s books, and the many facets of her personality are clearly discernible as components of characters his imagination created.

It has been estimated that the biographies, critical studies, psychological analyses, essays and theses dealing in the past twenty-five years with various aspects of Lawrence's life and work, together with the reissues of his books, rival in bulk the Shakespearian literature published during the same period. Inevitably Frieda plays a prominent part in these, and equally inevitably I must repeat much that has been told before, otherwise the story would not be complete. Besides, how could one write about Frieda's life without sketching Lorenzo's?

Thus I am happy to acknowledge my indebtedness to the research done by others. In particular, I wish to pay tribute to Professor Harry T. Moore, Professor E. W. Tedlock and the late Edward Nehls. Like every other author venturing into this territory, I have made copious use of their various works.

Above all, however, my thanks are due to those members of Frieda's family who have given me so much patient help and friendly encouragement in carrying out my researches and writing this book. I owe many valuable hints and pieces of information, here published for the first time, to Mrs Barbara Barr, Mr C. Montague Weekley, Dr Else Jaffe, Dr Marianne von Eckardt and Tenente Colonnello Angelo Ravagli who all, furthermore, kindly allowed me to include in this book photographs in their possession, many of them so far unpublished. Mr Laurence Pollinger has been my trusty guide and counsellor, proving once again how richly he deserved the confidence that Frieda herself placed in him and so warmly expressed.

It would be impossible to thank individually the many others who have helped me with their knowledge and advice, but I am particularly indebted to the following: Professor Dr Bolko Freiherr von Richthofen, Oswald Freiherr von Richthofen, at present German Ambassador in Singapore, Mrs Mary Middleton Murry, Miss Lucy I. Edwards of the City of Nottingham Central Library, which possesses an outstanding collection of material on D. H. Lawrence, Frau Mathilde Heizmann of the Stadtbücherei in Baden-Baden, Mrs Nancy Christoff and Mrs M. E. Welch of the BBC External Services Reference Library, Fräulein Inge Niemöller of the Library of the German Institute in London, and Mr R. Howard Brandenburg, Taos. Dr Keith Sagar, himself an authority on D. H. Lawrence, has very kindly placed a number of photos from his collection at my disposal.

Mr Laurence Pollinger, on behalf of the D. H. Lawrence and Frieda Lawrence Estates, has kindly allowed me to make use of passages from their writings. For permission to include other copyright material I am equally grateful to the authors and publishers listed in the bibliography at the end of this book.

Last but not least, I owe a great debt of gratitude to Geoffrey Skelton, who not only translated my book from the original German but also contributed many valuable suggestions.

Robert Lucas
Kingston Hill
Summer 1972

"One does not want to speak disrespectfully of the dead ..."

The voice of prosecuting counsel, as he spoke these words, became all at once cool and factual. If he was about to cast aspersions on the life of a man whom many (though not, it appeared, prosecuting counsel himself) considered to be one of the great figures of English literature, nobody should be allowed to think him lacking in deference. Mervyn Griffith-Jones, Attorney-General in Her Majesty's Government, would never in the heat of cross-examination forget the consideration due to the dead, nor, as one of Britain's foremost lawyers, had he any need to resort to cheap rhetoric. If his remarks seemed sometimes pompous or his sarcasm excessive, it was because he felt very strongly about the issue at stake. He feared that, if he were to lose this case, the social fabric of the British Isles might be irretrievably damaged. The effects might even be felt beyond Britain's shores, for moral climates can no more be contained than storm winds or sunshine. Could not the warning signals already be seen in the United States, where the flood of pornographic publications was rising alarmingly since the Federal Court had decided that *Lady Chatterley's Lover* was *not* obscene.

It was this very book that was once more on trial, this time at London's Central Criminal Court in Old Bailey. "*Lady Chatterley's Lover*," counsel declared, "sets on a pedestal promiscuous intercourse, commends sensuality almost as a virtue, and encourages and even advocates coarseness and vulgarity of thought and language."

The members of the jury, nine men and three women, sat in their narrow dark-oak box above the crowded press benches, listening to the proceedings with grim concentration. They were the thermometer with which the moral temperature of that elusive phenomenon called public opinion was to be measured.

Griffith-Jones took up a copy of the book to read out passages in which D. H. Lawrence had sought to capture the tenderness of secret caresses, the warmth of passionate embraces, all the mystery of a physical union between two human beings. His face with its sharp profile, the high forehead cut in half by the wig perched on his head, was completely expressionless, and words which once had bloomed and glowed dropped flat and lifeless from his lips. He turned the pages to read other passages containing those famous four-letter words which, in his submission, were proof of the book's coarseness and depravity. They were words with which all the members of the jury, all the men and women in the court's little public gallery, had been familiar since childhood; they could be heard every day in every pub throughout the kingdom. In this brown panelled courtroom, among the barristers with their black gowns and grey wigs, they took on a neutral, clinical quality. The huge lustreless glass roof did not fall in; the decorated white columns supporting it did not tremble under the shock.

The members of the jury had already read the book, singly, in the communal privacy of the locked jury room. D. H. Lawrence's attempt to express the inexpressible had been—for them—obligatory reading. Defending counsel was Gerald Gardiner, Lord Chancellor in a later Labour government, and he spoke with just as much passionate conviction as prosecuting counsel. Who, he asked, on reading the novel, could fail to recognise that Lawrence, the puritanic moralist, condemned sex without love? If the novel devoted a lot of space to descriptions of sexual acts, this was because the author felt deeply that society was too little concerned with the implications of physical union between a man and a woman—the normal, healthy sort of love that is part of a permanent, and not a promiscuous relationship. Was it really the business of the state to treat adult people as if they were children, to be kept under strict supervision?

A long procession of witnesses—church dignitaries, university professors, teachers, psychologists, historians, novelists—was called to speak in the novel's defence: seldom have so many famous people ever appeared together in one courtroom. Here is a sample of the cross-examination to which one of them, Joan Bennett, a lecturer in English at Cambridge and a rather excitable witness, was subjected by the prosecution:

PROSECUTING COUNSEL: The chief character in his book, who happens to be a married woman, is depicted throughout the book as going and having sexual intercourse. It may be satisfactory, it may be unsatisfactory, it may be that she is in love, it may be that she is not in love, but the fact remains she is depicted throughout the book as going off and having sexual intercourse with somebody other than her husband. That is the fact, is it not?

WITNESS: But the question, of course, that is of interest—

COUNSEL: Would you answer my question first? He [the author] shows the woman breaking it [lawful wedlock] without any conditions at all, without ever telling her husband, does he not?

WITNESS: Yes.

COUNSEL: And indeed one does not want to speak disrespectfully of the dead, but if one is talking about what the author's views were and what he was endeavouring to show, that is in fact, is it not, exactly what he himself had done? He had run off with his friend's wife, had he not?

WITNESS: Yes.

COUNSEL: And married her.

WITNESS: Yes.

COUNSEL: And it is just that type of behaviour, is it not, that is depicted in this book? ... The whole book is about that subject, is it not?

WITNESS: Yes.

At the time this trial—with its truly unforeseeable consequences—took place in October 1960, something like eight hundred books dealing with the life and work of David Herbert Lawrence, the author of *Lady Chatterley's Lover*, had been published. Today the number is probably nearer a thousand, among them biographies, critical analyses of his writings and annotated editions of his letters. No other writer of this century has been so thoroughly described, dissected, analysed, interpreted, praised and denounced by so many literary critics, sociologists and psychologists as D. H. Lawrence. Yet, curiously enough, there has not been one single biography of the woman with whom he had "run off", who became his wife and provided the model for that famous and much maligned character, Lady Chatterley. Again and again we meet her in his novels: she is Ursula Brangwen in *Women in Love*, Tanny Lilly in *Aaron's Rod*, Harriet Somers in *Kangaroo*, Kate Leslie in *The Plumed Serpent*. Possibly never before nor since has a great writer been so intensely and so permanently influenced by one woman as Lawrence was by Frieda von Richthofen. The greater part of his work is a continuous dialogue with Frieda, sometimes loving, sometimes full of hate. And certainly never before has one single woman, as interpreted by a poet, so radically changed the moral climate of her time.

2

It would be going too far to describe the barons von Richthofen as peers of an ancient lineage.[1] To find the family's origins we must go back to a certain Paul Schultheiss, who was born in 1521 in Bernau, near Berlin. Little is known of him beyond the fact that he was a Lutheran and that, being ambitious and (we may suppose) of considerable intelligence, he worked himself up to a position of some influence. His rise is reflected in his twofold change of name. At first, as a poor scholar, he followed the fashion of his time in latinising the commoner's name with which he was born. But when, many years later, he became political and legal adviser to the margraves Friedrich and Sigismund, the name Scultetus no longer suited either his ambition or his position, and so he changed it to Paulus Praetorius. He had every reason to look back with pride on his career. He held the title of *Geheimer Rat* (privy counsellor), possessed an imperial coat of arms* and was the owner of three considerable estates. He lacked nothing except a son to carry on his name and inherit his heraldic glory.

A year after his rise in the social scale he adopted Samuel Schmidt, the nineteen-year-old son of a deceased friend and Lutheran disciple. The young man brought honour to his new name, becoming in time mayor of the town of Frankfurt an der Oder in the province of Brandenburg. One might have expected so signal a recognition to have cemented the family's bonds to Brandenburg, but Samuel's son, Tobias Praetorius, rather surprisingly chose to move to the province of Silesia, and to transfer his allegiance to the King of Bohemia. There he became involved in the Thirty Years War and the Wallenstein conspiracy. But at last, after a long series of catastrophes, the family's fortune turned again. In 1661 Tobias's eldest son Johann was raised to the Bohemian knighthood and took the name of Praetorius von

---

* The Richthofen coat of arms shows, on a field of gold, a black-robed praetor (judge) sitting on a red chair and holding in his right hand a golden sceptre with an eagle.

Richthofen. Johann was Frieda's great-great-great-great-grandfather.

No one can claim that the Richthofen family, branching out in several directions, brought forth many remarkable men. There were some excellent farmers, certainly, a few eccentrics and a large number of distinguished Prussian civil servants. A few—a very few—went into the army. But as for great personalities there was none before Ferdinand von Richthofen, an explorer who, after Alexander von Humboldt, might be regarded as the founder of the German school of geography.[2] In the years between 1860 and 1872 this extraordinary man travelled through Ceylon and Japan, Formosa and the Philippines, Celebes and Java, Siam and India—no mean feat at a time when these countries had not yet been put on the tourist map with the help of Boeing jets, Hilton hotels and motorways. He was seven times in China, at that time an all but inaccessible country, and explored thirteen of the eighteen central provinces, observing and carefully recording his geological researches, with only one other man for company: his Belgian factotum and interpreter Paul Splingaert. Splingaert, on the run from the police on suspicion of murder, repaid Richthofen's trust with touching loyalty. He eventually married a Chinese girl and became a high mandarin. Ferdinand von Richthofen himself, after his return from China, took on a long succession of teaching posts and corresponded busily with his friend and pupil Sven Hedin. He died, much honoured and respected, in 1905.

Several members of the family entered the diplomatic service, thus establishing a tradition that has persisted right up to this day. One of them was Oswald von Richthofen, who succeeded von Bülow as State Secretary of the Foreign Ministry. In her early years Frieda spent a few happy winter months in Berlin as his guest. But most members of the Richthofen family lived on their estates in the country, far away from the big cities.

The main Richthofen territory was in Silesia. The family possessions lay widely scattered in the triangle of land (bounded by the rivers Oder and Neisse and the Sudeten mountains) which was colonised by German settlers in the twelfth century, and is now part of Poland. When the main town was still called Breslau the barons von Richthofen farmed no less than twenty thousand acres of fertile soil on the Neumarkt plateau to the west and south of the city, in addition to all their other estates.[3] Many of them were Catholics, though the great majority were Protestants. However, their religious convictions, inherited from generation to generation, were not rigid enough to impair family concord. Once every six years the male members of the Richthofen clan gathered together for their *Familientag*, and their celebrations included those traditional pastimes of the junkers: boar- and stag-hunting in the Riesengebirge and Carpathians, salmon-fishing in the Oder.

As far as the eye could reach across the flat or lightly undulating land, there lay the Richthofen estates, the rich, dark, humus-laden soil hidden beneath golden fields of wheat and barley or grey-green steppes of sugar beet. Silesia was the home of the sugar beet. As early as 1747 the Berlin scientist Marggraf had discovered that certain types of beet contained as much sugar as the canes of the West Indies, which at that time supplied the whole world market. But it was not until Napoleon's Continental System forced the price of sugar up to fantastic heights that the production of sugar from beet became economical. Marggraf's pupil Franz Karl Achard built the world's first sugar-beet factory in 1802. Situated in the Silesian district of Wohlau, it looked more like a large wash-house than an industrial factory. Encouraged by his example, many landowners hastened to cash in on the boom, and within a few years the industry had spread far beyond the bounds of Silesia.

But with the abolition of the Continental System the new-found prosperity came to a sudden end. Sugar from the colonies could once more be brought to Europe in British ships and, since it was so very much cheaper, it soon regained its old markets. The sugar factories were forced to close down, and the Silesian squires found themselves feeding their sugar beet to the pigs. It was not until the late thirties of the nineteenth century that the beet came back into its own, when careful seed selection and improved factory methods enabled Silesia to become one of the most important sugar-producing territories in the whole world.

However, Frieda's ancestors had no share in this new rise to prosperity. Her great-grandfather, Ludwig Praetorius von Richthofen, inherited the family property in an already run-down state, and he was too much harassed by Napoleon's wars and his own conjugal troubles to do more than barely keep his head above water. Four years after his first marriage his young bride had to surrender her place in the marital bed to a more mature Frenchwoman, and only a few years later the baron, an optimist to the end, married for a third time. As far as his business enterprises were concerned, his exuberance was to prove his undoing. He was one of the Silesian landowners who, inspired by Achard's visions and his own hopes of a quick profit, staked everything on sugar beet. When, with the end of the Continental System, the dream dissolved, he found himself drowning in a flood of beetroots and debts. Later speculations in which he indulged, along with his son Johann Ludwig, proved equally unprofitable. Even the elements seemed to conspire against the family: during a thunderstorm a whole flock of sheep was lost when lightning struck the pen.

Johann Ludwig married Amalie Luise von Laszowska, the daughter of an aristocratic German–Polish family.[4] In the summer of 1845, at the small Rashowa estate in Upper Silesia, she gave birth to a son. This was Friedrich von Richthofen, Frieda's father.

Although one of its members was to become the greatest fighter pilot of the First World War, the Richthofen family had no military leanings. It was thus surprising that Friedrich should have chosen, before he was even seventeen, the profession of a soldier. But conditions at home were far from good. His mother was dead, and his father, now in his sixties, had been speculating unwisely. He was forced to sell his lands and spend his remaining years at the home of his daughter and her landowner husband.

Thus nothing now stood in the way of young Friedrich following his own bent and joining a regiment of engineers. The year 1862, in which he donned his cadet's uniform for the first time, was a significant date in military history. In the elections of that year the conservatives, who were in favour of extending military service and increasing the army's budget, suffered a catastrophic defeat. Wilhelm I—himself an ardent admirer of all things military—had already been drastically reorganising his army behind the back of his elected parliament, and now he appointed a new minister-president to bring the rebellious members to heel. This was Bismarck. If parliament had emerged victorious from this struggle with the crown, world history might have taken a different course. But Bismarck ensured that this did not happen. "Blood and iron" was the new order of the day.

Bismarck's policies gave the army plenty to do, and Friedrich von Richthofen was every inch a soldier. We can be sure that he conducted himself with courage. After his death Frieda discovered the diary which he kept during the Franco-Prussian War of 1870–71. The entries provide a fascinating picture of an officer's everyday life during the campaign which culminated in the capture of Strasbourg: an endless succession of gun-fights and skirmishes; day-long marches through rain and snow; billets in country inns and farmhouses; drinking parties, ending often enough in violent quarrels; encounters with refugees;

7

band concerts in conquered towns; duels among the officers, suicides and funerals. The diary shows Friedrich to have been a typical Prussian officer of that era. To settle a quarrel with an artillery officer he resorted quite naturally to his sabre. After a whist party in his quarters, at which he and his comrades—and obviously his batman Heinrich too—took heavy toll of the grog, he wrote in his diary the laconic sentence: "Heinrich drunk; I beat him."

On New Year's Day the entries came to an abrupt end. Friedrich had been wounded and taken prisoner.

On the larger stage of history the tragedy of France continued to be played through to the last. One month after the fall of Strasbourg, its strongest bastion, Metz, the second strongest, also capitulated.

Friedrich von Richthofen's captivity was short, but the wounds he had received in battle crippled his right hand and put an end to his military career. He was discharged with the rank of lieutenant and an Iron Cross.

There are many indications that he never quite recovered from the shock. Being a man of courage, he must have reckoned with an early death, but not with the early termination of his army career. The injury to his hand soon healed, the wound in his heart never.

He was only twenty-five years old, and his life still lay before him— even if it was not to be the life he had dreamed of. His father was now seventy, and there was clearly nothing in Silesia that could tempt Friedrich to return there. Those territories in the west that had been snatched from France offered better opportunities for a brave German officer wounded in the service of his fatherland and Bismarck's power politics. Shortly after this dramatic turn in his destiny the young Baron Friedrich was comfortably settled in Metz, a member of the civil administration now governing the new German district of Lothringen. He was also married. His bride, Anna, was the daughter of a lawyer from Donaueschingen. Her maiden name, Marquier, reveals her French extraction. Her ancestors, fleeing from the terror of the French Revolution, had, it was said, entered Germany concealed in a haycart and found asylum in the Black Forest.

3

Frieda—or, to give her full name, Emma Maria Frieda Johanna Freiin von Richthofen—was born in Metz on 11 August 1879, nearly five years after her sister Else and three years before Johanna, the youngest. Frieda, as she herself later wrote,* was "a wild, sunburnt child with straw-coloured hair standing out from her head and scratched knees from climbing trees and falling into ditches too wide for her to jump."[1] Of the three sisters the dark-haired Nusch (as Johanna was called within the family) was the prettiest, and was in fact to grow into an outstanding beauty. When grown-ups called at the house, they usually began by remarking what a charming child Johanna was. Frieda stood nearby making faces. The visitors then looked at her—and said nothing. Frieda would respond by making even fiercer faces, and Nusch would begin to giggle. Mama would then decide that the time had come to send the "insufferable brats" out of the room.

They lived in a pleasant house in Sablon,† a suburb of Metz which at that time was still rural. Many years later, high up in the mountains of New Mexico, Frieda often found her lonely thoughts travelling back to the place of her childhood. It was all indelibly impressed on her memory: the old wistaria draping its leafy branches around the front door of her parents' house; her father's study with its huge writing-desk, on which lay, in strict symmetrical order, a seal and a letterweight, a small meteorite and an onyx ashtray. The shotguns on the wall, the boars' and stags' heads revealed that the baron, like his cousins on their estates in Silesia, was a passionate sportsman.

At Christmastime the shed at the back was always filled with the pungent scent of the game he had killed. On the floor lay a wild boar with massive tusks, from the beams hung partridges and hares. A smell of honey and spices came from the kitchen, heralding the approach of the festive season, and the larder was full of sausages and smoked

* This quotation and all subsequent extracts from Frieda's memoirs have been left in the original, if somewhat idiosyncratic English.
† Route d'Augny 205.

9

hams. When at long last Christmas Eve came, the girls in their new white dresses would be in their own room, impatiently awaiting the eight flaxen-haired children who belonged to Frau Seidel, their washerwoman. On a table covered with a white cloth stood a small lighted Christmas tree, and beneath it the presents for which Else, Frieda and Nusch had been saving up their pocket-money for months. At a given sign the Seidel children would come shyly in, to sing "Ihr Kinderlein kommet" and receive their gifts.

It was only afterwards that the real family celebrations began. Summoned by the silver dinner-bell, they would all gather in front of the brown-gold doors of the drawing-room, into which for days past mysterious parcels had been seen disappearing. Now the doors were flung open, revealing a Christmas tree gleaming in the light of innumerable candles. Frieda recited a short poem and then the girls rushed to the tables on which the presents lay piled up: dolls and books and toys that exceeded even the wildest of hopes.

Friends of the family came too—Baron K. and Doctor A. and Baron P., all loaded with gifts—and now the meal could begin. Wilhelm, the manservant, to whom the children could safely confide all their deepest secrets, served—in white gloves, of course. Even in summer, when lunch was taken under the cherry trees in the garden, Wilhelm always served in white gloves.

The baron set great store by style. He himself was always faultlessly dressed, from his highly polished shoes to his snow-white handkerchief with a coronet in one corner. It was a gesture not only to his aristocratic birth, but also to his official position. Like thousands of other Prussian officials, he regarded the swift rise of the new German Reich to world-power status as a personal triumph which obliged him to adopt an attitude of superiority. There was also another reason why he wished ostentatiously to stress the importance of his position, both to himself and to others: he was part of the administrative machinery of a conquered territory, whose inhabitants accepted their new overlords only under protest.

He had the advantage of speaking French fluently—indeed, if we can accept Frieda's own testimony, like a native. Some of his hunting companions were members of the aristocracy of Lorraine. "One of his friends," Frieda tells us, "was a Vicomte L.—who was also a writer and had one of those charming small chateaux in Lorraine. Many actors came to stay with him. Among them Sarah Bernhardt." Speaking of herself in the third person, as she does in her memoirs, Frieda goes on:

"Her father had returned from one of the shooting expeditions with the Vicomte ... From his visit her father was full of stories of Sarah: how she had given the village hairdresser a priceless ring because she liked the way he had done her hair." Frieda begged her father to take her with him: she too would like to meet Sarah Bernhardt. But Papa would not hear of it. Actresses belong to the *demi-monde*, he said, but his daughters were ladies.

In the baron's personal hierarchy—as in that of millions of his German contemporaries—the highest place was occupied by the military. His former regiment was stationed in Metz, and the officers, who knew his story, treated him with respect. Once, while celebrating the Kaiser's birthday, Richthofen's regimental comrades staged a dramatic scene in which they re-enacted the circumstances in which he had won his Iron Cross in 1870. The scene ended with them carrying him in triumph on their shoulders around the room—a hero's reception which filled his young daughters with understandable pride.

A photograph of the period shows him to have been a good-looking man with piercing eyes, thin lips half-hidden by a bushy moustache, a somewhat bristly beard combed forward and thick hair carefully parted above a clear forehead. But the masterful exterior concealed an inner lack of authority. What it was that had caused the loss of his self-confidence we can only attempt to guess. It was perhaps the feeling of having been uprooted not only once, but twice: his father's financial failure had deprived him of his birthright, and his career as an officer had been abruptly ended. Strangers might be taken in by his self-assertive manner, but his own wife had long seen through him. She knew the full extent of his inner uncertainty. The children became instinctively aware of his weakness long before violent scenes and a growing coldness between their parents betrayed secrets that could no longer be kept hidden in the family circle.

He was a gambler. Some sketches by Frieda, discovered after her death, contain certain reminiscences which, in spite of their fictional touches, are undoubtedly based on fact. One evening Friedrich von Richthofen did not return home. His wife stayed up all night awaiting him, and then, worry overcoming her reluctance to lay bare her humiliation before the servants, she sent Wilhelm into town to seek him. Two hours later the baron appeared, pale and weary, a picture of misery. He followed her, "a thing without a will", into the bedroom. There she dragged from him the admission that he had spent the night gambling in the officers' mess and had lost several thousand marks. He begged her to allow him to take out a mortgage on the house, in order to pay his debts. Frieda continues (anglicising her parents' names and inventing a new one for her elder sister Else): "From that day, Anne and Frederick hated each other, nothing but convention and the children kept them tied together ... The children vaguely felt the atmosphere of strife without understanding ... Especially in the sensitive Sybil the parents' war broke something that never healed in later life."[1]

For the warmth and tenderness that his wife no longer gave him the baron turned to his three daughters, on whom he lavished unstinted love. If others, unaware of his inner weakness, saw him as a typical autocrat, the three girls knew him as an indulgent and generous father, always ready to fulfil their fondest desires.

"I don't mind whom my daughters marry," he once said to them, though he immediately added the proviso: "as long as they don't marry a Jew, an Englishman or"—and at this point his warning assumed a tragic overtone—"a gambler."[2]

The remarkable thing is that this is exactly what subsequently happened. Else married a Jewish university professor, who in 1918 helped to depose the Wittelsbach dynasty in Bavaria; Frieda became the wife of a correct Englishman, a respected professor of modern languages; Johanna, the youngest, married a gambler. And all three marriages ended unhappily.

Being girls, they preferred their father's impulsive and highly strung masculinity to the more settled temperament of their mother. Anna seems to have inherited something of the affable fussiness of the little town in the Black Forest in which she was brought up. She loved to talk about her childhood, about the mailcoach that drove up every evening at nine o'clock, heralded by the postilion's horn. Then all the inhabitants would rush out, armed with lanterns, to collect letters, parcels and newspapers. She recalled the grocery store, the only one in the town, where the children would be given dried prunes, liquorice sticks and home-made sweets; and Joshua, the Jewish peddler, who called twice a year with a load of dress materials and was Donaueschingen's only link with the world of fashion outside; and sleigh rides to the hunting lodges of Prince Fürstenberg, who had his residence in the town.

But, whatever their relationship with their parents, the three girls were devoted to each other. Frieda and Nusch shared a bedroom, and every evening before bed there would be great goings-on, with pillow-fights and highly dramatic renderings of scenes from *Macbeth* or

Schiller's *Die Räuber*. Else was the most intelligent of the three, and the younger sisters' respect for her intellectual superiority persisted throughout their lives. But of course this did not prevent Frieda and Nusch from teasing her for her studiousness. As Frieda later wrote: "Home was barren. Only in school she lived." From her early years Else suffered from a social conscience, deploring the injustice that gave Frau Seidel, the washerwoman with eight children, no share in the pleasant things of life which were accepted by the Richthofen family as theirs by right. It had been Else's idea, only grudgingly adopted by her two sisters, that they should put aside a part of their pocket-money to buy Christmas presents for the Seidel children.

Frieda, the tomboy, and Johanna, for whom Else felt an elder-sisterly responsibility, were sent to a Roman Catholic convent school, although all the members of their family were Protestant. From this school, partly German and partly French, Frieda brought home good reports, but complaints about her unruly behaviour showed that she did not make life easy for the worthy nuns.

Metz, during Frieda's childhood, was a predominantly German town. Its French inhabitants were still weighed down with memories of the traumatic happenings of 1870, when, in its narrow confines between the Moselle and Seille rivers, the town had been besieged and its normal population increased fivefold by an influx of French troops and refugees. The capitulation of the besieged fortress—a shattering combination of scandal and catastrophe—followed by the humiliating entry of the Prussian victors, and the departure of 173,000 French soldiers to German prison camps, were experiences which, even after ten or twenty years, still filled French hearts with bitterness and shame.

But now, in Frieda's growing years, the French population of a city that had belonged to France for three centuries constituted only a minority. In the two years following the German conquest, no less than one in four moved across the new border into France. The vacated houses and apartments in the narrow crooked streets of the old town and in the outer residential districts were taken over by new arrivals from the German Reich. They included military officers and administrative officials of all sorts, tradesmen out to establish new business connections, and more than a few shady characters in search of a quick profit in the conquered territories. The huge forts which Napoleon III had reinforced were given German names, extended, and new bastions were added. The military had persuaded Bismarck that the retention and further fortification of both Metz and Strasbourg were vital to the nation's defence in the war which was soon to be unleashed by their insatiable lust for power.

As Germany's military power grew, the strength of the garrison in Metz increased with it.[3] In the first years of occupation it had comprised 10,000 officers and men. By 1905 their number had risen to 25,000—and that in a town of only 35,000 civilian inhabitants, most of them now German. It was small wonder that the few French-speaking citizens who had remained felt themselves squeezed into a corner. But many of the German-speaking Lorrainers were also embittered. Maybe it had now become rare for German pedestrians to be attacked in the streets by night, as had happened in the immediate post-war years, but hostile looks, flashes of temper and disorderly scenes in the council chamber were evidence enough that among the people of Lorraine resentment still smouldered.

Frieda saw nothing of the hatred beneath the smooth and orderly surface of affairs. Though, with a few short breaks, she spent all her life up to the age of twenty in Metz, and though her father's position placed him at the centre of many conflicts, both large and small, she never showed any awareness that all was not well between the Germans and the French. Nowhere in any of her reminiscences, in her surviving letters or in recorded conversations, is there any acknowledgment of it. National problems meant nothing to her. She ignored all the symptoms —until the First World War came to teach her better.

But what she could not ignore (and had no desire to ignore) was that Metz was full of officers and soldiers. Uniforms were to be seen everywhere—in the streets and at all social functions. At Christmas Frieda and Nusch would take time off from their own festivities at home to visit the nearby barracks. There they gazed wide-eyed at huge Christmas trees hung with gingerbread, sausages and cigars, and hugged the dolls which the soldiers had made for them. As time went on, the young men in military jackets began to pay Frieda attentions of a different sort. Meaning glances, a smart salute, a click of the heels, a flattering remark murmured to a comrade, loud enough for her to hear, an invitation to dance, followed by another and yet another—Frieda basked in the admiration of the young cadets.

She was sixteen when she experienced the intoxication of first love. Ensign Kurt von Richthofen was a distant cousin from Silesia, and he had been sent to Metz to study in the military school. He spent every

Sunday in the Richthofen house, where the baron and his wife spoiled him as if he had been the son whom fate had denied them. Else sought to convert him to her progressive political and social ideas, while Nusch pestered him adoringly and revelled in his friendly teasing. But Frieda was soon looking at him in a way she had never looked at a young man before. She led him through the garden and showed him the sixteen species of iris which were her father's special pride and joy. They went for walks together, passing the old citadel on their way to the esplanade, from which there was a splendid view across the valley of the Moselle, with its green meadows and vineyards and the twin forts on the steep slopes of St Quentin. Occasionally they would meet a troop of cadets on horseback, and then Frieda would blush, for she knew them all, and their smart salutes made Kurt tense with ill-concealed jealousy. They played tennis together and went rowing on the river, outings that culminated in luxurious picnics on the bank.

Everyday things suddenly took on a new beauty. When she entered the Roman Catholic cathedral, which looked "like the hollow skeleton of an enormous prehistoric animal", she noticed the dim spots of colour thrown by the rose window, like a medieval sun, on the stone floor. She loved to go there just before sunset, when the light was full of mystery and only a few women were present, kneeling in prayer before the little side altars. In the Protestant garrison church the light was always cold and grey. At a Good Friday service for the soldiers Frieda stood among the officers, and her eyes sought Kurt. He was standing close to the door, and he nodded to her. Outside in a side street a landau was waiting. He had hired it specially, and after the service, very conscious of their appearance, they drove along the banks of the Moselle. Passing the military school and the Kaiser Wilhelm Memorial, the citadel and the headquarters building, the officers' mess at the Prinz Friedrich Karl barracks and the Intendatur, they at last reached the quieter residential streets of Sablon.

They kissed each other for the first time on the evening of Easter Sunday. Saying good-night to her at the garden gate, Kurt touched her mouth shyly with his lips and whispered breathlessly, "Little one, sweet one." She tore herself away and ran wildly back into the house and up to her room, where she threw off her clothes and, slipping into bed, lay there in a state of blissful ecstasy.

They kissed often after that, until the dreadful day when she went to the station to bid him good-bye. As a parting present he gave her a box of macaroons, of which, to Else's and Nusch's utter disgust, she ate every single one herself. Afterwards she was horribly sick.

The kisses they exchanged were innocent. But the dictates of convention were so strong that Lieutenant Karl von Marbahr, who loved her and whose love she returned, did not once dare to advance thus far. This was a much more serious affair than Frieda's flirtation with her Silesian cousin. Marbahr genuinely wanted to marry her. But at that time a military officer needed a lot of money to maintain his position: this was the army's way of safeguarding itself against the invasion of undesirable elements from the "lower" classes. A young lieutenant, in order to keep up the high standards of living which convention demanded of a military officer, could afford to marry only a girl with money of her own. The three Richthofen daughters had no expectations. However much Lieutenant von Marbahr might admire Frieda, he was well aware that she did not constitute a "good match".

In the letters which he wrote to Frieda more than forty years later Marbahr recalled their youthful love affair with melancholy.[4] She had now lived through a lifetime as different as could be from the circumstances in which the young Prussian officer had met and fallen in love with her. He himself, at the time he wrote to her again, was a minor employee in the UFA film company in Berlin. He was married and had three children. "Twice I should have given you a kiss," he wrote, "once when you had stepped in the mud near the tennis court and you stood close in front of me, and then at the station in Metz when you were going away. I still see you at the open window of the car. But then at that time we would have got engaged and would have had to wait ten years for a captaincy ..."

Would Frieda really have waited ten years for him? She was eighteen when she met Kurt von Richthofen again, the ensign who, in contrast to Lieutenant von Marbahr, had dared to kiss her. From Berlin, where the meeting took place, she wrote to her sister Else: "Guess who was here today? Kurt, my first love, just like he used to be. It was very funny ..."

Already only "funny", when all that lay between was a single chaste love affair and a year in a boarding-school in the Black Forest.

This girls' school, Haus Eichberg, was to play an important role in Frieda's later life. It lay in an idyllic position on a mountain slope above Littenweiler, not far from Freiburg. The school was run by two unmarried sisters, Julie and Kamilla Blass, who had been childhood friends of the baroness, and this was the reason why the three Richthofen girls, one after the other, were entrusted to their care. The Blass sisters were ladies of very considerable intelligence, and they taught their pupils far more than just the good manners and other graces which a finishing school is expected to instil into gentlemen's daughters. Both had the gift of winning their pupils' lifelong friendship, and even after they had ceased to run their roomy house as a boarding-school it remained a meeting-place for their many young friends. Else, Frieda and Nusch spent many happy holidays there, as did their children in later years.[5]

The "funny" meeting with cousin Kurt took place in the elegant home of Oswald von Richthofen in the Tiergarten district of Berlin. Frieda called Oswald "uncle", though in fact the relationship was not quite so close. He was one of the diplomats of the Richthofen family, and a man of remarkable intelligence and vision. At that time he was working in the newly formed colonial department of the foreign ministry. It was in his company that Frieda first breathed the tingling air of the great world outside. He showed her the office in which he had worked as a young man under Bismarck, and she danced impetuously around the Iron Chancellor's formidable writing-desk. "You have no respect for high politics, my child," said Oswald, laughing. No doubt he was right.

At an earlier period of his life Uncle Oswald had held a diplomatic post in Egypt. While he was absent from Alexandria on a duty trip, his wife was stricken with cholera and died. The servants fled in panic—all but one, Ahmed, who stayed by the dying woman and took care of her three children, thereby possibly saving their lives. In gratitude Oswald gave him a permanent place in his household. Frieda found Ahmed "very decorative". He fitted well into the style of the house, which was hung with oriental carpets and copper lamps brought back from Egypt. One room looked just like an Arab tent.[6]

Oswald von Richthofen's two widowed sisters, Anna von Elbe and Elisabeth von Plessen, lived with him. Both of them wore severe clothes with high, tight-fitting collars edged in white. Frau von Elbe had been connected in some way with the court of Friedrich Wilhelm IV, doubtless at a time when he was beginning to show the first symptoms of madness. However, this did nothing to minimise Frau von Elbe's great admiration for him. Court life had been very simple in those days, she told Frieda. The royal couple liked to eat their supper of sandwiches and beer seated at one end of the dining-room, and afterwards the king would smoke his pipe while the queen sat knitting socks. The younger members of the court ate their sandwiches at the other end of the room. Aunt Anna made it clear that she admired these frugal manners far more than the arrogance and vulgar extravagance of Wilhelm II.

It was indeed a different world from her mother's cosy mailcoach idylls which Frieda heard described there, but how difficult it was to find one's bearings! On one occasion a friend of the two aunts, a countess from Baden-Baden, came to visit them. In the heat of their gossip the old ladies evidently forgot that a young girl was present in the room, for the countess proceeded to describe a dinner party which the Prince of Wales (later King Edward VII) gave for a number of his friends. When they came to the fish course, six lackeys entered, bearing a huge silver tray, on which, garnished with parsley and slices of lemon, lay a naked girl. Frieda wondered (as she recalls in her memoirs) "whether the lady looked more like salmon or more like halibut". She expected her aunts to be shocked by the scandalous story. But on the contrary, the two strait-laced old ladies were highly amused.

Yet they were genuinely upset when Frieda, ordered to bed on account of a cold, protested (no doubt with good Frau Seidel in mind): "If I were a poor washerwoman, I couldn't stay in bed just for a cold." How could she, a member of the Richthofen family and a baroness in her own right, so far lower herself as to compare herself with a washerwoman?

It was all very confusing—as, too, was the city itself. The Prussian capital, now the capital of the German Reich, drew the young débutante from Metz into its feverish activities with all the brash self-confidence of its founding days. The Berlin of 1898 was a huge bundle of nervous energy, a mixture of vitality and ambition, of speculation and fraud, of hard work and robust efficiency. Within a single generation the population had doubled. People had streamed in from the eastern plains in their hundreds of thousands, and hundreds of thousands more were on their way. For the *nouveaux-riches*, and those hoping to become so, huge new apartment blocks were built, each a would-be palace in itself, in rows extending for miles. A new *parvenu* style, compounded of a dozen other building styles, broke all records for ugliness—and that in a period in which, throughout the world, architecture had nothing to offer but sterility and execrable taste. But the new metropolis was not content to be simply the herald of a new age: its ambition was to become the cultural centre of all Germany. It was to achieve this ambition thirty years later in a final flourish of creative decadence. By that time the flamboyant pomp of Kaiser Wilhelm was no more than a memory of a distant past, and just around the corner a new barbarism was lurking.

At the turn of the century, however, Berlin was a magnet, drawing artistic talent from all parts of the country. Private art galleries catered not only for the vanity of snobbish upstarts, but also for the receptive minds of young people in search of experience. Liebermann and Slevogt were hailed as enthusiastically as Cézanne and Van Gogh. In the theatres the voice of a social conscience was raised for the first time in the works of Gerhart Hauptmann, Ibsen and Tolstoy, accompanied by noisy controversies in the press. Even the struggles of the theatre directors against the censorship mirrored and stimulated the ferment of the times. Curiously enough, it was a Richthofen—the Berlin police chief, Bernhard von Richthofen—who banned public performances of such "seditious" dramas as Hauptmann's *The Weavers* and Sudermann's *The End of Sodom*. His words justifying the banning have since become immortal: "*Die ganze Richtung passt uns nicht!*" (roughly, "We just don't care for that trend!")

The girl from Metz threw herself into the turmoil of the great city with delight. There were visits to the theatre and the opera, carriage drives in the woods of Grunewald, enchanting hours spent in the cafés of Unter den Linden and romantic *Weinstuben*, horse-racing in Karlshorst and occasionally a court ball. At one of these Frieda and Nusch, who happened to be spending a few days in Berlin, attracted the attention of the Kaiser himself. He wanted to know who the two young ladies were and, when told, he remarked: "Ah, the Herr Under-Secretary has very beautiful nieces!"

His Majesty was not exactly a connoisseur in this field, but this case was no great strain on his judgment. Frieda, high-spirited and flirtatious, thoroughly enjoyed the attentions paid her by young attachés and lieutenants. But she found scarcely less pleasure in fooling around with her uncle's thirteen-year-old son. Once, playing hide-and-seek with him, she hid herself in a niche on the landing of the staircase. Hearing steps on the stairs and thinking it was her young cousin, she rushed out of hiding with a wild redskin yell. The person coming up the stairs—not her cousin, but an imposing gentleman in dress uniform heavily hung with medals—almost fell down again to the bottom in his fright. He was the Grand Duke of Saxe-Weimar—a man known for his extreme shyness—on his way to visit Uncle Oswald.

At that time there was no indication that Frieda would follow a path different from that of innumerable daughters of "good" families. In her early years she was—and who can wonder at it?—entirely a creature of her own era, held fast in the conventions of her class. If she could shock her aunts by airily comparing herself with a washerwoman or hurrying down into the road to hitch up the nosebag of a straining cab-horse, all that we are entitled to deduce from that is that her parental home was less stuffy than the home of the two old ladies.

But she never forgot that she was a baroness or—at times when she felt irked by her family's strained financial situation—"only a poor baroness". She needed her aristocratic title to bolster her self-confidence. Her sister Else, whose sharp analytical eye missed no significant psychological detail, later said that Uncle Oswald used to tease Frieda for attaching too much importance to the aristocratic origin of her family. But who can take serious exception to the little vanities of a young girl still in search of her identity? Else, with her precociously developed social conscience, was of course never vulnerable to attacks of class-consciousness. While her sister was still uncertainly pursuing her youthful impulses, Else had already found a place among the elite of an emancipated youth. One of the first female students to be accepted at the University of Heidelberg, she was the favourite pupil of the celebrated sociologist, Professor Max Weber. Under his direction she wrote her doctoral thesis, which dealt with the attitude of the political parties to Germany's new social-security laws.

No subject could have lain further from Frieda's thoughts than this. But of course she was five years younger than Else—hardly more than a child, experiencing in Berlin for the first time the joys of liberation from the narrow confines of provincial life.

Eighteen months later she was a married woman.

4

At the time of their marriage Ernest Weekley was thirty-four, fourteen years older than Frieda. He came of an English lower middle-class family, his father being a poorly paid official whose job it was to distribute alms to the poor of Hampstead under the now superseded Poor Law. His mother, intellectually the dominant partner in their marriage, was the daughter of a schoolteacher and parish clerk in Uxbridge.[1]

Ernest was the second of nine children, brought up in an atmosphere of godliness and thrift. The role of eldest son devolved on him when his elder brother died at the age of eighteen, and it was not in his nature to take his duties lightly. A relation, a clergyman who had inherited a flourishing boarding-school, came to the aid of the hard-pressed family by offering free places in his school to three of the Weekley children, among them Ernest.

Such assistance meant a great deal at a time when elementary education in England left much to be desired, and no one deserved it more than this intelligent and studious boy. At the age of seventeen he himself became a schoolmaster. But in the ensuing years he worked late into the night, seeking through intense study of mathematical and philological textbooks both to improve his knowledge and to further his career. It was a great day, for the family as well as for himself, when his hard work was rewarded with an external degree from London University. Somehow or other money was found to send him to the University of Berne, where he took a year's course in German studies.

His ambition led him on to Cambridge, where he studied Middle English and modern languages, and then for a further year to the Sorbonne in Paris. Following that he was offered a position as lecturer in English at Freiburg University. He accepted it eagerly, not only for the excellent opportunity it gave him to perfect his German, but also because it would enable him to attend the lectures of Friedrich Kluge, a great German philologist whose personal charm captivated Ernest as much as his monumental *Etymological Dictionary of the German Language*.

Ernest did not stay in Freiburg for long. At the beginning of 1898 he was offered a professorship at University College in Nottingham, and he seized the opportunity with both hands. It seemed to him a wonderful reward for all his past labours and sacrifices, and at the same time a proof of the basic fairness of a world order whose divine origin he had never for a moment doubted. There was time to spare before taking up his new position, so he resolved to treat himself to a holiday in the Black Forest.

It was his first real holiday for many years—probably the first since his childhood. His solitary wanderings among the thickly wooded mountains put new life in him. Eagerly he drank in the beauty of the German countryside, which he had hitherto known only through the poems of Mörike and Eichendorff. He entered into lively conversations with farmworkers at the roadside, visited country inns to sit at spotless scrubbed tables, drinking the local wine. And in the little village of Littenweiler he met a girl who seemed to him the quintessence of all that was desirable. The girl was Frieda, who happened to be spending a holiday of her own with the Blass sisters in Haus Eichberg.

It is not surprising that she made so deep an impression on him. Ernest must at that time have been very conscious that he had reached a turning point in his life. Very soon he would be taking up a good academic post which, in contrast to all the short-lived jobs he had so far held, would last him for years (indeed, as it turned out, to the very end of his working life). He could face the future with confidence. Only one thing was needed to complete his happiness: a wife to love and care for. He had had enough of his solitary bachelor existence.

And now he met this enchanting girl. From descriptions and photographs we can form an idea of what Frieda looked like at that time, with her finely cut profile, straight nose and determined chin. No wonder his heart beat faster when those clear green eyes, flecked with gold, turned reflectively on him, or when he stole glances at her blonde hair, which still defied all efforts to tame it into curls or plaits. Her face and her rounded figure, with its tendency to fullness, radiated both girlish high spirits and womanly warmth. She was quite different from all girls he had met before—if indeed he had met enough to make any genuine comparisons. Certainly he was no bloodless bookworm—in his youth he had in fact been a keen sportsman—but he himself would have been the first to admit that his contacts with the female sex, outside his immediate family, had been only superficial. Study and hard work had left him no time at all for love, and in addition his whole upbringing, his family code and his religious beliefs were such that he was bound to look on any fleeting erotic adventure as sinful, and consequently quite out of the question for him.

But while it is easy to understand what Ernest Weekley saw in Frieda, it is harder to explain why Frieda fell in love with him. She too was confronting the unknown: never before had she encountered a man quite like this good-looking Englishman. True, he was no longer young, and his hair had already begun to turn grey at the temples. But how much finer did he seem in his deep moral earnestness than the frivolous uniformed cubs who had hitherto paid court to her! Maybe they were more decorative, but what had they got in their heads, those privileged scions of the officer class, beyond a cynical desire for a good time? Weekley told her about his family and the ungrudging sacrifices his parents had made to provide him and his eight brothers and sisters with a good home and a worthwhile education. Frieda thought of her own father, a gambler, despised by his own wife. What did the charm of her cousin Kurt and the sentimental love affair with Lieutenant von Marbahr count for, compared with the moral strength of this English-man, whose whole body trembled when he drew her to him and kissed her?

Ernest spoke to her of his sleepless nights in Cambridge, spent writing school textbooks and correcting his pupils' homework, in order to earn his livelihood. Yet in spite of it he had still managed to find time to prepare for a scholarship to Trinity College. He told her how he had gone home one day and surprised his family by telling them casually after dinner: "By the way, you had dinner with a scholar of Trinity." He told the story with modest pride, smiling, and she smiled too, knowing in this instant that she loved him.

She was overwhelmed by the depth of passion she had aroused in him. The knowledge that a man of his sort should pay attention to her had something unreal, something intoxicating about it. When he asked her to become his wife, she agreed joyfully, without hesitation.

After becoming officially engaged, they travelled together to England. Ernest wished Frieda and his parents to get to know each other before the wedding. For the sake of propriety the baroness accompanied them to Dover, where Weekley's father and mother had arranged to meet the young couple. As the ferry crossed the Channel, the sun was shining and the sea was calm. "Look, Mama, now you can see the cliffs of old England," cried Weekley excitedly as the chalk promontory emerged from the haze. He was always very respectful to his future mother-in-law, and she liked him. As the steamer sailed into the harbour he stood at the railing, looking for his parents on the quay. Thirty-five years later, in her fragmentary memoirs, Frieda wrote a description (in the third person, as usual) of her first arrival in the country that was to become her new home:

"There they are," he shouted; on the pier in the afternoon sun two old people stood arm-in-arm. He, a beautiful old man looking like Michelangelo's Moses toned down by an English frock-coat, she a round, little quick old lady in a cape and bonnet with a big forehead and beautiful blue eyes. They went to meet them. The mother had eyes only for the son; yes, he was happy ...

But the father had at once succumbed to the fresh, charming creature that came to meet them. He took her arm and walked to the hotel where they were to have a meal. Behind followed the two mothers and the son. The little Englishwoman talked busily away about all sorts of things, Anne [Frieda's mother] understanding only a word here and there, Ernest in a trance of bliss.[2]

The baroness was slightly put out. She could not follow the flow of words gushing from this strange woman, who was so unexpectedly to become a member of her family, but intuitively she sensed behind the language barrier the behaviour and manner of speaking of the lower middle class. When the time came for parting, the baroness saw tears in Frieda's eyes. "Don't weep, you goose," she whispered, and Frieda had to laugh.

In the train that took them to London the old lady chattered unceasingly about family affairs. Her son seemed scarcely to be listening. The Moses-like father sat with a stony face smoking his pipe. Frieda silently watched the gentle green countryside through the compartment window. "What a wonderful cow one would make here," she thought, "or a frog," and later she wrote:

Something of the atmosphere of a little church, the "dim religious light" seemed to hang round the landscape. She looked up at the sky. How near it was, how close! It frightened her. She looked at her lover. Suddenly he seemed quite strange, part of this domestic closeness of things, and she quite alone, out of it ... Like something heavy England came down on the lightness of her heart. The tears came ...

She had truly come into a strange world. Shortly before, Ernest's parents had moved into a house near Hampstead Heath. It had once been the home of the painter, John Constable. Every morning the father would read to the assembled family from the Bible, his arm around one of his grandchildren. With his huge white beard and his noble features he did look strikingly like an Old Testament prophet. But it was the small and lively mother who ran the household with discreet authority. The warm and cheerful atmosphere which filled the home seemed to emanate from her.

The wedding took place on 29 August 1899 in Freiburg.[3] One of Ernest's brothers, Bruce Edward Weekley, who was a curate, travelled from England to give the happy couple the blessing of the Church of England. A few hours later, they were seated in a train to Switzerland, where they were to spend their honeymoon.

Here is Frieda's own description, written down thirty-six years later. Though in this account she calls herself Paula, and elsewhere in the manuscript refers to Ernest as Charles, here in the heat of composition she gives him his real name—or at least the initial letter of it:

They travelled first-class and were alone. He sat in a corner, ill at ease, miserable, tired. He was married, this happy creature was his wife. Yet she felt so far away in her virginity, he was almost in despair. The question of sex relations was terrifying to him, he was almost virgin himself.

In spite of his age and strong passions he had never let himself go. Sex was suppressed in him with ferocity. He had suppressed it so much, put it away so entirely, that now, married, it overwhelmed him. His love had been of the ideal, pure adoration kind, sex he had not let enter consciously. How he suffered now! Paula saw it in his face. She got frightened suddenly. Perhaps after all the lovely thing that she expected would not happen. He hardly said a word. From time to time he gripped her hand with his long, beautiful hand tightly, while his body was held stiff and unbending ...

They were at Lucerne. The lights were reflected in the lake, a beautiful warm night. E. was strung to an unbearable pitch. Their two rooms looked out on the lake; carts and people and a happy life went still on under their windows. Paula sat down on the window seat and looked out, uneasy herself.

"Will you have something to eat?" he asked.

"No, thank you," she answered. "What nice big rooms they are."

"Yes. Paula," he braced himself to it, "I must tell you we aren't really married yet. Come to me."

She came and sat on his knee. She could feel his legs tremble underneath her, she could smell his homespun.

"My little love, you are not yet my wife. '

"Oh yes," she said. "I knew."

The cheerfulness, the frankness of the answer confused him.

"Go to bed, my child. I'll go and drink something, then I will come and say good-night to you."

He got up and went, almost relieved, Paula thought. She was sad, she had imagined it all so differently. "He used to kiss my feet in stupid boots," she thought, "why doesn't he kiss my real toes? He treats me like an old dowager Empress." A big old oak cupboard, beautifully carved with a stiff Eve and an ape-like Adam held her attention. She had taken some of her clothes off. Suddenly she climbed up the old cupboard, the frills of her knickers flapping from her climbing legs. Triumphantly she reached the top, and sat there, wondering what he would do if he couldn't find her ...

After a while her husband knocked, he came in, looked at the bed, and then saw her, her legs dangling from the cupboard. "He looks scared," she thought and climbed down.

Two hours afterwards she stood on the balcony in her light blue dressing-gown for only comfort. She was in an unspeakable torment of soul. It had been so horrible, more than horrible. "Oh God," she thought. How she would love to fling herself from the window! "Only housemaids jump from windows," she said disdainfully. Couldn't she get away? "No, I am married, I am married," rang in her ears. She had expected unspeakable bliss and now she felt a degraded wretch ...

And he slept. He slept. She stamped her foot in impotent rage. He was sleeping while she was in utter despair. Oh God, how she hated him for it, hated him helplessly, miserably.[4]

Such was the wedding night of the woman who was to become the model for Lady Chatterley.

5

No one but a fool with a malicious sense of humour would ever dream of recommending Nottingham as a desirable place of residence for an eager young German girl who had once tasted the joys of court life in Berlin. Frieda felt her heart contract as, on a grim November day, she drove with Ernest from the railway station to the little house that from now on was to be her home. How distant, how infinitely remote did the familiar lanes and promenades of her native town seem then! Certainly Nottingham, like Metz, could boast a citadel, but whereas in Metz she could feast her eyes on the ravishing slopes of the Moselle valley, here, from the hill on which Nottingham Castle stands, she could see nothing but the black slate roofs of warehouses and factories, railway sidings, smoking chimneys and the hopeless muddle of pokey workers' houses ranged in streets along the banks of the River Trent. It was true, of course, that Nottingham also had a warlike history. King Richard III had resided in the castle: from there he rode out to the battlefield at Bosworth where, fighting in defeat, he had suffered a more honourable death than he deserved. Nottingham also had its huge, cathedral-like Church of St Mary, but, while in Metz the cathedral was hemmed in by picturesque medieval lanes, here gaunt Victorian storehouses jostled the ancient church walls. In her native city Frieda could not move a step without bumping into fortifications or barracks, officers' clubs or military headquarters. In Nottingham, on the other hand, the way to the city centre led her past the bastions of the Industrial Revolution, the charmless brickwork of old stocking factories, the squat buildings of lace manufacturers with their steep roofs of glass and slate. Here there was nobody to boast of heroic deeds carried out on the battlefields of Vionville and Gravelotte, and no one told sad stories of humiliating sieges. The chronicles of Nottingham recorded battles of a different order—workers' risings and the clashes of the military with hordes of starving machine-wreckers. The hallowed names were not of generals, but of inventors and pioneers who had helped to set the town—and the world—on its industrial course: Arkwright and Hargreaves, Heathcot and Cotton.

Frieda's first uncertain efforts to run the household in their little home in Goldswong Terrace[1] were fraught with difficulties. She was unfamiliar with the local customs, and could not really understand them. She was amazed by the naturalness with which people followed their own individual philosophical and political leanings, by the openness with which subjects of the Queen proclaimed their republican views, by the violence with which they criticised the government for its treatment of the Boers. She was bewildered by the variety of religious sects to which her neighbours and her husband's new friends belonged. But side by side with this freedom of expression she discovered a rigid framework of social prejudices, based on hallowed tradition. There was a pattern of everyday behaviour to which she must adhere if she did not wish to appear a hopeless outsider. She was expected, as she was very soon given to understand, to conform to a standard of behaviour in keeping with her social position. When at first she occasionally went shopping in the afternoons, helpful neighbours dropped discreet hints that in Nottingham this was not considered good form. Shopping was something to be done in the morning, and the afternoons must be kept free for visiting. Every day of the week had its divinely appointed purpose. Monday was washing-day and Tuesday the day for ironing, and of the remaining days of the week, one was for doing out the kitchen thoroughly, and another for tidying the downstairs rooms. On Monday you served the cold remains of the Sunday roast, and both afternoon tea and dinner in the evening followed certain set rules. If Frieda went into the kitchen, she was treated by the cook almost as an intruder, and when once, in an effort to atone for past transgressions, Frieda asked the class-conscious kitchen tyrant about her family, she was given to understand that she should not meddle in things that were no concern of hers. Frieda did not make the same mistake again. For her the kitchen became foreign territory, and, since she was by nature anything but good at housework, she was unable after a dozen years of marriage to perform even the simplest of kitchen duties.

Frieda did her utmost to observe the unwritten laws of daily life in England. And after a while it all began to seem easier and more sensible. For, ten days before Christmas, she wrote joyfully to her parents in Metz: 'Weekleys will be three next year." Ernest added to the letter a proud postscript: "My wife is stubborn; she wants a boy, but I have ordered a girl."

Frieda's mother travelled to Nottingham to be with her daughter at the confinement, and she brought along a pretty young girl to help with the new baby. On 15 June 1900 Frieda gave birth to a strong and healthy boy. His parents wanted at first to give him three Christian names: Montague Karl Richthofen. But eventually they decided on two, and the boy was christened Charles Montague.

At suitable intervals two further children were born, both of them daughters. The first was named Elsa, after Frieda's elder sister, and given the additional names of Agnes Frieda. ("We can decide later what to call her," Ernest wrote jokingly. "If learned, it will be Elsa, if impudent, it will be Frieda.") The younger one was called Barbara Joy.[2] A second child-nurse was engaged from Germany, a strict Catholic called Ida Wilhelmy, to whom the children were soon as deeply attached as Ida herself was to Frieda. They were now a compact little family, reasonably like those of their neighbours, though Frieda's English unmistakably betrayed her German origin. She was trying to bring the children up bilingually and she told them fairy-tales in German, no doubt much to the approval of her language-loving husband. Ernest persuaded Frieda to join him in learning Italian—never suspecting under what circumstances she would later regret not having paid more attention to its grammar and vocabulary. They would sit together with their Italian textbooks whenever Ernest could find a free evening. That was a rare occurrence, for Ernest was forever taking on new commitments. From Monday to Friday he taught all day at University College, which was housed in a Victorian-Gothic building (now the City Library) in the centre of the city. Here he was not only professor of French, but also head of the modern languages department, a position which involved many additional administrative duties. University College in Nottingham had not yet attained full university status (that was not to happen until 1948). On three evenings of the week he taught languages in a workers' institute, and on Saturdays he lectured in Cambridge. In the time that remained he wrote a succession of school textbooks: *French Prose Composition*, *School French Grammar*, *Exercises in the French Subjunctive*, *A Higher French Reader*. His later books, *The Romance of Words* and *The Romance of Names*, became best-sellers.

He also encouraged Frieda to indulge in literary activity. For Blackie's series of Little German Classics she edited a volume entitled *Schiller's Select Ballads*. She wrote to her sisters: "A little exercise does my rusty brain good. I receive a hundred marks for very little work." In fact, she enjoyed the work so much that she took on another volume: *Bechstein's "Märchen". Selected and edited by Frieda Weekley.*

Did she really enjoy it or was it just a way of passing the time?

Certainly there was little work for her to do in the house: the servants looked after that. In the evenings she sometimes went out with Ernest, when colleagues or neighbours invited them to dine. They had made friends with a chemical scientist, Professor F. S. Kipping, and his wife, who lived in the Park, a well-to-do residential area not far from the castle and close to the huge market place, where the rich lace manufacturers had their palatial Victorian homes.* But Frieda was never at a loss for anything to do when the children were in bed and Ernest was out supervising his evening classes. She played the piano and read the English classics; in particular George Eliot and Thackeray. She wrote long letters to her sister Else, who was now married to one of her teachers at Heidelberg University, the economist Dr Edgar Jaffe, son of a well-to-do Jewish merchant family in Hamburg.

Nusch, the youngest of the three sisters, had been married two years before Else. Her husband, Max von Schreibershofen, was an officer on the German General Staff.[3] He was also a gambler. Had not Papa once warned his daughters not to marry an Englishman, a Jew or a gambler? It was as if the three Richthofen daughters had deliberately set out to spite their father.

But was Frieda happy? Certainly she wrote to her parents and sisters: "I am happier every day, we have no squabbles, much less quarrels" and "I have spells of absurd happiness." Her accounts of the children are tender and affectionate.

She knew that her husband loved her. But the warm feeling of security that this knowledge gave her contained at the same time a certain sense of obligation and dependence, even of frustration. Looking back later on these years, she wrote:[4]

> She believed he was good, better than she was herself, he felt so firm and going his way so sure of himself. Yes, he was better, he knew what was right and wrong, she didn't. She could understand how a person could steal, lie, murder, love another man when one was married. To him there was an absoluteness, she knew he simply could not have done any of these lawless things. It impressed her very much and yet somehow she felt so different herself; she knew for certain that never could she have his rigid code of morals, she even did not really want it. But it was nice to feel him at the back of her days, solid and firm, her rock of ages. He bored her a bit occasionally.

* Professor Kipping's work on organic silicon compounds was later to achieve world-wide recognition.

Boredom: that was the fatal shadow that gradually stole across her marriage. It struck her sometimes in the evening, when the children were sleeping.

She put on an old hat, ran out of the house, tore up the Mapperley hill. The lanterns gave a cheerful light; in rhythmic distances the burring noise of the trams as they boiled up the hill came near and passed again, and she had a glorious feeling of escape, of freedom as she ran on and on the dark road where the wind was catching the trees on the top of the plain. Then she would go back to her house quietly, sane again.

Johanna, her younger sister, came on a visit. But she was no longer the old Nusch to whom Frieda had once felt so close. Her voice had become hard and vulgar. She was now a woman of the world who fitted easily into the circles among which her staff-officer husband moved—though not for long, since he was soon forced to resign his commission on account of his gambling debts. Frieda admired her beauty and her elegant clothes. She was also amused, yet at the same time repelled, by Nusch's account of her glittering life and the conquests she made among the men. "It's something to be married," Nusch said. "How the men hate them, the poor virgins. We married women have a better time!" And then, with a hint of concern in her voice, she enquired of Frieda: "And how are you, tell me about you? Tell me, are you really satisfied in your life, have you got all you want?" She shot a glance at her sister's simple clothing, and, when she left, gave Frieda some of the Paris gowns for which she had no further use.

Frieda was irritated and unsettled by her visit. Was life passing her by? Her husband never seemed to have any time for her now. His whole life revolved around words, words, words—books about words, lectures about words. And Nottingham was not London. The slow tempo of provincial existence made her impatient, and the long, foggy Midlands' winters depressed her. But spring brought compensations. Never before had she enjoyed spring so much as here in Nottingham after the damp cold of winter. She wandered happily among the trees of Sherwood Forest to the north of the city, admiring the carpets of saffron yellow and azure blue spread by primroses and bluebells beneath old oaks and young birches. Its valleys hid coalmines and improbable rows of miners' cottages. Here, too, only a few miles from the city boundaries, lay Newstead Abbey, the ancient family seat of the Byrons.

31

All she learned about Newstead Abbey and its owners must have fascinated Frieda. Its lengthy chronicle of madness, genius and profligacy is of the stuff of which Shakespeare's dramas are made, yet here was evidence more substantial than mere theatrical make-believe. The little cottages whose tenants had once been terrorised by the "wicked Lord Byron" still stood, solid and unaltered, and their present occupants, in many cases the descendants of the oppressed victims, still told stories of the cruel tyrant, the fifth title-holder, who had stabbed and killed his cousin and neighbour, William Chaworth, the squire of Annesley, after some petty quarrel. He had done the deed, not in an honourable duel in a forest clearing by the grey light of morning, but in the back parlour of a London tavern, alone and by candlelight. He was accused of murder and brought to trial before his peers. It was a *cause célèbre*, and people paid six guineas for a seat in court. However, since in aristocratic circles dog does not eat dog, Lord Byron was found guilty only of manslaughter, and released. Nevertheless, he had to bear the enormous costs of the trial, and was obliged to raise a mortgage of thirty thousand pounds to meet them. From then on he was ostracised by London society. In blind rage the baron set about completing his own ruin. He had all the trees cut down in the Abbey grounds, including the centuries-old oaks, and he ordered his servants and tenants to kill all the game on his land; in the ensuing massacre thousands of stags and deer were slaughtered. The Abbey's state rooms were turned into stables and the building abandoned to decay.

It was in line with this unbridled eccentricity that the "wicked lord" always had two loaded pistols set alongside his knife and fork at table. To celebrate the coming of age of his son and heir, he had a complete and fully-rigged warship transported overland to Newstead and placed on the Abbey lake and there, with farmhands manning the twenty-one guns, it was used to fight simulated sea battles. The noise of the guns could be heard in the city of Nottingham itself. However, the son who was to assume this heritage died while his father was still alive, and the crumbling property passed to the old man's great-nephew, son of a neurotic mother and a blue-blooded scoundrel who gambled and drank his way through the fortunes of two noble heiresses before dying at the age of thirty-six. The crippled ten-year-old boy who so unexpectedly inherited both property and title was the Lord Byron who in later years won world-wide fame as a poet and fighter for freedom, and whom Goethe in the second part of his *Faust* celebrated as Euphorion, the Spirit of Light.

By the time Frieda came to visit Newstead Abbey the ravaged Park had long been replanted and the ruined house restored. But memories of the past still lay like a shadow over the Gothic walls and the clipped box hedges on the terraces. Here the poet had experienced his first love —unlike its successors a platonic affair—with Mary Chaworth of Annesley, a descendant of the William Chaworth whom his great-uncle had run through with a sword. Here, too, Byron spent some blissful days with his half-sister, Augusta, for whom his love was by no means merely platonic.

Handsome as a Greek god in spite of his club foot, as capricious as he was brilliant, Byron used Newstead as a picturesque setting for his excesses. It was to Newstead that he invited a dozen friends to celebrate the start of his journey to the Mediterranean. Dressed as an abbot, he drank claret from a skull, while his guests, clad in monks' cowls, strove to outdrink him. The housemaids whom he got with child faded into insignificance beside the aristocratic ladies whose love affairs with the writer of *Childe Harold* scandalised London society. He was "mad, bad, and dangerous to know," wrote Lady Caroline Lamb, wife of Lord Melbourne. But she also wrote: "That beautiful pale face is my fate," and as a token of her love sent Byron a few curls of her pubic hair. She begged him to repay her in the same way, though warning him to be careful not to cut himself. Only a few months after being hailed and courted as the darling of the gods, Goethe's Euphorion had to flee his native country to escape his creditors, pursued by accusations of repeated adultery, incest, homosexuality and other bizarre but unidentified transgressions. He moved on to new shores, to new excesses, to new poetic masterpieces and to an early death at Missolonghi.

Such intemperate behaviour provided an ideal topic of conversation on Frieda's walks through Sherwood Forest. For these she had a constant companion, a well-to-do lace manufacturer who lived in the Park. Will Dowson was married to an active suffragette, and it seems he took her crusade for emancipation as a welcome excuse to assert his own independence. He was a true admirer of the fair sex, whether entitled to vote or not, and his motor car (he was one of the first Englishmen to possess one) was a useful aid in his amorous adventures. Frieda drove out to the woods with him and "felt alive again". He was the first man with whom she deceived her husband.[5] The affair, beyond setting a precedent, was of little significance to her. After all, it was not Frieda who held rigid moral views, but Ernest—and he knew nothing at all about it.

A far more serious affair was to follow. Frieda often took the children to Metz to visit her parents. In the spring of 1907, however, when she went to Munich to see Else and her husband, Edgar Jaffe, she travelled alone. The Jaffes lived in Heidelberg and were firmly entrenched in the town's academic life. Edgar had achieved recognition as a lecturer and in a few years' time he was to be summoned to Munich University as professor of political economy. He had written a book about the British banking system which is still recognised as a standard work, and together with the sociologists, Max Weber and Werner Sombart, he was editing the leading periodical in this field, the *Archiv für Sozialwissenschaft und Sozialpolitik*. Small in stature, Edgar was a kind, shy man with a tendency towards pedantry: a mixture of Jewish inhibitions and Hamburg solidity. Else herself—as was to be expected from so brilliant a scholar—had gained her doctorate with honours and was on terms of close friendship with both Max and Alfred Weber. Professor Max Weber, Germany's foremost sociologist in this century, dedicated to her his great work on the sociology of religion. His wife Marianne was one of the pioneers of women's emancipation in Germany. In the ensuing years Alfred Weber was to become particularly close to Else.

At the time of Frieda's visit to Munich, Else was staying with an Austrian friend whom she had first met at the Blass sisters' boarding-school in Littenweiler. Friedel Schloffer, as this attractive, fair-haired girl had then been named, came of an upper middle-class family in Graz. Her friendship with Else had been as emotional and intimate as only the friendships of young girls can be. Friedel married a psychiatrist from Graz, Dr Otto Gross, the son of an Austrian university professor, and her marriage had brought her to the Bavarian capital.

Munich was at that time the centre for intellectuals in rebellion against convention. This was a period in which new ideas and new standards were striving to usurp the old, and in cafés and taverns endless debates were being fought over God and the state of the world. The district of Schwabing, where most of the literary cafés and artists' *Kneipen* were to be found, was a sort of Bavarian Montmartre. But the term "Schwabing" signified far more a state of mind and a way of life than a mere geographical concept. People showed by the very clothes they wore that they despised all convention. They spent their evenings and half their nights in the company of expressionist painters and futurist poets, homosexuals of both sexes, apostles of decadence and worshippers of violence—as well as many others who pretended to be all these things but were really just ordinary Schwabing citizens. There were infinite shades of belonging. One might be a member of the Verein Süddeutscher Bühnenkünstler (Association of South German Actors), to which, according to its rules (of which nobody took any notice) neither South Germans nor actors were permitted to belong. Or one could be a devotee of the political cabaret Elf Scharfrichter (Eleven Executioners), which made war on all Philistines. Frank Wedekind, the great German dramatist and prophet of a sexual Spring Awakening, was one of those who appeared on its stage. In the smoke and beer-laden atmosphere of Simplicissimus, the artists' tavern, one listened to the revolutionary *chansons* of Erich Mühsam.

Edgar had friends in Schwabing. He had money to spend on starting a collection of modern paintings, and the role of a Maecenas, distributing largesse to the needy artists, was one he enjoyed. But the noisy conviviality of the Simpl, as the Simplicissimus was familiarly called, was less congenial to the Jaffes than the quieter Café Stefanie. Here the tobacco smoke was mixed with the delicate aroma of coffee, not with beer fumes, and it had a curious musty odour which probably emanated from the stuffing in its tattered benches. The regular clientèle was as variegated as it was everywhere else in Schwabing: famous artists shared their tables with dilettantes, boys with their rich protectors, critics with their victims. Every day you could see Erich Mühsam, frail and full-bearded, sitting in a corner playing chess: he was a writer of brilliant ballad-songs and editor of a one-man periodical, *Der Anarchist*, which appeared at very irregular intervals. Among the art students, depending for their sustenance on the waiters' willingness to grant credit, was Leonhard Frank, who was to become one of Germany's most prominent writers.

Here Frieda made the acquaintance of an anarchist "with the most ferocious ideas, but he looked as though he would not hurt a fly", and of an "emancipated young countess" who wrote for the famous periodical *Jugend* (this was presumably the impoverished Franziska Gräfin von Reventlow, the gifted chronicler of Schwabing). Emancipation was in the air, and it seemed to Frieda that it was not only being preached, but also practised—as if the fight against bourgeois values, bigotry and militarism could only be won by unconventionality in sexual attitudes.

Dr Otto Gross, Friedel's husband, was a regular visitor to the Café Stefanie. He was thirty years old, tall and slim, and his hair was as fair as

35

that of his wife, who was now expecting a baby. Leonhard Frank portrayed him, under the name of Dr Otto Kreuz, in his novel *Heart on the Left* (*Links wo das Herz ist*), and this is his description: "The upper part of his face—the pale eyes with their childishly innocent expression, the hooked nose and the full lips, always slightly parted as if he were silently weeping for the world's misery—was at odds with the weak lower part, the chin that was scarcely more than indicated and receded completely out of sight. But nobody, once having seen that fantastic bird's head, ever forgot it."

Otto Gross exerted a powerful fascination on women, and Frieda proved no exception. She succumbed almost immediately to his personal magnetism. Though not really religious in outlook, she had hitherto regarded the world as divinely ordained and—notwithstanding Else's rebelliousness—unalterable. And now came this neurotic genius to conjure up for her a vision of a new way of life, based on the principles of abstract reason, and of a new social order in which the natural instincts would no longer be held in check by artificial taboos and ingrained prejudices.

Otto was a disciple of Sigmund Freud, who had already published his first basic works in the new field of psycho-analysis: *The Interpretation of Dreams, The Psychopathology of Everyday Life* and *Three Essays on the Theory of Sexuality*. Freud's theories and discoveries were by now beginning to influence thinking in intellectual circles, however vehemently, at the other end of the scale, they were being criticised or rejected. Frieda had never even heard of him, and when Otto Gross spoke to her of the man and his ideas, she felt as if the shutters of the dark house in which she had hitherto been living had been flung open. Her mind was in a turmoil; she seemed suddenly to have been freed of all her inhibitions. Both pupil and teacher were set ablaze by the experience, and Otto became Frieda's lover.

It was no momentary intoxication, no passing adventure, quickly enjoyed and as soon forgotten. After her return to her family and her housewifely duties in Nottingham, one of her little daughters said to her: "You are not our old mother. You have got our old mother's skin on, but you are not our mother that went away."

The words remained in Frieda's memory as proof of the uncanny second-sight of children. "The child was right," she wrote. She *was* altered. She continued to correspond with her lover. The Jaffes knew about the affair—possibly Else, fanatic advocate of women's liberation that she was, had even played a part in bringing it about. But Edgar, with greater circumspection, advised Frieda to be careful. She wrote to him from Nottingham:

I am very, very happy and can only now enjoy all my love. I had promised to burn all my letters from Munich, but I cannot do it: relieve me of my promise, I must still have something. I am nevertheless *very* careful.

Frieda never destroyed Otto's letters. They contain glowing assurances of his love—"I am grateful that you exist ... You give me the wonderful strength to make me a genuine human being, and at the same time live for an idea ... It is as if out of your letter streamed the warmth of your body, so sweet and powerful, like a wave of happy, liberating bliss, as you live and give, you whom I love with such joy ..."

They came together once again, and he accompanied her on the crossing from Holland to England. His letters became even more pressing, more passionate: "We have found each other ... Give your flame to me. Don't, for God's sake, reduce yourself to smouldering ashes! Think of the night on the boat. There we looked on this vision of a future happiness ..."

But finally the stream of letters dried up. In the last of them he wrote: "I can never lose you because you will never lose yourself."

Frieda never saw him again, but she never forgot him. Towards the end of her life she wrote in her memoirs that he had died in the First World War, serving, as she had been told, as an army doctor. "How he must have suffered!" she commented. "He, who had dreamed of a glorious coming day for all men, saw before him the torn bodies and broken spirits of the young that he had dreamed his dreams of happiness for! No wonder he died, as so many had died with their hopes denied and broken."

The reality was much crueller. Though Frieda never suspected it, Dr Otto Gross was already at the time of their meeting a drug addict. He could not have written his brilliant psycho-analytical essays without the stimulus of cocaine. He nevertheless managed for a long time to conceal his weakness from the people around him, all of them lost in admiration for his intellect, his nervous energy and the boldness of his theories. Gross believed it was not enough just to analyse sexual complexes: they had to be exorcised in bed. It was a recipe that he—whatever the state of his own complexes—personally applied, and his wife Friedel, who was utterly devoted to him, never made any serious effort to prevent him. On the contrary, she obeyed him when he decided to stay with the young woman painter with whom he had been living for some time and ordered Friedel to go and live with a Swiss anarchist. This man, who had spent two years in prison for robbery with violence, committed in the interest of his ideals, was presumably the young anarchist of whom Frieda Weekley had written: "... but he looked as though he would not hurt a fly." Friedel Gross went with him to Ascona, where they lived in great poverty and brought three children into the world. Ultimately, Friedel was left alone and had to live on her own resources, supported by a tiny allowance paid by her family on the condition that she should never return to Austria.

As for Otto Gross himself, his decline had meanwhile reached a pitiful level. He had lost all control over himself and would sniff the lethal white powder openly, even in the presence of strangers. His nostrils were eaten away. He died in a Berlin hospital in 1920. "He was a complete wreck," reported the doctor who treated him at the end.

But of all this Frieda knew nothing.[6] It would perhaps be going too far to say that her meeting with Otto Gross changed the direction of her life. Probably, it would be more correct to argue that the passionate erotic and intellectual experience she underwent with him strengthened tendencies already present in her, and swept away barriers which had hitherto restricted her emotional outlook.

"My marriage seemed like a success," Frieda later wrote sarcastically, and her letters to her parents in Metz must have given the impression that it really was. To friends and neighbours it also seemed to be a success. The Weekleys' financial position had improved. They had moved to a better part of Nottingham and were now living in Mapperley in a large, high-gabled house with Virginia creeper winding past the bay windows right up to the roof. The children were going to good schools. When young Monty left the house in the mornings, his schoolbooks under his arm, he would look up and wave to his mother, who stood with her nose pressed against the window, making faces to make him laugh. He would look around apprehensively, to make sure that nobody else could see her childish behaviour.

She had everything that a middle-class housewife in Nottingham could wish for: three children whom she dearly loved and who dearly loved her, a husband who commanded general respect through his position and his high moral principles, and a comfortable home. But was this "success"?

Though several years had passed since her last meeting with Otto, she still could not regain her peace of mind. That affair had differed in every way from those earlier adulterous motor drives to Sherwood Forest; these, the result of boredom, fitted well enough into the usual framework of provincial life. "I was living like a somnambulist in a conventional set life," Frieda wrote. But the affair with Otto had put an end to that by awakening in her what she later called "the consciousness of my own proper self". His visions of a better world gripped her imagination. As her sister Else Jaffe observed, she believed—somewhat naively, no doubt—in the goodness of mankind, and considered it her mission to give support to everyone who happened to arouse her interest and sympathy. Her lover had introduced her to the ideas of Freud, and, although perhaps he presented them in a distorted form reflecting his own excessive tendencies, he had succeeded in lifting the veil of secrecy from matters hitherto regarded as unmentionable. In consequence, her feelings had been aroused and her thoughts revolutionised. Her ideas were doubtless amateurish and undisciplined and led her to some absurd conclusions. But for her it was not a matter of whether Freud or Otto Gross were right in their theories; the important thing was to find her own instincts confirmed. The frustrated longings and the sexual urges —emotions which her marital vows and society's moral laws had bidden her suppress—had been vindicated. She wrote later:

Fanatically I believed that if only sex were "free" the world would straightaway turn into a paradise. I suffered and struggled at outs [odds?] with society, and felt absolutely isolated. The process left me unbalanced. I felt alone. What could I do, when there were so many millions who thought differently from me? But I couldn't give in. I couldn't submit.

The years dragged on—it was five years since that visit to Munich— and her life continued within the dreary confines dictated by the taboos of religion and hallowed custom. However much she may have chafed inside herself, however bored she may have been by the English form of social life, without intimacy or intensity of feeling, she still meekly obeyed the rituals of neighbourly relations and the rules of polite conversation at afternoon teas, at dinner parties and at school functions. She was now thirty-two years old—young by present-day standards. But according to the ideas of that time she was already on the threshold of middle-age. It was almost inevitable that she should begin to wonder whether she had missed her chance. Perhaps her revolt would remain a dream, and she would have to spend the rest of her life behind the prison bars of convention.

At the end of March 1912 Ernest Weekley told his wife to expect a guest for lunch. One of his former students at University College wished to discuss with him the question of a lecturer's post at a German university. "He is a young genius," Professor Weekley added.

The visitor was D. H. Lawrence. His meeting with Frieda was to change her whole life—and his.

6

The mining village of Eastwood lies on rising ground at the edge of Sherwood Forest, "just between the red sandstone and the oak-trees of Nottingham, and the cold limestone, the ash-trees, the stone fences of Derbyshire."[1] Externally nothing much has changed there since the end of the last century, apart from the cars on the main road to Nottingham and the groups of ugly new houses which have come to join the ugly old ones. At that time the coalfield was still relatively new, but pitheads and smoking coaltips were already beginning to spread, marring the lovely countryside like festering boils.

Here, in a small grey-slated worker's cottage, David Herbert Lawrence was born on 11 September 1885. His father, Arthur John Lawrence, was a coalminer. He was a remarkably attractive-looking man with lively black eyes, rosy cheeks and a full black beard. Never in all his life, he used to boast, had a razor touched his face. Like so many miners, he had an excellent singing voice and was also a graceful dancer. It was no wonder that he turned the heads of all the maidens. Among them was a quiet and shy girl named Lydia Beardsall. She met him in Nottingham and fell in love with him.

Lydia was twenty-three years old, six years younger than Arthur Lawrence. She came of a pious Methodist family, had been for some time a schoolteacher and had pronounced intellectual interests. She was also self-willed, and she insisted, against the wishes of her parents, on marrying the handsome dancer who had captured her heart. When, in the little parish church of Sneinton, he placed the wedding ring on her finger, she had no idea of how a coalminer lived. It was only after marriage that she learned what it meant to be a miner's wife.

She could hardly believe that the black-faced man who returned from the pit on the first day was the same man who had parted from her that morning with a kiss on the lips. She was even more dismayed when, after washing his hands, he sat down at table with his face still black and demanded his food. "Coal dirt is clean dirt," he said firmly. But there was an even greater shock in store. After the meal, in accordance

41

with miners' custom, he insisted on taking a bath in a tub in front of the kitchen fire, and he called on her to scrub his back. She considered such menial tasks beneath her dignity.

The abyss that opened up between them on that evening was never bridged. Arthur Lawrence was not prepared to be told by his wife how a man should behave. He expected her to conform to the usual pattern of a miner's wife. But Lydia could be equally unyielding. She was not going to give in to a man whom she considered both socially and intellectually her inferior. She spoke the Queen's English, and, even if she had wanted to—which she most emphatically did not—she never could have learned the local dialect. Her husband had little understanding for her cultural longings. He had started to work in the pits at the age of seven, and could barely write his own name. He could read a newspaper, though only with much effort, but during the whole of his married life he never once touched a book. It was bitter for Lydia to recall that she, the wife of this semi-literate man, had in earlier years seen poems of her own printed in the newspapers.

How often must she have cursed the evening when she succumbed to the charms of her handsome dancing partner! Perhaps the marriage could have been saved if she had shown a little more tolerance, but Lydia had a will of iron. Brought up in the strict faith of a puritanical family, she was not prepared to make any concessions to the devil. She had never touched alcohol, and now she insisted that no drop of the evil stuff should ever enter her house. Her husband, having realised all too soon that he could share nothing with his wife beyond bed and board, began to seek congenial company elsewhere. He found it in the pub only a few hundred yards down the road from his house.

They had five children, of whom Bert, as David Herbert was called by everyone in Eastwood, was the fourth. He was, as he later wrote, "a delicate pale brat with a snuffy nose". He was very thin and he tired so quickly that George, his eldest brother, would often carry him for miles on his shoulder. Most of the boys in the village despised him. They teased him because he was too delicate to join in their games and consequently stayed among the girls. "Dicky Dicky Denches plays with the wenches," they would shout in monotonous sing-song, marching behind as he walked home from school chatting with two little girls. He would try to ignore them, but after a while his squeaky little voice would falter and his chalk-white face would be distorted by frustration and rage.

He suffered his worst humiliations in the offices of the mining company, to which he had to go on Friday afternoons to collect his father's wages. As soon as Bert reached the counter in the room full of miners, miners' wives and children, the cashier would lean forward and call out in a loud voice inviting public approbation: "Ho, lad, where's your Pa—too drunk to come and collect the pay hissen!" Then the whole company would burst into mocking laughter and Bert would long for the ground to open and swallow him up.

The cynical cashier, whose portrait he later painted in his novel *Sons and Lovers*, was for Bert a living symbol of the anonymous power he so much hated. He saw Barber, Walker & Co., the owners of most of the coalpits in the district, as responsible for the poverty not only of his own family, but of all the other three and a half thousand inhabitants of Eastwood. They were also responsible for the ugliness of the village. Precocious and sensitive, as delicate children often are, he bitterly resented the brutal way in which the bare house fronts, the ash heaps and shaft houses at the pitheads, the high chimneys with their ragged plumes of smoke desecrated the countryside. He carried these early impressions throughout his life like scars. In one of his last essays he wrote:[2]

The great crime which the moneyed classes and promoters of industry committed in the palmy Victorian days was the condemning of the workers to ugliness, ugliness, ugliness: meanness and formless and ugly surroundings, ugly ideals, ugly religion, ugly hope, ugly love, ugly clothes, ugly furniture, ugly homes, ugly relationship between workers and employers. The human soul needs actual beauty more than bread.

Bert escaped from the ugliness of Eastwood into the beauty of the woods and meadows. He went for walks, either with his sisters or alone, to Brinsley, where his father's parents lived, passing the Brinsley mine in which, deep down in the bowels of the earth, his father worked and swore. He explored the cracked ruins of Beauvale Monastery and the woods of High Park, where Byron had once wooed Mary Chaworth. On Saturdays the children would often wander through the fields in search of herbs, which their mother turned into delicious beverages. There was not a single flower, tree or bird that escaped Bert's sharp eye, and the pictures and impressions stored up during those childhood days were later reproduced with astonishing freshness in his writings.

From the circle of close and happy harmony in which mother and children lived, the father found himself increasingly excluded. Lydia Lawrence was responsible for that. Having in a moment of inexplicable blindness married beneath her, she felt there was only one way to make good her tragic mistake: she must raise her children above their proletarian surroundings to the social level from which she herself came. She vowed that her sons should never become miners, nor her daughters maidservants. And having decided that this was the only path to salvation, she stuck to it with iron determination. She insisted on the children speaking the Queen's English, though of course she could not prevent them lapsing into the local dialect when they were with the other village children. She helped them with their homework and made their clothes, managing somehow to keep them always nicely and cleanly dressed. It was amazing what she managed to do on the scanty pay her husband earned.

She was small and by no means strong. Yet somehow she found the time and energy, beside her housewifely duties, to perform secretarial duties for the local Women's Guild, and to read the books the children brought home for her from the public library. She was determined not to allow the housework to get her down: for the sake of her sons she must not neglect her intellectual interests. She considered herself to be something more than a mother to her children: she was a torchbearer, charged with the duty of leading them out of the black night of ignorance and vulgarity into the sphere of light. The very magnitude of the task seemed to give her new reserves of strength. The minister of the Congregationalist chapel to which she took her family, took great delight in coming to the house to discuss religious and philosophical problems with her. She had a ready tongue, and he found her dry and sarcastic sense of humour captivating.

Arthur Lawrence was well aware that his wife was turning his children against him. Returning tired from work in the evening, he could feel the coldness, the disapproval, even at times the hostility with which his family received him. His visits to the pub down the road became more and more frequent. His wife would stay up until he returned, stammering excuses with a heavy tongue. Then she would set mercilessly about him, her bitter reproaches falling like whips on his ears, and he would respond with mounting anger and ever more violent curses. And while their parents battled in the kitchen, the children would lie trembling in their beds, praying that the horrible scene would soon come to an end.

Bert and the two girls, Emily and Ada, were still small when George, the eldest brother, left Eastwood. He was apprenticed to a framemaker in Nottingham. The second brother, Ernest, seven years older than Bert, was their mother's favourite. He promised to be the fulfilment of all her hopes. Attractive in appearance, as his father had been in earlier years, but endowed with the clear intelligence of his mother, he seemed destined to surmount the hurdles of life with consummate ease. His successes at sport and his brilliant examination results were constantly being held up to his younger brother as an example.

With a sensitive boy such as Bert pedagogical methods of this sort were of doubtful value, and certainly the occasional attempt to reinforce them with a touch of the cane did nothing to improve his self-confidence. But deliverance came when he won a scholarship that enabled him to enter one of the best schools in the county, Nottingham High School.

A few days after his thirteenth birthday Bert made his first rail journey to Nottingham and back, a journey that he was to make twice every weekday, except during the holidays, for the next three years. He left home every morning at seven and returned at seven in the evening. For so delicate a boy it was a very considerable exertion, particularly on the damp and frosty days of autumn and winter. It was at that time he first developed the dry cough that was later to plague him.

Nottingham High School had a continuous tradition going back over six centuries, and its headmaster was a man of outstanding ability and liberal ideas. Of course, it is impossible to say with any certainty what the formation of a child's character owes to the stability of a cultural tradition, just as no school report can be considered a reliable barometer of intellectual progress. David Herbert Lawrence's gifts could in any case only be expected to show in the subject of English, and what can be concluded from the fact that, in a class of twenty-one pupils, he was only thirteenth in English? Probably nothing at all, for such oddities are a familiar phenomenon in the life of many other great writers. One thing only can be stated with certainty: Lydia had achieved her goal and saved her son Bert from becoming a miner. The gates of the whole world were now open to him.

But when at the age of fifteen he left school and passed through those golden gates, he found nothing awaiting him. He could not continue his studies, for there was no more money available. The deprivations and sacrifices made so far culminated in nothing more than a clerk's job in a factory manufacturing artificial limbs and surgical stockings.

This grotesque episode in D. H. Lawrence's life lasted only three months, though it provided him with some material for his novel *Sons and Lovers*. He was still travelling to Nottingham six days a week. But, whereas he left in the morning with the same train as before, he now had to work until eight o'clock in the evening. For a working week of seventy-two hours he received the princely wage of thirteen shillings. However, this Dickensian interlude was soon brought to an end by family tragedy.

Bert's brother Ernest, so rich in talent and so adored by his mother, was now working in the London office of a large shipping firm. He had every prospect of a brilliant future. But besides the good fairy which had lavished so many gifts on him there was a wicked fairy at work. At the age of twenty-three he fell ill with pneumonia. A telegram sent Lydia Lawrence hurrying to London, where she found him lying in a coma. A few hours after her arrival he died.

The loss of her favourite son plunged Lydia into an abyss of despair. Her apathy was so great that when Bert returned from Nottingham in the evenings and pressed a kiss on her brow, she seemed scarcely aware of his presence. As he told her of the day's happenings she would listen with a vacant expression in her eyes, not taking in what he said. All his efforts to arouse her from her distraught condition proved unsuccessful.

Months went by, and still Lydia was unable to throw off her paralysing dejection. Then Bert, following his brother's example, came down with pneumonia. For days he hovered between life and death. His perilous condition at last tore his mother out of her lethargy. With an agonised cry, "I should have watched the living, not the dead!" she shook off her trance and exerted all her energies, day and night, in a superhuman effort to nurse him back to health. She saved his life, and with it her own.

There are many indications that Bert's illness was psychosomatic in origin. It could have been the subconscious culmination of his desperate efforts to win for himself the love that his mother was squandering on his dead brother. But there is another possible explanation.

In *Sons and Lovers* D. H. Lawrence portrayed the girls who worked in the surgical appliances factory in a warmly sympathetic light. But it seems his sentimental picture was not in accordance with the real facts. One of his closest friends at that time later revealed that these by no means strait-laced girls used to taunt the boy with his innocence; not surprisingly perhaps, for he was still tied to the moral principles of his

46

puritanical mother. One day they set on him in the storeroom and tried to open his fly-buttons—presumably with the intention of finding out if everything was as it should be. Only with the greatest difficulty did Bert succeed in tearing himself away and seeking safety. He was both exhausted and sickened by the experience, and it is possible that the shock led directly to his illness.

Whatever the cause, this crisis in his life enormously strengthened the bond between him and his mother. She took complete and exclusive possession of him, and he submitted gladly.

His friendship with the Chambers family at Haggs Farm, to the north of Eastwood, went back to his schooldays. In *Sons and Lovers* he has described his first visit to the farm after a long walk with his mother through the surrounding fields and woods:

> In front, along the edge of the wood, was a cluster of low red farm buildings. The two hastened forward. Flush with the wood was the apple orchard, where blossom was falling on the grindstone. The pond was deep under a hedge and overhanging oak-trees ... Some cows stood in the shade ... Then, in the doorway suddenly appeared a girl in a dirty apron. She was about fourteen years old, had a rosy dark face, a bunch of short black curls, very fine and free, and dark eyes; she, questioning, a little resentful of the strangers, she disappeared ...

That was Lawrence's first impression of Jessie Chambers, whom he calls Miriam in his novel. Jessie was the second oldest daughter of the farmer's family. That first summer, when Bert was fifteen, they took very little notice of one another. It was Edmund Chambers, her father, who first showed an interest in the pale and lanky red-haired boy.

A few weeks after Bert had recovered from his illness, Edmund Chambers called for him in his milkcart and took him to spend a day at the farm. As his strength returned, Bert began to make himself useful in the house and in the fields, and very soon he was being treated as a member of the family.

Besides Jessie Chambers' memoirs[3] there is an account of those days written by Jessie's youngest brother, David, who was then still a child; he later became professor of economic history at Nottingham University. His reminiscences, written down forty years after the event, provide evidence of the extraordinary impression that Lawrence made on people even at the early age of seventeen or eighteen:

I adored him for what he was: high spirited, infectiously gay, galvanising every company, whether at work or at play, into new and more intense activity, making them bigger, better, cleverer than they were by nature, and imparting to them some of his own inexhaustible zest for life. When he came into the hayfield, as he often did in those endlessly sunny summers of one's boyhood, work went on with an unaccustomed swing; he worked along with my father and brothers, staggering under massive forkfuls of hay and keeping up his side of the haycart by sheer nervous energy, for in physique he was not their equal, though he was taller. And at tea time, hampers would be mysteriously unearthed and tea time in the hayfield was turned into a picnic; how it happened I never quite knew, but I suspect the news got around that Bert was helping in Chambers' fields at Greasley and his sister or his friends, mainly girls studying at the Pupil-Teacher Centre at Ilkeston, would take the opportunity of bringing a contribution to a picnic that might well become an impromptu dance, a game of duck or hide and seek and would certainly be memorable for high spirits and reckless fun.[4]

Eighteen months before his death Lawrence himself wrote a nostalgic letter to David Chambers, recalling that happy time:

Whatever I forget, I shall never forget the Haggs—I loved it so. I loved to come to you all, it really was a new life began in me there ... Oh, I'd love to be nineteen again, and coming up through the Warren and catching the first glimpse of the buildings ... Because whatever else I am, I am somewhere still the same Bert who rushed with such joy to the Haggs.

After a while he began to take an interest in Jessie, attracted by her earnest, pensive and rather melancholy manner and her sensitive nature. She was so completely different from all the girls he had so far met in Eastwood and Nottingham. The others seemed unable to talk about anything except boy-friends and clothes, whereas with Jessie he could discuss all the problems with which he himself was preoccupied.

She listened in fascination when in his lively way he told her about a book he had just been reading, or when he talked about some occurrence he had witnessed. What might have seemed little more than an ordinary everyday experience became significant and colourful when he described it. Gradually a profound understanding began to form between the farmer's daughter and the miner's son. It was a process of mutual give and take, a contact of souls which had a determining effect on Lawrence's intellectual development, and for Jessie became the decisive experience of her life.

Every Thursday they would go together to the public library in Eastwood, and Lawrence would choose books for his family and also for Haggs Farm. Lying together in a meadow with their books, Bert and Jessie would eagerly discuss what they were reading. In the little kitchen at the farm, crouching over a book, he would insist on reading out some paragraph or chapter that had struck him to anyone who happened to be in the room. In these apprentice years Lawrence's feeling for style was nurtured by the dramas of Shakespeare and the poems of the *Golden Treasury*, the prose of Dickens, Thackeray, Stevenson and Hardy. He loved George Eliot and Jane Austen, for he recognised in their books the people and the countryside of Derbyshire, just across the border from Eastwood.

For Jessie he was the prince in the fairy-tale of Sleeping Beauty. On hot summer afternoons she would sit waiting for him in her little room above the stables, and, as soon as the click of the chain on the garden gate proclaimed that he had arrived on his bicycle, she would run out to meet him. She was in love for the first time, yet in an attempt to win his love in return she had to wage a bitter battle. She knew that in Lydia Lawrence she had an inexorable rival, who was not prepared to share her son's heart with any other woman.

Lawrence has placed his bitter-sweet friendship with Jessie Chambers at the centre of his novel *Sons and Lovers*, in which he himself appears under the name of Paul Morel. Jessie gave him some of her own notes to use in the book. Among them was this prayer, which betrays in its stammering fervour all her hopes and fears in those early days:

O Lord, let me not love Paul Morel: keep me from loving him, O Lord, if I ought not to love him. But, O Lord, if it's thy will I should love Paul make me love him—like Christ would. Make me love him splendidly—because he is thy son.

Lawrence had now taken a post as pupil-teacher at a school in Eastwood, a position he owed to the Congregational minister with whom his mother was friendly. From the autumn of 1903 onwards he attended the Pupil-Teacher Centre at Ilkeston, a little town nearby. There he was among friends. Both Jessie and her eldest brother, Alan, had followed his example and decided to become schoolteachers. Alan, who appears in *Sons and Lovers* under the name of Edgar, was at that time particularly close to Lawrence, and in fact there are certain indications that their friendship might have had an element of homosexuality about it. If so, that should scarcely surprise us in a boy of eighteen, knowing as we do how often such feelings arise during the stormy years of adolescence, only to vanish in later years.

His closeness to Alan has nevertheless given rise to a theory that Lawrence was always homosexual, and many scenes in his books have been cited to prove it: the bathing scene in *The White Peacock* is one, as well as certain chapters in *Aaron's Rod*, *Kangaroo* and *The Plumed Serpent*. But the most frequently cited evidence is the scene in *Women in Love*, in which Birkin and Gerald wrestle naked together. An unpublished foreword to the novel contains some sentences that refer ostensibly to Birkin, yet there are many who suspect that Lawrence was really writing about himself:

> All the time he recognized that, although he was always drawn to women, feeling more at home with a woman than with a man, yet it was for men that he felt the hot, flushing roused attraction which a man is supposed to feel for the other sex ... The male physique had a fascination for him, and for the female physique he felt only a fondness, a sort of sacred love, as for a sister.[5]

Compton Mackenzie also recalls in his copious memoirs that Lawrence once said to him during a conversation in Capri: "I believe that the nearest I've ever come to perfect love was with a young coalminer when I was about sixteen."

Inevitably, remembering his juvenile hatred for his father and his emotional slavery to his mother, one thinks of Lawrence in terms of an Oedipus complex. But his personality was in fact much too complicated to be reduced to a simple formula. If a tendency towards homosexuality was present in him, it was only one element among many others —a tendency that perhaps occasionally overstepped the threshold of consciousness, but certainly never sought a practical outlet. In all the mass of material describing every phase of his life in the most intimate detail, there is certainly no concrete evidence to the contrary. In fact, Lawrence repeatedly expressed his distaste for any form of homosexual practice. It would indeed be surprising if this were not so: no other modern author has treated the subject of physical union between man and woman in such a mystical, even religious manner as Lawrence.

That, however, still lay in the future. The friendship between Lawrence and Jessie Chambers—a rapturous union of two young souls

—was strictly platonic. As Jessie later wrote: "There was no thought of the distinction between body and spirit because each was perfectly pure." His puritanical mother was watching over his chastity, for she was as eager to preserve him from a "life of sin" as from the clutches of another woman. And on her side Jessie was deluding herself that in the end her "ideal love" would prove strong enough to overcome his mother's hostile resistance.

One evening Lawrence broached the subject of their relationship, and he spoke some bitter words about the "balance of strength" between them. "I could never love you as a husband should love his wife," he told her harshly.

Jessie's illusions were shattered. In his words she recognised the voice of his mother, her irreconcilable enemy. Still, she was not prepared to give in without a fight. She had a weapon which she thought invincible: her own unselfish and boundless love.

A few months later Lawrence and his mother went for a short holiday to the coast of Lincolnshire, and Jessie accompanied them. They went for a walk by the sea. It was windy, and Jessie took a silk scarf to tie down her hat. She saw that Lawrence was watching her; his eyes lighted up.

"Does the scarf suit me?" she asked with a hint of coquetry.

"What do you think?" he asked his mother.

Lydia gave Jessie "a bitter glance, and turned away, and the light died out of Lawrence's face."

That same evening the two young people went for a walk alone among the sand dunes. Suddenly Lawrence began to heap wild reproaches on Jessie's head. He appeared to be, in her words, "in great distress of mind and possibly also of body." [3]

If this was the most painful, it was by no means the last of the many stormy scenes that stood out like milestones in their friendship. Most of them ended with Lawrence in a mood of bitter self-reproach. Jessie had long since realised that she stood no chance of winning him for herself as long as Lydia was alive. All the same, she wanted to remain within his magic circle; for she believed in him implicitly. She could not imagine life without him, and she knew that he too needed her.

He had shown her some poems which he had written, and—more important still—the first pages of a novel. That was sometime around Whitsun 1906, when he was twenty years old. The novel was *The White Peacock*, on which he was to work for four long years; in it he attempted to reproduce the landscapes of his youth: Haggs Farm, Felley

Mill nearby, the steep cart-track beside the abandoned stone quarry, up which he pushed his bicycle on his way to the farm. As soon as he had completed a few pages, he would give them to Jessie to read. It was the beginning of her future role as his trusted literary adviser. Poor Jessie: he valued her criticism more than her love.

Lawrence was twenty-one when, with the help of a scholarship and some money he had managed to save during his months as a school-teacher, he entered University College in Nottingham to continue his studies. He had a very low opinion of his tutors—with one exception: the head of the modern language department, Professor Ernest Weekley, won his respect. But their contacts were confined to the lecture room and remained on an impersonal and superficial basis. How could they know that their paths were later to cross again—and this time disastrously?

Among the students at University College was a girl whom Lawrence had already known for some time. Louisa Burrows—or Louie, as she was always called—had studied at the Pupil-Teacher Centre at Ilkeston at the same time as both Lawrence and Jessie. She was a strong and pretty girl with black hair and lively brown eyes. Lawrence likened her to a pomegranate. He later used her as a model for Ursula Brangwen in *The Rainbow* (not, however, for Ursula Brangwen in *Women in Love*). Louie came from a happy home, combining intellectual interests with a strong streak of Christian piety. Her father was a talented woodcarver in the manner of William Morris. His masterpiece, an oak reredos, still adorns the church in Cossall near Eastwood, a little village in which the Burrows family lived for many years. Louie possessed more than average intelligence: her examination results in college were better than Lawrence's own. He found her warm naturalness very attractive, and in this case his interest was unmistakably physical. Even Jessie knew it—not surprisingly, for Lawrence, who could be malicious at times, showed her a poem which he had written under Louie's spell. The phallic symbolism of this poem, "Snapdragon", is very evident:

> I put my hand to the dint
> In the flower's throat, and the flower gaped wide with woe.
> She watched, she went of a sudden intensely still,
> She watched my hand, to see what it would fulfil.
> I pressed the wretched, throttled flower between

My fingers, till its head lay back, its fangs
Poised at her. Like a weapon my hand was white and keen,
And I held the choked flower-serpent in its pangs
Of mordant anguish, till she ceased to laugh,
Until her pride's flag, smitten, cleaved down to the staff.
She hid her face, she murmured between her lips
The low word "Don't" ...

And the reaction is exactly what one would expect from a girl of Louie's character and background:

I bade her eyes
To mine, I opened her helpless eyes to consult
Their fear, their shame, their joy that underlies
Defeat in such a battle.

However much this friendship might have aroused Jessie's jealousy, she was wise enough not to show Lawrence that she was hurt. She consoled herself that Louie stood no better chance than she as long as his mother was alive. He continued to spend many happy hours at Haggs Farm, but often a sudden flurry of bitter words would betray the tension that was threatening to destroy their relationship. They still sat together over their books or lay side by side in the meadows, eagerly discussing what they had been reading: de Maupassant, Balzac, Flaubert, Tolstoy, Meredith, Schopenhauer, Thomas Huxley and Haeckel. He showed her pages from *The White Peacock* almost before the ink was dry, and she freely criticised his immature work. Sometimes they met in Nottingham and went to the theatre together.

The great Sarah Bernhardt herself appeared at the Theatre Royal during a tour of England. Her playing in *La Dame aux Camélias* excited Lawrence to such a degree that, when the curtain fell, he stormed out of the theatre like a madman. He found her "wonderful and terrible".

"I could love such a woman myself, love her to madness, all for the pure wild passion of it," he wrote in a letter to Blanche Jennings, who belonged to a circle of socialists and suffragettes in Eastwood. Lawrence had made friends with members of this group, and through them he got to know some of the leading figures of the Labour movement: Ramsay MacDonald and Philip Snowden, who were both scarcely known at that time, and Beatrice and Sidney Webb, the two Fabians. It was in this circle that he also met Alice Dax, a staunch suffragette of radical ideas who was married to a chemist. Her friends later professed to see many of her characteristics in Clara Dawes, Miriam's rival in *Sons and Lovers.*

It was this married woman who did for Lawrence what Jessie, with all her inhibitions and devotion to abstract ideals, was unable to do. One day, in Alice Dax's house, he was wrestling with a poem, unable to find a satisfactory ending for it. Alice Dax at last took matters into her own hands. She led him to her bedroom and, as she later confided to a friend, "gave Bert sex. I had to. He came downstairs and finished the poem."

According to all accounts, Alice Dax was a woman who was not at all given to sexual impulses of this sort. Lawrence later became her lover over a period, as far as is known, of several months. From that first moment she was deeply devoted to him, and she hoped fervently that the child to which she subsequently gave birth was his. But her closest friends, who knew her secret, persuaded her that it bore an unmistakable resemblance to her husband. When Lawrence eventually broke with her, she made no attempt to hold him back. She was convinced that she owed it to his genius to make this sacrifice. But after their separation she allowed no man, not even her husband, to touch her again.[6]

7

"Here I am a stranger in a strange land," wrote Lawrence soon after his arrival in Croydon. His two-year course at University College had come to its end, and he had taken a job as a teacher in this south London suburb.

Leaving Eastwood had been a torture. He had spent very few nights away from home. The occasions in his life when his first and last acts on rising and going to bed had not been to kiss his mother had been rare. He paid a last visit to Haggs Farm to take leave of his friends. It was a still autumn evening, and Jessie accompanied him to the garden gate. She could not restrain her tears, and he took her in his arms and kissed her. He had seldom kissed her before.

He felt as if he were going into exile, and his first letter to Jessie was, as she expressed it, "like a howl of terror". But ten days later he was able to write: "I am rapidly getting over my loneliness and despair."

Croydon was then—less so today—a typical suburb on the periphery of the vast metropolis, with clean and pleasant, if characterless, streets, tidy front gardens and plain-looking houses jealously guarding their privacy. The elementary school, which was to be his place of work for the next three years, had been opened only twelve months previously. It was regarded as a model school, at least as far as its buildings and its facilities were concerned.

It is hardly surprising that Lawrence responded reluctantly to the dictates of school discipline. After all, he did not regard teaching as his mission in life; it was simply a means of earning his bread, and not a very easy one at that, for from his salary of ninety-five pounds a year he had to pay out almost half for board and lodging. But he was a good and conscientious teacher, particularly in the subjects that lay closest to his heart: English, natural history and art. He had taken drawing lessons and begun to paint even before he wrote his first poems, and the skills he had acquired were of use to him now.

He had to cope with a class of sixty pupils, but with his inborn sympathy for children he immediately established an excellent rapport. "I rebuke them sternly," he wrote in a letter, "but my heart is laughing." The headmaster was a friendly and liberal-minded man, and he allowed Lawrence to use his own methods of teaching, which were very unconventional and remarkably progressive. Many years later this headmaster, Philip F. T. Smith, wrote:

> Lawrence hated the slightest interference with his class work. On one occasion I followed a Ministerial Inspector into his room. The intrusion was unexpected and resented. A curious wailing of distressed voices issued from a far corner. The sounds were muffled by a large covering black-board. The words of a familiar song arose from the depths:
>
> > Full fathom five thy father lies,
> > Of his bones are coral made.
>
> The class was reading *The Tempest*. The presentation expressed the usual thoroughness of Lawrence's attitude to the exercise in progress. It must not be spoiled even by official comment. Lawrence rushed with outstretched hands to the astounded visitor: "Hush! Hush! Don't you hear? The sea chorus from *The Tempest*." Those were the days of conventional methods of instruction, and Lawrence's excursions into dramatic expression were not likely to meet with full approval.[1]

Whenever Lawrence could find time, he continued work on *The White Peacock*. His health was giving him some cause for concern. "I think it is my liver which is upset by nervous excitement," he wrote. His face, decorated at that time with a small, reddish-brown moustache, was unnaturally pale. One of his older colleagues, an elderly schoolmistress, decided to take him under her maternal wing, and she persuaded him to join her and another teacher, Helen Corke, in long rambles through the woods and fields of the surrounding countryside.

Helen was teaching at a different school. At first he regarded her simply as a pleasant walking companion, a lively, intelligent and sensitive woman who shared his literary interests and made no emotional demands on him. But in September 1909, returning to Croydon after spending the holidays with his mother, he discovered Helen in a state of profound spiritual distress. She had been involved in a tragic love affair, the circumstances of which were uncomfortably reminiscent of a formula very popular at that time with romantic novelists.

A young musician from whom she had been taking violin lessons fell in love with her, and she with him. But their happiness contained the seeds of tragedy from the very beginning, for he was already married. He persuaded her to go away with him during the summer holidays, but their days together proved a torture to them both, and shortly after their return to London he committed suicide.

For Helen, life had now lost all meaning. Lawrence was appalled, and he determined to do all he could to save her from a complete breakdown. The method he chose was both subtle and effective. Instead of trying to take her mind off her sorrow, he sought to place it in a wider perspective. He read the tragedies of Euripides with her, hoping to restore her will to live by identifying her personal grief with the sorrows of all mankind. But the further he penetrated into her mourning, the stronger became his own urge to take the place of her dead lover. The fight to save Helen turned into a struggle for her love, and in the effort to restore her spiritual peace his own passions were aroused. He wrote her one strongly sensual poem after another, but it was all in vain. He wrote:[2]

> Your radiance dims when I draw too near, and my free
> Fire enters your petals like death, you wilt dead white.

Helen refused him her love, but not her friendship. She was a remarkable girl, and the spiritual help which Lawrence gave her in her hour of need was not entirely unreciprocated. Her understanding for his personal feelings and her sympathy with his creative struggles were all the more valuable to him now that he was away from his normal surroundings and about to make his public début as an author. She herself had talent as a writer, and the books which she later wrote achieved a modest success.

Her own efforts to heal her wounds revealed her wisdom and strength of character. She began, almost as an act of personal psycho-analysis, to write a novel based on her traumatic experience. After she had shown Lawrence some chapters of her uncompleted manuscript, he resolved—himself already deeply involved in her tragedy—to make these fragments the basis of a novel of his own. Helen did not object. He had already finished *The White Peacock* and had begun work on *Sons and Lovers*, but now he put this aside in order to write *The Trespasser*, his second novel. Many years later Helen Corke completed her own book and it was published after Lawrence's death under the title *Neutral Ground*.

His contact with Helen faded out after he left Croydon, but she remained on terms of close friendship with Jessie Chambers, even after both of them had ceased to play a part in Lawrence's life.

On an August evening in the year 1909 a large, affable-looking man of about thirty-five was sitting in the drawing-room of his house in London. The dimensions of his body were so expansive that they must have been the cause of much doubtful head-shaking in life insurance companies. The room itself had the discreetly elegant proportions one expects of an eighteenth-century drawing-room, but its architectural felicities and the beauty of its Chippendale chairs were obscured by a muddled mass of books, manuscripts, periodicals and office equipment. Partly living-room, partly office, it constituted the editorial headquarters of a very reputable literary magazine that had not yet completed the first year of its short life. The magazine was the *English Review*, and the urbane, well-nourished gentleman was Ford Madox Hueffer, its editor.

Hueffer, as his name suggests, was of German extraction. His family were staunch Catholics from Westphalia, and his paternal grandfather had been mayor of Münster and member of the German National Assembly which met in Frankfurt in 1848. He had also sired seventeen children. One of Ford's uncles—this time on the maternal side—had been lord mayor of Bonn and a member of the German Reichstag.

The Prussian takeover of Westphalia drove several members of the Hüffer family to seek their fortunes abroad, but Ford's father was the only one of them to make England his new home. Dr Franz Karl Christoph Johann Hüffer became plain Francis Hueffer—not that that made it easier for his new British compatriots to pronounce his name. His boundless enthusiasm for Schopenhauer caused some alarm in London. Appointed music critic of *The Times*, he did much to further Richard Wagner's cause in London. He became friends with Carlyle and married a daughter of Ford Madox Brown, the Pre-Raphaelite painter. Francis Hueffer died when his son Ford was only fifteen years old. Though born in England, Ford's feelings for Germany were still strong, and he went to Bonn to study at the university. He lived with his uncle, a historian whose lectures he attended. He also made friends with a number of socialist students and learned by personal experience what it felt like to be attacked by soldiers on horseback. Up to the time of his death he retained a profound admiration for German culture and a loathing for German militarism.[3]

Hueffer was a writer of remarkable, if not of truly great talent; he wrote no less than sixty-seven books. But his real significance lay outside his creative work. He had good judgment and a sharp eye for budding literary talent. He encouraged and advised new young writers and supported, enthusiastically and at times eccentrically, all types of experiment. At a time when English writers were struggling to free themselves from traditional forms, he did much to define and clarify new ideas. Together with his close friend Joseph Conrad, the Polish seaman who became a classic English novelist, he laid down the foundations of the "Impressionist Novel". Today the form is completely accepted, but in the first years of the twentieth century it was a subject of violent controversy. Hueffer fought courageously and successfully for his conviction that the novel did not have to be cast in the conventional epic form. It could also consist, like life itself, of a series of impressions, in which chronology plays as unimportant a part as it does in memory itself: the psychological factor alone was decisive. Thus he condemned the traditional linear form of the novel as a falsification of human experience, and insisted that jumps in time, flashbacks and juxtapositions were legitimate tools in a writer's technique.

His friends called him a "literary saint"—and he had a great many friends. The first number of the *English Review*, which appeared in December 1908, contained new contributions by Joseph Conrad, H. G. Wells, Thomas Hardy and John Galsworthy. His friends and disciples then or later included Henry James (who used him as a model for Merton Densher in his novel *The Wings of the Dove*), as well as Ezra Pound, James Joyce, Ernest Hemingway, Wyndham Lewis and W. B. Yeats.

On that evening in August, Hueffer sat at his writing-desk reading a manuscript which began like this:

> The small locomotive engine, Number 4, came clanking, stumbling down from Selston with seven full waggons. It appeared round the corner with loud threats of speed, but the colt that it startled from among the gorse, which still flickered indistinctly in the raw afternoon, outdistanced it at a canter. A woman, walking up the railway line to Underwood, drew back into the hedge, held her basket aside, and watched the footplate of the engine advancing.

Hueffer was tired. His eyes were burning. Without reading any further, he placed the manuscript in the tray for accepted contributions and stood up.

"You've got another genius?" the secretary enquired ironically.

"It's a big one this time," Hueffer replied and went into his bedroom to dress for dinner.

The dinner was a literary one, and it was being held in the Pall Mall

Restaurant. At Hueffer's table sat G. K. Chesterton and Hilaire Belloc, H. G. Wells and Maurice Baring, diplomat as well as writer, who had just returned from the British Embassy in St Petersburg.

"I've discovered a genius," Hueffer remarked to Wells. "He is called D. H. Lawrence."

And before the dinner party broke up two publishers had already asked when they would be able to see the new author's first novel with a view to publication.

Lawrence at this time was on holiday with his mother on the Isle of Wight. He had not the slightest idea that his name was being talked about in literary circles. Indeed, he did not even know that Jessie had sent the *English Review* some of his poems and the short story *Odour of Chrysanthemums*.[4] She had taken a hand in his destiny behind his back and smoothed his path into literature without his knowledge.

On his return to Croydon Lawrence paid a visit to the offices of the *English Review*. Hueffer awaited him with a certain trepidation. He knew from his correspondence with Jessie that the author he had discovered was the son of a coalminer. He was of course quite used to dealing with geniuses, but all the same he had never had anything to do with a writer whose father worked down the mines. Then suddenly he saw a young man he had never seen before leaning against the door, panting. Like a fox, Hueffer thought to himself: sunshot tawny hair ... moustache, deepset luminous eyes—a fox! And the "fox", who was no doubt just as nervous as Hueffer, blurted out after a keen glance around the drawing-room cum office: "This isn't my idea, sir, of an editor's office."

In his next letter to Jessie, Lawrence described Hueffer as the kindest man on earth. "Last night I dined with celebrities," he added, "and tonight I am dining with two R.As., but I'd give it all up for one of our old evenings in the Haggs parlour."

But now he was launched. With one single leap—aided of course by Jessie's push—he had landed among the group of young writers who were then being talked about. Hueffer, concerned as always for the human side of things, had by no means forgotten the young schoolmistress in Eastwood. He invited Lawrence to bring Jessie along some time. And when she came to London at the end of November, Lawrence dragged her, ignoring her protests, to see Hueffer, who, like everyone else on that evening, took her to be the fiancée of his newly discovered genius. They all went to Kensington to visit Violet Hunt.

By this time Lawrence was aware that Hueffer's private life was in something of a mess. At the age of twenty-one Hueffer had fallen in love with a seventeen-year-old girl, Elsie Martindale. Her father, a well-known painter, was a man of strict Victorian principles, and his daughter was kept virtually a prisoner at home. With remarkable courage, Elsie, following the example of many fictional heroines of the time, cast her fetters aside and left her father's house, informing her lover of her whereabouts through a coded message in the personal column of a newspaper. He hastened to her on wings of love, and, with the help of influential friends and a little discreet blackmail, the marriage was finally sanctioned.

Sad to relate, Elsie's reserves of passion began to ebb as the years went by, and Hueffer grew tired of his former sweetheart. He left her settled at their home in the country and went to London to seek his literary fortune. However, his love of literature could not entirely compensate for the lack of love in other directions, and Hueffer succumbed to the charms and intellectual attractions of Violet Hunt, a lady seven years older than himself.

Violet was also the daughter of a well-known Pre-Raphaelite painter. Herself a writer, she was well endowed with the social graces, and her salon, to which Hueffer was now conducting Lawrence and Jessie, was the meeting-place of many famous writers and artists of the day.

Jessie found it all rather overwhelming. "Am I supposed to keep the hat on or not?" she whispered to the maid who opened the door for them and later, when they sat down at the candlelit dinner table: "Should I remove my gloves or keep them on?"

Among the guests was the American poet Ezra Pound, who was of the same age as Lawrence. In later years, like those two other expatriate Americans, Henry James and T. S. Eliot, Pound was to have a considerable influence on English letters. Maybe even at that time there were many who were intuitively aware of the fame that lay in store for him, for his mere arrival on the London literary scene had caused as much excitement as if a volcano had suddenly erupted on the flat fields of Holland. He had become a lecturer at Wabash College, Indiana, at the unlikely age of twenty-two, but four months after his appointment he had been dismissed in circumstances that bore some resemblance to a scandal. He had sinned against the strict moral code by providing shelter in his room to a homeless soubrette singer—partly out of compassion, but partly for less noble reasons. His subsequent boundless hatred for his native country seems to have dated from this episode. After a year spent on the European Continent acclimatising himself, he established himself in London as an expert on the poetry of old Provence. He published ballads of his own in the style of the troubadours and generally caused a flutter in the English dovecotes with his compendious, if inaccurate, knowledge of European literature, his ecstatic, indefinable form of mysticism, and the absurdity of his behaviour. He signed all his letters in the Chinese manner and played the harpsichord with dramatic abandon. To receive guests in his "attic"—in reality a luxurious top-floor apartment—he would don a flowing dressing-gown which impressively underlined the exoticism of his appearance. He had a pale complexion, green eyes like a cat's, a red beard and he wore an ear-ring in one ear only. He was a fascinating, highly gifted poet whose word-music, frequently pretentious and at times completely meaningless, fleetingly inspired a number of imitators. In later years his eccentricity assumed an increasingly unpleasant character. Having repelled many people with his anti-Semitic utterances, he became a propagandist for Mussolini on the Italian radio during the Second World War. Picked up by Italian partisans, he was handed over to the American military authorities and, while in solitary confinement, occupied himself with translating Confucius. Eventually he suffered a complete mental breakdown. He was put on trial in Washington on a charge of treason, but was found to be incapable of pleading. He was locked up in a sanatorium for the criminally insane, where he remained until his release in 1958.

All this still lay far in the future, however. At that first meeting Pound bowed low before Jessie and asked Hueffer, with a meaningful glance towards Lawrence, how in his opinion one should address a working man. Lawrence quietly asked the maid who was serving the dishes which knife he should take for the asparagus. This problem solved, he joined in the general conversation with complete ease. When, in the course of it, the names of Carlyle and Ruskin cropped up, he quoted passages from their works in support of his arguments.

Hueffer regarded him with undisguised wonderment. "You're the only man I've ever met," he remarked, "who really has read all those people."[5]

Lawrence could not resist taking the November 1909 issue of the *English Review* to school and laying it on the classroom table in full sight of his pupils. The blue-covered magazine contained six poems under his own name. It was his first token of fame to come, a first step on the path about which he had dreamed for years. For his mother it must have been a proud moment to read her son's verses in the best literary periodical of its day.

The *English Review* remained loyal to him. A short story appeared in February 1910, followed by more poems. Hueffer had by now relinquished the editorship to Austin Harrison, but he continued to sponsor Lawrence. He obviously enjoyed conducting his new discovery, this strange schoolmaster genius from the coalmining district, through the corridors of literary society. And since Lawrence could be fitted into none of the usual categories, the first impression he made on people had a lasting effect. Violet Hunt later described him in these words:

> He had the head of a child—the yellow hair with a "feather" at the back, much as if a school-mate had been having a game with it. His eyes, if I mistake not, were very blue, his lips very red, and his face very white—sinisterly so, for he looked consumptive. His manner was gentle, modest and tender, in a way I did not associate with his upbringing.

But the impression he left was not always favourable: men in particular were often critical. The school inspector in Croydon, Stewart A. Robertson, a man with literary ambitions of his own, painted a much less sympathetic portrait:

> He had a pale face, stooping shoulders, a narrow chest, febrile hands, and a voice which I can only describe as contralto. He coughed occasionally ... He was morbidly sensitive in himself, and even more morbid in his reaction to others. He did not like teaching, and found boys tiresome and meaningless. Indeed, he was never interested in any person before the age of puberty. It would be unfair to say that libido and life were to him the same, but it would not be wholly untrue.

Lawrence made no secret of the fact that he was heartily sick of teaching. He had given Hueffer the manuscript of *The White Peacock* to read, and Hueffer gave him his opinion of it as they were riding together on a bus. "It's got every fault that the English novel can have," he boomed, "but you've got GENIUS!" He did not hesitate to recommend the novel to the publisher William Heinemann, who instantly accepted it.

"I *do* want that book to make haste," Lawrence wrote to his publisher. "Not that I care much myself. But I want my mother to see it while still she keeps the live consciousness. She is really horribly ill."

63

He wrote this letter in October 1910. His mother had become ill in August. She had cancer, and he knew that no power on earth could save her. He spent every other weekend at Eastwood and bitterly resented having to return to his work in Croydon. He would sit for hours at his mother's bedside, studying the beloved face now so horribly distorted by illness. His grief induced in him a panic-stricken terror of being left alone. What would become of him when the woman who meant more to him than anyone else in the whole world was no longer alive? Who could ever take her place? Not Jessie, certainly: marriage to her was impossible to contemplate. As he himself once said, his mother would rise up even from her grave to prevent that.

Two weeks before Lydia Lawrence died, he met Louie Burrows in Leicester. Years had passed since the dark-haired Louie had inspired him to write passionate love poems. They had exchanged occasional letters after leaving University College in Nottingham, and they had also met a few times during the school holidays. Since then Louie had become headmistress of a village school not far from Quorn, where her family was now settled.

It was a Saturday, and he spent the afternoon in Leicester with Louie. At the end of it they got into the same train, she to return home, he to continue the short journey to Nottingham and Eastwood. At the last station before Quorn, as she was preparing to alight, Louie asked: "And what do you think you'll do, Bert, after Christmas?"

He knew very well that she meant: after your mother is dead. "I don't know," he replied. Then he added suddenly: "I should like to get married." She was silent.

"Should you?" he asked.

She hesitated. "I don't know."

"I should like to marry you," he said suddenly. It was like a despairing scream uttered during the wild flight from impending loneliness. "Should you?" he urged.

"What?" she asked in confusion, the blood mounting to her face.

"Like to marry me?"

The brakes screeched as the train drew into Quorn. She looked him straight in the face and laid a hand on his. "I'll go to Loughborough. I can come back by the 8.10," she said softly.

A warm feeling of happiness pushed back his sorrow and despair. He counted the money in his pocket. "My wealth is four pounds four shillings and twopence-halfpenny—and not a penny more."

"And I haven't quite twice as much," she replied. Was that enough to start a marriage on? They laughed as they stepped out of the train at Loughborough station into the streaming rain.

With the surprising openness he always showed in speaking of his relations with women, he wrote in a letter that very evening:[6]

> She [Jessie] loves me to madness, and demands the soul of me. I have been cruel to her, and wronged her, but I did not know. Nobody can have the soul of me. My mother has had it, and nobody can have it again. Nobody can come into my very self again, and breathe me like an atmosphere. Don't say I am hasty this time—I know. Louie—whom I wish I could marry the day after the funeral —she would never demand to drink me up and have me. She loves me—but it is a fine, warm, healthy, natural love.

It might have been a sudden impulse, yet it is clear that he had considered the possibility before. Some weeks previously, sitting at his mother's bedside, he had cautiously asked: "Mother, do you think it would be all right for me to marry Louie—later?"

The dying woman's answer came promptly, without a moment's hesitation, hard and implacable: "No—I don't!" But half a minute later, bowing to the inevitable, she added softly: "Well—if you think you'd be happy with her—yes."

Lydia Lawrence died on 9 December. A few days before that Lawrence had placed in her hands the first printed copy of *The White Peacock*. She gave the book an uncomprehending glance and turned away.

The day before the rain-drenched funeral, he met Jessie. They walked along the paths they had trodden together in earlier and happier days, and she said to him: "You should not have drawn Louie into things."

He answered her sharply, and her heart contracted. They walked on in silence, apprehensive. Then, "I've always loved Mother," he said in a strangled voice.

"I know you have—"

"I don't mean that," he interrupted her. "I've *loved* her, like a lover. That's why I could never love you."[7]

The year afterwards, 1911, was his "sick" year. He wrote:

> Then, in that year, for me everything collapsed, save the mystery of death, and the haunting of death in life. I was twenty-five, and from the death of my mother, the world began to dissolve around me,

beautiful, iridescent, but passing away substanceless. Till I almost dissolved away myself, and was very ill: when I was twenty-six.

To Louie he wrote; "It is true, I have died, a bit of me—but there's plenty left for you."

He was now back in Croydon and she was some hundred and twenty miles away in her little village school. He was listless and bitter. The protracted four months of his mother's dying had exhausted him in mind as well as in body. And something seemed to be compelling him to continue the destructive work that death had begun inside him. His break with Jessie severed other cords that bound him to his past life. He felt uprooted. He had nothing now to hold on to. He was at logger-heads with his younger sister and his father: his family was upset that he had become engaged while his mother was on her deathbed. Louie's parents were also against the marriage and treated him with silent hostility.

It was indeed on all counts a sick year, and the appearance of his novel did nothing to change the situation. He showed it to his father and watched as the miner sat down and read half a page, laboriously spelling out the words—like a Hottentot, his son thought contemptuously. The father wanted to know how much Lawrence had received for the book and, when he was told fifty pounds, he "looked at me with shrewd eyes, as if I were a swindler. 'Fifty pounds! An' tha's niver done a day's work in thy life!'"

Hueffer's belief that he had discovered a new genius was not shared by the critics. Though the immature novel was acknowledged to have some merit, praise and blame were at best equally balanced. "Impressive natural descriptions", "... no well-knit plot", "... aimlessness and banality of much of the conversation", "... a confusing, strange, disturbing book, but that it has the elements of greatness, few will deny"—were these signposts to the fame of which he had so sanguinely dreamed? True, the small first printing was soon sold out and was followed in spring by a new impression. But in America the book was a complete failure.

Hueffer continued to push him, and one evening took him to a literary supper at the house of Ernest Rhys, editor of the famous Everyman series of classics. Each of the guests was expected to read an unpublished poem or passage of prose of his own composition. The two most prominent guests were W. B. Yeats and Ezra Pound, between whom an unmistakable rivalry began to show in the course of the evening. Florence Farr, the very talented actress for whom Shaw had written his play *Arms and the Man*, had brought along a psaltery, a medieval stringed instrument, and, accompanied by its monotonous notes, she proceeded to recite some verses by Yeats. Yeats himself, the great apostle of the Celtic twilight, embarked on an endless monologue concerning the revolutionary significance of this attempt to wed music to poetry. Ezra Pound felt himself being pushed aside. His vanity wounded, he took a red tulip from the vase on the table before him, and absentmindedly, it seemed, began to chew it. Nobody paid him the slightest attention. By the time the Celtic flow at last came to an end, Pound had eaten all the tulips on the table.

The symposium proper began after supper. Lawrence, who had been sitting silently in a corner, was among those asked to recite a poem of his own. He rose awkwardly, crossed the room and sat down at a writing-desk. Pulling a book from his pocket, he began to read from it in a quiet, but expressive voice. He had his back to the audience, and the longer he went on reading, the more difficult it became to understand him. The listeners became restless, and soon the drawing-room was filled with whispered conversations. Lawrence did not appear to notice: at any rate he gave no sign of bringing his reading to a close. After this had gone on for half an hour, the host at last summoned up courage to approach and beg him not to over-exert himself. Lawrence rose quickly, stuffed his book in his pocket and with an awkward bow returned shyly to his corner.[8]

It was certainly a consolation to Lawrence in his desperate efforts to extricate himself from his labyrinth of grief and loneliness to find himself accepted in the magic circle of the successful. But all the same he felt an outsider. A wide chasm yawned not only between him, the schoolmaster writer, and those who had achieved fame, but also between him and all those eager imitators and hangers-on who, without being successful, famous and rich themselves, enjoyed basking in the atmosphere of success. He took his revenge by caricaturing them with bitter savagery. He made Helen Corke laugh with his imitations of Yeats, the Celtic prophet, and Florence Farr, his high priestess, and with his parody of the beauty-worshipping Ezra Pound eating tulips. Even his "discoverer" came in for some satirical attention. Hueffer had been tactless enough to condemn his second novel, *The Trespasser*, which was based on Helen Corke's tragic love affair.

Of course Lawrence was fully aware of the practical advantages his acquaintance with these literary figures could bring him. But it placed him in certain difficulties.

Ezra Pound invited him to dinner, but Lawrence could not repay his hospitality. When Hueffer asked him to a meal in the Reform Club, he had to refuse on the grounds that he did not possess a single respectable suit. "My shirts are patched, my boots are—well, not presentable," he wrote to Louie when she once again reproached him for not putting aside any savings. They had agreed to get married as soon as they had saved a hundred pounds.

It annoyed him that she was always reminding him of this pledge. He felt she was trying to limit his freedom of action. Did he have to account to her for every penny he spent? After all, they were not married—yet. And, although he loved her—in fact just because he loved her—he was irritated by her petty reproaches and her conventional views. He admitted that, being engaged to her, he owed her certain obligations, but did he not have rights as well? Louie thought these should not go beyond kisses. His passionate nature battered in vain against her deep religious convictions. "It is very damnable," he complained, "to have slowly to drink back again into oneself all the lava and fire of passionate eruption."

Sexual frustration drove him to despair. What tricks was fate trying to play on him that he found himself involved with three women, all of whom loved and admired him, yet kept him physically at arm's length? His friendship with Helen Corke was hopelessly overshadowed by the tragedy which had given rise to it. Prepared though she was to accept his declarations of love in poetry, any attempt to turn theory into practice was immediately repulsed. Poor Jessie, who in her puritanical way still adored him in spite of repeated humiliations, drew back as soon as his urges took on a sexual tinge. And Louie, his betrothed, refused to share her bed with him until their union had received the blessing of the church.

Since the summer of the previous year he had been working on his new novel, *Paul Morel*, to which he later gave the title *Sons and Lovers*. Most of Lawrence's writings have autobiographical features, but into none of them did he pour so much of his own life as into *Sons and Lovers*. Here he relived his life at home with his drunken father, his happy days at Haggs Farm, the crooked course of his first love, his mother's triumph over Jessie and her long drawn-out battle with death.

He sent Jessie the still unfinished first draft to read. She was not much impressed. "I was very surprised that you have kept so far from reality in your story," she wrote to him. "I think what really happened was much more poignant and interesting than the situation you have invented."

He begged her to write an account in her own words of the events and conflicts in which they had both been involved, so that he could use it as a guide when revising his own manuscript. Jessie did as she was asked, hoping in this way to help him free himself from the fetters still binding him to his dead mother. It was as if she were herself providing the instruments of torture for her martyrdom.

Nevertheless, this "sick" year brought Lawrence a ray of light in the shape of one new friend—Edward Garnett. Hueffer had served his purpose in introducing Lawrence into literary society, and now Garnett was to render him a much more valuable service: he became Lawrence's guide and adviser in the early years of his literary career.

Edward Garnett was a member of a famous literary family. His father, Richard Garnett, was director of the British Museum Library, and countless scholars and writers were indebted to his encyclopaedic knowledge in helping them to track down their sources on its vast shelves. Karl Marx, writing *Das Kapital* under the great cupola of the Reading Room, was one who owed much to his advice, and he repaid Richard Garnett's help with a signed photograph of himself.

If Richard Garnett's claim to immortality rests on the books of others, the same can be said even more emphatically about his son. Edward Garnett, who was forty-three at the time he first met Lawrence, wrote no original work of any importance, but his services to English literature in general were beyond price. He took a long succession of young writers under his wing, advised them, encouraged them and helped them through to success. His job as reader to a number of publishing firms earned him little, and he was constantly in financial difficulties, but this did nothing either to damp his enthusiasm or to prevent him winning the friendship and admiration of all the most famous writers of his time. Unusually tall and slim, he showed his contempt for all worldly vanities in the negligence of his dress as well as, more directly, in endless tirades. John Galsworthy erected an enduring monument to him in the figure of the architect Bosinney in *The Forsyte Saga*.

Edward Garnett's wife, Constance, who was six years older than her husband, was also filled with an inexhaustible energy, however fragile she might have looked. She, more than anyone else, was responsible for introducing the masterpieces of Russian literature to the British public. When Lawrence first met her, she was engaged in translating the novels of Dostoevsky. She worked with great rapidity and concentration. As soon as a page was completed she would throw it, without looking up, onto the pile of handwritten pages which rose up "almost knee-high" at her side, as Lawrence noted with astonishment. He was intrigued by the difference between her way of working and her husband's. Edward would often spend hours polishing a single sentence, until he found a formula that satisfied him.

Constance Garnett's shy and delicate features, hidden now behind spectacles, and her lovely complexion revealed that as a girl she must have been beautiful. In her early years she had been a keen socialist, and Bernard Shaw had been one of her admirers. Once, when they were serving together on the committee of the Fabian Society, he confessed that he would have liked to marry her. "I did not dare to ask you," he told her. "I could not afford the standard of living to which you were entitled." Constance was vastly amused by this revelation. Throughout her marriage to Edward Garnett it was only her scanty earnings as a translator that kept her family from the direst need; and even then she was not always successful. Once, when her husband had a prolonged spell without work, they and their son David lived for a whole summer on almost nothing but mushrooms.

Although her translations brought her fame, they were miserably paid. For translating all three volumes of Tolstoy's *War and Peace* she received no more than three hundred pounds, and she had to complete her translation within a year, which meant working day and night with hardly a pause. As a result of these superhuman exertions she temporarily lost her sight, and for a long time she had to employ a secretary, who read out the Russian text to her and then took down the translation which Constance carefully dictated to her, sentence by sentence. In the space of thirty-five years she translated the works of Turgenev, Chekhov, Dostoevsky, Tolstoy, Gogol, Goncharov, Ostrovsky and Herzen—seventy volumes in all.

The literary talents of this remarkable couple were inherited by their son David, whose first novel, *Lady into Fox*, sold half a million copies. This little book alone probably earned its young author more than his parents had managed to earn throughout their whole lives.[9] But this was much later. At the time Lawrence first met him, David Garnett was only twenty years old and was studying botany.

It was not easy to reach the Garnetts' house. They lived "away from it all" in the depths of Kent, and they had built their home, The Cearne, in the style of an old farmhouse. It lay in a meadow surrounded by woods, and the nearest road was half a mile away. Lawrence loved going there for an occasional weekend, sometimes perhaps only for a single evening. He felt far more at home in the Garnetts' living-room, with its dark oak beams and its crackling fire, than in his own room in Croydon. Waiting one rainy day for the train at Edenbridge, the nearest station, he contracted pneumonia. During this year he had been frequently ill. His mother's death had depressed and weakened him. His work on *Sons and Lovers* brought back all the conflicts which he had thought forgotten. Louie, he had hoped, would rescue him from the misery of loneliness. But, instead of that, his engagement brought him nothing but constant irritation and torturing doubt, and the ascetic living which her strict piety imposed on him caused him untold anguish. In addition, there was his disappointment over the scant success of his first novel and the depressing knowledge that he would have to continue his work as a teacher. It was all bound to lead to a crisis. Once again, as ten years earlier, he found himself at death's door.

A telegram brought his sister Ada to his bedside. Helen Corke came with her. Emily, his other sister, visited him, as well as Louie Burrows and Jessie Chambers. The doctor told him that he must give up his teaching job. Lawrence wrote to Edward Garnett: "I feel my life burn like a free flame floating on oil—wavering and leaping and snapping. I shall be glad to get it confined and conducted again."

However, many weeks were to pass before the flame of his life burned steadily again, and in the period of slow recovery and reflection he came to see that he must make a clean break with the past. He put *Sons and Lovers* aside and took up *The Trespasser* again, which he finished in a remarkably short time. He met Helen Corke, whose tragedy had inspired this novel, in London. It was a short meeting over a tea table. No hard words were exchanged, and no sentimental ones either, but each of them knew, as they said good-bye, that it was for the last time. They never saw one another again.

On the following day, 4 February 1912, he asked Louie to release him from his engagement. The doctors, he wrote, had urgently advised him not to marry, and in view of his precarious health he also felt that he could not take on the responsibility of a marriage. "My illness has changed me a good deal, has broken a good many of the old bonds that held me," he confessed.

He only had one further meeting with Jessie. But he continued to send her, page by page, the new version of *Sons and Lovers*, on which he was now working furiously. Back in her old role, Jessie faithfully returned the pages, with remarks scribbled in the margin. But she knew now that her last hope had gone. His work on the novel had not succeeded in reviving his early love for her. Even in the poetic recon-struction of their friendship, in the recollection of their struggle with his mother, he was never on Jessie's side. In these hastily written pages his mother's victory (so it seemed to her) was complete—even beyond the grave.

But not all the old ties had yet been severed. In Lawrence himself the feeling must have arisen that there was nothing he could do to extricate himself once and for all from the fetters of the past except to flee from them. Could he perhaps find a position as a lecturer in English in a German university? A post like that, he felt, would damage his health far less than his present job as a schoolteacher. He approached two people for help. The first, to whom he wrote, was his uncle Fritz Krenkow, who was married to one of his mother's sisters. A native of Mecklenburg in Germany, he was now running a business in Leicester. Krenkow was, however, a very unusual businessman, for his real interests lay in oriental languages. Articles by him appeared regularly in academic periodicals, and he was a respected member of a number of learned societies. Later—ten years after the First World War—he became professor of Arabic at the University of Delhi. Lawrence had been in contact with him for some time, and had translated several of Krenkow's German versions of Egyptian folk songs into English.

The other person to whom Lawrence turned for help was Professor Ernest Weekley, whose lectures he had once attended at University College in Nottingham.

8

"I see him before me as he entered the house. A long thin figure, quick straight legs, light, sure movements."

This was Frieda Weekley's first impression of Lawrence. Her husband had invited him for lunch, so that they could talk about his plan. Frieda led him into the sitting-room. There was still half an hour till lunchtime, and Professor Weekley had not yet arrived home. The french windows leading into the garden were open, and the red velvet curtains were swaying in the April wind. Outside on the lawn the children were playing.

Something about him, as she wrote later, attracted Frieda's attention to Lawrence from the very first moment. It might of course simply have been due to her husband's announcement, spoken half jokingly, that he was expecting the visit of a "genius". But in the half-hour they spent alone together she felt something more than mere superficial curiosity. Lawrence had no talent for small talk, and after only a few minutes he was telling Frieda vehemently that he wanted nothing more to do with women—nothing, nothing, nothing. Had she been an Englishwoman she would have regarded such a statement as out of place and tactless. It showed a distinct lack of manners to speak so indiscreetly about one's unsolved personal problems to a lady whom one had only just met.

But Frieda was not English. Lawrence could not have chosen a better way to arouse her sympathy and interest. It was obvious to her that he intended no such effect (at least at this stage): his behaviour sprang entirely from the spontaneity and intensity of his temperament. It was these things that particularly impressed her.

She was thirty-two years old and the mother of three children. Yet this astonishing young man, six years younger than herself, seemed suddenly to have opened up new perspectives, to have shown her a deeper, more intense aspect of humanity, against which the everyday conventionality of her surroundings looked flat and colourless. How had she come to allow the routine of her middle-class family life so completely to smother her longings for the wider horizons, of whose existence she had had vague glimmerings in her earlier youth?

Who was this man who could make her feel in the course of a single conversation that she had spent the twelve years of her supposedly happy marriage walking in her sleep? Was it conceivable that this lanky red-haired young man, so sickly in appearance and so vulnerable, had been sent to wake her? What was it about his burning eyes and his high, ugly, almost feminine voice that had the power to restore her so magically to life? She did not know, but she felt that the mysterious magnetism which was weaving its spell around her had also taken possession of him.

He must have realised from the very first moment that Frieda was different from all the women he had hitherto known. She seemed to possess more vitality, a more powerfully feminine aura, a relaxed naturalness of manner. During the meal he observed her with the acuteness he had kept alive since his childhood. Not the slightest detail escaped his perceptive senses. He noted the excitement in her greenish-brown eyes, the gloss in her fair hair, the wide range of facial expression, childishly naïve at one moment, wickedly mischievous the next. He savoured her natural grace and noble bearing, the foreign colouring in her speech and the dark seductiveness of her voice.

Afterwards he told her that during the whole meal she had paid hardly any attention to her husband. His brutal candour wounded her, but at the same time she was amazed that he had managed in the course of one superficial table conversation to see behind the façade of her marriage. He had only been invited to lunch, but he stayed until evening. Since leaving Croydon he had been living in his father's house at Eastwood. Instead of taking the train, he walked home—a journey of five hours through fields shrouded in darkness.

He wrote to her: "You are the most wonderful woman in all England."

She could have ignored his letter or simply replied: "One does not write such things to a married woman." But she responded instead with a light-hearted question: "You don't know many women in England, how do you know?"

Some days later he visited her again. It was Easter Sunday. The children were in the garden hunting for Easter eggs and the servants had been given the afternoon off. She went into the kitchen to put on a kettle for tea, but she did not even know how to light the gas ring. Her ignorance made him impatient, and he scolded her like a little child. Never before had she been treated in this way. She was, after all, a baroness and the wife of a university professor. But she accepted her scolding like a humble schoolgirl. It would be silly, she thought, to stand on her dignity before him; indeed it would be pointless to play any sort of role, for he obviously knew exactly what was going on inside her. "From the first he saw through me like glass," she wrote twenty years later, "saw how hard I was trying to keep up a cheerful front. I thought it was so despicable and unproud and unclean to be miserable, but he saw through my hard bright shell."

At that time Lawrence was spending frequent weekends at a farm near Eastwood. The farmer, William Holbrook, was married to Jessie's elder sister May. Lawrence invited Frieda to make an excursion there, for he wanted to show her the fields and woods in which he had spent his childhood. Frieda came, bringing her two daughters, and they walked happily through the burgeoning countryside. It was during this walk that she realised, with terrifying but blissful certainty, that the feeling Lawrence had aroused in her was no passing attraction, no mere flaring of physical desire. It was love.

After visiting the farm, Frieda returned to Nottingham with the children. Lawrence spent the night with the Holbrooks. On the following morning, Jessie turned up unexpectedly with her father. She found Lawrence in good humour, but quieter and more reflective than usual. He spoke of his intention of going to Germany, but said not a word about Frieda. When Jessie left, he rode a part of the way with her in her trap, then got out in order to return to the Holbrook farm on foot. He stood at the roadside watching the trap as it drew away. Jessie turned to wave to him, and he raised his hand in farewell. It was their final parting. The chapter of Jessie Chambers was now closed. A new one had begun.

On the Sunday, Lawrence was again with Frieda. Ernest Weekley was away, and Frieda asked Lawrence to spend the night with her.

His answer was clear and decided: "No, I will not stay in your husband's house while he is away, but you must tell him the truth and we will go away together, because I love you."

The thought of having to tell her husband filled Frieda with terror. He had no inkling of what had happened. It was not in his nature to be mistrustful, and he had no reason to suspect the mother of his children of infidelity. Certainly he knew that some Austrian disciple of Freud had filled her head with all sorts of "idiotic sex ideas" when she was in Munich, but he had never envisaged her putting these theories into practice. After over twelve years of marriage he belonged among those who were deceived by her "hard bright shell".

She would probably have been ready to continue with the deception, but she reckoned without Lawrence's character. This time it was the man whom she hoped to take as her lover who saw adultery as a moral problem. His view of the matter had nothing to do with any middle-class moral code. It was permissible, he thought, for a man to take a woman from her husband, if love compelled him. But it was immoral and contemptible to act behind the husband's back and to sleep with his wife in secret, just so that the marriage should appear intact from the outside. Honesty is more important than marital fidelity—that was the principle to which Lawrence now tried to convert Frieda: no half-measures, no falsehoods, no concessions to decorum, no hypocrisy. Frieda found herself suddenly faced with an appalling and tragic choice. She had to choose not only between her husband and the man she passionately loved, but also between her children, the security of her home, the comfort of her middle-class life and all the dangers of an unforeseeable future.

If Frieda still held back and tried to persuade Lawrence to accept a compromise, it was not simply for selfish reasons. She knew that the blow could destroy her husband, and she had no wish to hurt him. She respected him, and she knew how much he loved her. But through all her arguments she knew that, when it finally came to the test, she had already chosen between the respectable university professor whose whole life was words, and the poor elementary schoolteacher whose words could inspire life.

In the end Frieda abandoned all resistance. She agreed to tell Ernest the truth: that their marriage was finished. Once that had been done, once she had fulfilled Lawrence's conditions and put paid to the great lie, they would be free. They were in a daze of blissful but fearful anticipation. Nothing was yet fully clear, and they did not dare to plan beyond the next two or three weeks. In an atmosphere of feverish unrest, assailed by hopes and fears, they had only one fixed point to which to cling, and all further steps must stem from that: on 4 May 1912 Frieda's father was celebrating the fiftieth anniversary of his entry into the army. Frieda had resolved some time before to travel to Metz for the occasion. They now decided that Lawrence should go with her. Beyond that point they were quite unable to think, but Lawrence wrote to Edward Garnett, whom he had taken into his confidence: "We could have at least one week together." At least one week: the prospect filled them both with happiness. What would happen after that lay in the lap of the gods, but they felt the gods, whoever they might be, looked favourably on them. In any case Lawrence could travel on from Metz to Waldbröl near Bonn, where a brother of his uncle Fritz Krenkow was living.

They met in London and journeyed on together to Kent to visit Edward Garnett at The Cearne. Lawrence had written to him enthusiastically about "the finest woman I've ever met," and he had added: "She is the daughter of Baron von Richthofen, of the ancient and famous house of Richthofen." The rebellious son of a working-class family was, as one sees, by no means immune to the allure of an aristocratic name. He was now eager to introduce the baron's daughter to his fatherly friend.

Frieda put off the interview with her husband until the very last moment. But finally, in accordance with her promise to Lawrence, she went to him in his study to tell him the "truth" about their marriage. Whether it was her intention from the start, or whether, in his boundless fury, he wrung the confession from her, we cannot know, but she told Ernest that since her marriage she had been unfaithful with two men, Will Dowson and Otto Gross. But she did not tell her husband the full truth. The main point—that she was leaving him on the following day to go to Germany with Lawrence—she kept to herself.

Ernest's study was on the first floor. The two little girls, Elsa and Barbara, were playing on the stairs and were surprised to see their mother come with tear-stained eyes from their father's room and run sobbing past them.

After that events moved fast. The next morning, Monty, now almost twelve years old, went off to school as usual. He could not understand why his mother was in tears as she kissed him good-bye. Frieda had no fears of leaving him behind in Nottingham with her husband. She knew she could rely on Ida Wilhelmy, her faithful and dependable nanny, to look after him, but she took the two younger children, Elsa and Barbara, to London with her and, inventing some excuse, deposited them with her parents-in-law.

She met Lawrence at Charing Cross Station. They began their journey in a state of indescribable excitement. At Dover they took the night boat to Ostend. He had his entire fortune with him—eleven pounds—and their plans had still got no further than the vague hope of being able to spend a week together in Metz. What was to happen after that, neither of them knew.

They arrived in Metz on 4 May, a Saturday. Lawrence took a room at the Deutscher Hof Hotel, while Frieda went on to her parents' home. They were no longer living in the house in which she had spent her childhood, but had moved to the nearby residential suburb of Montigny, on the baron's retirement from government service.

Frieda found the house stuffed with relatives from Silesia and Baden gathered together to celebrate her father's jubilee. There was a regimental band in attendance, and wherever one went one stumbled over children and army officers. The bedrooms were filled with old ladies who had removed their corsets and stretched themselves out on beds to recover from the day's exertions. Servants flitted about keeping the guests constantly supplied with champagne. Nevertheless, among all the embraces and toasts the baron found an opportunity to draw Frieda to one side. Frantic telegrams from Nottingham were disturbing his festive mood. Professor Weekley had of course known of his wife's intended visit to Metz, but he had been alarmed by her unexpected action in taking their two daughters to London. As his telegrams showed, he had guessed that Frieda had not simply gone off on an innocent visit to her parents. "My child, what are you doing?" the baron asked. His agitation and concern revealed that, whatever his faults, his love for his daughter was as warm as ever. He added: "I always thought you had so much sense." Frieda told her parents that she had fallen out with her husband, but she did not hint with so much as a word that she had left him for another man. She certainly did not mention that Lawrence was with her in Metz.

Her parents tried to persuade her to sleep in their home, but, so great were the crush and confusion, that she preferred to take a room at the Deutscher Hof. Lawrence did not even know the number of her room. He was feeling completely displaced. All that the grand romantic elopement had so far brought him was the inside of a hotel guest room where he was obliged to sit for hours, lost and dejected, drinking one pint of beer after another. His occasional meetings with Frieda were furtive and short, for his presence had to be kept secret. She was desperately anxious to avoid scandal, and, besides, she had her hands full with the family and the jubilee celebrations. Johanna, her youngest sister, had also decided to stay in a hotel rather than in the chaos of her parents' house. Else, the eldest sister, had not yet arrived.

78

Frieda went to the station to meet her. Else, who was accompanied by her two small children, had hardly set foot on the platform when Frieda took the opportunity of their first embrace to whisper in her ear: "I have brought someone with me. You must help me." She knew that, whatever happened, Else would be on her side. Of Johanna she could not be so certain, but Else, by nature as well as on account of her emancipated views, would be her ally. The elder sister of course wanted to see Lawrence as soon as possible, and they arranged a meeting on the Esplanade. The little café in which they first met looked out across the Moselle valley, fresh and green in its spring colours. Lawrence was reserved and silent. Else was surprised by his youth, but she found him sensitive and full of a quiet self-confidence. He was a gentleman, she thought, and she liked him.

There was a fair going on in Metz at the time. Frieda and Johanna escaped from the confusion of their parents' home to plunge into the even greater jumble of decorated stalls, sausage and gingerbread sellers, boneless men and bearded ladies. Nusch was now, as Frieda assures us, more beautiful and elegant than ever before. All of a sudden, among the shooting-galleries and roundabouts, Lawrence appeared. With his shabby raincoat and his cloth cap he looked almost like a tramp. Frieda's heart missed a beat. Full of embarrassment, she introduced him to her sister. He spoke a few words only and then went on his way. To Frieda's great surprise, Johanna said: "You can go with him. You can trust him."

If this was the prelude to bliss, one could only conclude that some-one had blundered. At the merest thought of her children Frieda's eyes would fill with tears, and she did not even dare imagine what her husband was feeling. The situation might have been tragic, but it was also absurd. In order to preserve her secret, Frieda was obliged to limit her contacts with Lawrence to letters, even inside the hotel. His missives to her became more and more impatient and pressing. After all, what sort of elopement was this, when the woman who had abandoned her husband and children for his sake did not dare to acknowledge him openly? Why should they not leave Metz—which he hated anyway, because it was too full of uniforms? He was trying to revise his manuscript of *Sons and Lovers*, but was unable to make any progress; there was more pleasure to be found wandering through the vineyards. But on the Monday it was raining, and he wrote her a few anguished words: "This hotel is like a monastery." On the following day he told her in another letter that he simply could not bear it any longer. And he enclosed a letter to Ernest:[1]

I have written a letter to Ernest. You needn't, of course, send it. But you must say to him all I have said. No more dishonour, no more lies. Let them do their—silliest—but no more subterfuge, lying, dirt, fear. I feel as if it would strangle me.

Ernest Weekley wrote to Frieda:

I had a letter from Lawrence this morning. I bear him no ill-will and hope you will be happy with him. But have some pity on me ... Let me know at once that you agree to a divorce ... You have loved me once—help me now—but quickly.

But he had hardly posted the letter before he sent her a telegram telling her not to open it. He wrote to Frieda's parents: the desperate outburst of a man driven to the brink of madness. But, in spite of everything, there was no word of criticism against Frieda, no derogatory remarks about Lawrence:[2]

Today two letters came from Frieda; in one she speaks of a compromise, in the second she says she will come to help me with the moving. Dear Mama, please make her understand what a state I am in: I cannot see her hand-writing without trembling like an old cripple—to see her again would be my death. I would kill myself and the children too ... Today I had to lecture for four hours and take part in a long session of the Senate. I have desperately to stretch every nerve in order not to cry out hysterically, and then I am weak as a child and can only lie there and think—if only for a quarter of an hour I could not think.

Tragedy was turning into farce. Frieda went with Lawrence for a walk on the slopes between the fortifications; it seemed unlikely they would meet any acquaintances there. The bastions had been rebuilt in the days of her childhood. How she had once loved jumping across the ditches and hiding behind the walls! And now she was among them again, lying with Lawrence in the tall grass: it seemed the safest place to go to discuss their situation. Suddenly a policeman was standing behind them, and Lawrence was arrested on suspicion of being a British spy.

This was awkward, to say the least. Soldiers with no wars to fight console themselves with the next best thing, which is catching spies, and, once having laid hands on a likely suspect, they are very reluctant to let him go. Luckily, the baron had some influence with the military authorities: had they not just been fêting him with speeches and serenades? In the circumstances Frieda had no choice but to confess the truth to her parents. Shaking with anger, the old baron set out to intervene on behalf of the man who had seduced his daughter, wrecked her marriage and spoilt his own jubilee celebrations.

Lawrence was released, but he had to leave Metz at once. Before his departure Frieda took him to Montigny and introduced him to her parents. The old baron and the young miner's son stared grimly at each other. Then angrily the baron offered him a cigarette. Considering all that had happened, one could hardly have expected a more friendly gesture than that.

A few hours later Lawrence was in Trier, glad to have left "cursed Metz" behind him. He took a room in a friendly little hotel. Trier entranced him. In the streets there were more priests than soldiers, and the apple trees were in full bloom. He wandered happily through the vineyards on the banks of the Moselle and wrote Frieda affectionate letters, full of longing. After a few days she came to join him, and they sat together beneath the lilac in the hotel garden. She showed him Ernest Weekley's last letter, in which he came back to that dreadful scene they had had before she left him. Weekley in his desperation was now clutching at straws. He knew that Lawrence had accompanied her to Metz, but, if she could assure him that she had not again betrayed him, it was conceivable that a solution could be found. There would be no possibility of that, however, if she had been unfaithful to him quite recently.

Lawrence took Frieda at once to the post office and insisted on her wiring "GANZ RECENT" (quite recently). A telegram came back from Ernest: "KEINE MÖGLICHKEIT" (no possibility), and then followed another agonising exchange of letters.

As soon as Frieda left for Munich, where she joined Else, Lawrence went on alone to Waldbröl to visit his relatives, the Krenkows. The quiet village reminded him of England, and gradually he regained his equilibrium. He flirted innocently with his cousin Hannah, resumed work on his novel, warned Frieda in daily letters not to rush matters and showered her with questions. Was there to be a divorce? Did she need to return to England at all? Should they accept Else's invitation and pitch their tent permanently in Munich? Would they have enough money to live on? In three months time he was expecting a fee of thirty pounds —what about getting married as soon as the money arrived?

She was sick with longing for him, bombarded him with letters, did not understand how he could expect her to be patient. She tried to make him jealous, reproaching him for leaving her in the lurch.

But at last all their fears and hopes, all their agonies and uncertainties, all the muddles and the absurdities culminated in a week of perfect sexual fulfilment. "Frieda und ich haben unser Zusammenleben in Beuerberg im Isartal angefangen—im Mai 1912—und wie schön es war!" Lawrence wrote many years later in German to one of his friends. ("Frieda and I began our life together in Beuerberg in the Isartal, in May 1912—and how lovely it was!")

Beuerberg, where they spent this happy week in the Hotel Zur Post, lies twenty-five miles to the south of Munich. In the neighbouring village of Icking, Else's old friend, Alfred Weber, had an apartment where he occasionally spent his vacations. Else—who was now separated from her husband Edgar Jaffe, though still on friendly terms with him—persuaded Weber to lend it to her sister. Its four rooms were built on top of a typical village store, and it had a fine balcony, where they sat to eat their breakfast and lunch, looking out over the village street and the whitish-green glacier waters of the River Isar to the distant blue mountains beyond. Lawrence found the balcony an ideal working place and settled down to write. Frieda in the meantime busied herself in the kitchen, but her lack of experience and skill provoked Lawrence to an outburst: "You can't even make a decent cup of coffee. Any common woman can do lots of things that you can't do." Impatiently he took over the preparation of their meals himself. It was not difficult: since they had hardly any money, they lived on fresh eggs and berries and the dark local bread, which Lawrence loved.

Certainly as a housewife Frieda was completely inept. Lawrence had already discovered that in Nottingham, when she had been unable even to light the gas stove. She was slovenly, she left her dresses and underclothes lying untidily about the room, on chairs, beds, on the chest of drawers.

He was upset by her lack of discipline and tried to teach her: "Look, put your woollen things in this drawer, in this one your silk clothes and here your cotton ones." It was like an echo of his mother's voice. He took her things and folded them swiftly, laying them in the drawers with the careful pedantry and dexterity he had learned as a child in the little miner's home in Eastwood, in whose cramped rooms untidiness would soon have led to chaos.

They went for walks along the banks of the Isar. On one occasion the heel broke off one of her shoes. She took both off and threw them with a laugh into the river. He was deeply shocked by her thoughtless behaviour. "A pair of shoes takes a long time to make," he scolded her, "and you should respect the labour somebody's put into those shoes."

Yet every hour they spent together was pure enchantment, and every difference they noted in their reactions to the day's experiences only added spice to their happiness. "I love Frieda so much, I don't like to talk about it," he wrote home to Eastwood, "I never knew what love was before."

For Frieda it was as if her life had begun all over again. A strange radiance seemed to emanate from him, an aura which enabled her to look on the world with completely different eyes—his eyes.

> When Lawrence first found a gentian, a big single blue one, I remember feeling as if he had a strange communion with it, as if the gentian yielded up its blueness, its very essence, to him. Everything he met had the newness of a creation, just that moment come into being. I didn't want people, I didn't want anything, I only wanted to revel in this new world Lawrence had given me.[3]

But none of their problems had yet been solved. Anguished letters continued to arrive from her husband, and they were all the harder to bear because he behaved like a perfect gentleman. Even Lawrence admitted to Garnett: "He's rather fine—never for one moment denies his love for Frieda, and never says anything against her herself ... He says I am *ehrlich* and have a great future—good God, I reckon I'm an angel!"

Frieda wrote Weekley that she could never return to him, and he replied that in that case she would have to give up her children. That was the hardest part to bear. At times she felt that the separation from her children would break her heart. She would lie on the floor in a paroxysm of tears, vowing that she must return to them. Lawrence sat in a corner, clenching his teeth. He told her: "I won't say 'Stay for my sake.' I say, 'Decide what you want most, to live with me and share my rotten chances, or go back to security, and your children—decide for *yourself*—choose for yourself.' " Wild with hatred, she flung abuse at him, simply because he was too proud to say to her: "I love you—stay with me whatever happens." He did not speak the magic words, though he did love her and could not have borne it if she had left him. Yet, though she knew that, and knew that her own wounded heart was almost breaking for love of him, she continued to batter and rage against him.

They discovered within themselves the power to restore their spirits in floods of execration against one another. But, when it came to terms of abuse, Lawrence's superiority was undeniable.

The publisher, William Heinemann, sent the manuscript of *Sons and Lovers* back. He was not interested in publishing it, presumably because he found the novel "dirty". Lawrence relieved his feelings of disappointment in a wild letter to Garnett:[4]

> Curse the blasted, jelly-boned swines, the slimy, the belly-wriggling invertebrates, the miserable sodding rotters, the flaming sods, the snivelling, dribbling, dithering, palsied pulse-less lot that make up England today. They've got white of egg in their veins, and their spunk is that watery it's a marvel they can breed. They *can* nothing but frog-spawn—the gibberers! God, how I hate them! God curse them, funkers. God blast them, wish-wash. Exterminate them, slime ...

The tempest over, Lawrence added at the bottom of his letter a conciliatory postscript: "And Heinemann, I can see, is quite right, as a business man."

Now that Heinemann, the publisher of *The White Peacock*, had let him down, the connection with Garnett became doubly important. Edward Garnett was chief reader for the small but reputable firm of Duckworth, which on his recommendation had published *The Trespasser*. Its reception was encouraging. The literary critic of the *Athenaeum* reviewed it together with Dostoevsky's *The Brothers Karamazov*, which had just appeared in Constance Garnett's translation—and that was no small compliment. The *Saturday Review* wrote: "Had it been the work of almost any other man, it would have satisfied, for it is no common novel, but for some months we have been waiting for this book with the highest hopes."

Though the success of *The Trespasser* was not overwhelming, it strengthened Lawrence in his resolve to abandon the idea of seeking a lectureship at a German university. He would earn his living as a writer. If Frieda considered the prospect too insecure, if she did not believe in his talents, there was nothing to stop her returning to her husband. He sent the manuscript of *Sons and Lovers* to Garnett. In return Garnett sent them his son, David.

Bunny—that was David Garnett's nickname—happened just at that time to be staying in Munich. Consumed with boredom, he avidly seized his father's suggestion that he should visit Lawrence in the country. He had already read *The White Peacock*, and it had made a great impression on him.

David Garnett possessed a sharp and observant eye. He found Lawrence's appearance more proletarian than others have described it. He wrote of his hair as "bright mud-colour, with a streak of red in it … scrubby toothbrush moustache … his chin altogether too large … He was the type of the plumber's mate who goes back to fetch the tools." But, more kindly, he added: "The lightness of his movements gives him a sort of grace," and he was charmed by Lawrence's beautiful and lively eyes "dancing with gaiety". Frieda reminded him at, first sight, of a mother of five who had been sitting, sweating in the heat of July, in the same compartment with him on his journey to Icking by train—with the difference that Frieda was prettier.

She had the same sturdy body, as strong as a horse, the same magnificent shoulders, but her head and the expression of her eyes were very different. Her head and the whole carriage of her body were noble. Her eyes were green, with a lot of tawny yellow in them, the nose straight. She looked one dead in the eyes, fearlessly judging one and, at that moment, she was extraordinarily like a lioness; eyes and colouring, and the swift power of her lazy leap up from the hammock where she had been lying. I have always been particularly attracted by happy lovers and attached to them: Lawrence and Frieda were more than twice as attractive to me together than they would have been separately. I was completely charmed by each of them and at once worshipped them[5].

They were equally attracted by the young man. In the evening Bunny performed a wild redskin dance in their apartment. He wound red, green, yellow and orange scarfs from Frieda's wardrobe like snakes around his bare arms and legs and stamped around brandishing a huge kitchen knife above his head. Lawrence sat on the sofa, accompanying him with rhythmic noises and shaking with laughter. Frieda fled screaming on to the balcony. "Go and trample somewhere else," the woman from the stores below shouted up to her, and the three of them collapsed on the floor in helpless laughter.

They received another visitor—an entirely unexpected one—in the person of Frieda's mother, bent on recriminations. For a full hour Lawrence sat there as meek as a lamb, letting the German tempest rage about his head:

Who was I, did I think, that a Baroness should clean my boots and empty my slops; she the daughter of a high-born and highly cultured gentleman. No decent man, no man with a common sense of decency, could expect to have a woman, the wife of a clever professor, living with him like a barmaid, and he not even able to keep her in shoes.

Afterwards the baroness went on to Munich to see her daughter Else. Else wanted to know what she thought of Lawrence. "A lovable and trustworthy person," the baroness replied.

9

At the beginning of August 1912 Lawrence and Frieda began their march south: they had decided to spend the winter in Italy. They set off on foot, rucksacks, provisions and a spirit stove on their backs, and he with an old straw hat on his head. They crossed the border into Austrian territory, sleeping in barns and mountain huts and washing themselves in ice-cold brooks. They lingered to admire the wayside shrines (Lawrence's essay on wooden crucifixes in the Tirol is one of his finest) and lit candles in a wooden votive chapel. Sometimes Frieda would throw off all her clothes to sunbathe in naked bliss among the harebells, primulas and gentians.

They arrived at Mayrhofen in the Zillertal, and a week later David Garnett joined them there. Lawrence pointed out to him all the special features of the place: thanks to his extraordinary ability to absorb impressions swiftly and clearly, he could identify all the villagers by name and knew all about their characters and their love affairs. His powers of concentration were another thing that amazed David Garnett. While Frieda engaged Bunny in lively conversation, Lawrence would sit in a corner of their rented single room, shut off from them as if by an invisible soundproof wall, filling one page after another with his clear, neat handwriting. Occasionally he would jump up to attend to the cooking or to go to the window on Frieda's call to see some mules passing along the road with loads of cheese on their backs. Then he would return quietly to his corner and resume work on the manuscript of *Sons and Lovers*, which Edward Garnett had returned to him with a great many critical remarks.

But there were difficult hours whenever a new letter arrived from Ernest Weekley. On such occasions Lawrence would rescue Frieda from her inferno of self-laceration and despair by staging satirical one-man shows for her and Bunny's benefit. As Helen Corke had already discovered, he was a master of impersonation. His imitations of the speech and gestures of people like Ezra Pound and Yeats were so funny and so true that they turned the little room in Mayrhofen into a cross between a London literary salon and *Alice in Wonderland*. He could also poke fun at himself in hilarious scenes from his own life: "D. H. Lawrence being patronised by literary lions, Lawrence charming his landlady, Lawrence being put in his place by his landlady's daughter, a bad-tempered Lawrence picking a quarrel with Frieda over nothing." David Garnett later compared him with Charlie Chaplin—a bitter, completely unsentimental Chaplin. Watching him, Frieda and David rolled about in helpless laughter.

After a few days the three of them left Mayrhofen to climb along the Zemmtal to the Dominikus-Hütte. The following day they moved up to the Pfitscher Joch, a col more than six thousand feet high. Frieda submitted with good grace to the exertions of mountain climbing and the nights in primitive huts, though she was completely unused to this kind of hard outdoor life—as indeed Lawrence was, for he had never been out of England before, let alone undertaken Alpine tours. A steep descent on the south side of the mountain brought them in a couple of hours through the snowdrifts on the pass to the friendly houses of St Jakob. A few miles further on, Bunny left them for Sterzing, to catch the night train from Verona.

Six weeks after starting out they found themselves standing on the shores of Lake Garda. On the Jaufen Pass, in darkness and icy wind, they had lost their way; in Bozen they had slept on top of a pigsty; in Trient they had spent the night in such a squalid hotel that Frieda, tired out and horrified by the dirty sheets and the indescribable lavatories, had collapsed in tears on a bench beside the Dante memorial. But in Riva, then an Austrian garrison town, the world smiled on them again. Smart army officers, looking like figures out of an operetta by Lehar, stalked proudly along the lakeside promenade with elegant ladies on their arms. Frieda felt embarrassed by their own appearance, for she could see they both looked like tramps. All the same, they received a friendly reception in one of the boarding-houses. They had a splendid room, but it was too expensive for them—three kronen a day—and their money was almost exhausted. They cooked surreptitious meals on a spirit stove in their room, in constant fear that the chambermaid would catch them at it. But then their clothes arrived, packed in trunks, which they had sent on by rail to Riva, and Nusch also sent Frieda some cast-off Paquin gowns—much too chic even for the lakeside promenade. That day they both dressed up to celebrate their return to "civilisation".

Ten days later a cheque for fifty pounds arrived—an advance on *Sons and Lovers*, paid by the publisher Gerald Duckworth at Edward

Garnett's request. They received it rapturously—never had a remittance been more heartily welcome. Two days afterwards, acting on the advice of their landlady at the boarding-house, they moved to Gargnano on the other side of the Italian border.

They spent the next seven months in Gargnano. The modern road, which now runs through the village along the western shore of the lake, was not then in existence; Gargnano could be reached only across the water. They discovered a good apartment, "big enough for a regiment", in the Villa Igéa—rent eighty lire a month. It had a view over the lake, and there was a small garden with orange trees, persimmons and roses in front. Behind the house lay mountain slopes covered with vineyards, lemons and olives. The *padrone* brought them baskets of figs and grapes, and in the *osteria* in Bogliacco they could get a quarter of a litre of red wine for only fifteen *centesimi*. It was a good place to spend the winter.

Contentedly puffing cigarettes, Frieda lay idly in bed until lunchtime. Lawrence got up at eight o'clock and brought her breakfast in bed. He would stay sitting beside her the whole of the morning, chatting, discussing his work, quarrelling, making plans. *La signora* would play the grand lady, but at last she would rouse herself to climb out of bed and take up the role of housewife. It was the first time in her life that she had had a house to run without servants. Picturesque the kitchen undoubtedly was, with its huge stove and its gleaming copper pans, but it fell far short of modern expectations, as anyone will know who has ever tried to cook a meal over the glowing charcoal of a *fornello*. "The pigeons are burning, what shall I do?" screamed Frieda in horror, and Lawrence rushed in to restore order. He was always hurrying to the rescue—from fire or from water. "The first time I washed sheets was a disaster," Frieda admitted later. "They were so large and wet, their wetness was overwhelming. The kitchen floor was flooded, the table drenched, I dripped from hair to feet."

"Woman, are you out of your senses?" he cried in desperation. He dried her carefully, wiped the floor and hung the sheets out in the garden. He could have run the house quite easily by himself. As Aldous Huxley wrote: "He could cook, he could sew, he could darn a stocking and milk a cow, he was an efficient wood-cutter and a good hand at embroidery. Fires always burned when he had laid them and a floor, after Lawrence had scrubbed it, was thoroughly clean."

But Frieda was so helplessly naïve in regard to all little household problems that she would have been quite lost without him. "If you hear of us murdered, that also will be Frieda's fault," Lawrence wrote to Edward Garnett. "She empties water out of the bedroom onto the high road and a fat old lady who steals along under the wall. I had to keep all the doors locked ..."

When they arrived they knew only ten words of Italian. Now they began to take lessons from Signorina Feltrelline, who always wore black gloves, and squinted. Frieda immersed herself in *Anna Karenina*—as a sort of practical guide to the behaviour of a married woman who has run away with her lover. When she had finished the book she sent it to Ernest Weekley, possibly wanting to show him what terrible things can happen when a deserted husband decides to be unforgiving. Unfortunately—and this was typical of Frieda—she left between the pages a letter from Will Dowson, the car-owning lace manufacturer from Nottingham with whom she had once had an affair. In the letter Dowson said: "If you had to run away, why did you not do it with me?" Ernest Weekley was malicious enough to send this letter to Lawrence by return of post.[1]

During these months in Gargnano Lawrence worked with fanatic zeal. He revised the last hundred pages of *Sons and Lovers* within two weeks, and in the middle of November he sent the completed manuscript off to Duckworth. Since Jessie Chambers had called the first draft "tired and lifeless" he had completely rewritten the novel. He had sweated blood wrestling with the material, which was the story of his own youth, and his reward was that he managed to break through the fetters in which his love for his mother had bound him. Paul Morel, the hero of the novel, is his own naked self, stripped of all protective clothing. When he wrote the chapter describing the death of Lydia Lawrence, the old wounds opened again. His agony affected Frieda too, and made her ill. He told her: "If my mother had lived I could never have loved you, she wouldn't have let me go."

Sons and Lovers is an act of self-liberation. The same can of course be said of many works in world literature which reflect in sublimated form the inner conflicts and experiences of their authors. But *Sons and Lovers* goes further: it has been described, not unjustifiably, as a self-administered act of psycho-analysis. Lawrence was able to carry out this self-analysis because Frieda was standing beside him, giving him strength.

Sons and Lovers is the most significant and by far the most successful of his early works. In contrast to both the preceding novels, which were strongly imitative, it reveals that extraordinary and spontaneous mastery of expression which is characteristic of most of his writing. Lawrence's novels resemble wild open landscapes rather than carefully laid-out gardens. He created no new forms of expression. Unlike his contemporary and literary antithesis, James Joyce, he made no attempt to penetrate, with bold linguistic constructions and thought associations, into the realms of the subconscious where the myths and history of mankind fuse with the intellectual realities of everyday life. Lawrence's art is much more direct. It originates in a unique identification with nature and an intuitive feeling for character, and its effect stems from the vitality and spontaneity of his style. Lawrence was convinced that all true art springs from an impulse of self-expression, with all the flaws inherent in an impulsive act. The flaws are undoubtedly there: in his later works, side by side with whole pages of compelling beauty and conviction, one finds wearisome repetitions, long drawn-out sermons on his philosophy of life, and dialogue of embarrassing banality. Even worse, when the author's propagandist zeal pushes aside his artistic intuition, human relationships are sometimes distorted in order to prove abstruse theories. In *Sons and Lovers* Lawrence stood at the beginning of his artistic development. The novel might not reach the highest peaks of which he was to become capable, but neither does it descend into the later disappointing depths. The vivid descriptions of a Midlands' landscape scarred by the activities of the mine-owners, the picture of a miner's grim daily life, the restless urges of adolescence have scarcely ever been surpassed.

Jessie Chambers had been disappointed with what she had seen of the early draft of the novel, and she had urged Lawrence to keep to the true facts of their youthful experiences. When he at last found the strength to face the truth, it was not to her love that he owed it, but to Frieda's. Poor Jessie! She had had to stand helplessly by and see Lawrence's love for her stifled by his mother. Later, after the death of her pitiless rival, she had to acknowledge that his mother's influence still persisted beyond the grave. And now her cup of bitterness was filled to the brim: the book in which she had hoped to see him liberate himself from his mother's bonds seemed to her to have confirmed his mother's final victory. Twenty years later she wrote in her own reminiscences:[2]

So instead of a release and deliverance from bondage, the bondage was glorified and made absolute. His mother conquered indeed, but the vanquished one was her son. In *Sons and Lovers* Lawrence handed his mother the laurels of victory.

For Jessie the novel in its final form represented the last un-forgivable betrayal:

The shock of *Sons and Lovers* gave the death-blow to our friendship. If I had told Lawrence that I had died before, I certainly died again.

In this judgment Jessie was unfair to Lawrence. His book is not a glorification of his mother. It is true that when he blames the breakdown of his parents' marriage on his father's ignorance and drunkenness he is speaking with his mother's voice. But he does at least hint that the guilt might not have been exclusively his father's. Tribute is paid in many passages of dialogue to the father's warm and vigorous personality: evidence that the writer was touchingly concerned to give him the justice his wife had denied him. But many more years were to elapse before Lawrence reached the point of admitting: "I would write a different *Sons and Lovers* now; my mother was wrong, and I thought she was absolutely right."

In the novel Paul Morel cuts short his mother's death agony by giving her an overdose of morphia. It is feasible that this is a true account of what really happened and that Lawrence did in fact perform an act of euthanasia. But more important than the fact are the words in which the writer describes the deed:

That evening he got all the morphia pills there were, and took them downstairs. Carefully he crushed them to powder. "What are you doing?" said Annie [Paul's sister].
"I s'll put 'em in her night milk."
Then they both laughed together like two conspiring children. On top of all their horror flickered this little sanity.

But the dying woman lived through the night. Her son could no longer bear the rattling in her throat, and wondered whether this terrible wheezing would stop "if he piled the blanket and heavy coats on her."

One should not forget that even an autobiographical novel follows its own laws, independent of the reality behind it. Its characters may think and act in a way completely alien to the models on which they were originally based. But one would probably not be far from the truth if one were to recognise in Paul Morel's behaviour during his mother's last hours at least a symbolic significance which was valid for Lawrence himself—even if he did not realise it for some considerable time afterwards. It signified the final severance of the bond which tied him to his mother.

Jessie was much too embittered to appreciate that. She might be able to resign herself to the inescapable fact that the present life of the man she loved now belonged to another woman—perhaps the future as well. But she could not forgive him for robbing her (as she saw it) of her past. Nobody was permitted to break the web of her illusions—and least of all the admired companion of her youth.

What part Frieda played in the actual creation of the novel is far from clear. Her own accounts are contradictory, but it is certainly fair to state that her influence on Lawrence during those first stormy months was far too profound to be proved merely by pointing to some specific chapter or page. She was not his literary adviser, but rather the catalyst that set free his latent energies. She helped him to recognise the anaemia and sexual hypocrisy of the English middle-class life to whose standards and ideals his mother had clung. It is probable that she made no attempt to join directly in his struggle with the ghosts of his past. *Sons and Lovers* belonged to a phase of his life in which she had no part. In fact, she had no high opinion of the book and was convinced that he could do very much better. She later wrote to Edward Garnett with characteristic frankness:[3]

> The novel is a failure, but you must feel something at the back of it struggling, trying to come out. You see, I don't really believe in *Sons and Lovers*; it feels as if there were nothing *behind* all those happenings, as if there were no *Hinterland der Seele*, only intensely felt fugitive things. I who am a believer though I don't know in what, to me it seems an irreligious book.

The first months with Frieda belong to the most productive of Lawrence's life. She opened the floodgates of his creative powers, and there seemed to be no bounds to his energy. Besides the five hundred pages of *Sons and Lovers* he wrote a number of poems which he later included in the volume entitled *Look! We Have Come Through!* He began work on two important manuscripts. One was a draft of the novel *The Lost Girl*; the other, *The Sisters*, was later split up to provide the starting-point for his two most significant novels, *The Rainbow* and *Women in Love*. As a form of relaxation he scribbled down a four-act comedy, *Fight for Barbara*, in the space of three days. The play has no literary value, but it has some interest for the biographer.

The action, set in the Villa Igéa, is a fictionalised account of his own flight with Frieda, whom he has transformed into an Englishwoman. Barbara Tressider (otherwise Frieda) has eloped with James Wesson, the son of a coalminer. After they have been living together for some weeks in the Italian villa, Barbara's aristocratic mother, Lady Charlcote, suddenly turns up and overwhelms Wesson with all the reproaches which, a few weeks earlier in Icking, Baroness von Richthofen had flung in Lawrence's face. "You have not got even enough money to keep her. She has to have money from her sister ... the daughter of a high-born and highly cultured gentleman." The "high-born and highly cultured gentleman" also appears in the play and behaves in the way the old baron had probably behaved in Metz. Barbara's husband, a professor, arrives unexpectedly and urges her to return with him to their children. This leads to a highly dramatic scene, in which she reminds him of her catastrophic wedding-night in Lucerne. After several changes of mind and some violent quarrels with her seducer, Barbara-Frieda decides to remain with Wesson-Lawrence.

The husband's arrival is the product of the author's imagination, but it is almost certain that the passionate scenes of this play, with their alternations of love and hate, give an accurate picture of the disturbances which began at this time to arise with increasing frequency between Lawrence and Frieda. Gargnano may have seemed like the Garden of Eden, but it also had its moments of hell. Trouble came with the postman. There were days on which Frieda was misery personified; the mere thought of her children was enough to plunge her into an abyss of despair. At her request, Lawrence asked David Garnett to send Elsa a book on her tenth birthday. He was obeying Frieda's wishes, too, when he sent the children money for Christmas, but he was thoughtless enough to sign the money order with his own name. Ernest Weekley sent it back with a furious letter. The professor seemed gradually to be losing his self-control: he utterly refused to consider even the possibility of a divorce, and threats alternated with abject pleading, promises with vindictive attacks. Worst of all, he sent Frieda a photograph of her two daughters, and it almost broke her heart.

But even if Weekley's actions were now governed solely by his emotions it must by now have become completely clear to him that the old order could never be restored. He had dismissed Ida Wilhelmy, the nanny whom Frieda had engaged. Nothing that could be spared should remain to remind him of his unfaithful wife. At the prompting of his parents he had moved his home to London. Both households, his own in Nottingham and his parents' in the lovely Constable house in Hampstead, had been given up, and now Weekley was living with his three children in a large and ugly Victorian house in Chiswick, sharing it with his parents, an unmarried aunt and a bachelor uncle. His comprehensive library, consisting in part of old etymological works of considerable value, was installed in a large room on the ground floor.

The house symbolised the final break-up of his marriage. But it had one important advantage: it was not far from St Paul's School, which in the four hundred years of its existence has brought forth such distinguished pupils as Milton, Pepys, G. K. Chesterton, and Montgomery, the future Field Marshal. A place was found there for Montague, now almost thirteen years old, while Elsa and Barbara were sent to a girls' school nearby. For Ernest Weekley, however, the position of the house was much less advantageous. To spare himself the wearisome daily rail journey to Nottingham, he rented a couple of dismal rooms near University College as a *pied-à-terre*.

Edward and Constance Garnett sent "Mrs Anthony" to Gargnano. The name was a pseudonym: she was a young artist whose maiden name had been Antonia (or Anjuta) Cyriax. Her husband was a Swedish painter who—as she eventually discovered to her horror—suffered from maniacal delusions, and he had threatened her with violence. She fled to England, where the Garnetts took her in. When her husband followed her there, she was swiftly despatched to Italy under conditions of great secrecy. "Mrs Anthony" settled down in San Gaudenzio, a village situated above Gargnano, and in March 1913 Lawrence and Frieda left the lakeside to join her for a couple of weeks.

It was a sign of the way things were going. By the end of December the tension between them had reached a climax. For Frieda, ever since those distant childhood days in Metz, Christmas had always been a more sacred and more intimate festival than it seemed to be to her English friends and relations, and she had done her best to transmit her sense of its holy, comforting magic to her children. To be separated from them at such a time was almost too painful to bear, but the absence of the children was not the only cause of her distress. Apart from the Garnetts, not a single one of her friends had sent a Christmas greeting, and she felt more than ever before that she was being treated as a pariah. She began to make plans for seeing her children. If she was not allowed actually to speak to them and embrace them, at least she could look on them from a distance. Perhaps, she wrote to Edward Garnett, she could lie in wait for them on the street? When he suggested that this was not a good plan, she replied to him in desperation:

For the first time really in my life, I am undecided, *I don't know what to do*. Of course I don't think it's desirable that I should see the children in the street, but what can I do? I am entirely cut off from all, Ernest or the children ... He loved me absolutely, that's why he hates me absolutely; he will keep the children from me, I know he is a whole-hogger ... I know they will tell the children, "Your mother has left you"; I want to tell them, "I left your father, not you." If they ask Ernest, "We want to see our mother," I think he cannot say no.

Lawrence's behaviour was hardly calculated to soothe her over-wrought nerves. He could not bear her outbreaks of despair; he hated to be constantly reminded that she had made the greatest sacrifice of which a mother is capable for his sake. He had triumphed over Ernest Weekley, but now he was becoming convinced that his most dangerous adversary was not the husband, but the children. Frieda, he felt, was using Monty, Elsa and Barby, these distant offshoots of a marriage he had destroyed, to blackmail him into surrender. They were truly at war now. It was a war in which short, sharp battles were interspersed with long and happy periods of armistice and peace, in which the things that bound them were stronger than those that separated them. Love and hate existed side by side, though fortunately love triumphed time and again. The issue was not simply the children: it was as much Lawrence's insistence that she should acknowledge him as the dominant partner in their union.

He had no other grounds for his demand and no other excuse for it than that he was a man and she a woman. The argument was too facile, and it is no wonder that Frieda rejected it with haughty disdain. After all she had not given up her husband and children and her boring middle-class security in order to deliver herself into bondage: it was freedom she sought. She was convinced that Lawrence was a genius, but this did not mean that she was in the very least prepared to bow to his male superiority.

It was usually some mention of the children that would set a spark to the fire. At such times Lawrence could sink so low as scornfully to invite her to return to her husband if she was not prepared to give up her children. "Why aren't you going?" he shouted and then, his jealously turning to blind rage: "I wouldn't try to stop you. If you really, really wanted to leave me, you can go back to England today!" As outbreaks of this sort forced her to realise, there was undoubtedly a streak of cruelty in his character. In his *Fight for Barbara* he had put these words in Wesson's mouth: "I may hate you, I may rage against you, I may sneer at you—very well! It doesn't alter the fact that I love you." When the battle was over, their anger and desperation would give way to tears and ardent embraces.

As Frieda later wrote to Edward Garnett:[4]

> Over the children, I thought he was beastly; he hated me for being miserable, not a moment of misery did he put up with; he denied all the suffering and suffered all the more, like his mother before him; how we fought over this."

Their inner unrest drove them from Gargnano. In San Gaudenzio, which lies high above the lake, they shared the home of a friendly peasant family with the mysterious "Mrs Anthony". The peasant's cheerful young wife asked Lawrence how long he had known the *signora* before he married her, and he replied: "Six weeks." Here in Catholic Italy it would not do to betray the fact that he and Frieda were not married. The little pink cottage stood on a small piece of level ground, surrounded by vineyards and olive trees. Lizards flitted across the stones, and in the hollows there were grape hyacinths, "purple as noon, full of milk, and ripe, and sun-darkened, like many-breasted Diana". Lawrence would sit in the April sun beneath the blossoming peach and cherry trees, writing. In the evenings neighbours would drop in—among them young men preparing to emigrate to America to escape military service. There was music and dancing. "Mrs Anthony" called Lawrence "Lorenzo", and the peasants called him "Signor Lorenzo". Frieda liked the name, and he became "Lorenzo" to her from then on.

10

After much heart-searching, they decided to return to England. "Frieda wants to be within reach of the children," Lawrence told his sister Ada, and Frieda added: "Lawrence has made me so miserable that I began to think I was the scum of the earth ... *His* misery was all *my* doing."

They spent a few days in Verona and then made the journey back to Bavaria. Edgar Jaffe had lent them his brand-new chalet in Irschenhausen, not far from Icking. Here they lived in unaccustomed luxury, in rooms with fine Persian carpets, and Dürer prints hanging on the panelled walls.

Frieda was anxious to leave for England as soon as possible, but Lawrence still hesitated. He would rather have returned to Italy. Northerner as he was, he felt drawn by southern landscapes, which attracted him far more than his home country with its shades of his dead hopes and loves. But he was reluctant to let Frieda travel to London alone, possibly because he feared the effect which a reunion with the children might have on her. There was a risk that in her emotional confusion she might turn against him. He had only one yardstick for the power and egoism of mother-love, and that was his own mother. In attempting to loosen Frieda's bonds with her children he was once again struggling for his own freedom.

This time he did not feel happy in Bavaria, where a year ago he and Frieda had spent such relaxed and blissful days. He wrote to Edward Garnett: "I want to go back to Italy. I have suffered from the tightness, the domesticity of Germany ... The folk seem like tables of figures."

There were also other grounds for his feeling of uneasiness. While in Irschenhausen, Lawrence wrote two short stories with a German background, and both of them reveal his awareness of the militarist spirit that was to lead the Kaiser, fourteen months later, into his catastrophic attempt to find "a place in the sun" for himself and Germany. In June 1913 very few people realised that war was so near, but Lawrence had the power of grasping a situation intuitively.

His feeling for the psychological climate of the Kaiser's Germany certainly owed much to Frieda. Her father had been a Prussian officer, and her accounts of her early years in Metz, surrounded by military cadets, provided him with the colours he needed for his imaginative portrait. The first of the two stories, *The Thorn in the Flesh* (originally entitled *Vin ordinaire*) is set in Frieda's home in Metz, and one of its main figures, immediately recognisable, is the old baron himself: even the hand, disfigured in the campaign of 1870, is mentioned. But the second story, *The Prussian Officer*, set in the valley of the River Isar, is by far the more important of the two. It is a small masterpiece, written with an incomparable intensity of expression, and it provides an extraordinary insight into the motives of human behaviour. It deals with two aspects which go to the very heart of Prussian militarism: the aggressive brutality of its caste system and its mixture of sadism and homosexuality. At the time that Lawrence wrote this tragic story he was unfamiliar with the literature of psycho-analysis. What little he knew of Freud's ideas he had gathered at second-hand from Frieda, and it is possible that under her influence ideas crystallised which already existed amorphously in his mind. He was by no means uncritical of the Viennese school of thought. "I was a great Freud admirer," Frieda wrote later. "We had long arguments and Lawrence's conclusion was more or less that Freud looked on sex too much from the doctor's point of view, that Freud's 'sex' and 'libido' were too limited and mechanical, and that the root was deeper." Whatever his reservations about Freud, and however much his views might have developed later into a sort of sex religion of his own, one can understand how psycho-analysts have come to consider *The Prussian Officer*, like *Sons and Lovers*, to be an artistic affirmation of their ideas.

Sons and Lovers had by this time been published. The book's success was genuine, though by no means overwhelming—its reviewers would doubtless have been astonished to discover that fifty years later it is considered one of the really significant novels of its time. Reviews were nevertheless friendly and in some cases even enthusiastic, but with certain reservations. In these circumstances it would have been pointless to delay the journey to England any longer, and Lawrence at last yielded to Frieda's entreaties. In the middle of June they were installed at The Cearne as Edward Garnett's guests.

David Garnett, who was then living in his parents' home, later wrote that their presence did not make for a peaceful household. Quarrels were constantly breaking out between them, and in David

Garnett's view, the fault was invariably that of Lawrence, who did not show Frieda the sympathy and understanding she might have expected in her situation; indeed, his behaviour sometimes contained an element of spitefulness. David Garnett continues:[1]

> But he was ill. Once I caught sight of one of Frieda's handkerchiefs, marked with a coronet in the corner, crumpled in Lawrence's hand, after a fit of coughing and spotted with bright arterial blood— and I felt a new tenderness for him and readiness to forgive his bad moods ...
>
> Frieda's character was so full of love and she had such a genius for expressing it, that when she was suffering she was as painful to watch as an animal in a trap ... She could no more forget and abandon her children than a lioness or a puma can forget the cubs which the hunter has taken away, and her unhappiness in being separated from them was something simple and elemental, and like everything else in Frieda's nature, noble.

All her thoughts and feelings were now directed towards the one aim of seeing her children again. She had found out that the family had moved to Chiswick but did not know their address. So she wandered for days through the streets of that district in the desperate hope of catching a glimpse of the children. Suddenly, in the windows of a house, she recognised the curtains which she had once bought for their home in Nottingham. Without a moment's hesitation she entered the house and rushed upstairs. "We children had been told," Barbara recalls, "that our mother had brought shame and misery on our family. And suddenly there she stood in the doorway of the nursery where we were having supper with our grandmother and aunt. She appeared to us children like a terrifying apparition, while granny and aunt jumped up in great excitement and hurled abuse at her, as if she were the embodiment of evil. I am sorry to say that we children joined in. Frieda fled, shocked and humiliated."

She now devised another plan of campaign. David Garnett spent several afternoons with her, "hanging round St Paul's School". The writer Katherine Mansfield, whose acquaintance Frieda had just made, also joined in the conspiracy. For hours on end they walked to and fro in front of the ugly pseudo-Gothic school building, hoping to see the thirteen-year-old Montague for a few seconds or even exchange a few hasty words with him. Lawrence, deeply distrustful, was also there to keep an eye on them from a discreet distance. He thought it advisable to be on the spot: one could never know what silly things a mother might do in such a situation.

One day Frieda espied Monty among the boys as they streamed out of the school building. She spoke to him, then took him off to a nearby teashop to load him with sweets. Montague Weekley still remembers the occasion today: "A fascinating young lady with a charming and rather mysterious smile came with her. That was Katherine Mansfield." Monty was apparently discreet enough not to mention the encounter at home. But the two young girls, Elsa and Barbara, for whom Frieda lay in wait on their way to school, were less reticent. With no grandmother or aunt present they danced in delight around their mother and, between kisses and tears, asked when she would be coming home. A few days later Frieda set out once more to waylay her daughters. But it was obvious that they had now received strict instructions not to speak to her, and "only little white faces looked at me as if I were an evil ghost". Lawrence watched the humiliating scene from a distance, furious, but powerless to help.

Katherine Mansfield was born in Wellington, New Zealand. Her father, Sir Harold Beauchamp, was President of the Bank of New Zealand, and he sent her to London to acquire the intellectual and social graces of an English lady. The four years she spent at an exclusive private school in Harley Street changed the whole course of her life. She returned to New Zealand with only one thought in her mind: to get back to London, with its wide intellectual horizons and its brilliant theatre evenings, as soon as possible. But she had to resign herself to spending a further two years in the narrow provincial atmosphere of Wellington (which at that time had only seventy thousand inhabitants) before she could break down her family's resistance and win their consent. She returned to England with a yearly allowance of a hundred pounds from her father to protect her from the worst financial privations.

That was in 1908, when she was nineteen years old. She knew exactly what she wanted: to be a writer. But she felt she had led a far too sheltered life up to now. In order to work creatively, it was not enough just to think up the *nom de plume* of Katherine Mansfield; she must also learn what it meant to live in real freedom. Within a year she was pregnant, and she was also married—though not to the father of the child she was expecting. She had left her husband, the musician George Bowden, the day after they were married. Her mother came to London to visit her and, knowing nothing about the pregnancy, was appalled to find her daughter looking so ill. She sent her off post haste to a spa in Bavaria to recuperate. Here Katherine lost her child, which relieved her of at least one of her problems.

Katherine was certainly experiencing life with a vengeance, and the literary outcome was a handful of satirical sketches, which were brought out in volume form by a small publisher under the title *In a German Pension*. Immature as they certainly are, the stories show the beginnings of Katherine Mansfield's great talent. In them she pokes malicious fun at the standards of German middle-class life, and for this reason the book, though ignored by the critics, enjoyed a certain success with the public. Germany was not exactly popular in England in the year 1911, when the Kaiser was stirring up trouble with his naval rearmament and his sabre-rattling. Within a few months Katherine Mansfield's book had run into three editions. Then the publisher went bankrupt.

Later Katherine came to wish that she could blot out the book entirely. Even when mass hatred of the Germans was at its height during the First World War she refused to allow its reissue. After the war she wrote a number of stories, which, with their delicate pastel shades, are reminiscent of Chekhov in style and belong to the finest English prose work of their period.

Two years after the appearance of her first book she met John Middleton Murry, and for the first time in the stormy chronicle of her love life a bond was forged which did not soon end in tears, disappointments, miscarriage or abortion. Murry was ten months younger than Katherine. He came from a poor home in the south of London. His unusual intelligence began to show while he was still at school, and he was awarded a scholarship which took him to Oxford. However, after concluding his studies successfully, he suddenly fell victim to a severe mental crisis. At the very moment when all kinds of brilliant prospects were open to him, he lost the ability to decide what career to follow or indeed to make up his mind on any subject at all.

In his autobiography Murry explains his loss of self-confidence by pointing out that his academic training had severed his connections with his family and his social background, yet at the same time had failed to open the doors of the upper classes of society to him. He found himself, alone and uprooted, in a no-man's-land between the world of his birth and the realm of unfulfilled opportunities, without the strength or even the ambition to show what he could do. He possessed only a single talent: the ability to express his thoughts clearly in writing. Since he had to find a means of earning his living as soon as possible, he decided to become a journalist. As the years went on he came to be one of the leading literary critics of his day.[2]

But all that lay still in the future. Burdened as he was with his inferiority complex, his immediate need was to find another human being who, in contrast to himself, possessed a large measure of intellectual independence and will-power. Katherine Mansfield, scarred though she was with the wounds of her defeats, seemed to him to answer his needs. He was naïve and inexperienced, and he knew nothing of her past, but he was convinced he had found in her everything he required to restore his self-confidence. She gave him security as well as love, both maternal and sexual. Their life together was completely dominated in the first years by Katherine's stronger personality. Her husband refused to give her a divorce, so she could not marry Murry; but their partnership was so generally accepted that they were always referred to as "the Murrys". Together they launched an *avant-garde* literary review, *Rhythm*, and, when this came to an end after a very short life, they brought out another, *The Blue Review*, which was now also on its last legs. Short stories by D. H. Lawrence had appeared in both reviews. Soon after their arrival in England, Lorenzo and Frieda visited the Murrys in their little apartment, which served simultaneously as editorial office.

The two couples took to one another at once. Murry was not yet twenty-four—four years younger than Lawrence. According to the sculptor, Gaudier-Brzeska, he had "a magnificent head like a great god, an Apollo or Mars", though others were of the opinion that his broad mouth spoiled the symmetry of his features. Katherine Mansfield had the attraction of an unusual personality. In her appearance there was something slightly Slavonic, and her intense dark eyes gave evidence of great strength of will. She wore her brown hair in a style later to be known as a bob—in those days it was still unusual. She was a slight person, and she tended to be unconventional in her behaviour. When Frieda and Lorenzo made their first visit, they found Katherine sitting on the living-room floor beside a huge goldfish tank. Apart from this, the only furniture consisted of a number of cushions.

The similarity of their relationships—Murry, like Lawrence, was unmarried, Katherine, like Frieda, was waiting for a divorce before she could marry again—at once formed a strong bond between them.

Their friendship with the Murrys—and their enmity, too—became an important element in the future life of Frieda and Lawrence. For both sides the relationship brought rich rewards: it was "the only spontaneous and gay friendship we had," Frieda later wrote. But it was not without its dangers and moments of bitterness. Murry found in Lawrence during those first years the qualities he himself, with his inhibitions and his uncertainty, was painfully conscious of lacking: the intuitive ability to recognise and express the essence of a person, the nature of a landscape or a situation, coupled with an absolute confidence in his own talent, burning intensity and integrity of character. Murry absorbed Lawrence's vitality like mescalin—which, as we are told, heightens the vision and reveals the world in stronger colours, yet at the same time leads one to overestimate one's own powers. But presumably this stimulating friendship was to help him some years later to overcome his personal difficulties and to win esteem with a comprehensive critical study of Dostoevsky. That was the first of the books which were to make his name known beyond the bounds of England.

The Lawrences settled down in Kingsgate, a little resort on the coast of Kent. In "that half-crystallized nowhere of a place" Frieda sought solace in the waves from the bitter-sweet tribulations of her meetings with the children. Lorenzo, reacting to the exertions of the preceding months, looked ill and exhausted: "terribly ill," in the words of Edward Marsh who, like the Murrys, visited them several times in Kingsgate.

Edward Marsh had first made contact with Lawrence when he wrote asking permission to include the poem "Snapdragon" in an anthology he was editing. When they now met, Lawrence introduced Frieda as his wife—a white lie for which he later humbly apologised. "You do not look the type of man who would care for poetry," Frieda told him artlessly, not realising how tactless she was being. But Marsh was gentleman enough not to let her see he was hurt. He had made it his life's work to encourage and sponsor young poets, and he even helped them financially. He was closely associated with the "Georgian" school of poetry, consisting of a talented group of writers who sought inspiration in the spontaneity of poets like Blake and Wordsworth and whose work, though faintly romantic in flavour, reflected the social consciousness of their age.

Sir Edward Marsh belonged to that remarkable set of men, peculiar perhaps to England and France, who combine political activity at a high level with an active appreciation of the arts. He had been—and was later to be again—private secretary to Winston Churchill, who was at that time First Lord of the Admiralty in Asquith's Liberal government. His friendship was to be of continuing importance to Lawrence.

During those July days in Kingsgate it was to him that Frieda and Lorenzo owed their acquaintance with the young Asquiths, who had a summer holiday house in the immediate neighbourhood.

Herbert Asquith was the Prime Minister's second son. His wife, Lady Cynthia, a woman of unusual beauty and vitality, came of an ancient and noble Scottish family. Their marriage was a union not only of two dynasties, but also of two separate political spheres: Lady Cynthia's father, the eleventh Earl of Wemyss, represented the powerful world of feudal privilege and rigid Tory principle, while her father-in-law, a brilliant Oxford-educated lawyer of Liberal views, headed the government of the greatest empire of all time.

Malicious tongues might suggest that it was this bridging of the opposites that enabled Lady Cynthia to enjoy an almost endless succession of weekend parties in country houses of various political hues. Certainly she enjoyed the pleasures of high society and was not averse to flirting light-heartedly with prominent men. Much admired and much envied, she divided her time between the grandiose household in Downing Street, at that time the power centre of the world, and the noble houses of famous aristocrats. But it was becoming more and more difficult for her to keep up the style of life to which she was devoted and to preserve the appearance of ironically cheerful and carefree enjoyment. The difficulties had always been present, and now they were becoming even more menacing. Her arch-conservative father, who disapproved of her marriage to the Liberal "Beb" Asquith, had cut her off without a penny. Her gentle, well-meaning husband, the author of sensitive poems and unsuccessful novels, was following in the footsteps of his father, but his career as a barrister was interrupted by the war. When, wounded and shell-shocked, he returned from the Western Front, the main brunt of keeping things going fell on Cynthia. Only their closest friends knew that from the day of their marriage they had virtually never possessed a home of their own; and that the woman who always seemed so happy and untroubled was attempting in a stream of parties and banquets to divert her mind from the sorrows of caring for their mentally backward son.

When Edward Marsh introduced the Lawrences to her, she was twenty-six years old. From the very first moment she was attracted to Frieda, to her "health, strength and generosity of nature". It was the beginning of an enduring friendship. Lady Cynthia has provided a vivid account of the extraordinary impression which D.H.Lawrence made on her and her husband at this time:[3]

With his broad, jutting brow, and clear, sensitive, extremely blue eyes—very wide apart—he looked half faun, half prophet, and very young. He had not yet grown the tawny beard with which most people remember him ... Words welled out of him. He spoke in flashing phrases; at times colloquially, almost challengingly so, but often with a startling beauty of utterance ... You couldn't possibly be out of doors with Lawrence without becoming aware of the astonishing acuteness of his senses and realising that he belonged to an intenser existence, yet to some degree—and this was your great debt to him—he enabled you temporarily to share that intensified existence, for his faculty for communicating to others something of his own perceptiveness made a walk with him a wonderfully enhanced experience. In fact it made me feel that hitherto I had to all intents and purposes walked the earth with my eyes blindfolded and my ears plugged.

If Lawrence was for Cynthia Asquith something she had never experienced in her life before, a sort of elemental spirit who seemed to be in communion with the secret forces of nature, she was for him a feminine idol, and from the time of their meeting he worshipped her like a troubadour, platonically. This beautiful and much-courted woman—Frieda compared her with Botticelli's Venus—was the first *grande dame* he had so far encountered, and to feel, as he certainly did, that she responded to the magnetism of his personality and figured among his friends filled him with deep pride. The rebel against the values and conventions of his own time shared with the lower-middle-class masses he so much despised a reverence for the aura and social prestige of the nobility. Somewhere among the furnaces and abysses of his soul a snob lay concealed. However much he might poke fun at his own feelings, the snob in him was gratified that Frieda was of noble blood, and it was snobbish pride that made him, the coalminer's son, discern in Lady Cynthia, the aristocrat, the unattainable ideal of womanhood.

11

In August 1913 they were back again in Irschenhausen, and at the end of September in Italy.

This time they settled near Lerici on the Gulf of Spezia. A little pink house close to Fiascherino appealed to them so much that they at once rented it. It stood right on the seashore between vines and fig trees, and behind it were olive groves. Apart from that, it had the inestimable advantage of being cheap: sixty lire a month and twenty-five lire for the woman from Tellaro who kept it clean. They were hardly in a position to afford more, since once again they were in financial straits. *Sons and Lovers* had made the name of D. H. Lawrence widely known, but the novel was not a financial success.

Today the wooded foothills of Fiascherino are lined with hotels and *pensione*, and the narrow houses of the pirates' haunt Tellaro, perched on the cliffs above, have long since been transformed by architects into luxurious summer quarters for Milan industrialists. But Frieda and Lorenzo found both villages peaceful and unspoilt in their idyllic remoteness. "How beautiful olives are," he wrote, "so grey, so delicately sad, reminding one constantly of the New Testament. I am always expecting when I go to Tellaro for the letters, to meet Jesus gossiping with his disciples as he goes along above the sea, under the grey, light trees."

From Lerici the house could most easily be reached in a rowing-boat. But since Frieda once nearly upset the boat in the midst of a violent quarrel, Lorenzo preferred to take the land route, which was longer, but safer. One English poet had been drowned here already,* and that was enough.

Many visitors found their way to the pink cottage, among them Else Jaffe, Edward Marsh and Constance Garnett. Another was a wildly enthusiastic woman writer from England.

* On a stormy day in July 1822 Shelley, after a meeting with Byron, attempted with a friend to sail from Livorno to Lerici, where he was then living. In a sudden squall the boat capsized. It was several days before the two mangled bodies were washed up on shore. Shelley could be identified only by a volume of Sophocles in one pocket of his jacket and the poems of Keats in the other. Byron had the body burned on a pyre on the seashore according to the rites of Ancient Greece.

Ivy Low, a twenty-five-year-old Jewess, had already published two novels of her own. She came across a copy of *Sons and Lovers* in her mother's house. The moment she had finished reading it, she dashed off a dozen postcards to her friends, all proclaiming: "Discovered a genius! Be sure to read *Sons and Lovers*!" From now on Lawrence was her god and she his self-appointed high priestess. She wrote him, care of his publishers, a rapturous letter: "We of the younger generation believe you are the only English writer who represents our aspirations." He replied from Fiascherino on notepaper adorned with the Richthofen crest. Beside it the snobbish rebel wrote: "Don't let the crest upset you —my wife's father was a baron, and we're just using up old note paper."

Now Ivy Low was in Fiascherino, and she was to find the encounter with her idol an unnerving experience. The first week passed off happily enough. Ivy admired Frieda's un-English beauty, from which her rather untidy manner of dressing detracted not at all. The Lawrences liked their guest's lively ways and her capacity for enthusiasm. It did not escape Frieda's eyes that Ivy was wearing an embroidered blouse in the peasant style then in fashion among English intellectuals. Lorenzo never tired of talking to her. When he went to Lerici to do the shopping he asked her to accompany him, and they talked excitedly the whole way. No woman could have been more in love with her idol than Ivy Low.

But suddenly the mood changed, and the reason is not hard to guess: Frieda became jealous. All of a sudden, nothing that Ivy could do or say was right, and every moment Frieda and Lorenzo were discovering new defects in her character. When Ivy returned to England she had lost not only her belief in Lawrence, but also her own self-confidence. She was convinced she would never be able to write another book. And in fact fifteen years passed before she regained the courage to work on a new novel. By then her situation had changed entirely: she was living in Moscow with her husband, the Soviet Foreign Minister, Litvinov.

Lorenzo's work was making slow progress, and the surfeit of visitors was not the only cause. Frieda was again suffering from "moods": when her longing for her children was at its height, she became unbearable. But it was not these outward disturbances alone which were holding Lawrence back. He had made seven separate attempts to begin his novel *The Sisters*, and he was now well into what he—mistakenly—thought would be the final version. He was having considerable difficulty with the main female character. He had begun by basing Ursula on the girl to whom he had once been engaged, Louie

Burrows, but later he had invested her with the characteristics of Frieda. He sent the manuscript as soon as it was finished to Edward Garnett, remarking:[1]

I am sure of this now, this novel. It is a big and beautiful work. Before, I could not get my soul into it. That was because of the struggle and the resistance between Frieda and me. Now you will find her and me in the novel, I think, and the work is of both of us.

All the more bitter was his disappointment when Garnett told him that he did not like his *magnum opus*. He was evidently reluctant to follow Lawrence on the paths he had journeyed—to some extent under Frieda's influence, both conscious and unconscious—since *Sons and Lovers*. Also he felt that something in the psychology of the novel had gone wrong. Lawrence was ready to admit that he had perhaps not found the right expression for all he wanted to say, but all the same he reproached his old friend for not seriously trying to understand what he was aiming at.

All the time, underneath, there is something deep evolving itself out of me. And it is hard to express a new thing in sincerity ... But primarily I am a passionately religious man, and my novels must be written from the depth of my religious experience.

His vexation led to a cooling in his friendship with Edward Garnett, but he was sufficiently impressed by his old mentor's criticism to revise the novel yet again. He also gave the first part a new title, suggested by Frieda: *The Rainbow*.

Then an event occurred which profoundly affected their lives. On 28 May 1914, Frieda's marriage with Ernest Weekley was formally dissolved.

The knowledge that they were now at last free to marry had an electrifying effect on them. Within a few days they left Lerici to return to England. Frieda broke her journey in Baden-Baden, where her parents had moved from Metz. She found her father ill and disturbed in mind. "I don't understand the world any more," he complained, but presumably it was Frieda he did not understand. It was their last meeting. He died the following year, aged seventy.

The marriage took place on 13 July 1914 at the registry office in Kensington. There were three witnesses: John Middleton Murry, Katherine Mansfield and Gordon Campbell (later Lord Glenavy). In the taxi that conveyed all five to the registry office, Lawrence and Frieda were in a solemn mood. Murry, who was in a position to know, was probably right when he wrote:[2] "Perhaps it is those who have known what it is to live together unmarried who really do feel solemn about marriage, for they have known more nakedly the reality of the bond that binds a man and a woman. Precisely because they are, conventionally, free to leave one another, they know how closely they are bound."

On the way Lawrence, as if he had suddenly remembered something, stopped the taxi and hurried into a jeweller's shop. After a few minutes he came out again—with a wedding ring for his bride. Frieda looked at the ring she was still wearing on her left hand, the ring that Ernest Weekley had placed there fourteen years before. Slowly she drew it from her finger and gave it to Katherine Mansfield. It was a gesture of love, and Katherine was visibly moved. In the ensuing years she never took off that symbol of a broken bond between two other human beings. When she died in Fontainebleau at the age of thirty-three, she was still wearing Ernest Weekley's ring, and it was buried with her.

Despite his contempt for middle-class convention, Lawrence regarded marriage as a profound symbolic act, mystically sealing the union between man and woman:[3]

> When a man and woman truly come together, when there is a marriage, then an unconscious, vital connexion is established between them, like a throbbing blood-circuit. A man may forget a woman entirely with his head, and fling himself with energy and fervour into whatever job he is tackling, and all is well, all is good, if he does not break that inner vital connexion which is the mystery of marriage. But let him get out of unison, out of conjunction, let him inwardly break loose and come apart, let him fall into that worst of male vices, the vice of abstraction and mechanisation, and have a concern of working *alone* and of himself, then he commits the breach. He hurts the woman and he hurts himself, though neither may know why.

It may seem paradoxical that Lawrence, who lived for two years in an adulterous relationship with the wife of another man and who in his most famous book presented that kind of relationship as the highest fulfilment of sexual happiness, should at the same time proclaim the sacredness of marriage. But he was not conscious of the paradox. He was completely convinced that this "unconscious, vital connexion" and this "throbbing blood-circuit" had not existed between Frieda and Ernest Weekley. The mystery of which he spoke was not necessarily contained in every marriage. But between him and Frieda it had existed from that electric moment at their very first meeting when they recognised one another.

Could his irrational belief in a blood-circuit between a man and a woman, the idea that there existed a mysterious "blood-wisdom" which transcended the mind's wisdom, have been a reaction against the puritanical strictness of his mother? It is possible. Certainly Lawrence was following the "dictates of the blood" when, in direct and flagrant rebellion against all his mother's moral principles, he and Frieda lived together. For the same reason he felt no sense of guilt for having destroyed Ernest Weekley's marriage. Reason, the law and the church's commandments might condemn what he had done, but there was a higher law that approved and sanctified it. The simple and unimaginative ceremony at the registry office was for him a formal expression of the validity of his beliefs, the outward confirmation of his determination to protect the woman he loved and shield her from society's revenge.

For Frieda, marriage meant the ending of an irregular status within the social framework. She had hitherto received comfort from the sympathy and understanding of her friends, but very few people outside this small circle shared Else Jaffe's emancipated views or the Murrys' lack of prejudice. In order to avoid unpleasantness or hostility, Lawrence and Frieda had frequently pretended to be married, but they had found this humiliating, and had done it only in order to avoid possibly greater humiliations. It was good to know that there was no longer any need to dissemble.

Now that they were in England they were quite content to be drawn into the intellectual and social life of the great metropolis. The literary *avant-garde*, seeing Lawrence as a valuable reinforcement, welcomed him with open arms. The psycho-analysts, finding *Sons and Lovers* an impressive portrayal of the Oedipus complex at work, sought to make an ally of him in their efforts to win recognition for the ideas of Freud. One of the most significant pioneers in the field of psycho-analysis in England was Dr David Eder, who was a brother-in-law of Ivy Low. Frieda and Lawrence quickly made friends with him—much to the concern of Middleton Murry, who had little patience with the new teaching. He and Katherine had so far assumed somewhat naïvely that they were living a perfectly healthy sex life without the aid of any theories, and consequently they were rather baffled when Lawrence openly accused them of not taking the sexual side of their relationship seriously enough. In spite of many reservations, Lawrence was deeply impressed both by Eder's personality and his knowledge, and several years later he used him as a model for the hero of his novel *Kangaroo*.

Lawrence was one of the first English writers whose work was influenced by the theories of Freud. It was not until the traumatic experiences of the First World War opened minds to new thought processes, that these began to make a wide impact in England. The extent to which Lawrence was fascinated by the new discoveries—the acknowledgment that many of our acts are determined by forces over which we have no conscious control, the definition of the unconscious as "the true psychic reality", the recognition of the overriding importance of sexuality in the interpretation of dreams, in infancy and childhood, in trivial slips of the tongue, in the symbolism of primitive peoples —can be discerned from his later (and, it must be confessed, very amateurish) book of essays *Fantasia of the Unconscious*. Although in *Sons and Lovers* Lawrence instinctively anticipated ideas which he later found confirmed in psycho-analytical literature, his own psychological constructions differ radically from the teachings of Freud, both in matters of opinion and because of the dense emotional fog that overlays them. Generally speaking, it is not unfair to say that, while Freud attempted to throw a scientific light on mythological darkness, Lawrence snatched the soul from the claws of science and pushed it back into the twilight of myth. To a world that worshipped science this was a great, but dangerous boon. "All scientists are liars," he once told Aldous Huxley, when Huxley confronted him with certain inconvenient facts which had been experimentally proved. "Liars! Liars! I don't care about evidence."[4]

In the overlapping literary circles in which Lawrence and Frieda were now moving, Catherine Carswell and Richard Aldington represented new spheres. Both of them later wrote important biographies of D. H. Lawrence. Catherine Carswell, a Scotswoman and a friend of Ivy Low, was a slim, beautiful woman of unusual charm. She possessed the enviable gift of being able to awaken unreserved feelings of lifelong friendship in people who had known her for only a couple of hours. She established an instant inner contact with Lawrence, and her unquestioning admiration remained steadfast throughout his life and beyond. Since her friendship made no emotional demands, she never, in contrast to Ivy Low and others, aroused Frieda's jealousy. After his death she wrote:[5]

He had chosen ... a woman from whom he felt he could win the special submission he demanded without thereby defeating her in her womanhood. Sometimes it seemed to us that he had chosen rather a force of nature—a female force—than an individual woman. Frieda was to Lawrence by turns a buffeting and a laughing breeze, a healing rain or a maddening tempest of stupidity, a cheering sun or a stroke of indiscriminate lightning. She was mindless Womanhood, wilful, defiant, disrespectful, argumentative, assertive, vengeful, sly, illogical, treacherous, unscrupulous and self-seeking. At times she hated Lawrence and he her. There were things she jeered at in him and things in her that maddened him—things that neither would consent to subdue. But partly for that very reason—how he *admired* her! And to be ardently admired by Lawrence was something of a rarity, and it meant that the admired one was somebody rare. In Frieda, Lawrence found a magnificent female probity of being, as well as of physical well-being ... For myself, I find that in her own very different way Frieda is a person as remarkable as Lawrence, and that Lawrence knew it. Two things are certain: that in all his journeyings he never saw another woman whom he would or could have put in her place: also, that Lawrence cannot be accepted without acceptance of his wife.

Richard Aldington, then twenty-two years old, and his wife, the American lyric poet Hilda Doolittle (who signed her poems simply with the initials H.D.), belonged to the group of so-called Imagists, set up two years earlier by Ezra Pound and dedicated to certain aesthetic principles of no great interest today. Pound had abandoned his brain-child and transferred his allegiance to another clique, the "Blast" group. But, even worse, he had just proclaimed his intention of setting up a new "movement": the "Vortex" group. Such despotic fickleness could not be allowed to go unchallenged. The New World came swiftly to the Aldingtons' rescue in the person of Amy Lowell, leader of the American Imagists and a poet in her own right. Amy Lowell was a bundle of energy, and she also possessed apparently inexhaustible amounts of money, with which she generously supported a whole number of needy poets. As always when she came to London, she rented a whole suite in the sumptuous Berkeley Hotel. Here in the drawing-room she now staged a dinner to which she invited Ezra Pound and the leading Imagists (including the Aldingtons), in order to discuss "the immediate abolition of his despotism and the substitution of a pure democracy". To lend strength to her forces, Amy also invited the individualist, D. H. Lawrence.

It was a warm evening, and through the window of the drawing-room Aldington could look along the brilliantly lighted length of Piccadilly to Green Park and the front of the Ritz Hotel. On the corner a man was selling newspapers from a stand hung with placards proclaiming in huge letters: "GERMANY AND RUSSIA AT WAR—OFFICIAL". A boy brought a new bundle of evening papers, and the newspaper seller hung up another placard. It read: "BRITISH ARMY MOBILISED".

Up till then nobody had seriously believed in the possibility of a war. Three years earlier, during the Morocco crisis, a wave of nervousness had swept across the country. But now, in the summer of 1914, England was so quiet, so oblivious, so busied with its own domestic problems— Ireland, discipline in the Church of England—that the danger of becoming involved in a catastrophic armed conflict was quite unthinkable. It seemed so still to Aldington as he turned back to the room full of authors engaged in quiet conversation.

At that moment the door opened and Lawrence came in. Before he could be introduced, he said: "I've just been talking to Eddie Marsh. He says we shall be in the war."

There was an astonished pause. Then someone said: "Oh, nonsense!" Several others also cried: "Nonsense!" Then the dinner began. Lawrence was given the place of honour beside Amy Lowell, and in the ensuing battle between Imagists and Vorticists the poets forgot all about the other war.

12

At first, in spite of the war, things appeared to be going on in their accustomed way, and Lorenzo's thoughts were concentrated not on a uniform, but on a dinner jacket. H. G. Wells had invited him and Frieda to a party—proof conclusive that he had now "arrived".

Wells, whose popular reputation nowadays rests on his "science fiction" rather than on his social novels, stood in the vanguard of reformers and was one of the most active members of the Fabian Society. But he was fighting not only for a more equitable social order; he was also campaigning for the removal of traditional sexual taboos. Lorenzo and Frieda may well have found this an additional reason for looking forward eagerly to their meeting.

Wells had none of Lawrence's puritanism, and his struggle against Victorian hypocrisy had taken very different and much more radical forms. When he suddenly raised the banner of free love, the leading Fabians were scandalised. Their dismay was not surprising, considering who they were: the puritanical vegetarian Bernard Shaw, the strait-laced Philip Snowden (later Chancellor of the Exchequer in the first Labour government), the earnest theoreticians Sidney and Beatrice Webb, the future Archbishop of Canterbury William Temple and others of like mind.

But Wells was not satisfied merely with preaching the doctrine of free love. He had married his cousin Isabel Williams while still a poor assistant teacher in a London school. But Isabel could not keep pace with his intellectual and physical demands for long. Eighteen months after the wedding he fell in love with one of his pupils, Catherine Robbins, to whom he gave the name Jane in a symbolic act of pos-session. Jane was not content merely to return his love; she insisted energetically that he must face the consequences that arose from it. Wells consequently left his wife, gave up his teacher's job and settled down with Jane in a modest boarding-house. From now on his sexual life blossomed as actively, variously and successfully as his writing career. His outward appearance did not, admittedly, conform to the usual ideas of a Don Juan. He was short, his keenly intelligent eyes were set in a round and uninteresting face, and his voice was a shrill falsetto. But it was what he said that proved fascinating.

His marriage with the phlegmatic Isabel was dissolved. The relationship with Jane escaped collapse probably only because both partners had agreed in advance to grant each other complete freedom of action. Whether Jane made any use of this right is immaterial, but Wells himself, in spite of his bad health, launched out into an endless series of erotic adventures. When he began to draw the daughters of the Fabians into his net, Shaw felt the time had come to issue a serious warning. To this Wells replied: "Dear Shaw—The more I think you over the more it comes home to me what an unmitigated middle-Victorian ass you are." As if to demonstrate that he was not prepared to accept interference from anyone, he promptly seduced the pretty daughter of one of the most prominent Fabians. The girl's mother was a radical suffragette, but her revolutionary zeal vanished when it came to the matter of her own daughter. It was a highly dramatic affair which ended happily—on the surface, at any rate: the girl was hastily married off to another admirer, five months before giving birth to Wells's child. He had loved her passionately and was unable to forget her. The novel *Ann Veronica*, in which he drew her portrait, caused one of the most bitter literary scandals of the pre-war era.

That had all happened five years before. Since then Wells had published a further five books, his literary fame had penetrated into distant lands, and he had become a wealthy man. His invitation to dinner was a very important occasion for Lawrence and it justified, not to say demanded, some expenditure on suitable clothing. Lawrence, who had never in his life before worn a dinner jacket, let alone possessed one, looked rather out of place in it, but Frieda was too much occupied with the problems of her own toilet to notice. Wells and Jane, his second legal wife, made them cordially welcome in their fine old house in Hampstead, but as the evening went on Lawrence became increasingly silent and irritable. Probably he was put out by the fact that the attention of the ladies was firmly concentrated on their famous host. Not even the expensive dinner jacket helped.

However, there were far more serious reasons for feeling uneasy. The war had come so unexpectedly that it took Lawrence and Frieda some time to realise how seriously it affected their own plans. All of a sudden it struck them that they would not be able to return to Fiascherino. That, even under normal circumstances, would have been a bitter disappointment. But circumstances were not normal, and the prospect of having to spend the whole of the war in England was a depressing one. On top of that, Frieda was soon made to realise that her German birth raised a barrier between her and the people among whom she was living.

A fortnight after the outbreak of war David Garnett invited them to dinner in his father's London apartment. Edward Garnett himself was in Kent. David had asked a college friend to join the guests, and the mood was warm and friendly. Frieda began to speak of her divided loyalties. England had been her home for almost fifteen years, her children had been born in England, her husband was English and she loved her new home. But she had been born a German and she was still attached to Germany and to her family there. What had become of the celebrated British sense of fair play, when all this was held against her? David and his friend listened sympathetically to her complaints. Then Lawrence and Frieda left. They had gone down several flights of stairs to the ground floor and were standing outside the door of the ground-floor flat when David's friend cheerily shouted down to her in German: "Auf Wiedersehen, gnädige Baronin!" Frieda called back a light-hearted answer, also in German.

A few days later two detectives from Scotland Yard called on David Garnett. Distrustful and none too polite, they subjected him to a very embarrassing examination. Whom did the apartment belong to? What was the owner's profession? How many Germans lived there? Did he often have German visitors? Two days later two more detectives came and asked the same questions. A week elapsed, and then an older man from Scotland Yard came to the house. "Do you know," David complained, "that you are the fifth detective to come here to enquire about the same dinner party?" He would be grateful, he added, if his name could be removed from the list of people suspected of being German spies. The detective laughed and good-humouredly explained that the police received hundreds of denunciations every day, and they were obliged to investigate them all. That was the last David Garnett was to hear of the matter, but for Frieda and Lawrence it was only the beginning.

They had left London and were now living in a little house in Chesham, to the north-west of London. It was an ugly brick building surrounded by a sea of nettles. They soon discovered that the rooms were damp: it was no fit place for a man with a tendency to consumption. They were deeply depressed. The war was like a nightmare to Lawrence. He had no money and he was ill again. "My soul lay in

117

the tomb," he later wrote to Cynthia Asquith, "not dead, but with a flat stone over it, a corpse, become corpse-cold. And nobody existed, because I did not exist myself."

By roundabout routes Frieda received scraps of news from Germany. "Father seriously ill," "Dear Udo von Henning killed on 7 September at Charleroi ..." The nearness of London reopened old wounds. Her children were living there. Monty, Elsa and Barby flitted through her dreams.

Even when they were with friends, their cheerfulness was only precariously maintained. Katherine Mansfield and Middleton Murry had moved into a small cottage in the neighbourhood, and one evening they came to supper. The meal had to be cooked on a little paraffin stove—a job that usually fell to Lawrence. There were only two chairs in the house. If more guests were present, there was nowhere to sit except on boxes or trunks or simply on the floor: no obstacles to good cheer as long as the hosts keep their nerve. On this occasion the evening passed pleasantly until either Murry or Katherine unthinkingly mentioned the children. Frieda immediately burst into tears. Lawrence went as white as a sheet. He had now grown a beard, and the white face behind the red hair made him look uncanny—satanic and ill. The next moment his anger broke out in a terrifying explosion. Frieda must leave the house at once, he shouted. She was a misery to him, she would be his death. She must go—go at once! She knew how much money he had: he would give her half—more than half. Like a madman he ran up the stairs to the bedroom. Returning a minute later, he breathlessly counted the money out on the table. There, that was her share, and now she could go—what was she waiting for? Sobbing, Frieda put on her coat and hat and moved to the door, where she stood, helpless and weeping. She would have wandered out into the night if Murry had not succeeded in calming Lawrence down.

Such scenes were becoming increasingly frequent, and at length they realised that something must be done. Frieda must make a last attempt to reach an understanding concerning the children. They went together to Nottingham, and, while Lawrence was in Eastwood visiting his father and his sister Ada, now married, Frieda went to see Ernest Weekley at his *pied-à-terre*. She went unannounced, hoping to surprise him. She gave the landlady—who happened also to be a German—a false name, Mrs Lawson, and was shown in.

Weekley stared at her in amazement. "You—I hoped never to see you again."

Frieda went straight to the point. "I came to see you about the children," she said pleadingly.

His voice, as he replied, was full of hatred and contempt. "Aren't you ashamed to show your face where you are known? Isn't the commonest prostitute better than you?"

She flinched, as if he had slapped her in the face. "Oh, no."

But he went on inexorably: "Is there no place where I can have peace?"

She continued to plead with him. "I must speak to you about the children."

It was no use. His words became wilder and wilder. He called her the most despicable creature on the face of the earth. Under no circumstances was she to be allowed to see the children again. And then, with cold finality, he added that he had given his solicitors instructions to have her arrested if she attempted "to interfere with the children".[1]

The attempt was an utter disaster. Frieda returned to Lawrence, broken and despairing, and he consoled her with great love and understanding.

Friends came to see them. Catherine Carswell paid a visit, Amy Lowell descended on Chesham in a chestnut-brown limousine, driven by a chauffeur in a chestnut-brown uniform, and was horrified by the pokiness and dampness of the cottage. She gave Lawrence a typewriter. Samuel Solomonovich Koteliansky visited them several times. He was a Russian Jew who had studied political economy at the University of Kiev and who, on account of his radical views, had attracted some unwelcome attention from the Tsarist police. A scholarship had enabled him to come to England, where he was now working as a translator. Lawrence met him during a walking tour in the Lake District.

To Frieda and Lawrence—as equally to Katherine Mansfield and Virginia Woolf—Koteliansky was to become a lifelong friend, though his unflinching loyalty was often sorely tried. He was a man of the highest moral integrity, reminiscent in the passion of his convictions of an Old Testament prophet. He lived as far as possible according to the strict code of Mosaic law, and this may have been the reason why he had reservations about Frieda. He felt she was "not good enough" for Lawrence. At this time he was thirty-two years old. He had thick black hair and he walked with a slight stoop, peering through thick spectacles at the world with his sadly resigned, yet always burning dark eyes. His handshake reminded Leonard Woolf of the Commendatore in the last act of Mozart's opera, when, returning as a stone statue, he takes Don Giovanni's hand before consigning him to the flames of hell. Katherine Mansfield, to whom he was always a refuge in times of crisis, used sometimes to say to him: "Now howl like a dog." And Koteliansky would obediently imitate a watchdog—producing a noise which for some reason had a soothing effect on Katherine. He had learned this art in the Ukrainian village in which he grew up. At the time he had been in love with a girl who lived in another village five miles away, and he visited her once a week. When he was walking home in the night and the darkness and silence began to oppress him, he would start to howl like a dog, and all the mongrels in the villages round about would answer with a chorus of lamentation. Then he felt that he was no longer alone in a hostile world.

Besides Koteliansky, the Lawrences formed a whole succession of new friendships. Not far from Chesham lived Gilbert Cannan and his wife, the actress Mary Ansell, who were close friends of the Murrys. Cannan was Mary's second husband; she had formerly been married to the playwright James Barrie, and had learned only on their wedding night that Barrie was impotent. In spite of this she continued to share his life for many years, until one day he angrily accused her of having a lover. "Yes, I love another man," she cried out, "since you are incapable of loving me!" With these defiant words she left Barrie and went to live with her lover, who was Gilbert Cannan. Now they were happily married and living in a windmill. Here, perched at a high desk overlooking the surrounding woods and meadows, Cannan sat writing a thousand words every morning, never more and never less. He was a novelist of the "neo-realistic" school and he portrayed characters driven by ungovernable passions, set against the sombre background of Lancashire. In later years delusions of grandeur led him into increasingly ambitious projects, which finally proved his downfall. Now, a few years after his death, his work is not undeservedly forgotten.

The Cannans were also friendly with Compton Mackenzie, whose novel *Sinister Street* had fairly recently been published. The overwhelming success of this book marked the beginning of a literary career that was to be as brilliant as it was long. In the ten-volume autobiography in which he tells the eventful story of his life, Mackenzie describes his first meeting with Lawrence and Frieda in their little cottage:

When Cannan and I arrived, Lawrence was on his knees, with a pail beside him scrubbing the floor ... Rising and wiping his hands, he went to the bottom of the staircase and shouted, "Frieda!" A pair of legs in ringed black and white stockings came into view at the top of the curved staircase before the body they supported appeared. "Shut that door!" he called. The legs kept on their way down. "Frieda, shut that bloody door!" he shouted angrily. She turned back to shut the door, after which she descended into the sitting-room ...

Lawrence's rage with the war was fed by his having a German wife. I hardly exaggerate when I say that one might have supposed we had gone to war with Germany solely for the purpose of annoying Lawrence personally ...

In the course of the conversation ... I said: "I can't imagine anything more depressing than spending the winter in England as a special constable. I can't face the depressing view of these flat English fields surrounded by their melancholy elms without leaves."

"You're right," Lawrence exclaimed. "Those melancholy elms. Flat fields and elms! Frieda!"

"What is it, Lorenzo?"

"We can't stay in this cottage with these elms. We must get down somewhere to the sea."

Mackenzie ventured the opinion—held by most people in Britain and Germany at that time—that the war would be over by the spring, and then they could have his little house in Capri.[2]

Five years later Lawrence reminded him of this casual promise. But in the meantime he was dreaming, like so many others before him, of another island, somewhere in a strange sea, where he could found an ideal community far away from war-torn Europe. The members of his new Utopia—this was Lawrence's plan—should be given the opportunity to develop their natural talents to the full. They would live for their common ideals in unrestricted freedom. In this high-minded anarchic society there would be no money, communal life would be regulated by a code of moral integrity and not by riches, power and caprice, or the necessities imposed by poverty.

Lawrence had already decided on a symbol for his colony: it would be a phoenix, the legendary bird that rises from the ashes with its youth renewed. Later he adopted the phoenix as his personal emblem. He had also coined a name for the land of his dreams: Rananim. The inspiration for it came from some Hebrew words that Koteliansky had recited during one of their walking tours together. Lawrence wrote them down as "Ranani Sadekin Badanoi", but the correct form is "Ranenu Sadekim b'Adanoi": they are the first words of the 33rd Psalm—"Rejoice in the Lord, O ye righteous". In Lawrence's own mythology Rananim meant "the colony of lost souls". He held firm to his dream for the next eleven years.

In the following January they escaped from the cold and unhealthy cottage in Chesham. Viola Meynell, a friend of Ivy Low and like her an enthusiastic admirer of *Sons and Lovers*, lent them a small but comfortable house in Greatham in Sussex, and here Lawrence soon threw off the leaden weight of his depression. He made swift progress with *The Rainbow*. He had decided to divide his novel *The Sisters* in two (the second part appeared five years later under the title *Women in Love*), and this decision enabled him to complete *The Rainbow* by the beginning of 1915. Friends came to visit them: among them Murry, who was miserable because Katherine had left him to go off to France with a new lover (she soon returned, full of remorse). Other visitors were Ford Madox Hueffer, Ivy Low, Lady Cynthia Asquith and Lady Ottoline Morrell.

Lady Ottoline was a Cavendish-Bentinck and half-sister of the Duke of Portland. She had grown up at the family seat, Welbeck Abbey in Nottinghamshire, and the fact that they both came from the same county—she from a castle and he from a miner's cottage—quickly enabled her and Lawrence to get down to swopping sentimental childhood memories. They agreed about the romantic beauty of Sherwood Forest and the ugliness of the mining villages.

But the parental home belonged to a past part of her life which Lady Ottoline utterly rejected. Her place was now among the social reformers, the Bohemians and the intellectuals. Her husband, Philip Morrell, was a left-wing Liberal Member of Parliament, whose family had lived for generations past in Oxford and whose character and interests reflected its spirit of independence and its academic atmosphere. The Morrells had a town house in Bloomsbury, but, just before Lady Ottoline's first meeting with Lawrence, they had bought a country house, Garsington Manor, five miles outside Oxford. This house has been described countless times by writers who enjoyed Lady Ottoline's hospitality. A fine sixteenth-century building, it had been furnished with exquisite taste by the new lady of the house, and on the walls hung pictures painted by artists whom she had taken under her wing. Behind the house there was a rectangular lake, surrounded by statues and clipped yew-hedges, and from here the visitor enjoyed an enchanting view of the surrounding countryside—a view, incidentally, that today is somewhat marred by the chimneys of the new motor works near Oxford.

So much for Lady Ottoline's realm. What of Lady Ottoline herself? We know exactly what she looked like, for her portrait was painted often enough by artists such as Augustus John and Duncan Grant, and a succession of writers have described her in words. Her striking face— "horse-face" was Bertrand Russell's impolite description of it— seemed to be permanently covered with a thick layer of powder. She had a powerful nose, a massive chin, an expressive mouth, hair dyed "the colour of dark marmalade" (Bertrand Russell again) and an un-usually long neck. She was very tall and her imposing appearance was startlingly accentuated by the eccentricity of her clothing. She loved to wrap herself in long and brightly coloured shawls and loose fluttering cloaks, which gave her some resemblance to the peacocks on the Garsington lawns. Once when she was walking with Leonard and Virginia Woolf through the quiet streets of Bloomsbury, she attracted so much attention with her eccentric clothes, her enormous hat and her red hair that people stopped to look, while some workmen in the road roared with laughter and whistled after her. Lady Ottoline continued on her way, completely unconcerned. The poet Stephen Spender frequently saw her walking along in London with a whole troupe of Pekinese dogs, attached with brightly coloured strings to a shepherd's crook held in her right hand. Siegfried Sassoon thought she was trying to look like "a sort of modern Messalina", while Osbert Sitwell com-pared her with "a rather over-size Infanta of Spain".[3]

Lady Ottoline collected celebrities in the same way that a schoolboy collects stamps. Sir Maurice Bowra, the classical philologist, declared that part of the fascination of Garsington lay in the fact that one never knew whom one would meet there. In the gardens one might easily come across Herbert Asquith, the Prime Minister; almost certainly Bertrand Russell would be there—his fame at that time rested on his mathematical work, not, as later, on his philosophy and his champion-ship of controversial causes. Inside the house, always pervaded by the discreet fragrance of incense, one would meet a few brilliant Oxford undergraduates such as the twenty-year-old Aldous Huxley (who was later to portray Lady Ottoline in his novel *Crome Yellow* under the name of Mrs Wimbush), and his brother, the biologist Julian Huxley. In bizarre contrast to the pure rationalism of these super-intellectuals, W. B. Yeats would perhaps be telling a ghost story, or the post-

Impressionist painter Augustus John, red-bearded like Lawrence, might be engaged in noisy dispute with Stanley Spencer, the visionary painter with curious iconographic obsessions, or with Mark Gertler, the Jewish artist who looked like a Botticelli angel. Here one would often see the finely chiselled features of Virginia Woolf or recognise her close friend, the biographer Lytton Strachey. Another regular visitor was the composer Lord Berners, who always took a piano or a harpsichord around with him. It was said that he had once, during a tour of Italy, put the fear of God into the peasants by passing in his chauffeur-driven car through their peaceful villages with a horrific chalk-white mask over his face, and playing an elegiac melody on the piano.

There were people who took a malicious pleasure in declaring that Lady Ottoline, in her Christian charity and her encouragement of the artistic temperament, sometimes overstepped the bounds of convention. Desmond MacCarthy's wife, entering an apparently empty room, once, it was reported, surprised Lady Ottoline and the painter Henry Lamb in the middle of a passionate embrace. "I was just giving Henry an aspirin," Lady Ottoline explained with great presence of mind. And there was Bertrand Russell, who, while still a lecturer in mathematics at Cambridge, spent a night in the Morrells' London house. Philip Morrell had been unexpectedly called away to his constituency, and the guest found himself alone with Lady Ottoline, whom he then knew only slightly. After they had spent dinner in an animated discussion of politics, Russell, whose marriage was none too happy owing to his wife's frigidity, made a tentative pass at Lady Ottoline. To his surprise his advances were cordially received, and that night he became her lover. Returning home, he told his wife what had happened. She flew into a rage which lasted several hours, and threatened to make a public scandal. When the storm was over, Russell gave her niece, who was in the middle of school examinations, a lecture on Locke's philosophy, then mounted his bicycle and rode away. That was the end of his first marriage.[4]

Bertie, as Russell was known to his friends, remained Lady Ottoline's lover for five years. There was only one drawback to their happiness: Philip, bowing to the inevitable after many vain protests, made his acceptance of the situation conditional on his rival never spending a night with Ottoline. In that way outward appearances at least were preserved.

Like Bertrand Russell, the Morrells were both confirmed pacifists: Russell's convictions were later to land him in prison, Philip Morrell's to cost him his seat in the House of Commons. Mutual hatred of war forged a bond too between Lawrence and Lady Ottoline. With her usual enthusiasm whenever a creative talent crossed her path, she declared that his pale face and his red beard gave him a strong physical resemblance to Van Gogh. "Indeed, in many ways he resembled him in character, especially in the intensity of his imaginative insight into people and his power of seeing and even exaggerating the essence of what he saw, though, in fact, he was very English with a great love of English country and English ways."

Lawrence, always responsive to admiration in others, saw a chance here of bringing his Rananim plan a step nearer to realisation. Could Garsington not become the starting point of his ideal community? But Lady Ottoline, however eccentric she might have been, also had her shrewd side, and her reaction was cautious. Feeling no doubt that imaginative soap-bubbles are likely to burst quickest when brought into contact with a clear mind, she persuaded Bertrand Russell to accompany her to Greatham.

Russell's relationship with Lawrence ran a stormy course. "We were brought together by Ottoline," Russell wrote, "who admired us both and made us think that we ought to admire each other." At first they were mutually attracted: both loathed the war and were united in their rejection of the Establishment as well as the aestheticism of intellectual snobs. Russell was impressed by Lawrence's energy and his passionate conviction that some fundamental action was needed to set the world to rights. He invited Lawrence to visit him in Cambridge, and Lawrence, flattered though apprehensive, complied. The visit was not a success. At dinner in the august hall of Trinity College the author of *The Rainbow* sat, silent and morose, beside a lecturer in moral philosophy. To breakfast the following morning Russell invited the political economist John Maynard Keynes. Lawrence took an instant dislike to him, and sat silently sulking by the fire instead of joining in the conversation.

Notwithstanding this false start, Russell and Lawrence a few weeks later discussed the possibility of doing a series of lectures together. The plan fell through, for they came to realise that, apart from a few points of contact, they had really nothing in common. The mutual admiration which Lady Ottoline had hoped to arouse in them turned in the course of the following months into bitter enmity. Lawrence's letters became more and more aggressive. "Do stop working and writing altogether," he told Russell, "and become a creature instead of a mechanical instrument ... Do for your very pride's sake become a mere nothing, a mole, a creature that feels its way and doesn't think."

One might have expected Russell to take these unbridled outbursts of rage calmly. In fact, as he later admitted, they drove him to the brink of suicide. "When he said that my pacifism was rooted in blood-lust," he wrote in his autobiography, "I supposed that he might be right." But he recovered his equanimity when in the same breath with these accusations, Lawrence asked to be remembered in his will. The differences that drove them apart and turned them into enemies were in fact fundamental. Bertrand Russell was a profound believer in demo-cratic principles, and the vast gap between them became clearly apparent when Lawrence wrote: "I don't believe in democratic control ... The thing must culminate in one real head, as every organic thing must— no foolish republics with foolish presidents, but an elected King, some-thing like Julius Caesar." Russell's comment on this was: "He, of course, in his imagination supposed that when a dictatorship was established he would be the Julius Caesar. This was part of the dream-like quality of his thinking ... Gradually I discovered that he had no real wish to make the world better, but only indulge in eloquent soliloquy about how bad it was." Writing towards the end of his life, with the experience of later catastrophes behind him, Russell observed: "He had developed the whole philosophy of Fascism before the politicians had thought of it."5

He was utterly opposed to Lawrence's philosophy of blood-con-sciousness, which first found fictional expression in his novel *The Rainbow*. The idea had already begun to take shape in the Villa Igéa on Lake Garda—significantly enough during the first months of his living together with Frieda. In a letter written from there on 17 January 1913, Lawrence said:

My great religion is a belief in the blood, the flesh, as being wiser than the intellect. We can go wrong in our minds. But what our blood feels and believes and says, is always true. The intellect is only a bit and a bridle. What do I care about knowledge? ... I conceive a man's body as a kind of flame, like a candle flame, forever upright and yet flowing: and the intellect is just the light that is shed on to the things around. And I am not so much concerned with the things around—which is really mind—but with the mystery of flame forever flowing, coming God knows how from out of practically nowhere, and being *itself*, whatever there is around it, that it lights up.

And to Bertrand Russell he wrote:

> There is another seat of consciousness than the brain and the nerve
> system: there is a blood-consciousness which exists in us inde-
> pendently of the ordinary mental consciousness, which depends on
> the eye as its source or connector. There is the blood-consciousness,
> with the sexual connection holding the same relation as the eye, in
> seeing, holds to the mental consciousness.[6]

Not surprisingly, Russell regarded such views as utter nonsense.
And he believed he knew where these theories originated: in Frieda.
Lawrence, in his opinion, was the mouthpiece of his wife:[7]

> He had the eloquence, but she had the ideas ... Somehow she im-
> bibed prematurely the ideas afterwards developed by Mussolini and
> Hitler, and these ideas she transmitted to Lawrence, shall we say, by
> blood-consciousness. Lawrence was an essentially timid man, who
> tried to conceal his timidity by bluster. His wife was not timid, and
> her denunciations have the character of thunder, not of bluster.
> Under her wing he felt comparatively safe. Like Marx, he had a
> snobbish pride in having married a German aristocrat, and in *Lady
> Chatterley* he dressed her up marvellously ... His descriptive powers
> were remarkable, but his ideas cannot be too soon forgotten.

It cannot be disputed that Lawrence was gradually led by his ideas
into strange and dangerous byways, and François Mauriac was not
entirely unjust when he described Lawrence as a "ridiculous prophet".
His philosophy of blood-consciousness did lead him to some absurd
conclusions. For instance, in his novel *The Plumed Serpent*, written in
the middle of the twenties, he invited approval for a leadership that
demanded blind obedience and mass execution of "traitors". Ideas of
this sort earned him the reproach of having flirted with Fascist ideas.
But no other of his critics has ever gone quite so far as Bertrand Russell,
when he accused Lawrence of having "developed the whole philosophy
of Fascism".

Later, in the thirties, it became a fashionable pastime in Britain to
look for signs of Fascism in the works of prominent authors, and no
great degree of perspicacity was needed to find them. There were
plenty of cultural philosophers, irrationalists and neo-mythologists
active around the turn of the century who could be condemned on this
count. Only a few of them, such as Paul de Lagarde and Heinrich von
Treitschke, can be regarded as having been conscious pioneers of the

subsequent terror. Most of them were innocently playing with the fire of the new barbarism under the impression that they were lighting the way to man's recovery—or at least to their nation's recovery. Ideas which later, with the wisdom of hindsight, were held to contain "symptoms of Fascism" had been in the air at the time—particularly in Germany—and it is not improbable that Lawrence, who was susceptible to outside influence, was swayed by these ideas, as he was also, however, by others expressing the exact opposite. He described his novels as "thought adventures". Like many other writers, he was fascinated by the problem of power, and in two of his "thought adventures"—*Kangaroo* and *The Plumed Serpent*—he attempted to fathom the psychology of leadership. Dreams of power are not, after all, the prerogative of politicians. Bertrand Russell might have been right when he sarcastically remarked that Lawrence saw himself as the Julius Caesar of his imagined dictatorship. He was an individualist *par excellence* and could not have borne life in a dictatorship other than at the top. In his masterly story *St Mawr* he characterised Fascism as the embodiment of evil, and from Italy, where as a foreigner he was not directly affected by the measures of the regime, he once wrote:[8]

> One can ignore Fascism in Italy for a time. But after a while, the sense of false power forced against life is very depressing. And one can't escape—except by the trick of abstraction, which is no good.

Frieda herself, though one could hardly call her an objective witness, said in reply to Russell's attacks: "As for calling Lawrence an exponent of Nazism, that is pure nonsense. You might as well call St Augustine a Nazi."

Presumably, as long as Lawrence's philosophy of blood-consciousness was only a poetic conception, Russell had nothing against it. But for Lawrence it was far more than that: it was the very core of a new cosmology. His belief in the power of intuition, as distinct from intellect, and in the mystery of the relationship between man and woman led him to raise the sexual act to the status of a myth, to see it as the centre-piece of a pantheistic *Weltanschauung*. As he wrote in *The Rainbow*:[9]

> They felt the rush of the sap in spring, they knew the wave which cannot halt, but every year throws forward the seed to begetting, and, falling back, leaves the young-born on the earth. They knew the intercourse between heaven and earth, sunshine drawn into the

breast and bowels, the rain sucked up in the daytime, nakedness that comes under the wind in autumn, showing the birds' nests no longer worth hiding.

But were all these really Frieda's ideas? Was it really she who put into his mind all these emotional anticipations of Fascist ideology? Was he truly nothing but her mouthpiece? No, here Bertrand Russell wildly exaggerated. Certainly Frieda's influence with Lawrence was considerable. Lawrence himself once observed that Böcklin, "or some other artist," could only work when he sat with his back to a wall; and in the same way he himself could work only when he had a woman behind him. But Frieda was much more than just a shield for his back: she was also the ideal comrade and partner in those voyages into the unknown into which his "thought adventures" led him. This is, how-ever, not the same as saying that all his inspiration came from her. He might be compared with an infinitely sensitive aerial, receiving messages from countless other human beings and at the same time in mysterious communication with all organic things, even with inanimate natural objects. The essential factor was that he could speak to Frieda on the same wavelength and measure the inspirations relayed from a thousand sources against the scale of her reactions. She was his ideal partner because she submitted to him, yet at the same time fought against him; because she believed in his genius, yet preserved her independence as an individual against him; because she complemented him sexually and represented for him the perfect embodiment of the female principle.

However strained his relationship with Bertrand Russell, his friend-ship with Lady Ottoline continued unchanged. Frieda and he spent many days in Garsington. He helped to plant trees and bulbs, he built a wooden bower and wielded a paint brush, helping to redecorate the Red Drawing-Room. In the evenings he would sit down with the Morrells and other guests and talk about his young days or read the poems of Swinburne. It was as if he were trying to relive the sunny days of Haggs Farm on a higher plane.

Can one begrudge Lawrence his proud enjoyment of his hostess's admiration? He thrived on the company of admiring high-born ladies. Frieda, on the other hand, was less enchanted with Lady Ottoline's gushing enthusiasm. She had the feeling of being treated as a mere chattel of her husband, especially when her exuberant hostess tried to tell her how to handle "a genius, a being dropped straight from the sky". To tell her, Frieda, how to handle Lorenzo! She once told Philip

Morrell (according to his daughter) that she would not have minded if Lorenzo had had an ordinary affair with Lady Ottoline, but what she could not stand was "all this soul-mush"!

Across this slightly uneasy idyll the war continued to cast its gloomy shadow. "To him the war was not only the immediate horror it was to all of us," wrote Lady Cynthia. "He had the despair of prevision as well. Convinced as he was that one war must always breed another, he saw it as a suicide-pact between the nations, as the beginning of the end."

In his despair he could see for himself only one means of rescue: escape to Rananim. In Garsington he got to know a number of young intellectuals who were not averse to leaving a hopeless and decadent Europe behind and taking part in the building of an ideal community. A neurotic composer, Philip Heseltine, was full of enthusiasm (later, under the name of Peter Warlock, he achieved considerable success with his music before committing suicide at the age of thirty-five). The twenty-one-year-old Aldous Huxley, usually a coolly analytical character with a tendency towards caution, was stampeded into it by Lawrence's eloquence. Another surprising recruit was the Armenian Dikran Kouyoumdjian, who later, under the simpler name of Michael Arlen, became a popular best-selling author. The painter Dorothy Brett, a daughter of Viscount Esher, was all agog from the start. Lawrence continued to build his castles in the air, without bothering about Frieda's consent. Lady Ottoline was to be the uncrowned queen of Rananim, but, since basically the colony was to be a republic, Bertrand Russell would be invited at the same time to take over the presidency. In the absence of a suitable island, Lawrence had decided that his earthly paradise should be built in Florida. Contacts were made and he threw himself into preparations for the departure.

For the past few months they had been living in a small apartment in Hampstead. Frieda was more interested in being near her children than in distant Rananim, and during this time she did actually succeed in seeing them once or twice, with Ernest Weekley's consent. She owed this concession to Lady Ottoline, who had interceded with the inexorable father on Frieda's behalf. Obviously the professor did not consider it polite to snub the sister of the Duke of Portland. At last everything was ready. They sold or gave away many of the few poor articles of furniture which they had bought second-hand, one farewell party followed another, and passages were booked on a tramp steamer, which was to convey them to the West Indies on the first stage of their journey.

Then at the last moment Lawrence decided to put everything off—

though only for a month or two, he said. Huxley was convinced, however, that the project had fallen through. "Cities of God have always crumbled," he observed, "and Lawrence's city—his village rather, for he hated cities—his Village of the Dark God would doubtless have disintegrated like all the rest."

Why the sudden change of mind? It was not on account of the U-boat scare. Financial and other difficulties connected with the war had cropped up. And *The Rainbow*, the novel on which Lawrence had spent two long years and placed such high hopes, had been seized by the police as an indecent book.

The Rainbow is the first of Lawrence's major works which unmistakably shows Frieda's influence. The underlying social theme is the final destruction of a pre-industrial style of living in the rural areas of England, where in the second half of the nineteenth century it still lingered on. At that time even farm labourers were tending to become—in Lawrence's words—"town birds at heart", and before the First World War eighty per cent of the population of England and Wales were actually living in towns. The book is a sort of chronicle of the Brangwen family over three generations, and it may well have owed something of its form to Thomas Mann's *Buddenbrooks*, which Lawrence had read shortly before he began *The Rainbow*. The Brangwens' close ties with the land go back far in time, and their existence is geared to the rhythm of the seasons—"the marriage between heaven and earth".

The first chapters, for all their sensual intensity, convey an idyllic atmosphere, but into it "modern" life is beginning to intrude. This is the time of Ursula Brangwen's childhood and early womanhood. We meet her again, together with her sister Gudrun, in the ensuing novel *Women in Love*, but their characters have now changed. The Ursula of *The Rainbow* is based for the main part on Louie Burrows, the girl to whom Lawrence had once been engaged, but, as Frieda pointed out, "the inner relationship [with Anton Skrebensky] is Lawrence's and mine." In *Women in Love* Lawrence went even further: Ursula in that book is so faithful a portrait of Frieda that she has little in common with the Ursula of *The Rainbow*. It would possibly have been better if Lawrence had acknowledged his change of direction by giving this fascinating female character another name.

The Ursula of *The Rainbow*, emancipated and uprooted in the new industrialised world, has been called the first free soul of the English novel. She is depicted wandering through unknown emotional territory, with nothing to guide her except her belief in the existence of "an absolute truth and a living mystery" in the everyday world, in herself and in all living things. But not even physical love can satisfy her permanently: "Love—love—love—what does it mean—what does it amount to? ... As an end in itself, I could love a hundred men, one after the other. Why should I end with a Skrebensky?"

Frieda's comment on this was contained in a letter to Lady Cynthia Asquith: "In the end the man fails Ursula because he has no ideal beyond the old existing state, it does not satisfy her or him. For perfect love you don't only have two people, it must include a bigger, universal connection."

Other modern authors may certainly have produced more convincing characters than Lawrence, but none has succeeded to quite the same extent in penetrating so deeply into the mysteries of human relationships. F. R. Leavis, who is to Lawrence what Mohammed was to Allah, has drawn attention to this important aspect of his writing:[10] "The insistence on the individual, or 'fulfilment' in the individual, as the essential manifestation of life carries with it a corollary: ... it is only by way of the most delicate and complex responsive relations with others that the individual can achieve fulfilment." Leavis writes of "the peculiar Laurentian sense of the paradox of personal relations, especially of those between a man and a woman which make and validate a marriage." Lawrence, he maintains, insisted that "the more intimate and essential the relations, the more must the intimacy itself be, for the two lives that are brought into so essential a contact, a mutual acceptance of their separateness and otherness. Love for Lawrence is no more an absolute than sex is his religion. What, in fact, strikes us as religious is the intensity with which his men and women, hearkening to their deepest needs and promptings as they seek 'fulfilment' in marriage, know that they 'do not belong to themselves', but are responsible to something that, in transcending the individual, transcends love and sex too."

Lawrence dedicated *The Rainbow* to Else Jaffe (who later translated it into German). He had a new publisher, Methuen, who brought it out on 30 September 1915. The critics greeted the novel with a storm of righteous indignation. "A monstrous wilderness of phallicism," wrote one respected reviewer, Robert Lynd in the *Daily News*, while Clement Shorter in the *Sphere* declared it to be an "orgy of sexiness" and complained that it omitted "no form of viciousness, of suggestiveness". He recalled that Henry Vizetelly, Zola's English publisher, had been thrown into prison in 1889, and added: "But Zola's novels were child's food compared with the strong meat contained in an English story that I have just read—*The Rainbow*, by D. H. Lawrence." John Galsworthy wrote to Lawrence's agent that he was disgusted by the "overheated futuristic style" of the novel. "I much prefer," he declared, "a frankly pornographic book to one like this."

On 3 November an officer from Scotland Yard appeared in the publisher's offices, announced himself as Detective Inspector Albert Draper and ordered the seizure of all 1,011 copies of the novel still held by the publishers and the printers.

The publishers gave in at once. They took no steps at all to justify themselves or to protect the interests of their author. Philip Morrell, already branded as a pacifist, raised the matter with the Home Secretary at Question Time in the House of Commons. The case came to court on 14 November, when the publisher was charged—not the author. The solicitor representing the police declared the novel to be "a mass of obscenity of thought, idea and action throughout," expressed in language which apparently passed in certain circles for artistic and intellectual. He was unable to understand how so reputable a firm of publishers as Methuen could have lent their name to such a publication.

The magistrate ordered all seized copies of the book to be destroyed.

It is possible that the whole affair was politically motivated. Certain people (and not only the police) might well have seen advantage in blackening the reputation of a writer who had shown a remarkable lack of patriotic feeling and whose wife was suspected of sympathising with the enemy.

A reading of the book tends to confirm this suspicion. Its sexual content is of course undeniable, but Lawrence usually presents his love scenes in an impressionist and somewhat obscure poetic language. In recent years we have become so used to having even the most intimate happenings described in novels in complete clinical detail that it is hard to understand how the mild ecstasies of *The Rainbow* could even have been considered objectionable. But we must not forget how radically conventional attitudes have changed since those days.

The Anglo-Saxon world has never had the monopoly of prudery. Germany also banned Zola's *Nana*, and even in de Maupassant's stories ladies were held to be forward if they allowed their ankles to show beneath their skirts. But nowhere else, up to the First World War and beyond, was the moral climate quite so harsh as in the British Isles and the United States of America. This is all the more remarkable since the curiously zigzag course traced by public morals in England suggests that puritanism is by no means ingrained in the Anglo-Saxon character. Just as in political life Whigs and Tories, Conservative and Labour governments succeed each other in power, so too on the moral plane there has always been a ceaseless tug-of-war between strictness and laxity. The full-blooded lust for living of the Shakespearian era was followed by the bigoted tyranny of Cromwell's Commonwealth, which was in turn supplanted by the loose living that characterised the court of Charles II. But never did a change of direction occur on so broad a front and with such far-reaching consequences as in the half-century between about 1790 and the middle of the Victorian age. If one were asked to define the English character before that time, one would be obliged to call on words like "aggressive", "brutal", "coarse", "frank", "pleasure-loving", "uproarious" and "cruel". By the middle of the nineteenth century all that had radically changed: then it would have been no impermissible exaggeration to call the British one of the most repressed, most polite, prudish and hypocritical nations anywhere in the world. Queen Victoria, with whose name that new moral climate is inextricably bound, did not inspire it so much as reflect it. The remarkable change that took place is usually ascribed to the activities of religious sects such as the Methodists and the Con- gregationalists, as well as to the reforming zeal of organisations such as the Proclamation Society or the Society for the Suppression of Vice and Immorality and the Sunday schools of Hannah More. But Sunday schools, like revolutions, can succeed only when the social circum- stances are ripe for them. It was the rapid industrialisation of the country and the consequent emergence of slums that produced the right conditions. The valiant shock troops of morality were, it is true, inclined to confine their attentions to combating drunkenness, prostitution, crime and godlessness among the "lower classes", thus inducing that great social critic and wit, Sydney Smith, to speak sarcastically of a "society for suppressing the vices of persons whose income does not exceed £500 per annum." But terrifying accounts of the course of the French Revolution sent a wave of panic through the country. Was England immune against the bacillus of revolt? Many people asked themselves whether the British proletariat could be con- vinced of the blessings of a God-given order unless the property- owning classes themselves religiously followed the rules of the virtuous life they preached. When William Wilberforce, that noble destroyer of the slave trade, proclaimed, "God has set before me as my object the reformation of manners," he was thinking just as much of the manners of the rich as of the poor, and the moral ideas which he had in mind were those of the middle class. The evangelists began to distribute their religious tracts not only to the people who had nothing, but to the comfortably-off as well. Church attendances in "good" residential neighbourhoods rose steeply. A respectable way of life was regarded not only as a divine command, but also as a protective barrier guarding property. The family became the inviolable bastion of all morality, and prudery a part of the nation's defences.[11]

The main criterion of the new morality inevitably lay in the sexual sphere. Britons might like to regard themselves as citizens of the mightiest and freest nation in the world, but in fact at the height of the British Empire they were slaves to the most absurd and false of social conventions. In order to protect the family and preserve public law and order, old taboos were brought out and dusted, and new ones invented. The keystone of Victorian morality was the idea that sexual intercourse was permissible only between husband and wife. Thus everything that could feed the fires of sensuality was rigorously suppressed. Fashion reduced the amount of bare flesh that a lady might show to a few square inches. Clothing extended from the throat down to below the ankles—so that the merest glimpse of a woman's calf was enough to hurl elderly gentlemen into paroxysms of desire. No well-brought-up girl would dare to be caught reading the novels of Balzac, Georges Sand and Eugène Sue, or the poems of Baudelaire. No right-thinking man would dream of using offensive language in the presence of a lady, and what was then considered offensive seems to us today to be innocuousness itself. At a time when Darwin's theory of the origin of species was revolutionising thought, it was considered impermissible in "decent" society to talk of a person's legs—"limbs" was as far as one dared go—and at dinner nobody was ever offered the "breast" of a chicken. The result was that people began to see sexual connotations in the most curious places. What other generation could ever have come up with the idea of draping the legs of a piano to make them look less naked, or, on grounds of decency, separating the books of male authors from those of female authors on the shelves of their bookcases?

But human nature cannot be so easily repressed, and the concomitant of Victorian prudery was prostitution and pornography and a legally based double standard of sexual morality. There are no reliable estimates of the extent to which prostitution flourished beneath the hypocritical surface of Victorian England: the number of prostitutes active in London in the year 1869 has been estimated at anything between six thousand and eighty thousand. But the Victorian gentleman was adept at concealing other secrets as well as these beneath the cloak of morality. While Shakespeare's plays could only be printed in bowdlerised versions, there was at the same time a brisk trade in illicit pornographic literature. Books with titles like *The Decameron of Pleasure, The Romance of Lust, Intrigues and Confessions of a Ballet Girl*, passed surreptitiously from hand to hand in the period 1860–80, and even these pale into insignificance beside the sexual memoirs of a Victorian gentleman which, under the title *My Secret Life*, were clandestinely printed in eleven volumes containing a total of 4,200 pages. A police raid on two London houses in the year 1874 produced a haul of 130,248 pornographic photographs and five thousand negatives. Never before in British history had so much hypocrisy masqueraded behind so glittering and respectable a façade.

Even after Victoria had been succeeded on the throne by Edward VII, whose amorous adventures as Prince of Wales were no secret to anybody, the guardians of public morals persisted with their work. New organisations for the improvement of moral standards sprang up like mushrooms, clean-up crusades were launched, a play by Edward Garnett which would rate today as highly moral was banned by the censor, the publication of James Joyce's *Dubliners* was held up for eight years because publishers and printers were afraid of being brought to court, and H. G. Wells's novel *Ann Veronica* was boycotted by all the libraries. When D. H. Lawrence's friend, Dr David Eder, delivered an address to the British Medical Association in 1911 on the subject of clinical psycho-analysis—the first lecture on Freud to be given in England—the chairman sat listening, stony-faced; at the end he rose from his seat and left the room without a word, and the rest of the learned audience, without exception, demonstratively followed his lead.[12]

The intensity of Victorian morality and the pretence behind it explain the central position which sexuality occupied in Lawrence's creative work. The prudish atmosphere in which he had been brought up and the frustrations of his early love affairs turned him into a lifelong puritan and at the same time into a passionate rebel against puritanical mendacity; his revolt against its hypocrisy was equally a revolt against his mother. Frieda was the woman who rescued him from his inhibitions and in whom he found sexual fulfilment.

On 30 December 1915 Frieda and Lawrence arrived in Cornwall. This, as Lawrence hoped, was to be only a temporary stopping-place on the way to Rananim, but his "dark god" had other ideas. After the excitements and disappointments of the last months in London, the stillness and remoteness of the harsh Celtic landscape acted on them like balm. The old farmhouse near Padstow, in which they were living, overlooked a small bay, and they basked in romantic dreams of Tristan and Iseult and King Arthur, whom legend associates with this part of the country. Once again they were without commitments, free as air: their complete worldly possessions consisted of little more than the contents of their trunks.

At the end of February they had to leave the farmhouse. After a short search they found a cottage in Zennor, not far from the picturesque little harbour town of St Ives. It was a tiny cottage, with only two rooms—one above and one below—but they liked it, and the rent was only five pounds a year, so here they settled down to hide from the tumult of war—"like foxes under the hill".

Life was not exactly comfortable. The cold March winds blew across the grey hills and stony fields that separated them from the sea. The house was unfurnished, and they hurriedly sent for the few bits of furniture and utensils which they had stored with friends in London: a camp-bed, a kitchen table with four kitchen chairs, crockery, two paraffin stoves and a pair of brass candlesticks which Lawrence had inherited from his mother. He built a wooden cupboard and some wooden shelves—the manual work helped at least to take his mind off his gloomy thoughts. He was depressed and unwell. Apart from anything else, they had already used up all their money, and the prospect of receiving further royalties remained small, as long as the war lasted. Frieda endured all the discomforts with stoic calm: it was at difficult times like this that she always showed the reserves of strength inside her.

Yet in spite of all the difficulties they set out to persuade the Murrys to join them. It was quite a lot to ask, for the Murrys were now established in their refuge in Bandol on the French Riviera. But Frieda wrote coaxing letters to Katherine and Lawrence regaled Murry with tempting visions of a communal life among the black cliffs beside the sea—a sort of pocket-size Rananim. Vague though it might all sound, they managed to overcome Katherine's doubts, and at the beginning of April the Murrys arrived in Zennor.

Whatever illusions they may have had when they succumbed to the siren calls from Cornwall, the project was in fact doomed from the very start. Katherine's friendship with Murry was on the point of breaking up—not for the first and not for the last time. Six months earlier her adored brother had been killed on the Western Front and she was still wrapped in a cloak of deep melancholy. She continued to share her bed with Murry, but not her soul, and as always in such critical situations, he was incapable of coming to her aid. He could see that the woman he loved was threatening to slip out of his grasp, but he had not the strength to keep hold of her, and was hoping that the company of Frieda and Lawrence would have a beneficial effect: that was his main reason for yielding to their persuasions.

But on the very day of their arrival he had to acknowledge the prospect of failure. Katherine had left Bandol in tears, and on the rail journey to Cornwall her depression deepened. Was this the English spring so alluringly described in Lawrence's letters? After the smiling landscapes of the French Riviera she could find no comfort in the grim steeliness of the northern sky and the gaunt beauty of the barren hills.

Lawrence threw all his energies into helping them set up their home in the empty cottage nearby, and Frieda, radiating motherly warmth, did all she could for Katherine. But it was no use. Katherine did not now care for Frieda. "I am very much alone here," she wrote to Koteliansky. "I don't belong to anybody here." At times of crisis Koteliansky, with his Russian soul and his Jewish sensitivity, was the only person to whom she opened her heart. Murry knew it and began to sink in a morass of hopelessness.

It was no help either when Lawrence urged him to tell Katherine "not to be so queasy". With all his admiration for Lawrence's genius Murry was quite aware that his friend's ideas on the theory and practice of marriage could not serve as a model for himself. He soon received new proofs for his scepticism. During those long months in Cornwall, with Europe's agony tearing at their nerves and Lawrence's wilful moodiness clashing with Frieda's pride, the fights between them became more savage than ever before.

One evening Katherine and Murry were sitting beside the fire in their little house when they were suddenly alarmed by the sound of wild screams. The next instant Frieda burst into the room, her face contorted with fear. Behind her came Lawrence, white as a ghost. "I'll *kill* her!" he shouted, beside himself with fury. He began to chase her, scattering chairs to all sides and threatening, "I'll *kill* her! I'll *kill* her!" Murry felt that Lawrence really would have been capable of murdering her in his rage, but his own response was characteristic: he simply stood there as if nailed to the wall, while Katherine, completely apathetic, continued to sit motionless on her stool.

All at once Lawrence dropped down on a chair, breathing heavily, exhausted, his face drained of blood. Nobody dared say a single word. Some minutes went by, and then Frieda slipped out through the door. The others stayed where they were in silence, none of them seemed to have the energy to move. Then at last Lawrence rose uncertainly, softly said, "Good-night," and left.

The Murrys had no idea what had caused the explosion. Maybe Frieda had mentioned the children? They did not dare ask. On the following morning they went across to Lawrence's house, fearing the worst. They found him and Frieda sitting happily side by side, and he was busy decorating her hat with a ribbon.

Scenes like this occurred again and again, and usually the immediate cause was something completely trivial. Once, for instance, Lawrence made a derogatory remark about Shelley. Frieda, who knew perfectly well that Shelley (like Nietzsche) was one of the prophets whom Lorenzo had begun by admiring and then discarded, made as if to defend him—in an angelic voice, but with a far less innocent motive behind it. Lawrence, as if stung by a scorpion, jumped to his feet and shouted at her: "That's *false*! What do you know about Shelley? If you *dare* to say another word about Shelley, I'll ..."

In this he was being quite unfair, for all that Frieda had done was to quote a remark that Lawrence himself had made some time before.

He once spoke of the "sympathy of pure hatred". Catherine Carswell, who witnessed many of their battles, affirmed that these were never as painful as the conflicts between some married couples who, in the presence of others, simulate unclouded tenderness. She visited the Lawrences during this same summer, and tells in her biography the story of another outbreak in their love–hate relationship. In this instance the quarrel had been conducted with all the usual vehemence, but Lawrence was under the impression that it was already over, or at least that a truce had been declared. He went into the little kitchen and began to wash the dishes, his back to the door into the living-room. Two or three minutes later Frieda, still smarting from the quarrel, came into the kitchen carrying an earthenware plate. He did not hear her, and continued to hum a melody to himself, completely unconcerned and appeased. His carefree good-humour brought all her resentment back to the boil, and in the next moment she brought the heavy plate down on his skull. He was so surprised that it never occurred to him to strike back. "That was like a woman!" he hissed. "No man could have done such a thing when the quarrel was over, and from behind too! It was only lucky you didn't kill me."

This had happened before Catherine Carswell arrived in Zennor, but they both told her about it with complete openness, as if it had been the most natural thing in the world—which, as far as their marriage was concerned, it was.

The feud between them was always flaring up. There was a constant succession of violent quarrels and outbursts of hatred which, whatever the direct cause of each might have been, had their origin basically in one single source: Lawrence's absolute belief in the supremacy of the male.

In a letter to Katherine Mansfield he described his idea of the role of the sexes in marriage in the following way.[1]

> I do think a woman must yield some sort of precedence to a man, and he must take this precedence. I do think men must go ahead absolutely in front of their women, without turning round to ask for permission or approval from their women. Consequently the women must follow as it were unquestioningly. I can't help it, I believe this. Frieda doesn't. Hence our fight.

Frieda called his views antediluvian, and certainly they seem somewhat reminiscent of the Old Testament. Lawrence, regarded today as a pioneer in the sexual revolution, was preaching the idea which St Paul and Martin Luther had preached before him—that of the husband as a wise and benevolent despot. The apostle's command to women to submit to their husbands was also Lawrence's—and that at a time when England was well on the path towards complete emancipation and women were very shortly to be granted the right to vote!

The absolute authority of the man in the family was of course a Victorian concept too. Lawrence's obstinate adherence to the idea stands in such curious contrast to his dogged struggle against Victorian views of sexual morality that the origin of his *idée fixe* deserves further investigation.

We are of course venturing on purely speculative ground when we attempt to draw conclusions from the impressions we receive of his childhood and early youth. But it was certainly true that in the Victorian era the absolute authority of the *paterfamilias* was one of the cornerstones of marriage. At the time Lawrence was growing up, this particular cornerstone was beginning to show cracks. Even in the middle class, from whose new concepts of morality the upper classes and the lower classes at that time took their cue, the erosion of male authority had already begun. But it was not like that in Eastwood, nor in the other mining villages where—in contrast to many of the other industrial areas with a more fluctuating working population—there still existed a close-knit community with a subculture of its own, based on long-established traditions. Here (as Middleton Murry once suggested) the unquestioned authority of the head of the family persisted longer than elsewhere, not only because communities of this sort always tend to cling to traditional ideas, but also because it was a material necessity. People living under the constant threat of unemployment and only just above starvation level cannot afford to waste their energies by indulging in internal conflicts about the division of authority inside the family. Among the miners' wives in Eastwood, Alice Dax, the chemist's wife, was hard put to it to assemble even a handful of supporters for her ideas on female emancipation and equality between the sexes.

Lawrence's home was an exception. Thanks to her superior intelligence and her unbounded ambition, his mother usurped her husband's authority. The concept of a father figure that pursued Lawrence to the end of his life was that of a maimed authority, a man estranged from his children and driven to drink. It was not until he had freed himself from his mother's influence that he came to appreciate the extent of his father's tragedy. His rebellion against his mother brought a desire for revenge and a determination never himself to be humiliated and destroyed in the same way.

But Frieda had reasons of her own for resisting his claim to superiority. She also had been brought up at home in an atmosphere of crippled male authority. She knew what weakness of character lay concealed behind her father's aristocratic pride, his military bearing and his Iron Cross. She had been permitted to look behind the glittering mask, and what she saw had not increased her desire to submit to the abstract principle of male superiority. Lawrence, anyway, was most unsuited to assume the traditional role of a Victorian husband. His inability to protect her from need was obvious, and the childlessness of their union must have left no doubt in her mind—mother of three as she was—that the cause of it must be Lorenzo's sterility. Fate, with malicious irony, had decreed that the great apostle of sex should be incapable of producing any offspring.

Why then, did this woman, who had given such striking proof of her courage and her spirit of independence, continue to tolerate—even if cursing and fighting back—the humiliations he was constantly inflicting on her? There is only one explanation, and this lies in a single much-abused word—love. "Whatever happened on the surface of everyday life," she later wrote, "there blossomed the certainty of the unalterable bond between us."

Meanwhile their relations with the Murrys had sadly deteriorated. Katherine could not forgive them for having enticed her and Murry to Cornwall. She was also, though by no means a prude, becoming irritated by Lawrence's growing "sex obsession". She suggested that he ought to name his cottage "The Phallus", and Frieda heartily agreed. Murry himself was annoyed with Lawrence for trying to wheedle him, at the very moment in which their friendship stood in jeopardy, into bolstering it up with a symbolic act of "blood-brotherhood". The philosophy of blood-consciousness was indeed beginning to bear strange blossoms. At last, Katherine insisted on putting an end to the unpleasant situation. She and Murry left Zennor to settle on the south coast of Cornwall, where the air was warmer and the vegetation more luxuriant.

At the end of June, Frieda and Lawrence walked to Penzance. Five months earlier general conscription had been introduced, and he had been ordered to report to the district authorities. With his weak lungs, he was of course in no danger of being sent to the front line, but Frieda was afraid he might be called up for some sort of auxiliary service, which she knew he would find unbearable.

From Penzance he was sent to Bodmin for a medical examination, and there he had to spend two days and a night in a military barracks. He had not brought his sleeping things with him. It was "Lights out!" at nine o'clock and "Sweep the floors!" in the early morning. Thirty men in their shirt-tails were weighed like sheep, one after the other: he felt sick with shame and humiliation. The doctors declared him unfit and advised him to seek some work of national importance. The memory of this experience remained with him all his life: it cropped up again in the nightmare chapter of his novel *Kangaroo*.

On the warm summer days it was difficult to realise that terrible battles were being fought at Verdun and on the Somme. Frieda lay luxuriously sunning herself on the black rocks as the waves broke around them, or she walked to St Ives, a blonde Brunhilde in orange and pink or yellow and green stockings, to do the shopping. She managed to arrange another meeting with her children. She went to London and took them all to the opera in the evening. During the interval she gave each of them ten shillings, but when they were alone in the ladies' cloakroom Elsa, the eldest, said to Barbara: "You are not to *like* Mama, you know, just because we have got ten shillings." A few days later Ernest Weekley sent the money back to Frieda.

In feverish spurts of energy Lawrence lent the countryfolk a hand in the fields, and worked on *Women in Love*. "I have got a long way with my novel. It comes rapidly, and is very good," he wrote contentedly to Lady Ottoline Morrell. But he did not tell her that in it she herself was providing the model for the eccentric Hermione Roddice and that her home in Garsington featured prominently under the name of Breadalby. Several months later Lady Ottoline read the manuscript and angrily broke off all relations with Lawrence. Her threat to sue him for libel was the main reason why the publication of the novel was held up for several years.

It is not clear what caused Lawrence to paint his former friend and patroness in such magnificently satirical colours. He did of course always tend to put his friends and acquaintances into his books in some more or less veiled form, but, considering all that Lady Ottoline had done for him, his treatment of her does smack of ingratitude. Presumably Frieda was not entirely guiltless in the matter. She had never got on well with the mistress of Garsington, and at the beginning of the year they had fallen out completely. Lady Ottoline's vexation was understandable, and it was fully twelve years before she could bring herself to forgive Lawrence. But all the same the caricature she provoked Lawrence into drawing of her—the portrait of an overbred, neurotic intellectual, outwardly dictatorial but inwardly uncertain and empty—is a masterpiece.

Women in Love, originally designed to be the second part of *The Sisters*, provides other recognisable figures beside the larger-than-life portrait of Lady Ottoline. In the complicated relationship between the two Brangwen sisters and the two friends Gerald and Birkin we can catch flickering and ever changing glimpses of Frieda's and Lawrence's own uncertain relationship with Katherine and Murry. If Gerald Crich bears some traces of John Middleton Murry, Birkin is obviously identified in Lawrence's mind with himself. Gudrun, Frieda declares, was intended as a portrait of Katherine Mansfield, though Katherine herself said she could see no likeness at all. Gudrun's sister Ursula is of course Frieda. But the book is not directly autobiographical. In this, as in practically all his books, Lawrence wove real events, experiences and people like bright threads into the web of his story. In his mind's retort he sometimes mixed characters together or transposed them from their original setting to another.

In this novel too we find all of Lawrence's characteristic weaknesses as a creative writer: the neglect of over-all structure with its consequent shapelessness, a lack of objectivity, unevennesses of style, a tendency towards overemphasis due to obstinate repetitions of emotive words and phrases. But in none of his major works are Lawrence's visionary and poetic gifts more triumphantly and more convincingly displayed than in this novel. Within its magnetic field the personal is fused with the impersonal in a strange and sometimes mysterious way. Even inanimate objects are drawn into the stream of consciousness, and landscapes seem to be part of a subjective emanation. The sensual and the transcendental, realism and symbolism—all these are woven inextricably together. Aldous Huxley's penetrating analysis of Lawrence's peculiar gifts fits no other novel, with the exception of *The Rainbow*, more closely:[2]

> He was always intensely aware of the mystery of the world, and the mystery was always for him a *numen*, divine. Lawrence could never forget, as most of us almost continuously forget, the dark presence of the otherness that lies beyond the boundaries of man's conscious mind. This special sensibility was accompanied by a prodigious power of rendering the immediately experienced otherness in terms of literary art ... He had eyes that could see, beyond the walls of light, far into the darkness, sensitive fingers that kept him continually aware of the environing mystery ... Moreover—and in this he was unlike those others, to whom the world's mystery is continuously present, the great philosophers and men of science—he did not want to increase the illuminated area; he approved of the outer darkness, he felt at home in it.

Women in Love represents the peak of Lawrence's creative achievement. In none of his later works did he again reach such heights.

Even amid the stark pagan beauty of the lonely peninsula, in the white-washed cottage surrounded by beds of foxgloves laid out with Lawrence's own hands, they could not escape entirely from the world outside. Slowly but inexorably the war crept up and closed them in its cruel embrace. Its horrors could not be forgotten when, in the next village or on a nearby farm, they saw people going about in mourning for a son killed in France or drowned on a torpedoed merchant ship. Frieda and Lorenzo were becoming increasingly aware that the ever rising flood of patriotic hatred was affecting even their direct neighbours.

It is remarkable how much greater the hatred for all things German was in the Kaiser's war than in the war let loose by Hitler. After 1939 people were still prepared to distinguish between the criminal Nazi leadership and the German nation as a whole. Even in the winter of 1940–41, when the air raids on London were at their height, it was still possible—though perhaps not very tactful—to speak German on a bus. But in the First World War things were different. The German invasion of neutral Belgium not only brought Britain into the war, but also produced a wave of hatred that, even after the conclusion of peace, subsided only very gradually. The broad mass of the population was in no doubt at all about Germany's collective guilt or the complicity of every individual German. Even Beethoven and Brahms were banned from English concert halls. Prince Louis Battenberg, whose wife was a grand-daughter of Queen Victoria, had to resign his position as First Sea Lord because he had been born a German, and he found it expedient to anglicise his name into Mountbatten.

Ford Madox Hueffer also was made to suffer for his German name. Soon after the outbreak of war policemen approached him on a golf course and questioned him in the presence of other players, because somebody had denounced him as an enemy agent. He felt the humiliation all the more keenly since at the time he was working at the Ministry of Information on intellectual warfare directed against German militarism. Some months later he volunteered for service in the front line, although he was already forty-three. He subsequently eliminated the German element in his name by changing it to Ford Madox Ford.

The longer the war dragged on, the worse the spy scare became.

From the editorial offices of *John Bull,* the sensation-loving weekly periodical, a flood of patriotic hatred swept across the land, while Lord Northcliffe's dailies poured out in their millions, accusing the government of pursuing the war with insufficient vigour. Not even cabinet ministers were immune from suspicion and slander. In the drawing-rooms of Mayfair it was openly said that the Prime Minister, Asquith, possessed shares in Krupp's armament factories, and his daughter Elizabeth was engaged to a German admiral (in some versions a German general). His wife Margot, the gossips said, had been seen playing tennis with German prisoners of war. Margot Asquith was not the sort of woman to take such slanders lying down: she sued the *Globe* newspaper, and was awarded damages of a thousand pounds.[3] Mass hysteria rose to such a height that eventually the gentlemanly Asquith was swept out of office, and his place as Prime Minister was taken by Lloyd George. Frieda and Lawrence might have wanted to cut themselves off, but their isolation became much more extreme than they had bargained for.

At a hint from Lady Cynthia Asquith, Lawrence had severed his connections with Sir Edward Marsh. As he explained in a sad letter, he did not wish to burden a man in an official government position with the friendship of a writer whose attitude to the war was so negative. It did not need letters of this sort to encourage others to withdraw from them. Their circle of friends shrank, though a handful remained loyal even in the darkest hours—Catherine Carswell, Koteliansky, Mark Gertler and Lady Cynthia herself. Her husband, the gentle aesthete Herbert Asquith, was somewhere out in the trenches of Flanders, much to Frieda's amazement. "What is the good of being the Prime Minister's son," she wrote ungrammatically to Lady Cynthia, "and you can't be any different than other people?"

They could no longer even afford to travel to London together: the price of the fare had risen, and they had to watch every penny. Behind Lawrence's back Frieda wrote begging letters to friends from whom help might be forthcoming. They felt like prisoners in a hostile country and longed to be back in Italy. Lawrence made a final desperate attempt to escape to America, only to be foiled when his application for passports was refused.

In June 1917 he was again called up for medical examination, since the conscription regulations had now been sharpened. This time he spent only two hours in the military barracks in Bodmin. The doctors placed him in category C3, which meant that he was unsuitable for military service and fit only for light, non-combative duties. He returned the same evening to the isolation of Zennor.

Even in peacetime the Cornish people are not renowned for welcoming strangers with open arms. In wartime the presence of two such obvious interlopers must have seemed almost like a challenge. The disapproval of the farmers and fishermen was transformed by the insidious spy scare into open suspicion. What was this odd man with his red beard and his German wife doing in Cornwall at all—let alone within a few yards of the Atlantic coast? If he was one of those writers, why didn't he live in London along with the rest of them? If he was unfit for military service, why wasn't he being called up for some other sort of national service?

Why in fact was he not? John Middleton Murry, who had also been declared medically unfit, had been engaged for the past year in the censorship department of the War Ministry. Conscientious objectors, Quakers and others with pacifist scruples were working as farm labourers, postmen and milk roundsmen or doing other important but non-combative jobs. A whole host of intellectuals was busy ploughing and reaping the Morrells' fields in Garsington. Lawrence was doing nothing of this sort. Why not indeed?

Nobody could say why not. Only one thing was certain: Lawrence was against the war. He had never made a secret of that. And why was he against it? There seemed to be only one answer: his wife was a Prussian. And so, in the general atmosphere of hatred for all things German and in the midst of all the spy hysteria, the doors were opened to all sorts of suspicion. German U-boats were lurking off the Cornish coast, and immediately rumours began to fly: Lawrence and his German wife had been signalling to the U-boats and had supplied them with provisions.

Of course, the suspicions were completely unfounded. As Frieda angrily pointed out, even if they had been in touch with the U-boat crews, they could not in their poverty have spared them even a biscuit a day.

But mass hysteria inevitably wears down its chosen victim in the end, and somewhere in an obscure corner of her mind Frieda began to harbour a slight feeling of guilt. She had not forgotten that she was a German, a Richthofen. She could hardly have denied it, even if she had wanted to: anybody could see it with a glance, and even after eighteen years of British citizenship her accent betrayed at once where she came from. Deep within her she was conscious of her divided loyalties.

One evening two years before, when they were still living in London, she had been walking with Lawrence across Hampstead Heath when the guns began to roar. She heard the rumble of bombs, and high above in the cloud there appeared the long golden oval shape of a German zeppelin. It was the first air raid on London. "It was like Milton," Lawrence remarked, "then there was war in heaven. But it was not angels." Frieda's reactions were very different. She said: "In that zeppelin are perhaps men I have danced with when I was a girl, boys I have played with."[4]

One day—it was in August 1917—a German submarine was spotted not far from Zennor. Destroyers and planes closed in on it in a flash. The explosions of the depth charges could be heard on the coast. "How terrible such a war is," Frieda said to a neighbour, and again expressed the thought that she might have known some of the men in the submarine in earlier days. Soon afterwards a large patch of oil on the sea showed that one of the charges had found its mark.

The knowledge that the war was killing off her friends on both sides pursued her like a nightmare. Letters from her mother and her sister Else reached her via Switzerland, bringing news of the death of some friend of her youth: a cadet who had greeted her with a smart salute when she had met him on horseback in the streets of Metz had ended his life in Flanders, officers with whom she had danced in Berlin had fallen in Riga or on the banks of the Isonzo.

But it was not only mourning that bound her, across all the abysses of spiteful propaganda, to the enemy. In the English newspapers she read reports of Manfred von Richthofen's victories in the air, and they filled her with pride. To her he was only a name—but it was her own name. He was a distant cousin, whom she had never met. Manfred was only seven years old when she married Ernest Weekley and came to England—a schoolboy in Silesia, where she herself had never been, though it was the birthplace of her father. She felt herself drawn by their shared name to this Richthofen who, while still a young lieutenant, had flown to world fame on the wings of his bright red airplane. He was a cavalier who fought his chivalrous duels high up in the air above the mud and misery of the faceless ground warfare below. Had not the Kaiser himself, whom she loathed and despised, honoured him on his twenty-fifth birthday by placing him at an imperial luncheon to the right of Hindenburg? And did not the British themselves single him out for praise as the bravest and most chivalrous of their enemies—this fearless airman who bore her own name?

She was not cautious in her utterances. The simple farmers and farmworkers in Zennor were not at all pleased to hear her expressing sympathy for the crews of German submarines or admiration for a German air ace. And the neighbours did not appreciate her and Lawrence singing German folksongs at the top of their voices, as they frequently did.

They knew that they were being watched. Stooping figures lurked among the flowerbeds beneath the windows in the hope of overhearing them engaged in seditious conversation. Once, when they were returning from the village with their shopping, two coastguards sprang out on them from the bushes and demanded to know what Frieda was carrying in her rucksack, a relic of earlier wanderings in the Alps. One of the coastguards felt it from the outside and exclaimed: "Ah, a camera!" Frieda pulled out a small loaf of bread and held it out contemptuously for inspection, though in her heart she felt more like scratching out their eyes. From behind the stone walls surrounding the fields neighbours watched them intently through field-glasses, and felt no embarrassment if they were caught at it: after all, they were only performing a patriotic duty. When once, in a sudden outbreak of high spirits, Frieda began to dance on the beach, waving her white shawl in the wind, Lawrence cried out panic-stricken: "Stop it, stop it, you fool! Can't you see that they'll think you're signalling to the enemy?"

Fortunately they now had an ally. The Scottish composer Cecil Gray, a friend of Philip Heseltine, had come to live in a house near the beach. The military doctors had put him in category C2—suitable for office work. Lawrence and he took to each other like two hermits in a lonely desert.

During October he and Frieda spent a weekend with Gray in his house. After supper they sat down in front of the fire to entertain themselves with German folksongs—a form of protest in which they felt they could indulge without doing anybody harm. They had sung three songs together when Gray, seeking respite from their faulty harmonies, called for a rest. In the ensuing silence they heard a loud knocking at the front door. The next moment half a dozen men in uniform came charging in with weapons in their hands and demanded to search the house. A light had been seen in one of the windows overlooking the sea. It was much more than mere neglect of the black-out regulations of which they were suspected: the light had been intermittent, flashing on and off, and could have been a signal to the enemy in code (and Gray later found out that, as ill luck would have it, a German submarine had in fact been sighted off the coast shortly before). The unhappy accident of a curtain fluttering in the wind before a badly blacked-out window cost Gray a heavy fine. But the consequences for Frieda and Lawrence were even more serious.[5]

Some days later their cottage was searched while they were out. On the following day the visitors came again: a young army officer, the friendly village policeman and two ill-mannered detectives. They rummaged through all the drawers and cupboards and confiscated a notebook from Lawrence's college days in Nottingham. The officer then handed them an expulsion order. They were to leave Cornwall within three days and report to the police at whatever place they eventually settled.

"And that's what you call English justice!" Frieda said to the officer with bitter sarcasm. Lawrence told her to be quiet. What he himself said has not been recorded, but it is safe to assume that he showed little appreciation for the difficulties of the military authorities, who could hardly be expected in the middle of a war to show much consideration for the eccentricities of an author or the susceptibilities of a woman whose maiden name was Richthofen.[6]

Lawrence might, on this black day, have reflected ruefully on the ironies of fate. Once before he had been held on suspicion of being a spy. That was in Metz, and the Germans had taken him for an English spy; now it was the English suspecting him of being a German spy. But at the time he was hardly in a mood to smile over such coincidences. On the day they left Cornwall he looked ill and depressed. Frieda, on the other hand, felt as if a great load had been lifted from her shoulders.

Immediately on arrival in London they called on Lady Cynthia Asquith, who wrote in her diary: "He was in intense distress, not only terribly hurt, but utterly at a loss to know what to do next ... He looks terribly ill—as though every nerve in his body were exposed."

The police watch on them continued. When visitors left the room in Bloomsbury which Richard Aldington had lent them, they were stopped by Scotland Yard detectives and closely questioned about "the German woman and her husband". Even Ernest Weekley was approached on the subject of Frieda's political reliability.

In later years there has been much talk of the "scandalous persecution" to which Lawrence was at that time subjected. Yet is it really surprising that he was regarded with suspicion? As far as the police authorities were concerned, he was the author of a book that had been banned on grounds of immorality; he made no secret of his lack of

1 Friedrich and Anna von Richthofen at the time of their wedding

2 Frieda's father, Baron Friedrich von Richthofen, in 1872

3 Frieda with Ernest Weekley and his father

5 Frieda at 19

4 Frieda as a schoolgirl

6 Frieda in the early days o
marriage to Ernest Weekley

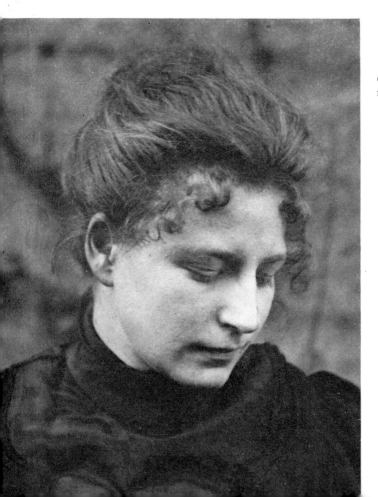

7 Else, Frieda's elder sister,
as a student

8 Frieda and Ernest Weekley, 1899

..lsa, Montague and Barbara (*left to right*),
children of Frieda's marriage to Ernest
Weekley

10 Montague Weekley as an Oxford
blue

11 D. H. Lawrence's Eastwood
birthplace, Victoria Street

12 The Lawrence family. *Left to right
front:* sister Ada, his mother Lydia,
D.H.L., his father Arthur John.
Standing: Emily, George, Ernest

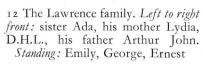

13 D. H. Lawrence in 1912 when he met Frieda

14 D. H. Lawrence in his early thirties

15 Lady Ottoline Morrell

16 Katherine Mansfield

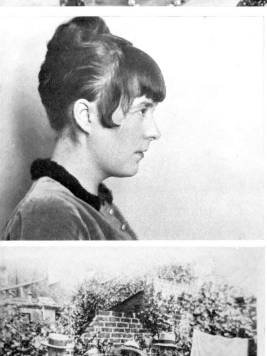

17 *From left to right*, D. H. Lawrence, Katherine Mansfield, Frieda, John Middleton Murry, in 1914

18 Compton Mackenzie in 1912

19 Frieda in Mexico, 1925

20 *Left to right*, Mabel Dodge, Frieda and
Dorothy Brett

21 Frieda and Angelo Ravagli outside the house he
built in Taos, 1956

22 Dorothy Brett in Taos

23 Frieda in old age at Taos

24 The D. H. Lawrence Memorial chapel at Kiowa Ranch, Taos. In the foreground is Frieda's grave

patriotism; he "publicly demonstrated his sympathies for the enemy" (for instance, by singing German folksongs); and he openly agitated against the war. Cecil Gray later admitted that he had agreed to take part in a nihilistic campaign in the industrial areas of North England, conceived by Lawrence as a means of bringing the war to a speedy end. Of course this was nothing more than talk, a pipe-dream on Lawrence's part. But were the authorities not justified in regarding him as a security risk, particularly since—another proof of his political blindness —he also attempted to offer his services in the Russian Revolution, seeking to get in touch with Ivy Low's husband, Maxim Litvinov, at that time the diplomatic representative of the Soviet government and later its foreign minister? Frieda's German origin tipped the scales of suspicion further still.

Meanwhile, in bursts of hectic activity, he was working on his new novel, *Aaron's Rod*, and trying in vain to find a publisher who would be willing to bring out *Women in Love*. Never before had they lived in such poverty. "In another fortnight I shall not have a penny to buy bread and margarine," he wrote to his agent. He wrote desperate letters, not only to friends, but also to people he scarcely knew; he applied to the Royal Literary Fund for support. Arnold Bennett, conscious of his own position as an eminent and successful author, offered to pay Lawrence a pension of three pounds a week, provided that H. G. Wells and John Galsworthy would do the same. Lawrence rejected the offer as an insult to his pride. But he was not too proud to consider making a new approach to Lady Ottoline Morrell. Only three months earlier he had written to Mark Gertler: "As for the Ott—why should I bother about the old carrion?" Now he was asking whether she would be glad to see them if they went to Garsington! Gertler's reply was not encouraging.

In the course of this year Frieda succeeded in arranging two meetings with her children. Monty, now seventeen years old, was dressed in cadet's uniform, and her mother's heart bled at the thought that he too might be sent into the inferno of the front line. "Let me hide you somewhere in a cave or in a wood," she said to him. "I don't want you to go and fight, I don't want you to be killed in this stupid war." Monty, who had always since the early days taken his father's side and regarded his mother with cold hostility, was profoundly shocked.

Frieda was still managing to maintain some sort of contact with her mother and sisters through an accommodation address in Switzerland, but she needed no private family bulletin to inform her of the death of Manfred von Richthofen. The London newspapers screamed it forth under huge headlines. He was shot down on 21 April 1918 east of Amiens after his eightieth victory in the air. He had already become a legend in Germany, a second Siegfried, and there he had to be depicted as triumphant even in death. The official death announcement stated that he was shot down by stray anti-aircraft fire. In fact Manfred von Richthofen's plane was brought down by a Canadian pilot, Captain Roy Brown, who belonged to Squadron 209 of the newly formed Royal Air Force and was flying a Camel 1 airplane.[7]

However, even to his enemies Manfred von Richthofen appeared as a knight in shining armour. He had been brought down behind the British lines, and his body was laid to rest with more pomp and ceremony than has been accorded to any other enemy soldier in this century. Fifty members of the Royal Air Force, officers and NCOs, marched beside the coffin, on which lay five huge wreaths of everlasting flowers bound with the German colours—tributes from RFC headquarters and neighbouring airfields—and three gun salutes were fired. After the war the body was exhumed and laid to rest in a new grave in Berlin.

Undoubtedly the emergence of Manfred von Richthofen as a hero owed much to the German Supreme Command, which glorified him for very deliberate policy reasons. Without this, his name would scarcely have become known outside a small circle, just as Hector and Achilles would be completely forgotten had it not been for Homer. But there is another reason why his fame survived. Richthofen's flights in his primitive machine to meet his enemy in single combat appealed to the twentieth century's imagination in much the same way that tales of individual heroism had stirred the hearts of men in ancient and medieval times. It was perhaps the last time in the history of warfare that "chivalry raised its lance on high"; air battles nowadays seem to have become mainly a matter of computers staffed by teams of specialists.*

Lawrence, however, was occupied at this time with another historical epoch. Inspired by Gibbon's monumental *Decline and Fall of the Roman Empire*, he wrote a school textbook with the title *Movements in European History*. At the same time he continued work on *Aaron's Rod*, dashed

---

* The fiftieth anniversary of Manfred von Richthofen's death in 1968 brought long articles in several British newspapers. The fascination the German pilot still exerts is all the more remarkable when one considers that the most successful British pilot during the First World War, Edward Mannock, with 73 victories to his name, is today completely forgotten. The reluctance of the British military to pander to the cult of hero-worship has consequently led, paradoxically, to the British finding a hero in the enemy camp!

off an unimportant play, *Touch and Go,* and began on a collection of essays, *Studies in Classic American Literature.* It was altogether a remarkable achievement in view of the struggle he was having merely to keep his head above water.

In spite of all the fears and humiliations, the poverty and the sickness, Lawrence and Frieda managed—amazingly—to remain what they had always been: enchanting, muddling, irritating, invigorating. Cecily Lambert, the owner of a farm in Berkshire at which they stayed for a time, has written a vivid account of her first meeting with them:[8]

> I was amazed to see coming towards me a most astounding spectacle—a tall, very slender creature clad in drainpipe khaki trousers, light shirt, scarlet tie, and what appeared, in the distance, to be a blue dressing jacket, but on closer acquaintance turned out to be a butcher blue linen coat. Above this shone the reddest beard I have ever seen, vivid and startling, a very pale gauntish face with deep blue penetrating eyes, and a shock of mousey blonde hair topped with a white floppy child's hat of cotton drill. Following a few yards behind was a very plump, heavily built woman, with strong features and blonde hair ... In her bold style she was quite handsome. She was dressed in a very full blue-and-white plaid skirt and a linen coat similar to Mr Lawrence's which afterwards we were told was copied and tailored by him. With this she wore a very wide brimmed straw hat, devoid of trimming but which suited her. She was hurrying along, panting and rather dishevelled, trying vainly to catch up with the man in front, who sped along on his toes almost as if he were being propelled by an invisible force and appearing as if he were trying to escape from the woman ...
>
> Our first visit to the cottage was a memorable one ... Frieda entertained while D.H.L. prepared the food, and very nice and tasty it was. For a sweet we had what appeared to be "toffee prunes" which we vainly tried to bite without success and ended in surreptitiously manipulating into our handkerchiefs. Afterwards there was a terrific argument between D.H. and Frieda, and we discovered later the reason was that Frieda had been responsible for the sweet course and had no idea that prunes needed soaking or at any rate some moisture and had placed them in a hot oven with sugar only ...
>
> Frieda was a good raconteur and had amusing episodes to tell of their wanderings and was in her element doing this. She hated work and was content to leave this and the chores to D.H. I can see her now

on that evening, sitting back on a low arm chair, purring away like a lazy cat and showing a great deal of plump leg above the knee encased in calico bloomers probably made by D.H. himself. She was not permitted to wear silk or dainties. Some time later when the Lawrences were staying with us, I was making up some crêpe de Chine which I had bought in my affluent days. To my amazement D.H. hurled some scathing remarks at me about using such material —"Prostitutey," he called it. It struck me at the time that it was a peculiar attitude to adopt regarding my underwear and much more so after I had read his novels ...

Cecily Lambert had plenty more opportunity to be amazed by Lawrence:

> He had a diabolical temper in keeping with his red beard ... On one occasion when staying at the Farm Frieda borrowed Miss Monk's sewing-machine and had inadvertently had some small mishap with it. I forget what it was really—not very serious—but anything happening to Miss Monk's possessions was a major calamity in her eyes. It was mentioned in front of D.H., and the result was a tornado so shocking that even we were terrified, fearing the outcome. He slated Frieda unmercifully, saying she was lazy and useless and sat around while we did all the work. He then ordered her to clean our kitchen floor which was large with the old-fashioned, well-worn bricks, none too easy to get scoured, in fact real hard labour. To our amazement she burst into tears and proceeded to work on it, fetching a pail of water and sloshing around with a floor cloth in a bending position (although he had told her to kneel), bitterly resentful at having to do such a menial task quite beneath the daughter of a baron, at the same time hurling every insult she could conjure up at D.H., calling him an uncouth lout, etc. He appeared to love an opportunity to humiliate her—whether from jealousy or extreme exasperation one could never tell. I was only surprised that she listened to his abuse or obeyed his orders.

And all the time Lawrence was continuing to dream of Rananim. For a while the happy colony of free men and women was to be set up in the Andes, then in some distant valley of Peru or Ecuador. Later still the surprising idea evolved of starting it in Palestine. But all this was merely a pipe-dream: the realities of life remained harsh and ugly.

Once again, for the third time, he had to present himself for a

154

medical examination—this time in a school building in Derby. He found it even more humiliating than before, feeling himself to be a miserably ridiculous figure, his nakedness scantily hidden beneath a short jacket. The room was full of other naked recruits and soldiers seated side by side at the long official table, and the air was alive with shameless mockery even before the young doctor placed his stethoscope to Lawrence's skinny, undernourished body and fingered his genitals. The result was category C2.

Six weeks later the war ended.

14

London, as soon as the news of the Armistice came through, erupted in a drunken frenzy. The streets of the West End were suddenly filled with singing, bawling and laughing crowds. Female munitions workers came in lorryloads from the arsenal in Woolwich, their faces stained yellow by the picric acid fumes. Jokes and ribald remarks flew to and fro like tennis balls between soldiers and overalled factory girls, men and women who had never before set eyes on each other copulated in doorways and on the pavements, affirming in this way the triumph of life over death. Groups stood on street corners singing hymns in a state of trance. Buses, commandeered by excited demonstrators, plunged off their routes in an ecstatic odyssey through unknown side-streets. Cars were filled to bursting with singing, screaming people, and from the roofs of taxis, passengers, drunk with victory and alcohol, slid down on to the road.

On Armistice Day, 11 November 1918, Frieda and Lawrence were also in London.[1] They pushed their way through the throng into Bloomsbury. The house they were making for belonged to Montague Shearman, lawyer, art collector and friend of Mark Gertler. It was already full of people when they arrived. The writers Osbert and Sacheverell Sitwell were there; Diaghilev, the ballet impresario, and Massine, the ballet dancer; Maynard Keynes, the political economist; Lady Mond, wife of the Minister for Munitions; the painter, Duncan Grant; and countless others.

And suddenly David Garnett was standing before them. They had not seen him for three years, and Frieda greeted him with enthusiastic warmth. But Lawrence merely said sourly: "So you're here." Garnett, surprised by his indifference, noticed that he looked depressed and ill: his was the only unhappy face in all that excited gathering. In the next instant Henry Mond started to play the piano, and David joined the dancing couples on the floor. Later he returned to Lawrence, who was still in gloomy mood, though now he was prepared to talk.

"I suppose you think the war is over and that we shall go back to the kind of world you lived in before it," he said. "But the war isn't over.

The hate and evil is greater now than ever. Very soon war will break out again and overwhelm you."

Lawrence was now speaking in a raised voice, and a circle of people began to form round him as he went on: "The crowd outside thinks that Germany is crushed forever. But the Germans will soon rise again. Europe is done for: England most of all the countries. This war isn't over. Even if the fighting should stop, the evil will be worse because the hate will be dammed up in men's hearts and will show itself in all sorts of ways which will be worse than war."

Who can say whether Lawrence realised how soon his dark prophecy was to come true? Or was he just taking a perverse pleasure in proclaiming his contrary views and placing a drop of gall in his companions' cup of pleasure? David Garnett, his close friend and long-standing admirer, was so revolted by his jeremiad that he broke off all personal relations with him from that moment.

Lawrence had been so long obsessed by his glowing hatred for the war that its sudden end threw him into an emotional vacuum. He felt uncertain, confused, perhaps even a little frightened to find himself standing in a world apparently heading for disaster. When he came to look back on what he had achieved in the past few years, he had reason to feel apprehensive about the future. *The Rainbow* was banned in England, although a slightly expurgated version of it had been published in New York, and in spite of intense efforts he had been unable to find a publisher for *Women in Love*. During all these years nothing from his pen had appeared in print apart from a few short pieces in periodicals, a little volume about his Italian travels and two books of poetry which had failed to please the critics. He was practically penniless, and possessed only a single pair of trousers, which through constant washing had shrunk to above his ankles. He had lost many of his friends, and his reputation had sunk to almost nothing. On top of that, his health was not what it should be: he was having trouble once more with his lungs. As usual, he found living in a large town unbearable. In order to work undisturbed, he hid himself away in a little cottage in Derbyshire, where he found "the world rather Macbeth-looking— brownish little strokes of larch trees above, the bracken brown and curly, disappearing below the house into shadowy gloom."

This landscape in sepia was sketched in a letter to Katherine Mansfield, who, though she had married John Middleton Murry in the previous May, was feeling spiritually closer to Lawrence during these winter weeks. It was perhaps their common tragedy that formed the link between them. She was also ill, though she did not yet know how far the tuberculosis in her lungs had advanced. Murry himself could have been under no illusions about it: the specialist had told him that, however carefully she was looked after, Katherine could not expect to live longer than three more years, or five at the outside. Frieda, who had remained behind in London and did not join Lawrence until shortly before Christmas, was often with her.

Frieda was feeling impatient and restless. But her mood was not due to the poverty in which she and Lorenzo were living, nor to the apparent hopelessness of their position. Whatever she might be charged with, if one feels the need to pass judgment on her, the scales tip heavily in her favour during these war years. The deprivations, the persecutions, the disappointments—none of them was sufficient to shake her belief in Lawrence's genius. If any one single factor saved him from going under, that factor was certainly her complete trust in him.

No, the cause of her unrest lay elsewhere. The continued separation from her family in Germany preyed on her mind. Since the baron's death her mother had been living alone in Baden-Baden. Else was in Munich, where her husband Edgar, from whom she had been separated for years, was now the Bavarian Finance Minister. Imposing as this may sound, it was really nothing more than a short and tragic chapter in his life, a curious episode in the turbulence that followed Germany's defeat. The end of the war found Edgar Jaffe, the shy intellectual, caught up in the glowing furnace of revolution. "Huge meetings in all the *Brauhaus* halls almost every evening," the poet Rainer Maria Rilke wrote on 7 November 1918 to his wife, Clara.[2] "Orators are springing up everywhere, foremost among them Professor Jaffe, and, when the halls are not big enough, thousands gather outside in the open air."

On the following morning Rilke added a postscript:

It has been a remarkable night. A council of soldiers, peasants and workers has now been set up here, with Kurt Eisner as its first chairman. The whole front page of the *Münchner Neueste* is taken up with a proclamation issued by him, whereby Bavaria is declared a republic and its citizens promised peace and security. The night's doings were preceded by a meeting on the *Theresienwiese*, to which one hundred and twenty thousand people came ... So far everything seems quiet, and one cannot help feeling that people are right in times like this to try to make big strides forward.

Edgar Jaffe was from the start a member of this revolutionary government, composed mainly of Independent Socialists and Social Democrats, which was attempting to build a sort of Bavarian Rananim on the ruins of the war. But it was an idealistic soap-bubble that soon burst when it came into contact with the harsh realities of terrorist movements. On 21 February 1919, five months after the abdication of King Ludwig III, the president, Kurt Eisner, was shot dead on his way to parliament by a right-wing radical, Count Arco-Valley.* Edgar Jaffe was already in the council chamber when the news of the assassination came through; the next instant he ducked as several bullets struck the ministerial benches. This time the terrorist, in private life a waiter, belonged to the extreme left wing. The Minister of the Interior, Erhard Auer, was severely wounded and a deputy killed.

"I am worried about my sister in München," Frieda wrote to Koteliansky. Several days passed before she received news of Else. Edgar had not been injured in the shooting, but the episode had put an end to his political career. A new government, to which he did not belong, was set up in Munich (including some anarchist writers, among them Erich Mühsam, whom Frieda in earlier days had seen playing chess in the Café Stefanie), and this government proclaimed a soviet republic in Bavaria. A month later the town was occupied by military troops, and the soviet republic expired in a sea of blood.

Apart from her worries about the Jaffes, Frieda had another reason for feeling "two hundred years old". Lorenzo was once again seriously ill, this time with Spanish flu, which was sweeping through the whole of Europe. His letters, when he recovered sufficiently to write them, looked like medical bulletins. His whole thoughts were now concentrated on getting away from England. He put his hopes on New York, but Amy Lowell, for all her faith in new ideas, wrote back in great alarm, urging him to think again. American writers nowadays can be as frank as they like in their descriptions of sex, but in 1919 the United States were, if anything, even more prudish than England. In Boston the famous Athenaeum library kept Lawrence's *Sons and Lovers* under lock and key and issued it only to privileged readers on request. In such

* The assassin was taken to Stadelheim prison and put in cell 70, where in the previous year Eisner himself had been locked up for several months for making a speech to strikers. In 1923 a young rebel named Adolf Hitler was an inmate of the same cell, and in 1934—also in cell 70—the Nazi SA leader Ernst Röhm was shot dead on Hitler's orders.

circumstances Lawrence could hardly expect to be received in the New World with open arms.

He dropped this plan, but he was still determined to leave his native land. Now peace was restored, England seemed to him like a corpse. "Damn it," he wrote, "we've been buried long enough, like toads under a muck-heap." Some payments came in, to his great relief, and their financial situation was temporarily eased.

At last the peace treaty was signed and they were able to apply for passports. It was as if the doors of their prison cell had been flung open. Lawrence had decided not to go to Germany with her, but Frieda awaited the day of her departure for Germany in a fever of impatience. Every new letter from her family threw her into a panic, and she was often in tears. Whenever she could, she sent off food parcels to Munich and Baden-Baden. When she left, Lawrence accompanied her to the station and put her on the train for Harwich.

Describing their farewells through the carriage window, Lawrence later wrote: "She had a look of almost vindictive triumph, and almost malignant love, as the train drew out." A few hours later she was in Holland, and there her baggage was stolen. After much excitement the trunks were found, but they were empty. The delay meant that she lost her train connections. But at long last she found herself seated in an unheated compartment in a German train, speeding beneath a grey October sky through the starved Rhineland.

Baden-Baden was a haven of peace in a land wracked by unemployment, hunger riots and political unrest. Frieda's mother had not returned to Metz on her husband's death, nor did she now the war was over, since the town was once again in French territory. The year before, on 19 November 1918, Marshal Pétain had taken the salute at a march-past of victorious French troops in the Place d'Armes. Girls dressed in the national costume of Lorraine had danced through the streets, laughing and singing as they filed past the stone figure of Kaiser Wilhelm, stretched out in comic stiffness in the road, beside the plinth from which it had been dislodged. The statue of Wilhelm II in the guise of a saint, which stood before the old cathedral, had been placed in handcuffs and hung with a placard inscribed *Sic transit gloria mundi*. In the city which for forty-eight years had been a bulwark of the German Empire not a single word of German could now be heard.

Baden-Baden, lying peacefully among its forests, looked grey and weary. No trams were running. Even the drinking-hall was closed, since it could not be heated, and all the shops shut at five in the evening in order to save gas and electricity. In any case, they rarely had anything to sell. Food could be bought only at official distribution centres, the weekly ration consisting of less than an ounce of butter, half a pound of meat or sausage and five pounds of potatoes. Hungry and freezing, people waited around in the streets for news of the next issue of fire-wood, exchanging spine-chilling stories about the misdeeds of the French, who were now occupying the Kehl bridgehead and the left bank of the Rhine.

Anna von Richthofen was living in the Ludwig-Wilhelm-Stift, a home "for ladies of the educated classes". However, hunger and cold being no respecters of persons, the educated, and for the most part aristocratic, ladies were no better off than anyone else, and Frieda was horrified to see the conditions under which her mother was now living. She did what she could to help. She stayed a month and then, appre-hensive and slimmer than she had been for a long time past, left for Italy, where she had arranged to rejoin Lawrence.

After an endless and exhausting journey, he had at last reached Turin. There he spent two nights as the guest of a well-to-do Englishman whom he later savagely portrayed in *Aaron's Rod*. He continued his journey to Florence on a cold and wet November day. Norman Douglas had procured a room for him in the boarding-house on the Arno in which he himself was staying. Douglas had been on the editorial staff of the *English Review* when Lawrence first met him ten years earlier. Since then he had become a famous author and was regarded as the uncrowned king of the British colony in Capri, whose eccentricities he portrayed with scintillating wit in his enormously successful novel *South Wind*. When Lawrence met him again in Florence, Douglas was accompanied by a curious individual, elegantly though shabbily dressed. This fawning, rakish homosexual, Maurice Magnus by name, was an American, though he seemed to be at home in all the main cities of Europe.

Douglas, who was staying in Florence at Magnus's expense, told Lawrence that his companion had once been Isadora Duncan's manager and before the war had been responsible for the *Roman Review*, the English-language newspaper in Rome. Lawrence was repelled by the plump little man with his sycophantic manners. When, a few days later, Maurice Magnus left for Rome, Lawrence was shocked to see that he travelled first class. "Travelling is so beastly anyhow, why not go in style?" simpered Magnus complacently. Lawrence thought of the agonising nights he and Frieda had spent in third-class railway compartments and was not amused.

Frieda arrived in Florence on 3 December at four o'clock in the morning. It is hardly the best time of day to admire the sights of a city, but Lorenzo insisted on taking her at once in an open one-horse carriage on a tour through the streets, pointing out the famous statues, churches and bridges to her in the misty moonlight. Six days later they moved south.

Who in his right senses would choose a God-forsaken village in the Abruzzi region as a place to stay at this time of year? But they had promised an acquaintance to inspect a farmhouse in Picinisco, six miles above Cassino, and give an opinion on its suitability as a holiday place. Both house and village turned out to be so primitive that a prolonged stay was unthinkable. Then Lawrence remembered that five years ago Compton Mackenzie had invited him to Capri, where he had a small holiday house in addition to his own home. Lawrence wrote to Mackenzie that the "melancholy elms" had driven him from England (he had never forgotten Compton Mackenzie's remark made in that terrible, damp little cottage in Chesham): could he come to Capri with Frieda? Just before Christmas it snowed for a whole day. Two freezing days later they made their departure before daybreak, picking their way carefully through the chickens sleeping on the kitchen floor and the dung heaps which the mules, tethered to the doorpost, had deposited on the threshold. They began their journey back to civilisation.

Compton Mackenzie had, as it happened, let the little holiday house to the writer Francis Brett Young and his wife, but he found a two-room apartment for the Lawrences in the old Palazzo Ferraro quite close to the Piazza. Frieda and Lawrence were enchanted: from the flat roof of the Palazzo they had a magnificent view of the sea, and behind it a picture-postcard panorama of Ischia and Naples swimming on a hazy horizon, Vesuvius with its plume of smoke and in the west, between terraces and gardens, the mighty limestone mass of Monte Solaro. To the south-east, above the houses with their white domed roofs, the Gulf of Salerno stretched away into the distance. Lorenzo wrote enthusiastically to Lady Cynthia Asquith: to "look down on a blue day and see the dim-sheer rocky coast, the clear rock mountains, is so beautiful, so like Ulysses!"

At their feet lay the maze of streets in the town of Capri itself, "about as big as Eastwood". They felt, if they were to stretch out a hand, they could touch the *Duomo*.

A narrow flight of steps led them down to the Café Morgano,* the nerve centre of the island and meeting place of all its eccentrics and Bohemians—English, German, American, Scandinavian and Russian—most of them homosexuals. Here Frieda and Lawrence spent New Year's Eve, drinking punch with an ancient Dutchman and an out-at-elbows Englishman who was a friend of Somerset Maugham and Norman Douglas. Just before midnight Compton Mackenzie came to join them with a number of already tipsy Americans in tow, and ordered champagne all round. The islanders sang ballads and two youths danced a tarantella—"a funny indecent pederastic sight," Lawrence observed.

Well, of course, the siren isle of Capri had always been a pederastic haven—from the time Emperor Tiberius built the finest of his villas high above the sea on the cliff facing Sorrento, and not only from the days when Friedrich Alfred Krupp was a regular visitor to the Café Morgano. The German arms magnate liked to share his table with fishermen and mule-drivers—so long as they were well-built young men: a highly democratic gesture, one might think, on the part of a man whose yearly income, during the four years in which he honoured Capri with his presence, rose from seven to twenty-one million marks. He always lived in the exclusive Hotel Quisisana, which had been extended and improved at his expense. It was hardly fair, therefore, that the *maître d'hôtel* once refused to admit Oscar Wilde and his scandalous friend, Lord Alfred Douglas, into the restaurant because a number of English guests objected to their presence: after all, what is good for one homosexual should be good enough for another. But Krupp was no ordinary pederast. Germany's richest millionaire, and a personal friend of Kaiser Wilhelm II, he was also the island's great benefactor.[3] He paid for the building of the magnificent road that encircles the cliffs high above the Marina Piccola, he showered gold coins on all and sundry and even had the owner of the Quisisana, Federico Serena, elected mayor. One might justifiably say that he had the whole of Capri in his pocket. How else could those bacchanals in the notorious Fra Felice Grotto have been tolerated so long? Here in the grotto Krupp would sport with his young favourites in a state of classical nudity, with three fiddlers providing romantic music in the background. Every orgasm was greeted by the firing of a rocket. The arms magnate was indiscreet enough to have his orgies photographed, and copies of the pictures were still being offered for sale in Capri at the time Frieda

* Now known as "Zum Kater Hiddigeigei".

163

and Lawrence were there, long after the scandal had been exposed and the corrupter of Capri's youth had committed suicide in the Villa Hügel, the palatial family residence outside Essen.

The reputation the Krupp scandal had given the island served to attract many more distinguished refugees from the laws on homosexuality to its shores. At the time the Lawrences arrived Comte Jacques d'Adelswärd-Fersen, probably the most notorious libertine then around, was enjoying similar delights in his Villa Lysis, with some additional opium-smoking into the bargain. Norman Douglas was temporarily absent from the island, but it was impossible to visit the Café Morgano without hearing of his exploits.

Lawrence declared that Douglas looked like a fallen angel. That was when he met him in Florence, and to compare a fifty-year-old man with an angel, even a fallen one, is certainly unusual. But many things about Norman Douglas were both unusual and impenetrable. Like Lawrence, he was a rebel against society, but his revolt took a completely different form.[4]

He came of an upper middle-class Scottish family, though he had inherited some German or Austrian blood through his grandparents on his mother's side. He spent his childhood in the Austrian province of Vorarlberg, where the family owned cotton mills, and went to school in Karlsruhe. All his life he spoke German as well as he spoke English: Frieda indeed declared that his German was even wittier and more amusing than the English language in which he wrote his books. After completing his education in an English public school he joined the diplomatic service and was sent to the British Embassy in St Petersburg. The reason for his hasty departure from Russia is, like so much else in his life, unclear. From hints he gave it might well have had something to do with his relationship to "Helene", a Russian lady of high social standing.

Equally obscure are the reasons that later led Douglas to abandon his native country and settle in Italy. It is reasonable to deduce from the sort of life he led in exile that they were concerned with his amorous adventures. Before Oscar Wilde was exposed and banished, Douglas was held to be the most dissolute of the British literary expatriates, but even those who condemned him as a libertine had to admit that there was something very fascinating about him.

He was tall, with the body of an athlete. Long after he was sixty (he died in 1952 at the age of eighty-three), and his hair was as white as snow, he still held himself strikingly erect as he strode along, a stick always in his hand, with the firm and deliberate tread of a mountaineer. He had one of those handsome Scottish faces which seem to reflect the proud free spirit of the Scottish Highlands as much as delight in intellectual achievement. And the impression was by no means false, for Douglas, with his high forehead, bushy eyebrows and thin lips, really was a master of the English language, a classical scholar, a distinguished botanist and an acknowledged expert in the art of landscape gardening at which the Scots have always been so remarkably adept. In addition to all these he was also a gifted pianist and composer (he had studied under Anton Rubinstein), a gourmet and above all a wonderful raconteur. Somehow he managed to combine the manners of a *grand seigneur* with the carefree style of a Bohemian. Women found him irresistible, and the attraction—at least in his earlier years—was mutual. Despising everything that stood for "morality" in the Britain of Queen Victoria and her son Edward VII, Douglas explored the heights and depths of sensuality with Epicurean enjoyment and scientific thoroughness. The word "libertine" is certainly much too harsh to apply to so sensitive a connoisseur of beauty and enjoyment, yet it is the word that is most frequently used by all who disapproved of his uninhibited sexual appetites and his rejection of any form of organised religion.

Douglas declared that the change in his erotic tastes had been sudden and almost incredible: it took place in a narrow side-street in Naples in the year 1897. From then on he plunged eagerly and shamelessly into the life of a homosexual. The sight of this distinguished Scotsman in his elegant, if sometimes shabby, clothing walking through the streets of Naples with ragged urchins at his side belonged for years to the curiosities of the city. It was in the circumstances inevitable that he should choose Capri as his favourite place of residence. Here he could abandon himself, uninhibitedly and among others of like mind, to a style of life which appeared to Richard Aldington "as if he were living in Eastern Mediterranean countries at some period between the age of Plato and that of Hadrian." No one was better fitted than Norman Douglas to chronicle the gay life of his siren land, and his witty autobiographical novel *South Wind*, as soon as it appeared in England, was seized on with avidity by readers whose eagerness was not unmixed with a degree of malicious curiosity.

Since Douglas was still in Florence, it fell to Mary Cannan to acquaint the Lawrences with Capri's chronicle of shame. Mary, whom they had first met in Chesham at the same time as Compton Mackenzie, was alone: her husband, Gilbert, was on a lecture tour in America. A year later he was certified insane. The Lawrences came across Mary quite by chance, but it was inevitable that everybody living in the area between the Marina Grande and the Marina Piccola should sooner or later meet in the Piazza. Mary was full of spicy little anecdotes. "I didn't like Capri," Frieda wrote later. "It was so small an island, it seemed hardly capable to contain all the gossip that flourished there." Compton Mackenzie, on the other hand, had the feeling that she tended rather to encourage gossip. It is certainly clear that Capri brought out the worst in both the Lawrences. It was from there that Lawrence wrote a dreadful letter to Katherine Mansfield, containing the unforgivable sentence: "I loathe you. You revolt me stewing in your consumption."[5]

But they were very happy to be with Compton Mackenzie. He was a man after Frieda's heart and also very congenial to Lawrence. Tall, handsome, with an aristocratic bearing and exquisite manners, he looked every inch a Scottish nobleman, though in fact he came of a distinguished family of actors. A precocious child, he learned to read at the age of two and decided while still at school to become a writer. He found no difficulty in adapting himself to the various contradictions in his character: he was a socialist, yet at the same time he founded the Scottish Nationalist Party; in 1914 he became a Catholic, and a year later was Britain's most successful Secret Service agent in Greece. On an average he wrote two books a year, among them his immensely successful novel *Sinister Street*. Their total number reached nearly a hundred and in 1970, at the age of eighty-seven and two years before his death he brought the crowning achievement of his literary life to an end with the publication of the tenth and last volume of his autobiography, in which he drew fully on his phenomenal memory.

Compton Mackenzie lived with his wife, Faith, in the Casa Solitaria, a villa in a superb position immediately opposite the Faraglioni, those three romantic cliffs which are the emblem of the hermaphroditic isle. In this house Frieda and Lawrence spent many lively afternoons: a homosexual neighbour would play the piano while Compton Mackenzie and the Lawrences sang "Sally in our Alley" and other music-hall ditties at the tops of their voices.

One day Lawrence and Compton Mackenzie were strolling around the Piazza discussing Greek philosophy.[6] Lawrence suddenly stopped and declared solemnly: "What we have to learn is to think here."

He bent over to point a finger at his fly-buttons, to my embarrassment and the obvious surprise of other people strolling on the piazza. "You'll be getting a jobation presently from the *guardia*," I said, and went on to tell him how the old *guardia* had one evening seen one of the English visitors being rather too familiar with a young Caprese. He approached from behind and tapped him on the shoulder. "Queste cose, signore, si fanno in casa privata," he gurgled in a reproachful vinous voice.

Lawrence reacted to this story like a maiden aunt. His puritanical prudery had a way of coming to light at unexpected moments. Compton Mackenzie lent him some numbers of the American *Little Review*, in which James Joyce's *Ulysses* was appearing as a serial. Lawrence returned the copies to him a few days later with the shocked remark: "This *Ulysses* muck is more disgusting than Casanova. I *must* show that it can be done without muck."

Many years later Compton Mackenzie remembered this conversation and wondered whether it was at this moment that *Lady Chatterley's Lover* was conceived. If so, Mackenzie had done all he could to discourage him:

> I told him that if he was determined to convert the world to proper reverence for the sexual act by writing about it in a novel he would always have to remember one handicap for such an undertaking.—"What's that?" he asked impatiently. "That except to the two people who are indulging in it the sexual act is a comic operation." I see now Lawrence's pale face grow paler as he turned round and hurried off ...
>
> Next day he came into my room and said abruptly: "Perhaps you're right. And if you're right ..." He made a gesture of despair for the future of the human race.

Lawrence had come to Italy with nine pounds in his pocket, but since then his financial situation had somewhat improved: he had received some fees for his writings and Amy Lowell, helpful as always, had sent him some money. Thus, when he heard that Maurice Magnus, Norman Douglas's homosexual friend, was in difficulties, he did not hesitate to send him a small sum. The American had made an unpleasant impression on him in Florence, but this did not prevent Lawrence travelling to Monte Cassino to visit him (he would be able at the same time to view the famous monastery). Magnus was at the door of the fortress-like building to greet him. He was a Catholic convert and had made friends with the monks.

Next morning Lawrence experienced that unique miracle: the view of Monte Cassino, with its monks in the monastery garden and its farmworkers busy with their ploughs and oxen on the steep slopes behind them, the mountain peak with its crown of snow. It seemed to belong to the world of the sixteenth century, like the monastery itself with its long vaulted corridors, its marble church, its courtyard and Bramante's magnificent colonnades. But down in the valley, at the other end of the winding mountain road, lay the railway station of Cassino, locomotives puffing smoke into the pure air. The impact of the technical age destroyed the illusion of an idyllic bygone era. "To see all this from the monastery, where the Middle Ages live on in a sort of agony, like Tithonus, and cannot die, this was almost a violation to my soul, made almost a wound."

Lawrence had intended to spend a week there, but he left after only two days, unable to put up any longer with having to sit wrapped in a borrowed coat in the unheated rooms of the stone building. Two years afterwards he wrote down his impressions of these two days. A quarter of a century later the monastery was destroyed in one of the bitterest battles of the Second World War, but, as Harry T. Moore remarks, Lawrence's description of it conjures up the medieval building and the life inside it far more graphically than any photograph. To him Monte Cassino represented the "last foothold of the old world" in a time of "democracy, industrialism, socialism, the red flag of the communists and the red, white and green tricolour of the *fascisti*." And he added: "That was another world ... barren like the black cinder-track of the railway with its two steel lines."

The description of the monastery is contained in the long introduction that Lawrence wrote for Maurice Magnus's book, *Memoirs of the Foreign Legion*. The worthless, yet sharp-witted American plays an important role in this paean on the world of yesteryear. In Lawrence's mind he became the symbol of "modern man", the alienated city dweller, the cosmopolitan parasite who knows all the short cuts, but never his destination, who is always in search of something to hold on to and incapable of giving expression to a sincere emotion. Magnus hated Germany and had enlisted in the Foreign Legion at the beginning of the war. In some tortuous way he had reached the conclusion that in this way he would be striking a blow against German militarism, but after a few months his desire for the romantic desert life was assuaged, his sense of duty exhausted, and he deserted.

Frieda and Lawrence had now grown heartily tired of all the gossiping in the Café Morgano. The island, Lawrence remarked, was "a microcosmos that does heaven much credit, but mankind none at all."

They got on very well with Compton Mackenzie and his wife, and Francis Brett Young they liked too, but, as Young himself later observed: "Capri was rather too small for three novelists at once"—an uncharitable remark when applied to an island that has sheltered and given inspiration to an unending stream of *scrittori*, from Turgenev to Gorki, from Ivan Bunin to Axel Munthe, from August Kopisch to Rainer Maria Rilke, from Norman Douglas to Richard Aldington, not to speak of such later arrivals as Graham Greene. It was the astute and much-travelled Magnus who, when Lawrence broached the matter, suggested Sicily as a place to settle down, adding encouragingly: "Sicily has been waiting for you since the days of Theocritus." The idea took root, and five days after his return from Monte Cassino Lawrence went to Sicily, accompanied by Francis and Jessica Brett Young, to look for a suitable place to live.

He found it in the shape of a pleasant apartment in a villa north of Taormina, which he immediately rented for a whole year. Frieda joined him there a few days later.

From the high Gothic windows of the Villa Fontana Vecchia, as the house was called, they looked across a deserted bay to the coast of Calabria. It was the middle of March, and the ground was carpeted with gay spring flowers. The house was surrounded by almond trees in full blossom, and in the garden was a tiny ruined Greek temple. Frieda was entranced. It was the first time in six years that she had spent the spring outside England. "Living in Sicily after the war years was like coming to life again," she later said. The dawns filled Lawrence with happiness: "I open my eyes at 5.0 and say, Coming; at 5.30, and say, yellow; at 6.0, and say, pink and smoke blue; at 6.15, and see a lovely orange flare and then the liquid sunlight winking straight in my eye. Then I know it's time to get up."

But not everything was orange sky, carpets of anemones and azure-blue sea. One morning Lawrence heard a suspicious noise on the terrace. It was Magnus. "A terrible thing has happened," he groaned. He had had to leave Monte Cassino in a hurry, for the police were after him: "I couldn't let myself be arrested up there, could I? So awful for the monastery!" Lawrence did not ask in what new swindle his un-invited guest had now become involved, but nor did he offer him a bed in the villa. Magnus had in any case booked himself into the most expensive hotel in Taormina, and he left the bill for Lawrence to settle. Frieda, who had so far known Magnus only from Lawrence's descriptions, found him repulsive—"anti-social, a poor devil without any pride, and he didn't seem to matter anyhow." The way he made use of them made her very angry, but Lawrence, who was usually so pedantic and particular in money matters, was curiously disturbed and impressed by the bare-faced cadging of his "modern man". He was conscious of sharing with Magnus a profound contempt for the bourgeois and their obsessions with property and gain. Whereas he himself was only a victim of the despised system, the slippery American had managed to devise a method of his own for "fleecing the capitalists".

After three days Magnus moved into an elegant villa, in which he proceeded to live in great style. When the landlord began to press him for the rent, he declared himself to have been mortally insulted and took his departure, much to Lawrence's relief.

Mary Cannan, following their example, also moved to Sicily, and she persuaded them to join her on an expedition to Malta. Naturally they travelled second class. On the boat Frieda noticed a first-class passenger talking to one of the ship's officers and behaving as if the whole world belong to him. It was Magnus.

Immediately on their arrival a strike broke out and brought all shipping to a standstill, thus trapping them on "that beastly island" for eleven days. Inevitably they ran into Magnus, who greeted them like long-lost friends and introduced them to two young Maltese who turned out to be protégés of the hospice manager in Monte Cassino. It did not need much imagination to guess that the American was fleecing them, too.

But at last they were able to return to the Villa Fontana Vecchia. The terrace was covered in scarlet bougainvillaea and the ground beneath the almond trees was a bright yellow. The wheat had now been cut and Frieda looked on with great interest as the corn was ground and turned into bread in the primitive oven of Signora Cacopardo's kitchen. Frieda herself, under Lorenzo's guidance, had by now become a quite respectable cook. Her tardy housewifely pride manifested itself in the piles of homemade cakes, tarts and pastries laid out on the sideboard in the dining-room.

Lawrence was also in his element here. After the sterile months in Capri his urge to write had returned. "Frieda watched him doing most of the work, smiling securely," wrote Jan Juta, a South African painter, with whom they had made friends.[7]

[She was] preparing her armour for her next attack on the defences of this elusive man, her husband. For I soon discovered that even she who loved him, disturbed by his continual fight against the world which he waged in order to stick to his principles, was not prepared to let him thus elude her. He admired the fighting spirit in her, but was confident he could always beat her down. And there were scenes of cold anger and floods of tears which gave rise to the rumour that they were not happy together. It was not true, for they were amazingly happy through every sort of difficulty, welded in a way most people could not understand.

Lawrence was working again with fanatical intensity. He wrote poems blazing with the burning colours of Sicily, he completed his novels *The Lost Girl* and *Aaron's Rod*, and prepared his fascinating *Studies in Classic American Literature* for the printer. Thanks to Compton Mackenzie's help he had found a new publisher, Martin Secker.

The Lost Girl, published by Secker in 1920, is one of Lawrence's weakest works. Its deficiencies can probably be attributed to the chequered course of its creation. Lawrence began to write it in Bavaria before the war. When he returned to England in the summer of 1914, he left the manuscript, two-thirds completed, with Else Jaffe. His efforts to recover it via Switzerland proved fruitless. When it at last reached him in Capri in February 1920 he decided—not surprisingly—that the whole thing would have to be rewritten. This he did in great haste in the Villa Fontana Vecchia, bringing several of his latest experiences into the last chapter. Pescocalascio, for instance, can be identified with Picinisco, the primitive village in the Abruzzi where they had lived the previous winter, while the unfortunate Maurice Magnus appears in the shape of Mr May, the American impresario. The basic theme of the novel is the same as in many of his other works: Alvina, a girl from the industrial Midlands (Eastwood) marries an Italian, Cicio, who is socially far beneath her. She has intuitively realised that Cicio, with his human warmth and understanding, is vastly superior to her friends in her own social class. The whole thing is of course a variation of Lawrence's own, highly personal theme: his relationship with Frieda, the marriage between the gifted miner's son and the aristocratic woman.

The hot sun of a Sicilian summer was now beginning to beat down unmercifully on their heads. Frieda was longing for her mother, for the pine trees of the Black Forest and the dewy grass. Since Lawrence was still reluctant to show himself in Germany, their ways divided: she went off to Baden-Baden, while he journeyed in slow stages to the north of Italy.

They returned to Taormina on 20 October 1920. It was pouring with rain, and the rain continued for weeks. "It rains with such persistency and stupidity here that one loses all one's initiative," wrote Lawrence.

During this period the rake's progress of Maurice Magnus in Malta came to a tragic end. The two Maltese who had stood surety for him had at last learned the full extent of his debts, and they withdrew their surety. A few days later two detectives came to see Magnus. He spoke with them on the door-step, and they asked him to accompany them to the police station. He slammed the door shut, turned the key, wrote a few hurried words to the hospice manager in Monte Cassino—"I cannot live any longer. Pray for me"—and swallowed a dose of cyanide. By the time the police broke down the door there was nothing more to be done except to fetch a priest to administer the last rites. On a piece of paper Magnus, true to himself to the end, had scribbled the words: "I want to be buried first-class." His last wish was granted: the two Maltese paid up generously for the funeral.

The Lawrences learned of the tragedy through the newspapers. Lawrence was tortured by remorse. "I could, by giving him half my money, have saved his life," he said.

In the ensuing course of this bizarre story there emerged a further twist which seems to belong to the Victorian novel rather than to the Lawrentian world. Magnus's loathing for Germany turned out to have been a case of Freudian over-compensation: his native language was not English, but German. As Lawrence discovered from the hospice manager in Monte Cassino, Magnus had been on his mother's side an illegitimate grandchild of Kaiser Friedrich III. Wilhelm II, the Kaiser against whom he tried to fight, was his own uncle.[8]

But even with that the story is not yet finished. Magnus had appointed Norman Douglas his literary executor, but the two Maltese creditors sent the manuscript of his *Memoirs of the Foreign Legion* to Lawrence. In the hope that publication would at least make good some of their losses, Lawrence agreed to edit the confused and formless manuscript. He was also anxious to perform some last gesture of friendship, even perhaps of remorse. It took him four years to find a publisher, and even then the book was accepted only on the strength of Lawrence's long introduction. Publication led to a bitter attack by Norman Douglas, who was annoyed with Lawrence for having portrayed him un-sympathetically in the novel *Aaron's Rod*. Now he accused Lawrence of having purloined royalties which belonged by rights to himself; Lawrence's reply was dignified and convincing. The brilliant battle of words that ensued, with Frieda herself joining in towards the end, has become one of the celebrated literary feuds of the century.

At the end of January they went to Palermo to board a ship for Sardinia. They had no reason to leave their beloved Villa Fontana Vecchia on that grey wet day except that Lawrence had once again been bitten by his incorrigible urge to travel. What was it that always made him take flight the very moment he had lighted on a comfortable nest? Was it the burning sickness in his lungs that filled him with such an insatiable greed for experience? Or was it because he was homeless, classless and rootless that he sought to find in new impressions the security that familiar surroundings and a home of his own would have given him? Rebecca West, to whom he spoke of his wanderings when he met her in Florence shortly afterwards, has put forward yet another explanation for his constant unrest:[9]

These were the journeys that the mystics of a certain type have always found necessary. The Russian saint goes to the head of his family and says good-bye and takes his stick and walks out with no objective but the truth. The Indian fakir draws lines with his bare feet across the dust of his peninsula which describe a diagram, mean-ingless to the uninitiated, but significant of holiness. Lawrence travelled, it seemed, to get a certain Apocalyptic vision of mankind that he registered again and again and again, always rising to a pitch of ecstatic agony.

Whatever the deepest motives of his unceasing pilgrimage, Frieda was his indispensable and at this time willing companion. She was his partner in a lasting dialogue in which he measured his thoughts and impressions against her reactions before laying them aside in the treasury of his memory for later use. Looking at his creative processes in chemical terms, she was not only the catalyst, but also the filter with whose aid he purged the substance he sought of its dross. He may have demanded her subservience and she may have rebelled against his tyranny, but as far as his literary work was concerned she fulfilled a necessary function, and his reliance on her was total.

The result of their ten-day-long excursion to Sardinia was *Sea and Sardinia*, one of his masterpieces. It is, to use the modern phrase, a travel book, but a travel book written by a poet in vital, inspired language. With a few words he can conjure up, with all the clarity of a painting by Cézanne, a visual image of the harbour town of Cagliari or the experience of a rail journey into the interior in a compartment full of miners and farmworkers, the feel of a frosty clear morning after a night spent in an indescribably dirty inn, or the bright silhouettes of men in narrow knee-breeches dancing in a dark wine-parlour to the sound of an accordion until, inflamed by wine, they fall on each other in a wild scuffle. Frieda, his travelling companion, is always referred to in the book as the Queen Bee, or simply q.b.

In May, Martin Secker brought out *Women in Love*.

A telegram arrived from Else: the baroness was seriously ill. Frieda hastened to Baden-Baden. By the time she arrived her mother was already on the road to recovery, but Else was at her husband's death-bed, and Frieda went to Munich to see Edgar Jaffe for the last time. Since the ruin of his political hopes he had been only a shadow of his former self. A prey to deep melancholy, bereft of the will to live, he fell a swift victim to pneumonia.

Lawrence, alone in Taormina, began to feel restless again. "The house is very empty without F. Don't like it at all," he wrote to his mother-in-law. Friends asked him to their houses, but he turned down their invitations. After a month of loneliness he decided to follow Frieda to Germany, but as usual he travelled by stages. He made a detour to Capri, where he got to know an American couple, Earl and Achsah Brewster, both of them painters. He soon discovered that they thought along the same lines as himself, and they quickly became friends. Brewster told him he was intending to go to Ceylon in the autumn to continue his studies in Buddhist philosophy. It was a conversation that was to have important consequences for Lawrence and Frieda.

On arrival in Baden-Baden he took a room in a small hotel in Ebersteinburg for Frieda and himself, and here he at last found peace to write the last chapters of *Aaron's Rod*.

Occasionally he accompanied Frieda when she visited her mother. Grinning behind his beard, he would bow politely to the "ladies of the educated classes" living out their days in the Ludwig-Wilhelm-Stift. The thought that any of them might have read one of her son-in-law's books made Frieda's mother shudder with apprehension. A curious rapport was developing between her and Lawrence. The baroness was an open-minded woman, and he had not forgotten how swiftly and courageously she had ranged herself on his side when he was still fighting Ernest Weekley for the possession of Frieda's soul.

At the beginning of July they visited Frieda's younger sister Nusch in the Tirol. Johanna's marriage with the ex-staff officer, Max von Schreibershofen, was not going well, and only the need to keep up outward appearances in front of the children still held them together. Frieda and Lawrence spent six weeks with them in their lakeside villa in Thumersbach opposite Zell-am-See. Nusch had lost none of her old infectious gaiety, and she and Frieda were soon back on their old intimate footing, from which Lawrence felt himself increasingly excluded. But it was not until the summer heat yielded to cool wet weather that Frieda could be persuaded to return south. Lawrence first of all dragged her to Capri to meet his new Buddhist friends, the Brewsters, and it was not until the end of September that they at last found themselves back in a wet and stormy Taormina.

If Frieda had suffered during the journey from Lorenzo's bad moods, there was still worse to come. The mail awaiting them in the Villa Fontana Vecchia plunged him into deep gloom. The sensation-seeking weekly *John Bull* was now turning its puritanical fury on *Women in Love*, which it described as an "analytical study of sexual depravity" and an "epic of vice". Beside itself with righteous moral indignation, it thundered: "If *The Rainbow* was an indecent book this later production is an obscene abomination. The police must act." The composer Philip Heseltine, whom Lawrence had portrayed satirically under the name of Halliday, was threatening a libel action. Lawrence vented his rage in a letter to Brewster: "It is a world of Canaille, absolutely, Canaille, cagnalia, Schweinhunderei, stinkpots. Pfui!" And in another letter to Brewster he wrote: "I feel rather gloomy. Europe is my own continent, so I feel bad about it. I feel as if it was dying under my eyes."

He began to dream vaguely and longingly of another escape.

Only Europe, with which he was out of sympathy, and only England, which he loathed during these weeks, could have produced a man like Lawrence. Equally, a woman like Mabel Dodge could have come from nowhere except America. Born in Buffalo on Lake Erie, she was the only child of an extravagantly rich banker, Charles Ganson. His marriage did not last long, and Mabel, the heiress to his vast fortune, passed through a series of boarding-schools. Reaching adult years, she ran through three marriages in ten years, ecouraged art—or, to be more precise, artists—turned Paris and Nice upside down, and set up literary salons, first in Florence and later in New York, to which famous authors and artists contributed international glamour. Among them were John Reed, author of the well-known report on the Russian Revolution, *Ten Days That Shook the World*, with whom she had a lengthy love affair; Walter Lippmann; the Marxist author, Max Eastman; Frances Perkins, later Labour Secretary in Roosevelt's administration; Amy Lowell, the poetess; and Isadora Duncan, the dancer whose life ended so tragically when she was strangled by her own scarf. Mabel Dodge was, so to speak, a sort of transatlantic Lady Ottoline Morrell, with the difference that Lady Ottoline's eccentricity and openhanded-ness were rooted in England's aristocracy and intellectual elite, whereas Mabel was the product of America's *nouveau riche* society.

When the war ended, Mabel Dodge—as she was generally called, though by this time she was Mabel Evans Dodge Sterne—joined forces with an artists' colony which was at that time being formed in Taos, New Mexico. She was now forty-two. Her last marriage—to the painter Maurice Sterne—had broken up, and she was living with a muscular Red Indian named Antonio Luhan.[1]

Mabel Dodge had read *Sea and Sardinia*, which had just appeared in New York. Lawrence's ability to convey the essence of a landscape or of a person in a few sentences made such a deep impression on her that she immediately wrote him an urgent and pressing letter. Would he be prepared to come to New Mexico with his Queen Bee and do for her beloved Taos what he had already done for Sardinia?

Frieda was delighted with the invitation, but Lawrence was more cautious and wanted to know who would pay for it. Mabel Dodge cabled back at once: from San Francisco onwards they would be her guests. From then on she bombarded them with letters and telegrams. Lawrence's replies indicated that he was not averse to the idea, but there were a number of things he wanted to know first. Was there not "an arty and literary crew" in Taos, nothing but "smoking, steaming shits"? And weren't the Red Indians dying out, and wasn't the whole thing a bit of a farce? What were rich Americans doing in Taos anyway? He could not make up his mind, and the correspondence dragged on for months. He wanted to know more about this odd woman before he committed himself to anything. Mabel described the psycho-analytical treatment she was undergoing. He wrote back rudely that as far as he was concerned all neurotics could be left to rot. "A real neurotic is half a devil, but a cured neurotic is a perfect devil."

Mabel Dodge, convinced of the irresistibility of her own peculiar mixture of wealth and will-power, tried to entice Lawrence to New Mexico through long-distance hypnosis. "Before I went to sleep at night," she later wrote,[2] "I drew myself all in to the core of my being where there is a live, plangent force lying passive—waiting for direc-tion. Becoming entirely that, moving with it, speaking with it, I leaped through space, joining myself to the central core of Lawrence ... 'Come, Lawrence! Come to Taos!' became, in me, Lawrence in Taos. This is not prayer, but command." To make doubly sure, she got her Red Indian friend, Tony (Antonio Luhan), to exercise his magic gifts. He showed little enthusiasm for the operation, but who could with-stand Mabel's persuasion?

But Lawrence still hesitated. At last Frieda suggested a compromise: how about a rendezvous in Ceylon? The Buddha-seekers, Earl Brewster and his wife, were already there and were writing them tempting letters. Lawrence was not at all keen on the idea of Ceylon—"Buddha is so finished and perfected and fulfilled and *vollendet*, and without new possibilities," he wrote to Brewster—but if that was the only way to get away from Europe, why not take it?

They embarked at Naples on 26 February 1922. Their luggage con-sisted of four trunks (one containing nothing but books), two suitcases, two travelling bags, a hatbox, baskets full of apples and oranges and the side panel of a Sicilian cart, decorated with bright paintings of a medieval joust and of St Genevieve. Frieda insisted on dragging this along, in spite of Lawrence's protests.

They stayed seven weeks in Earl Brewster's large bungalow in Ceylon. It lay at the top of a hill, and from the verandah there was a view across the jungle to the lake of Kandy. The first impression was overwhelming. The forest besieged the house, creeping up to within two or three yards of the verandah and filling the air with intoxicating smells and a discordant jangle of screaming, howling and twittering animal noises. It was the hot time of year, and the sky was a white-hot furnace. The slightest movement left one bathed in sweat.

They sat on the verandah, idly watching the lizards and chameleons scampering across the floor, and the birds and tree-lizards in the coconut palms and bread-fruit trees. Frieda, stretched out lazily, was working on a highly coloured piece of embroidery; a Sinhalese servant was fixing a bamboo fence and Lawrence, watching his fluid, graceful movements and the changing expressions of his handsome bearded face, said reflectively: "That man reminds me of my father." All at once a connection was established between the lonely bungalow in a tropical jungle and the miner's home in Eastwood as Lawrence compared the two men, speaking of "the same clean-cut and exuberant spirit". His father, he thought, had also been "a true pagan", a quality which, under the fateful influence of his mother, he had failed to recognise. Bitterly he admitted that his mother had poisoned his soul with her Christian rectitude, and he went on to recall the times when late in the evening, before the miner had returned home, Lydia Lawrence would collect her children round her and speak contemptuously of their father as a drunken sot. How fearfully he and his brothers and sisters would then await the homecoming, as if it were the devil himself and not their father who would appear through the door!

Lawrence had come far since the days when his memories of his father had been coloured by his mother's opinions. Now, watching a Sinhalese servant mending a fence, he remarked that he had not done justice to his father in *Sons and Lovers*, and he felt like re-writing it.[3]

Scarcely a week after their arrival the Prince of Wales paid a visit to the island. Frieda and Lawrence went with the Brewsters to the nocturnal *perahera* staged in his honour, and watched, in the flickering glare of coconut torches, the procession of elephants in their colourful regalia, the dancers with their half-naked bodies hung with jewels, and the fireworks on the lake. The prince sat opposite them, looking frail and nervous.

But Lawrence very quickly tired of Ceylon. "The East is not for me," he wrote to Lady Cynthia Asquith, "the sensuous spiritual voluptuousness, the curious sensitiveness of the naked people, their black, bottomless, hopeless eyes—and the heads of elephants and buffaloes poking out of primeval mud—the queer noise of tall metallic palm trees: *ach!*—altogether the tropics have something of the world before the flood." Incapable of creative work, he spent his time translating the novel *Mastro Don Gesualdo*, by the Sicilian author Giovanni Verga, for his American publisher. Frieda sat opposite him, bent over her embroidery. She found this exotic world fascinating. When Lorenzo bought her a little pile of sapphires, rubies, emeralds and moonstones in a small jeweller's shop in Kandy, she felt as if she were living in a fairy-tale.

The steamy heat made Lawrence ill, and they made up their minds to leave. In the meantime Mabel Dodge had been applying all her efforts of will to the task of spiriting him and Frieda to Taos. He answered her letters and her parcels of necklaces and books with the dry remark: "I still of course mistrust Taos very much, chiefly on account of the artists. I feel I never want to see an artist again while I live." At the end of April they were on their way to Australia.

It was a strange decision, and the only reason for it seems to have been the curiosity aroused in them by the accounts of a young Australian woman whom they had got to know on the ship on their way to Ceylon. Now, once again aboard a steamer, Lawrence wrote to Lady Cynthia: "We are going to Australia—Heaven knows why." A Spanish priest was playing Chopin on the piano, flying fish glistened in the sun. "Don't know what we'll do in Australia, don't care ..."

Australia, when they first caught sight of it, lay beneath a brilliant blue sky. Greyish-white gumtrees stretched out endlessly above low scrub—"like a Sleeping Princess on whom the dust of ages has settled." Would it, Lawrence wondered, ever awake? The lively Australian girl whom they had met on the ship to Ceylon was waiting for them in Fremantle, and she took them to Perth, where Lawrence established his headquarters in the local "Booklover's Library". There he received the local intelligentsia. One woman writer who had read two or three of his books was so overcome by excitement that she gave birth prematurely to a baby. Less than a day after their arrival in Sydney they rented a bungalow on the coast, about forty miles outside the city. The place was called Thirroul and it consisted entirely of bungalows with corrugated-iron roofs. The inhabitants were miners, thus establishing a link with Lawrence's youth. But they knew nobody "within a radius of a thousand miles".

Why this escape into anonymity? It was all Frieda's doing: she was tired of wandering about and wanted a settled home, if only for a few months. If Lorenzo was a storehouse of nervous energy that had constantly to be replenished by new impressions, there was in her, this composed, full-bosomed Valkyrie, an elemental quality of inertia.

She was happy here. She felt as if she and Lawrence were the only people in the world. The sun as it rose over the Pacific was for her "a wonder of the uncreated world". In the geography lessons of her distant schooldays in Germany she had known the Pacific as *Der Grosse oder Stille Ozean*, and she kept repeating the name in a mood of curious excitement. It was June, the middle of the Australian winter, and a coal fire was burning in the grate.

"It is a queer, grey, sad country—empty, and as if it would never be filled," wrote Lawrence to the baroness in Baden-Baden.[4] Whatever Frieda's feelings, he did not really like it here. "It is so raw—so crude. The people are so crude in their feelings—and they only want to be up-to-date in the 'conveniences'—electric light and tramways and things like that. The aristocracy are the people who own big shops— and there is no respect for anything else."

He could of course expect his complaint about the absence of a true aristocracy to be sympathetically received by the well-born widows in the Ludwig-Wilhelm-Stift. To Else Jaffe, the socialist, he wrote however: "This is the most democratic place I have *ever* been in. And the more I see of democracy the more I dislike it. It just brings everything down to the mere vulgar level of wages and prices, electric light and water closets, and nothing else."

What had previously been a snobbish preference for the company of aristocrats hardened in Lawrence, faced with Australian materialism, into an openly undemocratic attitude. He had already, as we may recall, expressed similar views to Bertrand Russell, who had thereupon dubbed him a forerunner of Fascism. Here in Australia his ideas found expression in the novel *Kangaroo*, in which he attempted to deal with the problem of power and leadership. To call it a novel—as Lawrence did— is slightly misleading, for the book is a strange mixture of the epic story and political fantasy, travel impressions and autobiographical reminiscences.

With the exception of the short final chapter, Lawrence wrote the whole four-hundred-page book in Thirroul itself, among the surroundings that provided him with his material, and he completed it in the amazingly short period of six weeks. Contrary to his usual habit, he made no subsequent revisions in the manuscript, which explains the extraordinary freshness and directness of the work, but also some of its most obvious weaknesses: the lack of inner cohesion, the passages of irrelevant material—such as, for example, the biographically interesting but artistically unjustified war reminiscences—and the occasional prolixity. Here, in a remarkably swift transformation process, Lawrence was making use of impressions only just absorbed.

The problem of power had already come up in some of his other books, particularly in *Aaron's Rod*. It was characteristic of Lawrence that in *Kangaroo* he discovered an inner relationship between a man's use of political power and his dominant position in marriage. The book concerns a married couple, the writer Richard Lovat Somers and his non-English wife Harriet (they are of course Lawrence and Frieda), who have just arrived in Australia. The political movement into which Somers allows himself, not entirely willingly, to be drawn is simply one of the author's "thought-adventures", a fantasy of power, projected, without regard to facts, into Australia. It is possible that the inspiration for it came from post-war Italy, for the Diggers, his organisation of conspirators against the existing democratic order, consisting mainly of soldiers returned from the war, is undeniably Fascist in flavour, with its worship of power, its contempt for the civic virtues, its military training and above all its devotion to the idea of a leader.

The leader of this movement is a lawyer, Ben Cooley, who has been given the nickname of "Kangaroo" on account of his massive body and his peculiar manner of walking. He is a man of fanatical integrity, an idealised dictator type—that was in the days before Hitler gave the word "Leader" its criminal associations—and Somers immediately falls under the spell of his prodigious charisma. Basically of course the book is simply a projection of Lawrence's own ideas for setting the world to rights, as manifested in his Utopian dream of Rananim. An interesting feature of *Kangaroo* is that Lawrence made his idealised "leader" a Jew. In this he was probably influenced by the almost legendary figure of Sir John Monash, a Jewish lawyer and engineer who became commander-in-chief of the Australian forces during the First World War. It was certainly from him that Lawrence borrowed the long "Jehovah-like" face, the massive body and the stooping shoulders. For the rest Ben Cooley is an amalgam of Koteliansky and Dr David Eder.

Lawrence could have had no ideological reasons for picking on his two loyal Jewish friends to provide the basis for his superman. Both were passionately opposed to the very idea of dictatorship. Koteliansky had indeed left Russia as a protest against Tsarist autocracy, while the psycho-analyst, Dr Eder, was a socialist and, following the Balfour Declaration, a close associate of the Zionist leader, Dr Chaim Weizmann. In the book, the leader figure fails to achieve his goal and Somers withdraws his support. Nevertheless he (and therefore by inference Lawrence himself) continues to regard the non-democratic solution as the right one. From *Kangaroo* a direct line leads into the blind alley of *The Plumed Serpent*.

The political theme of the book is closely integrated with the second main theme, Lawrence's favourite one of the roles of husband and wife in a marriage. But the connection between the two threads is incomprehensible unless one relates it to the personal issue between Lawrence and Frieda. In the chess game of their marriage they had now reached a position of stalemate. The idea of living their lives separately outside the framework of marriage was to both of them unthinkable—so much so that they did not even threaten each other with this vainest of solutions. But Frieda was bitterly aware that hers was a marriage without a settled home and without children.

The children of her marriage with Ernest Weekley were growing up on the other side of the globe. She tried, laboriously but with little success, to keep in touch with them by affectionate letters, but the affection was one-sided: the wounds caused by the initial separation had not yet healed. The consciousness of her sacrifice continued to strengthen Frieda's resolve to uphold her claims against Lawrence: she was not prepared, and would never be prepared, to subject herself to him entirely, and she insisted on him sharing his interests and his experiences with her absolutely. In *Aaron's Rod*, the novel that preceded *Kangaroo*, Rawdon Lilly and Tanny are again for the main part Lawrence and Frieda. Lilly makes this complaint against her:[5]

> She does nothing really but resist me: my authority, or my influence, or just *me*. At the bottom of her heart she just blindly and persistently opposes me ... She thinks I want her to submit to me. So I do, in a measure natural to our two selves. Somewhere, she ought to submit to me.

And the struggle was still continuing. Its reflection can be seen in *Kangaroo* in the conflict between Harriet and Somers. Harriet is deeply hurt because he will not initiate her into his political activities, and because—for the first time in their married life—he turns away from her whenever matters of an impersonal male nature arise. Somers, whose identity with Lawrence himself is continually emphasised by biographical details, has to acknowledge the justice of her reproaches, and he is seriously worried. His disturbed state of mind finds its way into his dreams, leading to the following highly significant sentences:[6]

Somers knew from his dreams what she was feeling: his dreams of a woman, a woman he loved, something like Harriet, something like his mother, and yet unlike either ... That was how the dream woman put it: he had betrayed her great love, and she must go down desolate into an everlasting hell, denied, and denying him absolutely in return, a sullen, awful soul. The face reminded him of Harriet, and of his mother, and of his sister, and of girls he had known when he was younger.

It was a feeling of guilt that made the picture of his wife merge in Lawrence's mind into the picture of his mother.

16

Mabel Dodge stood with Tony, the Red Indian, on the railway station at Lamy, twenty miles from Santa Fe. They were waiting for the Lawrences to arrive.

She had got her way at last. Every night the millionairess had sent her American soul winging across the ocean, to unite with Lawrence's inner core and force him to come to her in New Mexico.

She had sent Lawrence a telegram: "EXPECTING YOU." It was less a statement than a command. On 4 September 1922 Lawrence and Frieda arrived in San Francisco. They had less than twenty dollars in their pockets. After spending four nights in the Palace Hotel they travelled on towards the voice that bade them come, and they arrived on Lawrence's thirty-seventh birthday.

Mabel Dodge has described their meeting. Although her account as a whole has to be read with a very great deal of caution, the following eye-witness description might be allowed to speak for itself. Lawrence and Frieda had just got off the train in Lamy and were hastening along the platform:

> He was agitated, fussy, distraught, and giggling with nervous grimaces ... Frieda was over-expansive, vociferous, with a kind of forced, false bonhomie, assumed (it felt so to me, at least) to cover her inability to strike just the real right note.

Tony Luhan, her friend, stood by in respectful silence; Mabel, who was not usually at a loss for words, did not feel quite up to the situation, and she led the arrivals straight into the refreshment room. Here everything became clear to her: the vibrations were disturbed— Tony's presence had disconcerted the Lawrences.[1]

> I made out, in the twinkling of an eye, that Frieda immediately saw Tony and me sexually, visualizing our relationship ... In that first moment I saw how her encounters passed through her to Lawrence— how he was keyed to her so that he felt things through her and was obliged to receive life through her, vicariously; but that he was irked

by her vision; that he was impatient at being held back in the sex scale. He did not want to apprehend us so and it made him very nervous, but she was his medium, he must see through her and she had to see life from the sex center. She endorsed or repudiated experience from that angle. She was the mother of orgasm and of the vast, lively mystery of the flesh. But no more. Frieda was complete, but limited. Lawrence, tied to her, was incomplete and limited. Like a lively lamb tied to a solid stake, he frisked and pulled in an agony.

In other, less neurotic words: Mabel felt that Frieda was the wrong partner for Lawrence, and she at once laid claim to him herself.

Can it be possible that it was in that very first instant when we all came together that I sensed Lawrence's plight and that the womb in me roused to reach out to take him? I think so, for I remember thinking: "He is through with that—he needs another kind of force to propel him ... the spirit ..." The womb behind the womb—the significant, extended, and transformed power that succeeds primary sex, that he was ready, long since, to receive from woman. I longed to help him with that—to be used—to be put to his purpose.

By the time they got into the car Frieda was already aware what the American woman was up to. The car had a breakdown on the way and consequently it was very late at night by the time they reached Santa Fe. After a long search Mabel managed to find accommodation for herself and Luhan with friends, and she persuaded Witter Bynner, the American poet who lived in Santa Fe, to give the Lawrences a room for the night in his little house. The car drove into the narrow courtyard, Lawrence got out and struggled to unload the Sicilian cart panel which he and Frieda had dragged from Palermo to Naples, from there to Ceylon, through the length and breadth of Australia and now across to America. As he was wrestling with it, Luhan set the car moving backwards, and the precious painting got caught and split along its whole length. Lawrence threw it to the ground with one of his characteristic explosions of rage. "It's your fault, Frieda! You've made me carry that vile thing round the world, but I'm done with it. Take it, Mr Bynner, keep it, it's yours! Put it out of my sight!" Ignoring him, Frieda smiled radiantly at her unknown host while the Red Indian sat by in stony silence. As Mabel made the introductions, Lawrence shook Witter Bynner heartily by the hand. He seemed completely to have forgotten what had occurred only a moment earlier.

Next morning they continued their journey to Taos. In the clear light of morning they drove north beside the Rio Grande. Indian farm labourers waved to them from the fields of wheat and lucern, and the air was fragrant with the smell of apples and apricots. The narrow road, leading to the Rocky Mountains, rose steeply upwards between the rugged cliffs of a canyon. Tony Luhan, intent over the steering-wheel, drove them across patches of rock debris and around hair-raising bends with a sheer precipice to one side. Then, suddenly, they reached the plateau on top.

Frieda and Lawrence held their breath: the first sight of the Taos valley was overwhelming. The mountains formed a semi-circle, like the dark sides of a huge bowl, and its flat floor—the "desert"—was covered in sage-brush with grey-green leaves and yellow blossoms. In the middle lay the town of Taos, an emerald-green oasis, and behind it the Sacred Mountain of the Indians.

The valley lay quiet and peaceful in the evening sun, but above the Sacred Mountain black clouds were massing with ominous rapidity. Suddenly a flash of lightning lit the dark line of mountains, and in the next moment they were startled by a huge roar of thunder. Tony just had time to put up the top of the car before the heavens opened above them, hurling rain and hailstones with terrifying force against the stationary car. As the storm continued the mild September evening turned into an icy winter's night. It was an inauspicious welcome.

Lawrence and Frieda would have found it unbearable to share a house with Mabel. Quite apart from her forceful personality, there was always a stream of pseudo-artists and writers coming and going. But Mabel had been prudent enough to provide them with a home of their own. It was, as Frieda wrote, "a charming adobe house with Mexican blankets and Indian paintings of Indian dances and animals, clean and full of sun."

Before they even had time to recover their breath Mabel insisted that Lawrence should go to a fiesta in the reservation of the Apache Indians, in the company of Tony Luhan and Bessie Freeman, a friend of her youth. Mabel remained at home with Frieda, since there was no more room in the car. Mrs Freeman was a widow, white-haired and, to Mabel's way of thinking, completely harmless. In other words, she felt there was no danger that Tony Luhan or Lawrence would be enticed away from her. All the thoughts of this energetic millionairess had a sexual flavour: as soon as she met a person, she began gauging his sexual radiations, testing his potency, letting her imagination run on with one inevitable goal in mind—bed. Frieda was often amused and often irritated by Mabel, who was the same age as herself. When Lawrence was absent, they got on quite well together, and in the course of these five days there was no direct clash between them. The American reached down into her rich store of experience to pour over Frieda a flood of intimate mystical and practical detail. She spoke about her life with her first husband, who died early, her two subsequent marriages that had ended in divorce, and her relations with Tony. Frieda, encouraged by her example, said more about her life with Lawrence than was discreet. Mabel cleverly led her on, and afterwards wrote:[1]

> So long as one talked of people and their possibilities from the point of view of sex, she was grand. She had a real understanding of them. But one had to be careful all the time—to hide what was antagonistic to her. The groping, suffering, tragic soul of man was so much filthiness to that healthy creature.

The moment Lawrence returned from his visit to the Apache Indians, Mabel raised with him the possibility of writing a book about New Mexico. It was for this reason that she had employed all the arts of long-distance seduction to get him there. She wanted him to find and give expression to the soul of America—not the false and decadent, meretricious world of Greenwich Village, but the undiscovered soul of native America, the primitive ancient civilisation that lived on beneath the Sacred Mountain "in the bloodstream of the Indians". She suggested he should write a novel in which she herself would be the central figure. She wanted to give him "every part of the untold and undefined experience that lay in me like a shining, indigestible jewel that I was unable either to assimilate or to spew out."

This meant of course that they would have to collaborate on writing the book. Surprisingly Lawrence agreed.

They began at once. Lawrence went to her house in the early morning. Mabel was sunning herself on the flat roof, and she called to him to come up. To reach her, he had to go through her bedroom, which he did, "averting his eyes from the unmade bed as though it was a repulsive sight, though it was not so at all." Mabel went on to remark: "Lawrence, just passing through, turned my room into a brothel. Yes, he did: that's how powerful he was." Mabel was dressed in nothing but a loose cloaklike housecoat, with moccasins on her naked feet.

If Mabel's report is to be trusted (and it very seldom is), a conversation took place on that hot roof in which Lorenzo poured out his heart to her. He complained that Frieda did not understand him and added: "It's the German mind. Now, I have always had a sympathy for the Latin mind—for the quick, subtle, Latin spirit—but the north German psyche is inimical to it." In this hour, Mabel maintained, he came closer to her psychically than any other human being before: it was "a complete, stark approximation of spiritual union".

The goal might have been an unusual one, but the method has been well tried, ever since Eve used it in the Garden of Eden for purposes other than spiritual union. With brutal frankness Mabel later wrote:[2]

> I did not want, particularly, to touch him. There was no natural physical pleasure in contact with him. But I actually awakened in myself, artificially, I suppose, a wish, a wilful wish, to feel him, and I persuaded my flesh and my nerves that I wanted him. I did this because I knew instinctively that the strongest, surest way to the soul is through the flesh. It was his soul I needed for my purpose.

Whatever Mabel was after, Frieda was not prepared to let her have it. Over her rival's attempts to add Lorenzo to her gallery of lovers, Frieda simply smiled. But to surrender his "soul" to Mabel, to stand passively by while she wrote a book with him and usurped Frieda's own role within a creative partnership—that was more than she could tolerate. The storm that burst within the walls of their little house rivalled the thunderclaps that had greeted their arrival in Taos. A state of open war developed between the two women. Mabel, supposedly so sensitive in picking up the vibrations of the soul, told Frieda she didn't think she was the right woman for Lawrence; Frieda, thoroughly roused, exclaimed: "Try it then yourself, living with a genius, see what it is like and how easy it is, take him if you can."[3]

Lawrence exploded when Frieda told him about this conversation. He vowed to break off all relations with Mabel right away, to pay rent for the days in which they had enjoyed her hospitality, and to leave Taos. But the storm blew over, and they stayed.

However, the great American novel dedicated to the Indian bloodstream and the soul of Mabel Dodge was never written.

They stayed because the fascination of New Mexico was more than they could resist. The beauty of the country entranced them. They loved the yellow aspens on the mountains, the scarlet leaves of the wild plum trees, the snow on the mountain peaks, the hot days and the icy nights. As soon as they arrived in Taos, Tony Luhan taught them to ride, using Mexican saddles, and now they could gallop happily on their

Indian ponies, across stubble fields and up mountain slopes, accompanied by Indians or a solitary Mexican, sometimes even by Mabel. One day Apache and Navajo Indians came flocking in from miles around to celebrate the feast of their patron saint, San Geronimo. The chiefs took the statue of the Virgin Mary from the altar of the church and carried it to the *pueblo* through a long alleyway lined with bonfires, while the young men fired their muskets, and traditional battle cries drowned the hymn-singing.

But it was not easy to keep out of the way of the painters and writers who lived in Taos under Mabel's protection. Lawrence and Frieda soon discovered that the indefatigable millionairess was using them as showpieces. On such occasions they tended to behave at their worst: "Take that dirty cigarette out of your mouth!" Lawrence once yelled at her in front of several astounded guests, "And stop sticking out that fat belly of yours!" Whereupon Frieda hissed back: "You'd better stop that talk or I'll tell about *your* things." The guests, appalled or maliciously intrigued, were convinced the marriage was on the point of breaking up. A few minutes later they were astonished to see Frieda and Lawrence walking arm in arm in front of the house, from which they had slipped unseen, contentedly chatting together in the moonlight.

They rode to the Lobo Mountains to visit a lonely ranch which belonged to Mabel's twenty-year-old son, John Evans. It lay only fifteen miles away from Taos, but what bliss to have fifteen miles of mountainous country between them and Mabel and her chattering mob of hangers-on! "Here we must live!" Frieda cried. A few weeks later they moved into an old log-cabin on the neighbouring Del Monte Ranch.

Overcome by the magic of the landscape, Lawrence later wrote:[4]

For a greatness of beauty I have never experienced anything like New Mexico. All those mornings when I went with a hoe along the ditch to the canyon, at the ranch, and stood, in the fierce, proud silence of the Rockies, on their foothills, to look far over the desert to the blue mountains away in Arizona, blue as chalcedony, with the sage-brush desert sweeping grey-blue in between, dotted with the tiny cube-crystals of houses, the vast amphitheatre of lofty, indomitable desert, sweeping round to the ponderous Sangre de Cristo mountains on the east, and coming up flush at the pine-dotted foothills of the Rockies! What splendour!

They were not completely alone. The married couple to whom the ranch belonged lived five minutes away, and there were two Danish painters staying in another small log-cabin. But higher up there was not another house within two hundred miles. They led a primitive and divinely uncomplicated existence. The ranch supplied them with food and the forest provided the firewood, while everything else was brought up from Taos. They went riding with the two Danes, and swam in the hot springs of the Rio Grande valley in the middle of December.

Their financial situation had improved. Royalties and fees came flowing in, and Lawrence was able to send small sums of money to his mother-in-law in Baden-Baden and to Else Jaffe. And on top of that his New York publisher, Thomas Seltzer, had won an important victory. The New York Society for the Suppression of Vice had taken Seltzer to court on a charge of publishing obscene literature. The works which the Society was trying to have banned were Lawrence's *Women in Love*, Arthur Schnitzler's *Casanova's Homecoming* and the anonymous *Diary of a Young Girl*, to which Sigmund Freud had written an introduction. The courageous publisher was, however, completely exonerated. "I do not find anything in these books which may be considered obscene, lewd, lascivious, filthy, indecent or disgusting," said the judge, George W. Simpson. "On the contrary, I find that each of them is a distinct contribution to the literature of the present day."[5]

It was now 1923, and in February of that year they received from John Middleton Murry the news of Katherine Mansfield's death. In the last four years of her life she had exhausted her energies in a despairing attempt to find relief from her sufferings. Finally she had dragged her tuberculosis-ridden body to the Gurdjieff Institute in Fontainebleau. Even in death she still wore the wedding ring with which Ernest Weekley had sealed his marriage with Frieda and which Frieda had given to Katherine as she drove to the registry office with Lorenzo.

After receiving that inexcusable and inhuman letter from Lawrence two years before, Katherine had broken off all contact with him and Frieda. But when, on their journey from Australia to America, they went ashore in New Zealand, Lawrence sent her a picture postcard of Wellington, her birthplace. On it he wrote a single word: "Ricordi". As if by telepathic communion, Katherine thought of him on the very same day: she drew up her will, leaving him one of her books as a token of forgiveness. Now that her cruel pilgrimage had ended, Lawrence wrote to Murry: "It makes me afraid. As if worse were coming. I feel like the Sicilians. They always cry for help from their dead. We shall have to cry to ours: we do cry."

Lawrence had once again become restless. On 19 March he and Frieda slipped secretly through Taos, avoiding Mabel. Arriving in Santa Fe, they called on Witter Bynner, who promised to follow them, together with his friend, the journalist Willard Johnson.

Four days later they were in Mexico City.

17

Frieda was disappointed with her first sight of the Mexican capital. The modern streets reminded her of a *demi-mondaine* putting on a not very convincing show of high breeding. She much preferred the poorer parts of the city. To Lorenzo's indignation she immediately hurried off to the *volador*, the flea market where stolen goods were offered for sale, in the hope of picking up some bargains. In the National Museum they gazed on the state carriage of Emperor Maximilian, that brother of Emperor Francis Joseph of Austria who paid for Napoleon III's dreams of power and his own obstinacy with his life. The sight of the resplendent carriage reminded Frieda of Count Geldern, one of the heroes of her childhood in Metz. The lean and melancholy colonel of the Death's Head Hussars had been a member of Maximilian's staff in Mexico and had returned to Germany after Maximilian's execution by the rebels.[1]

Together with Witter Bynner and Willard Johnson—known to everybody as "Spud"—they went to a bullfight. Lawrence found it sickening: he was disgusted as much by the pleasure the public took in it as by the obscene brutality of the spectacle itself. He jumped up angrily from his seat and flung abuse at the toreadors and the audience, who (luckily for him) did not understand his Spanish. Then, together with Frieda, he fled.

He was irritable and restless, unable to make up his mind. One day he was vowing to leave "this loathsome country", the next he was planning to rent a *hacienda*. An American woman archaeologist invited them to live in her house in Coyoacán, the elegant suburb in which Trotsky was later assassinated. It was a splendid house, built by the *conquistador* Pedro de Alvarado, that lieutenant of Cortéz who subsequently became governor of Guatemala. However, Lawrence disdainfully refused the offer. His roughness towards Frieda reached new heights. In the presence of strangers he yelled at her: "Why do you sit with your legs apart that way? You're just like all the other dirty sluts!" Frieda pretended not to have heard him. Bynner was convinced he had gone out of his mind.

It was all very unfortunate, for they had chosen a particularly favourable time to visit Mexico. A surge of hopefulness was passing through
the country. The series of revolutions and armed revolts between 1910
and 1917 had produced a new and enlightened constitution that was
designed to provide the foundations for a new civilisation. Its inspiration owed nothing to Leningrad and Moscow, nor to any ideological dogma; rather, it was an attempt to express the indigenous spirit
of the Mexican people. The aim was not only social reform and the
elimination of dependence on foreign capital, but also the creation of
an alliance of culture and nationalism. The architect of this cultural
revolution was José Vasconcelos, a philosopher who was also Education
Minister in Obregón's government. In the space of three years, from
1921 to 1924, he transformed the educational system and the cultural
life of Mexico. New schools were built throughout the land, measures
introduced to integrate the Indian population into the cultural development of the nation, and the country was flooded with books printed by
the state (with the somewhat absurd result that the classics of Ancient
Greece and the works of Goethe came into the hands of peasants who
could neither read nor write). Musicians were encouraged to form
orchestras and folk-music groups, revolutionary painters like Diego
Rivera and Alfaro Siqueiros were commissioned to decorate ministerial
buildings with gigantic wall paintings. At the same time Vasconcelos
left the artists to find their own sources of inspiration—in the native
traditions of the pre-Columbian era as well as in modern *avant-garde*
techniques. Mexican artists, he declared, ought not to regard themselves as "intellectual slaves of Europe", yet on the other hand he did
not expect them to reject all European ideas absolutely.

It was a programme, one would have thought, after Lawrence's own
heart. It must surely have raised an echo in him when Vasconcelos
proclaimed the superiority of the artist "who intuitively recognises the
rhythm uniting all elements of the universe". Only persons who were
free of egoistic materialism, the dynamic philosopher-minister declared,
could discover this rhythm.[2]

Obviously Lawrence was anxious to meet this remarkable man whose
thoughts ran parallel to his own and who possessed the power—the
power of which Lawrence had dreamed in *Kangaroo*—of putting them
into effect. Witter Bynner managed to make contact with some influential people, who arranged a meeting. José Vasconcelos invited
Lawrence, Frieda, Bynner, Johnson and two other Americans to have
lunch with him. At the last moment, when the guests were already

assembled, Vasconcelos had to send apologies for his absence: an unexpected crisis had arisen and he was obliged to attend an urgent cabinet meeting. He asked his guests to do him the honour of returning on the following day. All (including Frieda) agreed—all, that is, except Lawrence, who sprang to his feet, his eyes glittering, and cried out: "No, I do not agree!" Furious, he left the room and spent the next ten minutes marching up and down a balcony on the third floor of the Education Ministry, nursing his injured pride. At length Frieda managed to persuade him to leave. The lunch party took place on the following day, but without Lawrence, who had not yet got over the "insult" and stayed away.

His irritation, bordering on hysteria, seems to have had an identifiable cause: he was planning a new novel, the first to be set against an American background. The strangeness of the country both fascinated and awed him. After all, this was not Australia, in whose empty spaces the descendants of British convicts and other immigrants had built up a civilisation that simply copied and caricatured the British way of life. The spirit of Australia he had been able to grasp in the space of a few days; here, however, he was in a land whose mysteries were rooted in many civilisations now past and gone. Even in its decadence it had preserved the violent urges which had led it once to propitiate its ancient gods with streams of blood, and its Christianity was often no more than a thin veneer over a dark pagan interior. Lawrence had not yet penetrated beneath the surface, but he could feel the underlying threat, the presence of a secret he was not yet able to solve.

The excursions they made with Bynner and Johnson at first stuck all too closely to the recommendations in the guide-book. Frieda, looking like a Cleopatra by Rubens, lolled in flower-bedecked, flat-bottomed boats and delightedly sampled hot *pavo con mole*—turkey with a deliciously aromatic dark-brown sauce made of a hundred kinds of chillies and other sharp spices, sesame seeds and, curiously, chocolate. They climbed the pyramids of Teotihuacán and photographed each other like ordinary sightseers. Lawrence spent long periods poring over representations of the god Quetzalcoatl, the plumed serpent, that mysterious being in whom the cunning of a reptile was combined with the boldness of an eagle. The stone effigies inspired him to something larger than just the title of his new novel.

But the well-trodden streets of the tourist industry were not leading him towards the Mexico whose secrets he desired to fathom. He journeyed alone to Guadalajara, and thirty odd miles outside it he found what he was looking for: a Spanish-style house standing in a neglected garden, not far from the shores of the huge silver-grey lake of Chapala. This was before the days when it became an overcrowded cluster of hotels and villas filled with retired business people. Frieda joined him in his new home, while Bynner and Johnson took a room in an inexpensive hotel nearby.

Every morning Lawrence would spend working on his novel, leaning up against a tree on a little wooded peninsula. Before him lay the lake which he had made the centre of his fictional story. Frieda enjoyed swimming in the milky water, until one morning a huge snake suddenly rose up from it just beside her and ruined her pleasure.

They often walked with the two Americans to the village of Chapala, where the white obelisk-shaped twin towers of the church rose high above the pepper trees. At the weekends they enjoyed watching the noisy young people from the town, the *fifi*-boys, who commandeered the pier or danced with their girls to the sound of fiddles and guitars on the *plaza* before the little café, studiously ignored by the young *peons* in their white blouses, broad-brimmed hats and red *serapes* draped over one shoulder. But behind the idyll, the bright colours and the laughter they sensed the constant presence of fear: in Mexico death and the sun are kin. The humid atmosphere was heavy with reports of marauding bands looting and killing, for in those years banditry and politics were inextricably intermingled. Soldiers rode on the roofs of trains, their muskets at the ready, and even the Lawrences had a guard with loaded revolver sleeping beside their bedroom door.

All this was welcome raw material for Lawrence's new novel, in which he was again providing his imaginary figures with the characteristics of real persons. Among these are their two homosexual companions: Witter Bynner stalks through the book under the name of Owen Rhys, while his friend Johnson is Villiers.

In Chapala they learned, to their general amusement, that Mabel Dodge had married her Indian lover. "Why?" asked Lawrence, unable to understand what greater degree of intimacy or other advantage the indefatigable millionairess could expect from the formal sealing of her relationship with Tony Luhan. "Why not?" replied Frieda cheerfully.

At the beginning of July 1923 they left the silver-grey lake and went to New York. The first draft of *The Plumed Serpent* was now done, though it was to take Lawrence another eighteen months to complete the novel in its final form.

The Plumed Serpent contains chapters of breathtaking intensity, such as the description of the bullfight which Lorenzo and Frieda attended in Mexico City, the evocation of the country's glowing colours and the strange beauty of the landscape around the lake of Chapala. The hot breath of violence, concealed and open, is palpably evident between the lines. Whenever Lawrence was drawing directly on his own experience, the power of his writing reaches the heights attained in his best work. Yet beside these there are many, all too many, pages of dubious banality. Taken as a whole, *The Plumed Serpent* is an unsatisfactory book, and there must be a great many readers who have laid it aside in disappointment half-way through. It is fair to hazard a guess that the deficiencies of the novel spring from the same causes as Lawrence's own extreme irritability throughout his stay in Mexico, and his aggressive attitude towards Frieda. There were probably two reasons: first, he might have been becoming uneasily aware, while still working on the book, that his philosophy of power—begun in *Aaron's Rod*, continued in *Kangaroo* and intended to attain its crowning point in *The Plumed Serpent*—had led him up a blind alley; and, secondly, his marriage had reached a point of serious crisis.

The revolution Lawrence envisaged in *Kangaroo* was less a political upheaval than a revolt against the industrialisation and commercialisation of the world. It was a revolution concerned with the pattern and meaning of life. From here the path led straight to the greatest "thought-adventure" of all: the attempt to depict the creation of a new religion, or—to put it more precisely—the resuscitation of an ancient mythology in new clothing. Two years before he first set foot on American soil, Lawrence had already written the following words:[3]

> Americans must take up life where the Red Indian, the Aztec, the Maya, the Incas left it off. Montezuma had other emotions, such as we have not known or admitted. We must start from Montezuma, not from St Francis or St Bernard.

Lawrence was convinced that it was absolutely necessary to return to the ancient gods if Mexico were to be saved—and here Mexico is meant as a symbol for the whole of humanity. (He was in no doubt that mankind needed saving.) The millions of mestizos and creoles were in his eyes a degenerate race of hybrids. The church was inert and lacking in influence, its representations of the crucified saviour satisfying nothing but the community's sadistic tendencies. Only the Indians possessed beauty and sensitivity, but "their black eyes are centre-less, and in them lurk malice and insolence".

196

To this "high plateau of death" comes Kate Leslie, a forty-year-old widow, who feels Europe is lying in a kind of death agony. She is the book's heroine, and she contains a great deal of Frieda's character. The theme of the novel is Kate's struggle for deliverance, and on her the work of the new national leader and founder of a new religion, Don Ramon, is tried out. Through her marriage with Cipriano, the leader's adjutant, she is even received into the innermost circle of the dark gods, for in these two leading figures the old divinities of Mexico are reborn. Don Ramon is Quetzalcoatl, the plumed serpent, the Aztec god who flung himself into a volcano when Christianity came to Mexico and who now, rising like a phoenix from the ashes, returns to earth in the form of a man. His companion Cipriano, an Indian general, is Huitzilopochtli, another of the ancient gods. Both figures are unconvincingly portrayed. Since Lawrence could discover no other leading personality in Mexico, he chose José Vasconcelos as his model for Ramon, and Vasconcelos was uncongenial to him (probably only because of his wounded vanity); besides, he had not even met the man (certainly because of his wounded vanity). The result is a wooden figure who never comes to life.

But it is what happens to Kate that is of particular interest to us. The transformation process, to which she submits only reluctantly, leads to the complete abandonment of her individuality. The slim and supple, dark-skinned Cipriano—in his potent masculinity, a sort of Mexican Pan—takes on the aspect of a "phallic mystery" to which she must unconditionally submit. A pagan wedding ceremony, conducted in the rain by Ramon-Quetzalcoatl, seals her capitulation: kneeling, she kisses Cipriano's feet and soles, and he, proudly taking possession of her, kisses her forehead and breast. From now on he is her absolute lord and master, whom she must obey. And not only that—Lawrence takes his tenet of the husband's supremacy in marriage to the absurd length of making Kate agree to dispense with an orgasm in the sexual act.

Although some critics have begun in recent years to praise the book, it is hard to regard *The Plumed Serpent* as anything else but an aberration. There can be no doubt, however, that it does reflect Lawrence's personal outlook at this period of his life. One is certainly also justified in drawing conclusions from it concerning the development of his own relations with Frieda, and the verdict can only be that his dictatorial ideas on marriage had now assumed an extreme form. Whether this was due to a conscious feeling of superiority or (more probably) to a sense of weakness is immaterial. The important point is that Frieda was not the sort of woman who would be prepared to consent to a complete abandonment of her own individuality. Her subsequent behaviour shows unmistakably that this time something more serious was happening than had arisen in any of their many previous conflicts. Their marriage was truly on the point of collapsing.

The steamer *Orbita* left New York harbour on 28 August 1923 with Frieda on board. She was alone: contrary to his original intentions, Lawrence stayed behind in America.

It was four years since Frieda had seen her children. They were now grown up. Monty was at Oxford, still reserved in his attitude, still the upholder of his father's honour. Elsa too showed little sympathy for the mother who had abandoned her children. Only the youngest, Barbara, now eighteen, had forgiven her (if indeed she had ever harboured a resentment against her, for what the members of her father's family had told her about her mother's "sinfulness" had only served to make her curious). When Frieda and Lorenzo were still in Sicily Barbara had written her mother a charming, chatty letter: "Don't go too near Etna, for Heaven's sake!" She was then living with her Uncle Ted, vicar of Great Maplestead, Essex, and Uncle Ted was none other than Bruce Edward Weekley, who had joined Frieda and Ernest Weekley in matrimony in Freiburg. All the same, Barbara had been prudent enough not to mention in her letter to her mother why she had been banished to the vicarage: at the dangerous age of thirteen she had been dishonourably expelled from St Paul's Girls' School for drawing "erotic nude pictures" and passing them round during the algebra lesson. Frieda, when she at length heard of it, must have reflected wrily that Ernest Weekley was unlucky with his womenfolk. Now, in 1923, Barbara was studying at the famous Slade School of Fine Art in London, and her pictures were being displayed in a gallery.

Frieda did not see her son until some years later but meetings with her daughters and old friends were balm to her heart, filled as it was with bitterness against Lawrence. She stayed some time with Koteliansky and then moved to an old house in Hampstead; on the floor below were Catherine and Donald Carswell with their little son John Patrick, and Catherine's brother, who owned the house, lived on the floor above. Surrounded by friends, she made a comfortable home for herself. John Middleton Murry was living in the vicinity, and he at once came to see her. Uncertain as always, forever analysing himself, he had since

Katherine Mansfield's death been carrying his wounded and bleeding soul about open for all to see. He had sought refuge from grief in his work. He had started a literary magazine, the *Adelphi*, which soon won high acclaim, and he wanted to publish Lawrence's work in it: indeed, as he enthusiastically told Frieda, the real purpose of the magazine was to be Lawrence's mouthpiece.

She felt happy in the reflected glow of Murry's hero-worship. However indignant she might be over Lorenzo's mania for male domination, she was delighted to hear his genius admired. Her enthusiasm for the *Adelphi* project surprised Catherine Carswell, who, though she respected Murry as a literary critic, had serious reserves about his personal qualities, and did not care at all for the intimacy that appeared to be developing between him and Frieda.

When would Lawrence be coming to England to join her, she asked. Frieda's replies were vague, and sometimes the dark hints she threw out gave the impression that she had left him for ever. The truth was that he refused to come to Europe, and insisted that she should return to him in America. But this time she was not prepared to bow to his will. She was no Kate Leslie, finding her happiness in subjecting herself to the despotism of a reincarnated Huitzilopochtli. If Lawrence wanted to be with her, he could come to England. She was grimly resolved not to capitulate in this marital tug-of-war. She had to prove to herself that she was as independent now as she had ever been, that she still possessed the courage of ten years ago and that she was still as free to make her own decisions as she had been on the day she walked out on Ernest Weekley and her children to go to Lawrence. Whatever the future might hold in store, her pride demanded this act of self-confirmation.

She went to Germany to visit her mother in Baden-Baden, hoping to see her sister Else again, too. She did not go alone: Middleton Murry accompanied her. At this time he was friendly with the poet T. S. Eliot, whose marriage was now set on its long and tragic downhill course. Eliot's wife Vivien suffered from severe neurosis, alternating with an addiction to drugs, and her life was finally to end in a condition of hopeless mental derangement. Murry, it appears, had acceded to Eliot's request to consult a specialist in Freiburg about Vivien. He parted from Frieda in Freiburg and went on to Switzerland for a short holiday.

More than twenty years later, long after Lorenzo's death, Frieda gathered up the broken threads of her friendship with Murry and wrote to him from New Mexico. In the ensuing correspondence their thoughts returned to that journey they made together in the autumn of 1923.

John Middleton Murry to Frieda, 27 May 1946:

I continually think about the old times: the pain of them has gone, and only the joy remains. I wish I had understood life then as well as I understand it now; but that's an impossible and childish wish. *Si jeunesse savait, si vieillesse pouvait!* How terribly we hurt one another: how utterly was I bewildered! But I think back, with nothing but love and gratitude, to lovely moments with you ... Those moments of blessedness when I lay beside you fed something in me that had been utterly starved.

Frieda to Murry, 4 June 1946:

I agree with you: why, oh why did we have to go through all those agonies and fights? We were fond of each other, the Lord knows. No blame that I can see—that's how it was. *Guilt* is stupid anyhow!

Murry to Frieda, 4 September 1946:

It's only since I found Mary* that I have entered into my inheritance of love—to the full. The only glimpse I had had of what it meant were those I had with and from you ... Looking back, I think that my shrinking from letting Lorenzo down, though it was a genuine feeling, was merely an excuse. I didn't take what you had to give because I was afraid of love itself. It's like taking a tremendous plunge—into a strange, new world. One has to surrender oneself entirely and absolutely to love—at any rate with a woman like you. And I dimly felt this, and was scared: not of you, but of the new world, the new life.

The correspondence eventually dried up, and it was not until November 1951 that Frieda, now seventy-two, wrote again to her old friend. In his reply, as if driven by an irresistible longing, Murry harked back to the same theme.

Murry to Frieda, 9 December 1951:

Do you sometimes think happily of the times when I was your lover? I often do. You gave me something then that I needed terribly: as it were opened a new world to me. And I sometimes wonder, when I think of that journey of ours to Germany together, and we wanted each other so badly, whether I was not a fool in

---

* Mary Gamble, John Middleton Murry's fourth wife.

feeling (or rather thinking) that it would have been disloyal to Lorenzo. Looking back, it seems only an "idea"—something in my *head*—and that the right and true thing would have been to stay with you, if only for a day or two. Anyway, I felt horribly sad when I left you: and the sadness lasted a long, long while.

Frieda to Murry, 19 December 1951:

Yes, indeed, I often think of our friendship first and later of our intimacy with great satisfaction. In the early days you were a friend and I am quite sure both L. and I never had friends like you and K. Then when there grew a greater intimacy when I stayed at that beastly place of Catherine's it was wonderful. On that journey to Germany I also felt sad but without bitterness because I had a hunch you were fond of me too. There was a lot of good will and understanding between us. It was very free, no *arrière pensée*, no suspicion, no vanity. Maybe it was right that way, after all it was my job to see L. through to the bitter end.[2]

Lawrence had in the meantime been spending several weeks in Los Angeles. Now he was back in Mexico, which fascinated him anew. He even visited Chapala, but here the old magic had fled: he missed Frieda. No one knew better than he that her refusal to return to him was more than a passing whim, something far more serious than the countless quarrels which had strewn the path of their marriage like milestones. This time it was all or nothing.

He received a telegram from her, urging him to come to England. She had sent it only because Murry, Koteliansky and other friends insisted, and she regretted it as soon as it was done. Lawrence complied: the champion of male hegemony in marriage capitulated. At the beginning of December he arrived in London.

Frieda went to the railway station to meet him, accompanied by Murry and Koteliansky. Almost before he got out of the train Lawrence had convinced himself that he had made a mistake; he should have insisted on Frieda returning to him in America. He looked ill and his face had an unnatural greenish pallor. He groaned, and practically the first words he spoke on the railway platform were: "I can't bear it."

That mysterious sixth sense of his, which enabled him to get to the bottom of things with the speed of lightning, detected the easy intimacy between Frieda and Murry within a few minutes—a "chumminess", as he termed it, which could not be left unchallenged.[3] Did he guess how far the intimacy between them had gone? Two months later he wrote a short story, *The Border Line*. Its hero is a British army officer, Alan Anstruther. He is tall and red-headed: in fact he is D.H.L. himself, raised to the stature of a superman. The woman he marries, the daughter of a German baron, is unmistakably Frieda. Anstruther is killed in the war, and his wife marries a second time. The new husband is a journalist with the characteristics of Murry. Lawrence certainly knew how to get his own back: not only does he portray Murry's fictional double as a weakling, ailing, sexually inferior and full of self-pity; but he also brings Anstruther back from the grave to avenge himself. After extinguishing the puny life-flame of his rival, he triumphantly unites with the baron's daughter, more potent even as a ghost than his sickly supplanter.

In this connection Aldous Huxley's later comments are of interest:[4]

Frieda and Lawrence had undoubtedly a profound and passionate love-life. But this did not prevent Frieda from having every now and then affairs with Prussian cavalry officers and Italian peasants, whom she loved for a season without in any way detracting from her love for Lawrence or from her intense devotion to his genius. Lawrence, for his part, was aware of these erotic excursions, got angry about them sometimes, but never made the least effort to break away from her, for he realised his own organic dependence upon her. He felt towards her as a man might feel towards his own liver: the liver may give trouble from time to time, but it remains one of the vital organs absolutely necessary to survival.

Lawrence wrote to Witter Bynner soon after his arrival: "Here I am. London—gloom—yellow air—bad cold—bed—old house—Morris wallpaper—visitors—English voices—tea in old cups—poor D.H.L. perfectly miserable, as if he was in his tomb."

Murry's hopes of interesting him in the *Adelphi* were dashed to the ground within a very few days. Lawrence declared that the magazine's true job was to attack and blow everything up. Murry could not agree: he had, he observed, outlived his nihilistic phase. In that case, Lawrence replied, the whole thing was pointless. Murry should give up the *Adelphi* and come with him to New Mexico to set up Rananim.

The old dream had not yet been abandoned. Lawrence invited his friends to a dinner in the Café Royal, and hired a small and elegant private room for the purpose. This was not at all in character, but he was anxious to show that, whatever they might think, he was not averse to conviviality. The dinner was, however, far more than a mere gesture of friendship: it was the starting point for a new campaign on behalf of

Rananim. Lawrence proved a charming host. For all his thirty-eight years, he still took a youthful pleasure in receiving his guests amid such opulent surroundings. Frieda, swathed in gossamer, radiated warmth and well-being. But the reunion stood under an unlucky star: between the guests there were hidden tensions which began to show through. Lawrence was reckless with the port wine, which did not agree with him. He looked pale and ill when he rose to make his little speech. He had to return to New Mexico, he said, and then he asked each of his guests, one by one, whether he or she would be prepared to go with him and help to found Rananim. He put the question with such urgency that everybody must have felt how important the answers were to him: he expected no less than an expression of faith in himself personally and a commitment to a new way of life. Mary Cannan was the only one who answered the vital question with an honest and outright "No." She added, "I like you, Lawrence, but not so much as all that." All the others promised to join him, but he must have noted by the tone of their replies that they were merely trying to avoid hurting him. Only Dorothy Brett's "Yes" was meant sincerely.

Koteliansky in his drunken exuberance smashed several glasses against the wall. Murry embraced and kissed Lawrence, then said to Catherine Carswell, who was looking rather shocked: "Women can't understand this." She cynically replied: "Maybe. But anyhow, it wasn't a woman who betrayed Jesus with a kiss." Whereupon Murry embraced Lawrence once more and told him: "I *have* betrayed you, old chap. In the past I *have* betrayed you. But never again."

That, at any rate, is how Catherine Carswell describes the famous scene.[3] Murry himself later disputed its accuracy. What he had really said, as far as he could remember, was: "I love you, Lorenzo, but I won't promise not to betray you."

Whatever it was that was said and done, Frieda watched the goings-on with apparent coolness and detachment. In the next moment Lawrence was sick over the table and fainted away.

Frieda's daughters, Elsa and Barbara, came to visit them. The two girls had seen their mother's "seducer" only once before. That had been in their school days, and had been no more than a fleeting glimpse of a man standing some distance away. All they could remember was a lean, restless figure and a dab of red hair. But now they got to know him properly and, chatting with him, felt he was treating them with especial attention and kindness. They were confused and at the same time fascinated. Barbara in particular felt there was something of the superman about him, some elemental quality "like a rock or mountain stream". From this day on she succumbed to his influence. Frieda watched them happily, and the room was filled with the sound of her loud laughter. She knew that her daughters now at last understood why she had felt impelled to leave them for this man. That evening she could feel she had been exonerated and forgiven.

After a few dismal days in Paris they went on to Baden-Baden to visit Frieda's mother among the grey-haired aristocratic ladies. It was now February 1924. Germany had just emerged from the nightmare of inflation, when a single tram journey cost one hundred thousand million marks, and people were still going about in a sort of daze. Lawrence sensed a kind of threat in the air. Prophetically he wrote:[5]

It looks as if the years were wheeling swiftly backwards, no more onwards. Like a spring that is broken and whirls swiftly back, so time seems to be whirling with mysterious swiftness to a sort of death. Whirling to the ghost of the old Middle Ages of Germany, then to the days of the silent forest and the dangerous, lurking barbarians.

They returned to London in a mood of depression. Even Frieda had now had enough of the old world. "I am glad to be going to America again," she wrote. "Except for seeing my children and mother here, it's cold and weary and sad." She had won her great battle with Lawrence when she had forced him to come to Europe—but in later years she realised remorsefully that it had been a mistake.

At the beginning of March they were on their way back to America— and Rananim.

It is unlikely that Lawrence still seriously believed that his ideal community would ever arise. At that unhappy evening in the Café Royal he must have guessed that the embarrassed assent of his friends meant nothing at all, and he was certainly not surprised to see them subsequently falling away one by one. True, Middleton Murry gave the impression up to the very last day that he would be taking part in the venture, but then he too withdrew. Only Dorothy Brett, the painter, was with Lawrence and Frieda when they left.

Such loyal devotion was only to be expected from Dorothy Brett. Lawrence had won her over to Rananim at the very start, when plans were being worked out on Lady Ottoline Morrell's estate during the early days of the war, and she had remained true to the project through all its subsequent phases. Lawrence was her idol, and in her shy admiration for his genius she was prepared to dedicate her whole life to him.

Like Lady Cynthia Asquith and Lady Ottoline, she belonged to the aristocratic section of Lawrence's entourage. Her father was the second Viscount Esher, a remarkable man whose interests spanned practically every aspect of civilised life, from politics to the fine arts and from military science to administration. She grew up in a palatial mansion on the edge of Windsor Park, surrounded by servants and celebrities. Two subsequent kings of England—Edward VIII, afterwards Duke of Windsor, and George VI—were her childhood playmates; Queen Mary supervised her dancing lessons; and Kaiser Wilhelm II conversed with her after a hunt. Such an upbringing would lead one to expect Dorothy and her younger sister, Sylvia, to become typical society ladies. But neither of them were made of common material. Sylvia's literary ambitions became evident when, while still in her teens, she entered a competition organised by a woman's magazine for the best love story. In spite of her lack of expertise and practical experience, she won the first prize of twenty pounds, not least because she had the brilliant idea of making the hero of her sweetly sentimental tale a stutterer of irresistible charm. Since he repeated everything he said two or three times, she had no difficulty in bringing her story to the required length of four thousand words. This success gave her the courage to enter into correspondence with Bernard Shaw and James Barrie, and so charming, beautiful and witty was she that she managed to make lifelong friends of them both. At the age of twenty-four she married Vyner Brooke, the almost legendary white Rajah of Sarawak. As wife of this enlightened autocrat and (as she liked to call herself) "Queen of the Headhunters" she spent the best months of every year in that idyllic part of Borneo, which even today is still unspoilt by the dubious blessings of the tourist trade.[6]

Dorothy, too, went her own unusual way. Hardly had she "come out", with the traditional round of parties and balls and presentation at court, than she cut off her hair, put on trousers and abandoned the drawing-rooms of Mayfair and the aristocratic country houses for the studios and artists' pubs of Chelsea. Inevitably this aristocratic Bohemian was in time "discovered" by Lady Ottoline Morrell. With her large ear-trumpet—for fate had condemned her to deafness, a contributory factor perhaps in her rebelliousness—and her chestnut hair surrounding a face totally devoid of sex appeal, "Brett", as she was generally called, had become almost a part of the furniture in Garsington and Bloomsbury. Now, following the call of Rananim, she gave up the world of Bertrand Russell and Virginia Woolf, Aldous Huxley and Augustus John for a lonely life on an American ranch.

19

A day after their arrival back in Taos, its uncrowned queen, Mabel Evans Dodge Sterne Luhan, herself returned from California. Things started badly. Mabel looked on Dorothy Brett as an interloper, an unwelcome rival for Lawrence's attentions. When Dorothy pointed her huge ear-trumpet towards Lawrence—and that was now its usual direction—the American had the feeling that it was sucking in words that should have been hers alone. She was convinced that the harmless instrument was being used to spy on them all. Brett, in her eyes, was an enemy.

Lawrence and Frieda moved into a two-storied house opposite Mabel's on the other side of a lucern field. Dorothy Brett made her quarters in a studio alongside. "The wide double door faced their house," wrote Mabel Luhan later, "and in it Brett sat all day long, apparently sketching the view of the Truchas Mountains, but in reality watching every move of Lorenzo to and fro between our houses." The presence of this woman artist who had ears (such as they were) for no one but Lawrence drove Mabel into a state of desperation. Soulful conversations with Lorenzo were now out of the question. If Frieda was not there getting in the way, Brett was sure to be in possession, sitting in silent worship at the master's feet. "I wanted to flow along alone with Lawrence," Mabel mourned, "in the sympathy and under-standing we had together. And each of the others, of course, wanted the same thing!"

Lorenzo and Mabel went riding together. Dorothy looked on enviously: although her father had a large racing stable, he had never permitted his daughters to ride. But Mabel's triumph was short-lived, for a few days later she came on Lawrence giving her rival riding lessons. The indefatigable American could soon, however, celebrate a new victory: Lawrence allowed her to trim his beard—and he was sitting in Dorothy's studio at the time. As the red strands of hair fell on to the white towel she had fixed around his neck, she felt a voluptuous sense of power, such as Delilah must have felt when she cut Samson's locks. Lorenzo sat silent, smiling, his eyes "soft and blue like lupins".

Some days afterwards Mabel decided that she herself needed a hair-cut. "I hate the town barber," she wailed. Lawrence pretended not to hear. Quick as lightning Dorothy cried: "I'll do it!" Grim-faced, Mabel sat down in the chair and Brett applied the scissors while Lawrence stood by giving directions. All of a sudden Dorothy snipped a piece off Mabel's ear and stood there, alternately laughing and crying, as the blood ran down her victim's neck. Later Mabel wrote: "She hated me, and she was deaf, and she tried to mutilate my ear! That seemed so interesting that I forgot to be indignant."[1]

Frieda watched the warring rivals with amused lethargy, but Lawrence at length began to find the situation unbearable. The millionairess chose that moment to produce her trump card: she offered to make Lawrence a present of her son's ranch. Lawrence refused. He hated both presents, which carried obligations, and property, which restricted his freedom. But Mabel was not giving in so easily: she offered the ranch to Frieda, who quickly found a way of overcoming Lawrence's objections. She would not accept the ranch as a gift, but "paid" for it with the manuscript of *Sons and Lovers*, which Else Jaffe had recently discovered in her old house in the Isartal and returned. Mabel showed little appreciation of its value: she later handed the priceless handwritten pages over to her psycho-analyst in part-payment for treatment.

Kiowa, as Lawrence and Frieda named the ranch, lay fifteen miles distant from Taos. Eight thousand feet above sea-level, it comprised one hundred and sixty acres of wild woodland on the slopes of the Rocky Mountains. It had three log cabins. The largest one was in such a bad state of repair that Lawrence immediately set to work to restore it, helped by four Indians and a drunken reprobate of a Mexican carpenter. The roofs of the two smaller cabins had also to be repaired. Frieda and Lorenzo settled into the large one, while Dorothy selected the smallest for herself. The third cabin was set aside for occasional use by Mabel and other guests.

After a month of hard work the buildings had been made habitable and weatherproof, and the Indians returned to the valley. The Lawrences remained behind in their remote mountain fastness, together with Brett and five horses. There was a rough cart track that petered out below the ranch, and the nearest road ran two miles downhill past the Del Monte Ranch, where the Hawk family lived. They rode down to it every morning to fetch milk and butter and collect the mail.

Isolated and primitive though it was, the ranch transformed Frieda's life. In all the ten years she had been married to Lawrence she had never possessed anything but the luggage she carried about with her on their wanderings. Now at last she had a home of her own, her own trees and her own animals.

It was not Rananim of course—not by any means. It would need more than three people to form the ideal community of which Lorenzo was always dreaming—quite apart from the fact that Frieda found living with Dorothy Brett anything but attractive. The constant presence of the charmless spinster with her ear-trumpet got on Frieda's nerves, though she did all she could at the beginning to hide her growing irritation. Brett was so selflessly devoted to them, so innocent in her dog-like worship of D.H.L., that it was very hard to be angry with her. She had borrowed a typewriter from Mabel, and now she sat there woodenly and laboriously typing out Lorenzo's manuscripts. Frieda did the cooking, stretching herself out between times on her wide bed in the living-room and smoking one cigarette after another. Most of the work was done, as always, by Lawrence himself. He cut down trees and sawed them up, he made cupboards and shelves, he fixed up the chimney, he baked bread according to methods learned from the Indians, he bottled strawberries picked by Brett, he looked after the horses—and wrote. Down in Taos, in Mabel's oppressive company, he had been unable to jot down even a single thought. Now he sat for hours on end in a clearing among the trees, his thick red fountain-pen flying across the pages.

Occasionally they would ride down to Taos to spend a few hours with Mabel and her clique. One Sunday the Luhans took them in their car to Hotevilla in Arizona, where three thousand people had assembled to watch the famous snake dance of the Hopi Indians. On another occasion they rode across country, through canyons and forests, to the top of the Lobo Mountains.

Then something unexpected and frightening happened. Lawrence coughed and spat, and there on the stone lay a blob of blood-flecked saliva. He cast a dismayed glance at Frieda, who was staring in horror at the ominous red stain. In the afternoon Lawrence felt so wretched that he allowed himself to be persuaded to go to bed. Next day he spat blood again. Without telling him, Frieda sent for the doctor. When the sick man heard what she had done he flew into one of his frenzied rages. He took up an iron ring which he used as an eggcup and flung it at Frieda's head, missing her by only a fraction of an inch. "You *know* I dislike doctors," he cried. "You *know* I wouldn't have him or you wouldn't have sent for him behind my back!"

The doctor came in the evening. After examining Lawrence, he allayed Frieda's anxiety with the words: "Nothing wrong; the lungs are strong. It is just a touch of bronchial trouble—the tubes are sore."

The warning signs were ignored. But Dorothy Brett recalled that the illness of her friend, Katherine Mansfield, had first revealed itself in just the same way—and how terribly it had ended.[2]

Here at the ranch Lawrence completed one of his masterpieces: the long short story *St Mawr*. The beauty and power of this tale—and particularly the descriptions of the scenery in the last part, based on the Kiowa Ranch—have rarely been equalled anywhere in modern English literature. Simple and straightforward as the surface story is, it possesses an underlying ambivalence which is as disturbing as it is overwhelming. Broadening out into almost metaphysical realms, it poses, unspoken, the vital question of our age—the problem of the meaning and value of our civilisation. The bay stallion which gives its name to the story is one of Lawrence's most astounding creations. The horse is an incarnation of the powers of Nature: half Pan, half Lucifer, it symbolises that emotional spontaneity which in Lawrence's mind had been pushed aside, crushed and corrupted by the destructive forces of modern life. St Mawr's opponent is the Australian Rico. Lawrence describes him as a painter, but it is obvious that he represents the sort of artist whom Lawrence despised and saw as a danger. Clever, superficial, good-looking and well-mannered, he is a poseur of the kind Lawrence had encountered often enough in Mabel's entourage.

He had hardly finished writing the story when he again felt the urge to move. It was the beginning of October: the first flurries of snow were signalling the approach of winter and the nights had become bitterly cold. It was time to escape south. Down in Taos they took leave of Mabel, who had just returned from one of her frequent visits to the psycho-analyst. The rules of politeness were observed, but beneath the smooth surface they felt the tensions which the past months had aroused in them, the mistrust and the jealousy, the disappointments and the wounded feelings. Mabel was smarting under a sense of being misunderstood and ungratefully treated. A few days afterwards she wrote to Lawrence, accusing him of being mean and deceitful. It was their last meeting.

Three weeks later the Lawrences and Dorothy Brett were in Oaxaca, south-east of Mexico City. They pushed their way inquisitively through the crowded market-place, its stalls bursting with exotic flowers, fruit and vegetables, bright-coloured *serapes*, earthenware jugs, sandals, basketware and poultry. The women in their wide coloured skirts, the little Zapotec Indians in their white tunics stared at Lawrence's tall lean figure, his pale, red-bearded face, and whispered excitedly *"Cristo! Cristo!"* They had done the same in Mexico City, to Lawrence's great annoyance.

It was warm and sunny, and the town still preserved all of its old primitive charm. Ox-carts rolled heavily through the streets, mule-drawn trams trundled noisily along and parrots screeched among the bougainvillaeas and roses of the luxuriant gardens. But the idyllic air of peacefulness was an illusion. The Lawrences were warned not to go far out of town. They might be robbed of everything they had on, they were told, or even murdered, for there was no clear dividing line between the terrorism of the armed revolutionaries and the violence of the armed bandits. All three of them went to see the ruins of the ancient temple of Mitla. Beside a sacrificial altar that still seemed to smell of blood there was a stone pillar which was said to possess magic powers. If they put their arms round it, the guide told them, he would be able to tell them how long they still had to live. Frieda felt uneasy and refused to consult the oracle, but Lawrence did as he was bid. "Eighteen years," the guide told him. It was a wildly optimistic prophecy.

Frieda and Lawrence had rooms in the house of an Anglican padre, while Brett put up at a little hotel. Frieda was by now thoroughly weary of her and treated her with growing unfriendliness. But, now as before, Dorothy still managed to spend several hours of the day alone with Lawrence. Together they walked to the edge of the town, where they would settle down among the bushes within calling distance of one another, she with her box of paints, he with writing-pad and fountain-pen. He had begun to revise *The Plumed Serpent*, and back in her hotel room she would type out his handwritten pages.

In the end it came to open battle. Lawrence and Dorothy had been spending the evening with some English residents, and Lawrence returned home late. Suddenly all Frieda's pent-up resentment culminated in an outburst of rage: she had had enough of Brett, there was no place in her marriage for a permanent hanger-on. Lorenzo, quickly convinced that she was right, sat down and wrote Dorothy a grim letter, which he sent with the houseboy to her hotel the next morning. Brett was deeply wounded, but she tried to pretend that nothing had happened. She visited the Lawrences in the afternoon at the usual time.

With her soulful gaze she soon won Lorenzo round, but Frieda remained cold and stand-offish. Dorothy did not stay long, and after her departure Frieda exploded again. Lawrence dashed out and caught up with Dorothy. Humble and conciliatory, she agreed to leave Oaxaca and return to the ranch.

On the following morning Frieda herself burst into Dorothy's room and thrust a letter into her hand. Brett read it with growing astonishment. In it Frieda charged her—not with having an affair with Lawrence, but with something almost the very opposite:

> She accuses us, Lawrence and myself, of being like a curate and a spinster; she resents the fact that we do not make love to each other. She says that friendship between man and woman makes only half the curve ...
>
> "But Frieda," I say, "how can I make love to Lawrence when I am your guest; would that not be rather indecent?" She stares at me suspiciously.
>
> "Lawrence says he could not possibly be in love with a woman like you—an asparagus stick!" she answers. I laugh.
>
> "He is none too fat himself," I reply.

The quarrel became so grotesque that it ended in laughter. Some days later Dorothy left for Taos.[3]

Lawrence continued to work on *The Plumed Serpent*, but every day he found writing more difficult. He was ill again and feeling increasingly wretched. The doctor diagnosed malaria, and he was given powerful injections of quinine. An earthquake shook the house in which he was lying and, terrified that the roof might fall on them, they crept under the bed. It was as if the cruel old gods, Quetzalcoatl and Huitzilopochtli, were trying to take revenge on him. Lawrence was convinced that his end was near. "You'll bury me in this cemetery here," he told Frieda bitterly. She bravely attempted to laugh his fears away: "No, no, it's such an ugly cemetery, don't you think of it!"

After recovering slightly, Lawrence had a relapse. Never before had he been as close to death as now. The Mexican doctor washed his hands of him: he was superstitious and wanted nothing to do with foreigners. The only help in their desperate situation came from a handful of English and American mining engineers and their wives who lived nearby. The wife of an English missionary came to bring Lawrence soup and to pray for him. They had already met the missionary himself: he lived in the mountains among the most primitive of the Indian tribes. Frieda wrote about him in her reminiscences: "He didn't look like a missionary but like a soldier. He told me he had been an airman, and there far away in Oaxaca he told me how he was there when Manfred Richthofen was brought down behind the trenches and in the evening at mess one of the officers rose and said: 'Let's drink to our noble and generous enemy.'"[4]

They made up their minds to return to England. Lorenzo's fever had now abated. It was the end of February 1925, and the heat in these arid regions was intense. Lawrence was so weak that it was all they could do to reach Mexico City. On the way there they spent a night in a hotel, and Frieda, herself feverish, broke down. "I cried like a maniac the whole night. And he disliked me for it."

In Mexico City they took a room in the Hotel Imperial and sent for a doctor who had been recommended to them. Dr Uhlfelder examined Lorenzo with German thoroughness and took blood and sputum tests. When, some days later, Frieda returned to the hotel from the town, where she had been doing some shopping, she found the doctor in their room. He looked at her and said, in the presence of the patient, with brutal frankness: "Mr Lawrence has tuberculosis." Lawrence gave her a look which she never forgot for the rest of her life.

The doctor went on to tell them that the illness was far advanced. Frieda replied bravely: "Now we know, we can tackle it. That's nothing. Lots of people have that." But she knew it was Lawrence's death sentence. He had only a year to live, Dr Uhlfelder informed her, or at the most two years. A return to England was out of the question. The climate there would kill him; even the sea journey would make matters worse. What about the ranch near Taos? Yes, that would be ideal: mountain air, pine forests.

Lawrence spent the next three weeks in bed. In letters to his friends he said he was suffering from malaria and influenza: not a word about tuberculosis. In fact he had such a superstitious dread of it that he never once, right up to his death, mentioned his illness by name. When he was able to get up and go out with Frieda for the first time, people looked at his greenish, emaciated face as if he were a ghost. He found their horror-stricken glances unbearable, so Frieda bought some rouge and painted his cheeks. The artificial freshness of his complexion could not, however, get him past the American immigration authorities on their journey back to Taos. In El Paso they were held up for two days because the officials refused to let him enter the United States. "Canaille of the most bottom-doggy order," he called them later in his fury, "and filthy with insolence." An intercession on Lawrence's behalf by the American Embassy in Mexico eventually broke down the medical officer's resistance, but Lawrence never got over the shock caused by this traumatic experience. They were thoroughly exhausted by the time they reached Kiowa Ranch. The woods behind their log cabin were still covered in snow, but in the fireplace a cheerful fire was burning.

Brett, after Frieda had given her to understand that she was no longer wanted at Kiowa, had settled in with the Hawk family on the neighbouring Del Monte Ranch. After three cold and windy days spring came at last, and Lorenzo was able to lie, heavily blanketed, on a camp bed out in the April sun, while Frieda looked after the house. She had two willing Indians to assist her—Trinidad and his wife Rufina, who lived in the second log cabin.

As the days became warmer Lorenzo's zest for life returned. He began to write again, though only an unimportant Biblical drama, *David*. They were homesick for Europe and hoped to make the trip they had originally planned for the spring in the coming autumn.

Like a messenger from home Frieda's nephew arrived for a visit in May. Else Jaffe's son Friedel had been attending one of the American universities as an exchange student. Twenty years later he was to return to the United States as an émigré. This time he brought the freshness of youth, family affection and a touch of German sentiment to the lonely ranch. It was no wonder that Frieda's spirits revived—and that her homesickness was multiplied a hundredfold. They returned to England once more.

"One's native land has a sort of hopeless attraction," wrote Lawrence at the beginning of October, adding sarcastically, "when one is away." In the dismal greyness of foggy London they longed for the sunshine and mountain air of Kiowa Ranch. Not even the reunion with Barbara could lighten their mood. Barbara, now twenty-one, was engaged, and she brought her fiancé to dinner in the hotel. He was fifteen years her senior, an idle, parasitical good-for-nothing, and Frieda and Lorenzo were soon resolved to prevent the marriage.

Nottinghamshire was even more dismal than London, and not only on account of the weather. There were one and a quarter million unemployed in the country, and the industrial parts of the Midlands were particularly hard hit. Lawrence found the people lifeless and disspirited: "My God! this country isn't an isle in the sea, it's under the sea, and the people are all marine specimens ... they're about as active as seaweed." They had come to visit Lawrence's friends and relations. His father had died in the previous year.

They stayed with Ada Clarke, his younger sister, in her new house at Ripley, near Nottingham. Frieda felt out of place and uncomfortable in the conventional household. Ada's hostility towards her was only thinly concealed. She still looked on the German noblewoman as an intruder, a wicked woman who had trapped her much admired brother with her seductive wiles.

Barbara happened to be spending several days in Nottingham at the same time, and she came to visit them in Ada's home. Lawrence had caught another cold—not surprisingly, considering the horrible weather—but this did not stop him sitting up in bed, giving Barby a friendly step-fatherly lecture about her proposed marriage. "He's a cadging dog," he said, dramatically gesturing. "He's a bit inferior somehow. Just shake him off, like a dog shakes off his fleas."

After supper was over, Barby got up to go. The others loudly protested: why shouldn't she stay the night? Barby wavered: she had promised the people with whom she was staying in Nottingham, a university professor and his wife, to be back by evening. She telephoned Nottingham, and the professor's wife, slightly startled, declared she must consult her husband. The professor, in great alarm, refused his permission. The thought of Barbara spending a night under the same roof as Lawrence horrified him. What would he say if he should meet Barbara's father, Professor Weekley, in college? Barby had shame-facedly to tell her mother that she had promised her hosts to return to Nottingham at once. Lawrence, white as a sheet, sprang to his feet, crying furiously: "These mean, dirty little insults your mother has had to put up with all these years!"

With a feeling of profound humiliation Barbara went back to the professor and his wife. However, some good did come out of the visit. Lorenzo's friendly warnings had fallen on fruitful soil: she broke off her engagement.[5]

And how was it with their friends? Catherine and Donald Carswell were "buried alive in a horrid little cottage in damp and dismal Bucks"; Lady Cynthia Asquith, in dire financial straits, had been charitably taken on as secretary by James Barrie; Mark Gertler was in a sanatorium. Koteliansky they did not see at all.

But they could not ignore Middleton Murry, who continued to cling to them like a leech. Murry had married for the second (though not the last) time. His wife, another assistant on his magazine, was Violet de Maistre. They had a baby and Violet, who was frail and delicate, was expecting another. Murry was eager to introduce his wife and baby daughter to Frieda and Lorenzo but, since he was now living in Dorset, his invitation was not enthusiastically received. Murry was hurt, but he came to London by himself to see Lawrence. Frieda does not appear to have been present at this meeting—presumably she thought it wiser to stay out of sight on this occasion—and Murry was not unnaturally disappointed. The whole reunion, as he observed later, was "a little sad and ghostly".[6] What he learned about Taos and Frieda's quarrel with Dorothy Brett seemed to him to prove he had been right in having doubts about the Rananim plan. How would it be if Frieda and Lorenzo were now to settle down near him in Dorset? Lawrence's emphatic rejection of this suggestion hurt him anew, and he would have gone off in a huff if Lawrence had not softened the blow by inviting Murry to visit them in Italy with his whole family.

The visit never in fact took place. Murry did not see Lawrence again. But it was by no means the end of his contact with Frieda.

Why Italy? Why did they not return to New Mexico and Frieda's beloved Kiowa Ranch, for which both of them were homesick? In none of the letters Lawrence wrote, in none of the conversations recorded by his friends in all those volumes of memoirs, was the real reason touched upon, and Frieda herself never spoke of it. But there can be no doubt that it lay in Lorenzo's unacknowledged and all too justifiable fear that the American immigration authorities would refuse him entry. The tuberculosis they neither of them mentioned, the mortal disease he superstitiously strove to overcome by dismissing it from his thoughts— the taboo they both recognised made it impossible for him ever again to tread American soil.

20

Italy seemed to hold out the only hope of bringing Lawrence alive through the winter. But there was Germany to be visited first—their usual stopping-place on their journeys between England and the south. It was more than a mere duty visit: her mother was still a source of strength to Frieda, and she never missed an opportunity of visiting Baden-Baden, where she usually found Else Jaffe too.

In the Ludwig-Wilhelm-Stift Lawrence once again elegantly played the role of the distinguished visitor, bowing with exaggerated polite-ness to the old ladies—"Good morning, Baroness!" "A very good morning to you, Dr Lawrence." "Slept well, your excellency?" Lawrence playfully mimicked the old baroness, for in this little corner of the country the old titles, officially abolished in the Weimar Republic, were still valid currency. Anna von Richthofen had markedly aged since their last visit, and Germany was as grey and dismal, as wintry as England. They hastened off south.

Martin Secker, Lawrence's London publisher, had recommended Spotorno to them: at that time it was hardly more than a fishing village between Genoa and the French border. Below the castle ruins Frieda discovered a pink villa which pleased her. Could it be rented? "Si, signora," was the reply, and a few days later the house-owner came to the little hotel in which they had temporarily taken rooms and intro-duced himself. Angelo Ravagli, lieutenant of the *Bersaglieri*, was dressed in full regalia—plumed helmet, sword, sash, epaulettes and all—for it was the queen's birthday. He was such a splendid, fairy-tale sight that Lawrence immediately fetched Frieda to have a look at him. When he next came, however, the *tenente dei Bersagliere* looked much less imposing. Lawrence had in the meantime rented the Villa Bernarda, the kitchen stove was smoking, and the landlord came to attend to it in workman's overalls. As he worked aloft, Lawrence stood below, catching the soot in a bucket.[1]

"This man would be useful on the ranch," he remarked to Frieda, with a glance at the soot-stained Italian. He little knew how right he was. Ravagli later became Frieda's third husband.

They enjoyed the mild winter sun of the Ligurian coast. They went on long walks, and Lawrence gave Lieutenant Ravagli English lessons when he visited them on Sundays. Frieda tried her hand at painting, and she also translated Lorenzo's play *David* into German. Middleton Murry, who had been expected to join them with his wife and baby, cancelled his visit on the grounds that his wife's precarious health made a long journey inadvisable. Lawrence, convinced that Murry was only making excuses, wrote him a furious letter. Had Murry ever kept to his word? This time, however, Lawrence was being unfair—Violet, a victim of tuberculosis like himself, died shortly after giving birth to her second child. An angry correspondence put an end to the friendship between Lawrence and Murry, leaving nothing but mutual bitterness behind.

At Christmastime Barbara came. After a long battle Ernest Weekley had given her permission to visit her mother, provided that for the sake of decorum she did not stay in Lawrence's house. Barbara obediently rented a room in a boarding-house run by two old English spinsters in nearby Alassio. However, she had inherited her mother's wilfulness and spirit of independence, and after a few days she had had enough of the *pensione*. She moved into the Villa Bernarda. Life with the Lawrences was certainly less boring than in Alassio, as Barbara's own account bears witness:[2]

> The next morning I was awakened by loud bumping noises overhead. I was half prepared for this, as I had heard that the Lawrences threw saucepans or plates at each other. I hurried upstairs to intervene.
>
> Frieda, her neck scratched, was in tears. "He has been horrid," she said with a glare at the glum, pale man sitting on the edge of his bed. She had told him that, now I was with her at last, he was to keep out of our relationship and not interfere. This had infuriated Lawrence. I was exhilarated, rather than shocked.
>
> It soon blew over, but a few days later the sparks flew again when Lawrence, after inveighing bitterly against Frieda, flung his wine in her face. This time I joined in, shouting, "She's too good for you; it's casting pearls before swine!"
>
> After Frieda had gone out of the room in anger, I asked Lawrence, "Do you care for her?"
>
> "It's indecent to ask," he replied. "Look what I've done for your mother! Haven't I just helped her with her rotten painting? ...
>
> "Why does your mother want to be so *important*?" he demanded.

"Why can't she be simple and talk to me naturally, as you do, like a woman?"

But once the storm was over the waves soon quietened down and love and understanding returned—if not always peace and quiet. Barbara soon found life in the Villa Bernarda so exhilarating that she began to take interest again in her own painting. Lawrence made fun of her academic style. "Forget all you learned at the art school," he urged her.

The year 1926 began, and in the middle of January the weather changed. The friendly winter sun gave way to icy rain and Lawrence went down with influenza and bronchial catarrh, which kept him in bed. It could hardly have happened at a worse moment: Elsa, Barbara's elder sister, was on her way to Spotorno and Lawrence's sister Ada was expected at almost the same time, accompanied by her friend, Mrs Booth. Frieda was convinced that Lorenzo had invited them solely in order to provide a counterbalance for the two Weekley girls. Anyway, Elsa and Barbara were booked into a little hotel on the sea-front so that the guestroom would be free for Ada and her companion.

The moment the five women were assembled around Lawrence, the Villa Bernarda turned into a wasps' nest. Frieda had every right to regard the presence of her two daughters as a personal triumph. True, her son Monty held aloof—still disapproving after fourteen years—but the reunion with Elsa and Barbara, of which she had so long been dreaming, had at last been achieved. For Lawrence to fill the house in this glorious hour with allies of his own seemed to Frieda to be a deliberate challenge. What was he trying to do—divide the Villa Bernarda into two enemy camps?

Unlike Barbara, who was always ready to spring with flaming eyes into the fray, Elsa, now almost twenty-three years old, hated family scenes. When she was forced to witness a marital squabble, which was almost unavoidable in the Villa Bernarda, she at once assumed the role of a referee. On one occasion, after the noise of battle had subsided, she noticed that Lawrence's eyes were full of tears. She drew her mother aside and gave her a severe lecture.

As the mutual antagonism grew, Frieda became convinced that Ada was trying to draw Lawrence back into the past—away from her. One evening she went to his room and, after they had talked it over and reached an understanding, Frieda felt that victory was hers. Next morning she had a bitter scene with her sister-in-law. "I hate you from the bottom of my heart," Ada hissed at her. When, in the evening, Frieda went up once again to Lawrence's room, she found his door locked. Ada had the key. "It was the only time he had really hurt me," Frieda recorded many years later. In the end Lawrence took refuge in flight. He went off with Ada, leaving Frieda and her daughters behind.

Lawrence and his sister spent several days in Monte Carlo and Nice, and then Ada returned to England. He journeyed on alone to Capri.

In the circumstances this was certainly a wise decision, and not only because of the island's milder winter climate. He had friends in Capri: first and foremost the Brewsters, with whom he could stay, and Dorothy Brett was there too (he himself had recommended the siren isle to her when she decided to leave New Mexico). So he could be certain that Frieda would not follow him to Capri, since the mere thought of Brett and her horrible ear-trumpet was unbearable to her. As things now were, he considered a temporary separation from Frieda and her two daughters would be the most effective way of restoring his own peace of mind.

Brett was absolutely delighted to see him: she could imagine no greater joy than to have the man she idolised to herself for a few precious weeks. Never mind that their relationship was strictly platonic: she found complete fulfilment in her selfless efforts to serve her god loyally and uncritically. As for Lawrence, it did him good to be so devotedly cared for. Illness and family discord had played havoc with him: he was thinner than ever, and on the walk between the Marina Piccola and Monte Tiberio he had sometimes to stop to regain his breath. Earl and Achsah Brewster were glad to have him as a guest in their villa, even though they were in the middle of preparations for a trip to India, and other friends and acquaintances of all three sexes greeted him like a long-lost honorary resident now repentantly returned. Mary Cannan was there, as well as the Brett Youngs and Faith Compton Mackenzie. Faith was alone, her husband having discovered his own personal Rananim—not in Ceylon or the South Seas, the mountains of New Mexico or the lakelands of Chapala, but in the English Channel. Herm and Jethou, two of the smallest of the Channel Islands, had belonged in 1914 to Count Blücher, who, though a warm Anglophile, had retained his German citizenship. It would clearly not have done to have left islands of potential strategic value in "enemy" hands, and so Blücher was deported and the island of Herm provided with a British garrison. Two years after the war Compton Mackenzie, a great lover of islands, was able to rent Herm, where he had since spent several months of the year in splendid isolation. Faith was happy to accept Lorenzo's invitation to dinner in a restaurant; the wine loosened her tongue, and some years later she and Compton Mackenzie were annoyed to find that Lawrence had used her indiscretions as material for a short story, *The Man Who Loved Islands*.

In the middle of March, his physical and mental strength restored, Lawrence moved back to the mainland with Brett in tow. They went to Ravello, where they ostentatiously occupied separate rooms. After a few days Dorothy was notified that the American entry visa she had applied for was awaiting collection at the British consulate in Naples. She wanted to put off the parting from her idol, but he insisted she should go. With a heavy heart she started on her journey back to the Kiowa Ranch, while he himself went north, to Rome, Perugia, Assisi, Florence and Ravenna.

Meanwhile in the Villa Bernarda harmony prevailed. Frieda had not entirely overcome her anger. She managed to push her resentment of her sister-in-law to the back of her mind, but it never entirely vanished. As for Lawrence, her ill-feeling gradually shrank back to what, in the ups and downs of their relationship, might be called the negative norm. From Capri he sent her a drawing of Jonah confronting the whale, and underneath it he wrote: "Who is going to swallow whom?" She knew it was meant as a conciliatory gesture, but she could not bring herself to laugh.

All the same, these two weeks in which the three of them were alone together were like a gift from heaven. Spring came, and Frieda walked proudly with her two long-legged daughters among the blossoming almond trees and the budding figs, or lay with them in the sun, savouring the sight of their youthful beauty. Barby, armed with palette and brushes, roamed the hills in search of subjects to paint. Ravagli came to flirt with both mother and daughters. These blissful weeks were a wonderful reward for the agony of those many sleepless nights spent vainly crying for her children.

When Lawrence sent news of his imminent return, she was afraid that the precious, hard-earned idyll would now come to an end. Her daughters strove to put heart in her, reminding her, as if they knew all the answers to life's problems: "Now, Mrs L [for so they jokingly called her] be reasonable, you have married him, now you must stick to him."

Before they left for the station they urged her: "Make yourself look nice to meet him!" It was the Saturday before Easter. Lawrence was surprised to see them standing on the platform so ceremoniously clad. "For the moment I am the Easter-lamb," he wrote to his mother-in-law.[3] "When I went away, I was very cross, but one must be able to forget a lot and go on ... Barby has painted one or two quite good pictures. I also feel much better, almost like in the past, only a little bronchitis."

Two and a half weeks later they said farewell to Angelo Ravagli and the Villa Bernarda. They wanted Elsa and Barbara to see Florence before they returned to England. And then what of themselves?

The weather in Florence was miserable, and they could not make up their minds. Lawrence had for some time been toying with the idea of writing a book about the Etruscan tombs in Tuscany and Umbria. Then a happy accident put an end to their indecision. About six miles outside Florence, near the village of Scandicci, they came on an old house. Topped by a small tower, it was part villa, part farmhouse. Frieda fell in love with it on the spot. In the middle of May they moved in.

What did it matter that the Villa Mirenda was rather primitive and that the furnishings of its six rooms left a lot to be desired? Their apartment lay on the top floor and the view from the windows was breathtaking. To the north-west the rivers Greve and Arno wound their way towards the suburbs of Florence through valleys lined with olive groves and vineyards, while dark cypresses, upright as Prussian grenadiers, stood sentinel over them. To the south lay the pine forests of Valicaia, and on clear days one could see the long ridge of the Apennines on the horizon. The rent was so low—three thousand lire a year—that Lawrence took the apartment for a full year. In fact they stayed there two years, and here *Lady Chatterley's Lover* was written.

In that first spring, however, he did little work. The unfavourable reviews of *The Plumed Serpent* had discouraged him. The weather continued cold and wet, but Frieda felt so well in the heart of Tuscany that she even kept putting off her projected visit to Baden-Baden. Within a few days they had made friends with the three families who worked on the farm connected with the Villa Mirenda. Dino, a mischievous lad with the face of an angel, was soon Frieda's particular favourite. When she found out that the boy had suffered since birth from a double rupture, she arranged for him to go into a hospital in Florence, where an operation was successfully performed, and Lawrence paid all the expenses. Giulia, a sixteen-year-old girl, looked after the house: never before had Frieda had such a cheerful and willing assistant. In addition there was Pietro, who came every morning to do the heavy work in the house, to feed the hens, the goats and also Stellina. Stellina was the pony who drew the little cart in which Frieda drove to Scandicci with Pietro.

Once or twice a week they would ride into Florence on the tram: it took only half an hour to the *Duomo*. There they would make straight for Orioli's bookshop on the Lungarno Corsini. Their friendship with Pino Orioli went back a full ten years. They had met him during those harsh war years in Cornwall, and whoever once got to know this remarkable antiquarian remained his friend for life.

Pino—his real name was Giuseppe—was a magnificent teller of anecdotes, and his conversation was so amusing that Frieda put him on a level with Boccaccio. He shared his birthplace, Romagna, with Mussolini—an act of malice, he considered, on the dictator's part. His father had been engaged in a thoroughly patriotic profession: he was a salami manufacturer. Pino himself had worked from the age of fourteen until he was twenty in a barber's shop, but after his military service he decided to seek his fortune in the wide world. He went to London, where he kept his head above water at the start by giving Italian lessons (one of his pupils, as he delighted to tell, had been the murderer Crippen); later he opened a bookshop in Soho. His father had impressed upon him that, if ever he needed a business partner, he should choose a Jew, for then success was assured. Pino followed his advice, but, to his great surprise, he ended his first year as a bookseller with a loss. "What is the good of you being a Jew if you do not make money for us?" he asked his unfortunate partner indignantly.[4]

Pino was a member of the homosexual underground, and his friends included Reggie Turner, Oscar Wilde's crony, as well as Norman Douglas. Since the Maurice Magnus affair, Douglas had been at daggers drawn with Lawrence, but Orioli strove good-naturedly to reconcile them. One day Douglas entered Orioli's stronghold while Frieda and Lawrence were there. The distinguished Scotsman stood rooted to the spot in surprised silence, then the stiff expression faded from his face and, with a charming smile, he held out his snuffbox to Lawrence, saying: "Have a pinch of snuff, dearie!" Friendship was restored— though it would be a mistake to imagine that a reconciliation with Norman Douglas was worth much more than a pinch of snuff.

No paradise was ever so perfect that Lawrence's restlessness would not eventually drive him from it. On 14 July he was again in Baden-Baden with Frieda, but this time there was a family reason for their visit: the seventy-fifth birthday of the baroness. It was celebrated in the Ludwig-Wilhelm-Stift with all the mixture of emotions—sympathy, envy, solidarity—which one would expect, in view of their similar situation, from its aristocratic inmates. "We old people are still here!" declared Frieda's mother triumphantly, provoking her son-in-law to a cynical comment in a letter: "'Wir Alten, wir sind noch hier!' she says. And here they mean to stay, having, through long and uninterrupted experience, become adepts at hanging on to their own lives, and letting anybody else who is fool enough cast bread upon the waters. Baden-Baden is a sort of Holbein *Totentanz*: old, old people tottering their cautious dance of triumph: 'wir sind noch hier: hupf! hupf! hupf!'"[5]

In spite of all that, they remained a further two weeks in Baden-Baden. They were both very fond of the baroness, who was still very lively, and, besides, Else and Nusch and their dependants were also there for the family reunion. After it Frieda and Lorenzo went on to London. They rented a little studio flat in Chelsea for their short stay, and Frieda invited her son, Montague, to visit them there. She was understandably nervous, for the invisible barrier between them had not yet been removed. But her mother's heart yearned for him: it was eight years since she had last seen him, and it was her dearest wish that he should accept not only her, but Lawrence too. When they returned to their apartment at the appointed time, they found Monty waiting for them on the steps. Before they had time to collect themselves, Monty put out a friendly hand to Lawrence, and their shyness and nervousness vanished at once. "This is what I have always longed for," Frieda wrote happily to Koteliansky, "and feel 'Lord, let thy servant depart in peace!!' But not too soon!"

Over forty years afterwards Montague Weekley described how at that first meeting he succumbed to Lawrence's charisma: "Lawrence and Henry Moore are the only men of genius whom I have met. Although, in the course of my life, I have made the acquaintance of many famous writers and artists, there was no other who made such a profound impression on me as Lawrence."

Frieda remained in London, while Lawrence made the first visit of his life to Scotland and then went on to Eastwood.

Could he have known that this would be his final farewell to the surroundings of his childhood? It was a gloomy leave-taking: the General Strike was over, but the miners were continuing the fight. The entries to the shafts were guarded by pickets and policemen, the huge pulleys of the pithead gear were still, and in Eastwood the miners were sitting idly in front of their houses, staring into space. Their wives were bitter and rebellious: they had nothing to give their children except bread, margarine and potatoes.

With William Hopkin, his childhood friend, he walked over the fields to Felley Dam, from which he could see across to Haggs Farm, the former home of Jessie Chambers, whom he had called Miriam in *Sons and Lovers* and whose love for him—like so much else—had been destroyed by his mother. Hopkin sat down at the edge of the reservoir and left his friend to his own thoughts. When he looked round after a while, Lawrence was still standing in the same place, motionless, and his face was contorted as if in deep pain. They walked back in silence. Then, suddenly, Lawrence began to speak—confused, fantastic, witty nonsense. They passed the house in which the Lawrence family had once lived, and he walked by without so much as a glance. As they parted, Hopkin asked him when he would come to Eastwood again. "Never!" Lawrence replied. "I hate the damned place!" He had often before vowed never again to return to Eastwood. But this time he kept his word.

And then it was time to say farewell to London. Catherine Carswell expressed concern about his appearance, but he reassured her: "It's nothing serious, not lungs, you know, only bronchials—tiresome enough, but nothing to worry about, except that I *must* try not to catch colds."

21

At the beginning of October 1926 they were back in Scandicci. The wine harvest was over and the Villa Mirenda was filled with the sour smell of grapes lying crushed in the huge vats. It was sunny and warm, wild strawberries were ripening in the woods and St Francis's fellow-countrymen were busy shooting down the little singing birds. Lorenzo worked on *Lady Chatterley*. He loved writing in the open air, but sometimes he would take his writing-pad and climb up the narrow stairs to the little room in the tower, through whose unglazed arched windows he could see the wooded hills and the towers and cupolas of Florence. Between times he painted "miles of window frames, acres of doors," and piled up firewood for the winter evenings.

At Christmas, Frieda decorated a large tree and all the workers at the farm were invited in to see it: they had no less than twenty-seven guests. It was an idyllic life of the kind that Frieda loved. She had a "peasant complex", and even when she was living in town she would strive to create an atmosphere of country life by dressing in some sort of national costume: what country or what quirk of her own imagination lay behind it was of no importance at all.

They had only a few visitors, among them the Aldingtons, friends since those distant pre-war days when Imagists and Vorticists fought their curious battles. Richard Aldington, always helpful and reliable, later wrote one of the best biographies of Lawrence.

Aldous Huxley came with his wife, driving up the bumpy cart-track to the Villa Mirenda in their gleaming new car. It was not of course their first meeting: during the war years Lawrence had once spent a grey winter afternoon trying to persuade him to join the Rananim venture. That meeting had taken place under the aegis of Lady Ottoline Morrell, by whose magnetic personality the young Oxford student had inevitably been drawn. It could scarcely have been otherwise, for how could a member of one of the foremost intellectual dynasties in England have escaped the attention of the mistress of Garsington? Aldous was the grandson of the zoologist Thomas H. Huxley, Darwin's great champion, and son of a much-respected man of letters; on his mother's side he was related to the poet Matthew Arnold; the eminent biologist, Sir Julian Huxley, is his brother.

Aldous was still a schoolboy in Eton when he was stricken with an inflammation of the cornea which robbed him of his sight for a number of years. He learned to read Braille and to work a typewriter, and with its help he wrote his first novel at the age of eighteen. Before he was able to read it with his own eyes the typescript had been lost, but all the same the improvement in his sight enabled him to study at Oxford, and news of his academic brilliance spread throughout all the university's colleges. It also reached the ears of Lady Ottoline in her insatiable search for conquests. After the war he attempted in his novel *Crome Yellow* to reproduce and satirise the eccentric atmosphere of Garsington, and the book brought him fame overnight. His dry analytical style, full of wit but lacking in emotion, seems more suited to the essay form than to imaginative fiction, but all the same it was his novels that took the English post-war generation by storm. With his tall lanky figure and his narrow don's face, its intellectuality magnified by the thick lenses of his spectacles, he seemed to be the living embodiment of a youthful generation which enjoyed seeing itself portrayed in the characters of his books. At cocktail parties, which had now become the rage in London, one had only to mention Huxley's name to be identified at once as a member of the *avant-garde*, as one of these knowledgeable and disillusioned young people who allowed themselves to be carried along aimlessly by the prevailing currents. At this time Huxley still carried his encyclopaedic knowledge with sophisticated nonchalance, his aloof clarity and his almost snobbish aesthetic feeling still had the power to captivate as he cynically analysed the weaknesses and stupidities of his contemporaries. The macabre humour and pessimistic Utopianism of his *Brave New World* and the final flight into mysticism and mescalin still lay in the future.

Those days spent under the wing of Lady Ottoline had been important to him for other reasons as well. At Garsington he had got to know a young Belgian war refugee, a charming, blue-eyed girl named Maria Nys, who after the war became his wife.* Now, together with Maria, this member of the intellectual aristocracy had come to visit the miner's son.

They arrived from Cortina d'Ampezzo, where they rented a house. Thus began a friendship which the Huxleys and Frieda kept up even

* His brother, Sir Julian Huxley, also met his wife, Juliette, at Garsington.

after Lawrence's death. But friendship had not been the only reason for Huxley's visit. He had just brought out a volume of short stories, in one of which he drew a satirical portrait of Lawrence.[1] Lawrence, of course, was not all that difficult to caricature, and, having used the same method so often himself, Lorenzo was in no position to complain because someone had paid him back in his own coin. But the story had in fact been written some years earlier, and since then Huxley had learnt to view Lawrence's books with different eyes. Brought up in the Huxley tradition of rationalism, he had been trying to combat social prejudice with purely intellectual arguments, and he had now been forced to recognise that he was a prisoner of his intellect, hopelessly entangled in the conflict between sensuality and asceticism. He came to Scandicci in the hope that Lawrence's "blood-consciousness" might provide the key to release him from his inhibitions.

Two years later his novel *Point Counter Point* impressively demonstrated the profound effect of Lawrence's ideas on him. Beside an ironic and clear-sighted portrait of Middleton Murry he had placed, in the figure of Rampion, another portrait of Lorenzo, but this time one drawn with sympathetic understanding. After Lawrence's death he collected the letters of his friend and published them with a long introduction which remains to this day the finest and profoundest testimony to Lawrence's greatness and humanity.

In their house in Cortina Maria Huxley had come across four untouched canvases. She brought them with her and presented them to Lawrence, who at once reached for the brushes and paints which he and Frieda had been using to decorate their furniture. Lawrence had, as we already know, taken lessons in drawing in his youth, but his urge to express himself in visual terms had been confined at that time merely to copying the landscapes of Corot and Brangwyn. Since then he had occasionally dashed off a sketch or so in colour, but it was this chance meeting with Maria Huxley that first seriously revived in him the urge to give expression to his creative energies and ideas in terms of colour and form. Seriously as he now began to take his pictures, it is difficult to grant Lawrence more than a certain amateurish measure of artistic talent. Yet his pictures have a recognisable style of their own. Almost every female nude that he painted was an idealised version of Frieda, just as every male nude was a no less idealised version of himself. As expressions of a philosophy of life these pictures have a definite documentary interest. Three years later they were dramatically to engage the attentions of the police. That Lawrence reckoned with this possibility from the start is evident from the sentences he wrote in a letter dated 27 February 1927:

> I paint no picture that won't shock people's castrated social spirituality. I do this out of positive belief that the phallus is a great sacred image, it represents a deep, deep life which has been denied in us, and still is denied.

Huxley has himself described what Lawrence was to him in these days of budding friendship. In the introduction to Lawrence's collected letters he wrote:

> To be with Lawrence was a kind of adventure, a voyage of discovery into newness and otherness ... He looked at things with the eyes, so it seemed, of a man who had been at the brink of death and to whom, as he emerges from the darkness, the world reveals itself as unfathomably beautiful and mysterious ... Wherever he looked, he saw more than a human being ought to see; saw more and therefore loved and hated more.

In March 1927 Frieda went once more to Baden-Baden, while Lorenzo joined his American friend, Earl Brewster, now returned from India, in a long-projected visit to the Etruscan tombs in Cerveteri, Tarquinia, Grosseto and Volterra. Hardly were they back in the Villa Mirenda when Barbara arrived for a three weeks' holiday. In the evenings they sat together in the whitewashed living-room, with logs crackling in the stove and an oil-lamp throwing out circles of warm and cosy light. Frieda would sit down at the hired piano and all three of them would sing Hebridean folksongs.

One of Lawrence's recent paintings hung on the wall. Barbara, the art student, examined it with critical eyes, finding it lacking in technique, but full of a mysterious vitality. Fired by Lorenzo's example, Frieda also tried her hand at painting. Barbara took a picture of hers—depicting hens in a yard—back to England and hung it over the mantelpiece at home, where her father saw it. "I like that," Ernest Weekley declared. "Who painted this picture?" His daughter replied evasively: "Oh, I don't know—somebody—I forget who."[2]

And then there occurred a curious episode, which assumes significance only in the light of later events. Angelo Ravagli, their former landlord in the Villa Bernarda, came one day to visit them. Since they had left his house in Spotorno the lively *Bersaglieri* officer had been

230

transferred to Gradisca and promoted to captain. The Lawrences had already seen him again some weeks earlier: on that occasion he had informed them by telegram that he would be in Florence on duty, and they met in a restaurant to celebrate the reunion over an enjoyable meal.

This time, however, Capitano Ravagli dropped into the Villa Mirenda unannounced, and Lorenzo's suspicions were at once aroused. He had the feeling that Ravagli had come only on Frieda's account, and took his explanation that he was again in Florence on official duty as a clumsy fabrication. His mistrust was dispelled only when Ravagli showed him a piece of paper ordering him to Florence to give evidence at a court martial.

It was the end of June and a heat haze lay over the Arno valley. The Huxleys had moved from Cortina to Forte dei Marmi on the Ligurian coast, and Frieda and Lorenzo spent a couple of days with them. They found the place "beastly", although it was only a few miles south of Fiascherino, that village of happy pre-war memory. Now they were back again in the Villa Mirenda. Lawrence had been picking peaches in the garden and had come indoors with a full basket. Suddenly Frieda heard a terrible cry from his room, uttered in a gurgling, half-suffocated voice. She rushed to his room and found him lying on the bed. Blood was flowing from his mouth, and he looked at her with panic-stricken eyes. Terrified, she took his head in her hands and urged him to lie quite still, but the trickle of blood continued to flow out between his lips. A doctor came from Florence and prescribed coagulen and mountain air. Giulia, the maid, went into Scandicci at four o'clock in the morning to fetch ice, wrapped in a scarf and packed in sawdust. The Huxleys, deeply concerned, hurried over from Forte dei Marmi, and Pino Orioli and other friends visited the sick man. "It's nothing to worry about," Lawrence wrote reassuringly to England; "only one must lie in bed when they [haemorrhages] come on." The terrible word tuberculosis was not mentioned—never, never.

After some weeks he had regained sufficient strength to undertake the journey to Carinthia in Austria. In the previous month it had looked as if the whole of Austria was going up in flames. Some members of the Fascist *Heimwehr* organisation had shot and killed a child and a disabled ex-serviceman at a socialist meeting. Charged with murder, they had been acquitted, and this strange verdict led to a gigantic demonstration of protest in Vienna. The law-court building was stormed and set on fire, and the police fired into the unarmed crowd, killing eighty-eight demonstrators. Austria stood on the brink of civil war. However, though not yet three weeks had elapsed, the Gasthof Fischer in Villach, in which Frieda and Lawrence had taken rooms, was full of care-free holidaymakers from Vienna, men in *Lederhosen* and women in *Dirndl* frocks. Nobody had any money, most of the banks were shut down, and the shop windows had nothing but a few shabby goods to show. It was a typically Austrian approach: fight during the day and amuse yourself in the evening—the situation, as a famous Austrian war communiqué is supposed to have said, was hopeless, but not serious.

Frieda's sister Johanna, who was still always addressed as Nusch, was spending her holidays at a hotel on the Ossiacher lake, about six miles away. She had divorced her good-for-nothing gambler of a husband four years before and had recently married a respectable banker from Berlin, Emil Krug. He was ten years older than Nusch, and he bored her. Lawrence was convinced that the switch of husbands had been a mistake. As a woman of the world, he declared, she should have stayed in the *demi-monde*. Frieda spent her birthday with her sister at the lake, while Lawrence, who was not allowed to swim or take long walks, remained behind in Villach. His cough bothered him, but he enjoyed sitting on a bench on the banks of the Drau, watching the fast-flowing river glide by.

At the end of August they went to Munich to meet Else Jaffe, who took them on to her country cottage in Irschenhausen. It was still the same friendly little Swiss chalet in which they had lived fourteen years before, and everything seemed unchanged, except that the trees on the other side of the sloping meadow had grown taller. The house was still Edgar's in spirit, though he had now been dead for six years: Else had altered nothing. Edgar's Dürer etchings still hung on the walls, the old Persian carpets still covered the floorboards and even Anna, his maid-servant, was still there. A few days after their arrival Johanna came to join them. While the three sisters endlessly chattered and gossiped, Lawrence would look on in amusement from a corner of the room or go walking through the meadows full of autumn crocuses. Sometimes, too, he would indulge in a little flirtation with Nusch, of whom he was very fond.

A little later on Else Jaffe sent them a friend of hers from Munich, Franz Schoenberner. He had long been a warm admirer of Lawrence's work and was eager to get to know him and Frieda. Schoenberner, the son of a Protestant pastor, represented the best side of the artistic coterie in Schwabing. Service during the First World War had cured him entirely of the rabid militarism that remained alive in so many of his Bavarian compatriots right up to the next war, but he was far more than just a vociferous advocate of the policy of live and let live. Schoenberner was one of the leaders of an independent intellectual movement in Munich: he was bound to no political party, but was an unflinching opponent of all forms of hypocritical servility and obscurantism. Since 1926 he had been editor of the Munich weekly *Jugend* (Youth), a lively and influential periodical which lent its name to the artistic movement known in France and England as *art nouveau*: in Germany it is called *Jugendstil*. One of Schoenberner's aims in coming to Irschenhausen was to persuade Lawrence to contribute to *Jugend*. Two years later he was to become editor of *Simplizissimus*, the periodical that strove with its sardonic wit to keep Germany on an even keel in a period when it was becoming increasingly vulnerable to the insanity of Hitler. In 1933, his spirit unbroken, he emigrated—first to France and then to America.

The meeting with Lawrence impressed itself permanently on his memory. Seventeen years after his visit to Irschenhausen he wrote:[3]

> It was the first time I had shared the afternoon of a faun, a sick faun who out of sheer friendliness had left his mysterious woods, adapting himself for some hours in manner and appearance to the usual human pattern; but one felt him likely to disappear at any moment with a light caper over the tea table and through the window, to return to the company of other goat-footed half gods waiting for him behind the next bushes.

In spite of this mythological flight of fancy Schoenberner was sufficiently concerned by the unmistakable signs of tuberculosis in Lawrence's countenance to beg him most urgently to submit to an examination by his friend, Dr Hans Carossa.

Carossa was not only one of the leading lung specialists in Munich, he was far more: a poet and short-story writer. This combination of talents overcame Lorenzo's usual resistance to medical examinations. "If a poet who is a doctor can't tell me what to do with myself, then who can?" he asked.

Schoenberner lost no time in getting Carossa to Irschenhausen. The doctor-poet examined the poet-patient, then quietly and reassuringly discussed with him the advantages of various kinds of treatment. Lawrence decided that Carossa's face, with its soft and gentle eyes, looked "mild, like mashed potatoes", and he reported to Else Jaffe: "He listened to my lung passages, he could not hear my lungs, thinks they must be healed, only the bronchi, and doctors are not interested in bronchi."

On the way to the station, Schoenberner asked the doctor for his true opinion. Carossa hesitated a moment, then said: "An average man with those lungs would have died long ago. But with a real artist no normal prognosis is ever sure. There are other forces involved. Maybe Lawrence can live two or even three years more. But no medical treatment can really save him."

Carossa was to be proved tragically right.

Yet another doctor who was also a writer paid Lawrence and Frieda a visit. Dr Max Mohr lived with his wife and daughter not far away in Tegernsee. D.H.L. had been his idol even before he met him personally. Mohr had an open boyish face that made him appear even younger than his thirty-six years, and he was an indefatigable, though harmless practical joker. Several of his plays enjoyed a success on the stage, and he also published a number of novels. Four years after his visit to Irschenhausen he brought out his novel, *Die Freundschaft von Ladiz*, in which Lawrence is the central figure.

Mohr was immediately accepted by Frieda and Lorenzo, and he proved to be a true and loyal friend. In later years the debasement of Germany was to become his own personal tragedy. Two years after Hitler came to power, Mohr said to his wife: "Let me go away. I cannot go on living in the Third Reich—it is like being in hell." He was neither a Jew nor a socialist but, like Schoenberner (and unlike Carossa), he preferred exile to life in Nazi Germany. He arrived in Shanghai with only ten dollars in his pocket. Hitler's war was still in progress when he was smitten in China with one of the diseases he was trying to cure, and died of it.

September was now nearing its end and the cold dampness was beginning to affect Lawrence's lungs. "Sometimes it pours with rain," he wrote to Pino Orioli, "and then we feel like two lonely pale fishes at the bottom of a dark sea."

Back in the Villa Mirenda, Lawrence finally completed *Lady Chatterley's Lover* at the beginning of January 1928.

He had completely rewritten it twice since he first began work on it in October 1926. At that time, as we recall, he had just returned to Tuscany from England. After his last melancholy visit to Eastwood he again set a novel in the surroundings of his youth—for the first time since *Women in Love*. Once more he conjured up the bewitching beauty of the Sherwood Forest in the springtime, with its silent trees, its golden crocuses and its tender anemones "bobbing their naked white shoulders over crinoline skirts of green". But he also did not forget the mining village, disfiguring the countryside like a carbuncle:

> ... the blackened brick dwellings, the black slate roofs glistening their sharp edges, the mud black with coal-dust, the pavements wet and black. It was as if dismalness had soaked through and through everything. The utter negation of natural beauty, the utter negation of the gladness of life, the utter absence of the instinct for shapely beauty which every bird and beast has, the utter death of the human intuitive faculty was appalling ...

The destruction of the natural environment was accompanied by the annihilation of everything that makes life worth living, and it was Lawrence's passionate conviction that this happened everywhere when industrial civilisation mechanised and commercialised life and estranged it from its natural sources of strength. In the introduction to his book of poems, *Pansies*, he later wrote:

> We all have our roots in earth. And it is our roots that now need a little attention, need the hard soil eased away from them, and softened so that a little fresh air can come to them, and they can breathe. For by pretending to have no roots, we have trodden the earth so hard over them that they are starving and stifling below the soil. We have roots; and our roots are in the sensual, instinctive, and intuitive body, and it is here we need fresh air of open consciousness.

Clifford Chatterley, the aristocratic mineowner of the novel, is the living embodiment of this mechanised and castrated civilisation, robbed of all its natural instincts and intuitions. His return from the war as an impotent wreck of a man only serves to emphasise, in an almost unnecessarily drastic way, the fact that even before his physical paralysis he had been spiritually paralysed, devoid of any sort of creative energy. But his injury has deprived Connie (Lady Chatterley) of her sexual partner. What marriage now has to offer her is mere co-existence with a man, but no physical relationship, no fulfilment of her life as a woman. Her roots, starving and stifled, are threatened with extinction.

All the great words, it seemed to Connie, were cancelled for her generation: love, joy, happiness, home, father, mother, husband, all these great dynamic words were half dead now, and dying from day to day. Home was a place you lived in, love was a thing you didn't fool yourself about, joy was a word you applied to a good Charleston, happiness was a term of hypocrisy used to bluff other people, a father was an individual who enjoyed his own existence, a husband was a man you lived with and kept going in spirits. As for sex, the last of the great words, it was just a cocktail term for an excitement that bucked you up for a while, then left you more raggy than ever.

In *Lady Chatterley's Lover* Lawrence was no longer concerned, as in *Aaron's Rod*, *Kangaroo* and *The Plumed Serpent*, with the problems of power. The new novel was to be his warning against the fatal consequences which, he passionately believed, flowed from the twin evils of industrialism and intellectualism: the destruction of man's vitality and the numbing of his creative spontaneity and sensual awareness. The cure which he prescribed was a return to fundamentals in the relationship of men, both to each other and to the universe, a revitalisation of the natural instincts and the "phallic consciousness" which puritanism and the hegemony of the intellect had stifled. He proclaimed "the phallic consciousness versus the mental-spiritual consciousness," leaving no doubt on which side he stood, and insisted that "the two things must be reconciled in us." The taboos and hypocrisies which falsified and besmirched sex must be swept away. "The result of taboo is insanity. And insanity, especially mob-insanity, mass-insanity, is the fearful danger that threatens our civilisation," he wrote with startling foresight in the preface to *Pansies*.

In *Lady Chatterley's Lover* Lawrence raises the banner of freedom in his crusade for the liberation of sex from falsehood, prudery and the fears and repressions of a puritan tradition. He is protesting against the defilement and debasement of physical love by an unnatural prurience. "Whoever the God was that made us, he made us complete. He didn't stop at the navel and leave the rest to the devil." So, with this thought in mind, Lawrence set out to write the Song of Songs of physical love.

None of his other novels is in outline so clear and simple, and in none of them does the writer's basic purpose lie so close to the surface. Connie seeks refuge from her torturing sexual frustrations in a short and unsatisfactory love affair with a young writer. Her husband wants a son and heir, and she is revolted by his cold-blooded proposal that she should become pregnant by another man. "But you do agree with me, don't you, that the casual sex thing is nothing compared to the long life lived together? After all, do these temporary excitements matter?" Soon after this conversation she meets Oliver Mellors, her husband's gamekeeper, who lives in a wooden hut on the estate. Because of his disappointing experiences with women, Mellors, the son of a coal-miner, has become a misanthropist, preferring a lonely existence in the woods to a life in a community. Connie is attracted by him and finds with him both the sexual happiness which her marriage has denied her and the fulfilment of her personality. At the end of the book she is expecting a child by him, and she leaves her husband and the social class to which she belongs, itself as sterile as Clifford, in order to live with the man she loves.

Lady Chatterley finds fulfilment with a man who is socially her inferior: the recurring theme in Lawrence's work, and clearly a reflection of his own marital situation. Lawrence, like Mellors, was the son of a coalminer, and Frieda was of noble birth and had, like Connie at the end of the book, given up the comfortable security of her home. It was "blood-consciousness" that had led her to Lawrence and brought about her own awakening, and she in turn had liberated him from many of his puritan inhibitions. The ecstatic descriptions, almost religious in tone, of the sexual act, which occupy a large part of the novel, are a panegyric on the physical satisfaction he himself had found in his marriage. Lawrence had originally considered calling the novel *Tenderness*—and it is beyond dispute that it reflects much of the tender-ness of his own relationship with Frieda. Since writing *The Plumed Serpent* his outlook had been transformed in a remarkable way. He no longer demanded the complete subjection of the woman to the man's will, a one-sided surrender of identity within the sexual union. Both Connie and Mellors find complete fulfilment in their love: it is not only she who "loses herself", but he too. Since those days in Mexico when his marriage was heading towards disaster, Lawrence—if Mellors can be taken to reflect the writer's own attitude—appears to have gone far towards overcoming his fears of losing his own identity. The ideal is no longer subjection and the exercise of power, but reciprocal tenderness.

What was the reason for this change in Lawrence's most intimate feelings towards Frieda? Had he realised that his ideas concerning the woman's role in marriage were leading him in the wrong direction? Certainly after completing *Lady Chatterley's Lover* he admitted that he no longer held to the attitudes expressed in *The Plumed Serpent*. Was it fear of his marriage breaking up (a fear, as we now know, which was well-founded)? Or was it the fact, later revealed by Frieda, that towards the end of 1926 he had become sexually impotent? Whatever the reasons, his change of attitude finds clear expression in his final novel.

Just as the gamekeeper Mellors is Lawrence himself—or at least a figure in whom Lawrence liked to see himself—so too Lady Chatterley, though certainly not identical with Frieda, has many of Frieda's characteristics. Long after Lawrence's death Frieda exchanged several letters with Karl von Marbahr, the sweetheart of her youth. He had not seen her since those distant days in Metz and knew nothing of her life in the ensuing forty years except that her name was now Lawrence. Could her husband, he asked her, have been the writer D. H. Lawrence? He had just read *Lady Chatterley's Lover* and, though he was not aware of any connection, the character of Connie had brought his early love back to mind.[4]

Lady Chatterley's Lover is Lawrence's most famous and most widely read book, but it is far from being his best. Sir Clifford Chatterley is a cardboard figure, a sketchily drawn symbol of the twin evils of Mammon-worship and impotence. Within the framework of the book he has only a negative role to play: Lawrence clearly considered it of no importance that, as a crippled war victim, he might have been entitled to a certain measure of understanding and sympathy. Rich as the book is in fine passages, the rapturous descriptions of the sexual act—an attempt to express the inexpressible—are not entirely free of unconscious humour. There is no full human relationship between Connie and the gamekeeper: the only contact between them lies in the act of copulation. This is all Mellors, in his male egotism, is interested in, while Lady Chatterley obviously does not expect from him any spiritual understanding. Thus the loving communion between them and the "tenderness" of the novel's original title are restricted to the area of greatest intensity.

In his battle against middle-class prudery, Lawrence not only makes his nature-loving hero, Mellors, relapse frequently into Derbyshire dialect, he also places in his mouth certain good old Anglo-Saxon words which at the time of writing were considered obscene: even in the more permissive climate of today their use is still not considered good manners in certain company. These "four-letter words" did not appear in the first version of the novel (which Frieda, incidentally, preferred to the later versions), though its style was more realistic than the two subsequent texts. Lawrence doubtless made use of them in order to emphasise the spontaneity and earthiness of the gamekeeper's speech, but he must have known that they would shock many of his readers. Presumably this is what he wanted, as a gesture of defiance, to do. Words were his tools, and so he considered it of vital importance that they too should be rescued from the hypocritical dictates of good manners. "What is obvious," he declared, "is that the words in these cases have been dirtied by the mind, by unclean associations. The words themselves are clean, so are the things to which they apply. But the mind drags in a filthy association, calls up some repulsive emotion. Well, then, cleanse the mind, that is the real job. It is the mind which is the Augean stables, not language."

Lawrence's reasoning appears somewhat faulty. Through the deliberate use of these forbidden words, which often seems forced, he introduces a note of vulgarity which is in blatant contrast to the under-lying purpose of his book. It was an error of judgment which delivered a useful weapon into the hands of his opponents.

Since Lawrence launched his crusade against Anglo-Saxon prudery there has been such a vast revolution in moral attitudes that he now appears to be merely stating the obvious. In fact his final novel con-tributed a great deal to this revolution, even if the *Lady Chatterley* trials themselves later resulted in developments completely opposed to what he himself had intended.

22

It was one thing to write *Lady Chatterley's Lover*, to rewrite it and then to rewrite it yet again, but it was quite another to get it published. Lawrence was obviously under no illusions that he could find a publisher for it in England or America: publishers are not usually given to committing suicide. He consequently devised a plan of arranging the publication himself and talked Pino Orioli into bringing it out in Florence in a private edition. Pino was of course a bookseller and not a publisher but that was of no consequence. Lawrence, the Mammon-hater, suddenly developed a remarkable talent for business. He made out a contract whereby Pino should receive ten per cent of the proceeds as publisher, while ninety per cent should go to the author, who was responsible for the printing and distribution costs. Since a thousand copies were to be printed and sold at two guineas each, Lawrence looked forward hopefully to a swift turn in the ebbing tide of his finances. But first of all the manuscript had to be typed. An English lady living in Florence gave the job up after only a few chapters, concerned for the salvation of her soul. Catherine Carswell, helpful as ever, undertook to copy the first half in London, while Maria Huxley made herself responsible for the second half.

The yearly battle against the onset of winter had now begun. Lawrence, constantly coughing and occasionally spitting blood, was not alone in his anxiety to escape from the cold December dampness of Tuscany—Frieda too was restless. She was now forty-eight, a dangerous age for a woman. They fled from Scandicci to Les Diablerets in Switzerland, where the Huxleys were taking a skiing holiday. Lorenzo indulged in dreams of a return to New Mexico—though he was perfectly aware that the American immigration authorities would have a word or two to say about that. At the beginning of March 1928 they returned to the Villa Mirenda, but three months later were back in Switzerland, this time in Chexbres-sur-Vevey in the mountains above Lake Geneva. After three weeks they moved even higher to a place near Gstaad, which at that time had not yet lost its rural innocence. They spent the summer in a little farmhouse outside the village of Gsteig, on

.the north side of the Pillon Pass. Earl and Achsah Brewster, their American friends from their distant days in Capri, moved into a hotel in the village, kept a watchful eye on them and joined them in singing folksongs; and Else Jaffe came on a visit. Lawrence kept himself busy painting—for the most part male and female nudes (not always Frieda). In September they went to Baden-Baden, taking the Brewsters with them.

Lawrence, always inclined to put on lordly airs in the presence of his mother-in-law, this time invited the old lady to stay with them in the Goldener Löwe Hotel in Lichtenthal. To celebrate Brewster's fiftieth birthday he hired two landaus, and they all went for a long ride through the autumnal Black Forest. Nobody could have recognised the author of *Lady Chatterley's Lover* in the slim, well-dressed gentleman who appeared punctually every morning at the Storchenbrunnen fountain with his drinking-glass to take the waters, who sat listening to the Kurhaus orchestra and spent his evenings in the wine-parlour of the Goldener Löwe, playing patience with the baroness.

The numbered private edition of the novel had meanwhile appeared in Florence and was causing Lawrence considerable—and not entirely unexpected—difficulties. Copies, paid for in advance, were despatched by Orioli through the post. Many of them mysteriously disappeared *en route*; a London bookseller declared indignantly that he was returning the thirty-six copies he had ordered, and others followed his example. Lawrence asked Koteliansky and Richard Aldington to collect the returned copies and send them on to other customers. His friends performed this labour of love, though they themselves had serious reservations about the book. In this way many of the copies reached their destinations in England before the customs officers, advised of the book's "pornographic" content, began to confiscate them. The American authorities also seized the packages as they arrived. On Lawrence's instructions Orioli took to despatching copies disguised in dustjackets bearing the apposite title *Samuel Butler: The Way of All Flesh*. Lawrence received angry letters from shocked readers and sad and concerned ones from friends such as Koteliansky, but other friends nobly took his side. These included the Huxleys, of course, as well as Lady Ottoline Morrell, with whom he was now reconciled, and David Garnett. Firms in America with an eye to a profitable deal brought out pirate editions, using a photographic process to produce copies which they could sell as the genuine article at fifty dollars apiece.

Increasingly weak as he was now becoming, Lorenzo looked after the business aspects of the enterprise with all the feverish energy of a consumptive. He wrote hundreds of letters, besides magazine articles and short stories, and he continued to paint new pictures. But his rapid decline was filling Frieda with great concern. One day she told him that a famous specialist she had met had promised to visit him on the following day. "I shall not be in," Lawrence retorted angrily. "He'll not see me!" And so it was. They visited the Cistercian abbey in Lichtenthal and, talking with the nuns, were told of a sister who was reputed to perform miraculous healings. Frieda implored Lorenzo to visit Sister Maria, but he shook his head obstinately: "All I need is the south and the sun."

They went in search of the southern sun, for another winter was looming in front of them. Frieda journeyed to Florence alone to wind up the tenancy of the Villa Mirenda. Lawrence went straight to Le Lavandou on the Côte d'Azur, where Else Jaffe was on holiday with her daughter, Marianne, and Alfred Weber. There he remained impatiently awaiting Frieda's arrival. She came later than expected. Not only had she been visiting Barbara, who was back in Alassio, but she had also had to go to Trieste, as she said, to settle some matters relating to the move.

Understandably she concealed the true reason. She had been with Angelo Ravagli, the *Bersaglieri* captain. She had made this part of the journey for the express purpose of meeting him, and she put up at a hotel near where Angelo was stationed. If he had not previously been her lover, it was here that he became so.*

Frieda had always felt attracted in some strange way to this gay Lothario in uniform, ever since she first met him in Spotorno. It is impossible to explain her infatuation in rational terms. Angelo—or Angelino, as he soon came to be called—was no youthful Adonis: at the time of this meeting he was thirty-seven years old. He was smaller than Frieda, but well-proportioned, and his movements were graceful. His virile, open features betrayed his peasant origin, but were otherwise in no way remarkable. It was the face of a man who had worked himself up from below and who set great store on outward appearances. He did not allow the fact that he was married and had three children to stand

---

* Barbara Barr, Frieda's younger daughter, to whom the author is indebted for this information, thinks it possible that the meeting took place in Gradisca in the province of Udine, but she cannot remember the name of the place for certain. According to Ravagli's own account he had been stationed in Gradisca since 1926.

in the way of his erotic adventures: his wife, a schoolteacher, lived far away in Savona, in the neighbourhood of the Villa Bernarda.

What can one say about Frieda's behaviour at this time? It is not necessary to seek excuses for her: the biographer's task is not to pass judgments, but to present the facts as they are and to seek where possible to explain them. The explanation here, presumably, is that Frieda was spiritually exhausted. Lawrence's physical decline was so sharply evident, his irritability so pronounced and his coughing so agonising (sometimes he coughed the whole night through, and they once had to leave a Swiss hotel on account of it), that living together with him had become an almost impossible burden. In addition, as she did not fail to inform her closest friends, he had for two years been impotent. "I can't stand it any longer!" she groaned. Her nerves were no longer equal to the strain—and she sought momentary relaxation with the primitive and uncomplicated Ravagli.

It can be assumed that the affair aroused no moral qualms in her. Lawrence himself was certainly wholeheartedly—and consciously— monogamous, but his philosophy of "blood-consciousness" unmistakably proclaimed that the laws governing sex were not those of Christian morality. Frieda might have felt able to discover in this some justification for giving way to a certain erotic laxity which was part of her nature. If this was so, it was neither the first nor the last time that Lawrence's message came to be misinterpreted.

She arrived in Le Lavandou on 12 October, by which time Else had already departed. Their Odyssey continued. They spent some weeks with Richard Aldington on the Ile de Port-Cros, until the November storms drove them from the tiny island. Back on the mainland, they settled into a quiet and friendly hotel in Bandol, the same Hôtel Beau Rivage in which ten years earlier Katherine Mansfield had had her first severe haemorrhage, but they were apparently unaware of the grim coincidence.

A young writer, Rhys Davies, visited them there. He came from a Welsh mining district and had just published his first novel. It was no doubt the similarity of their proletarian backgrounds that won him Lawrence's sympathy. In the ensuing weeks Rhys Davies frequently came over from Nice to see them, and it is to him we owe a description of Frieda during those days of growing uncertainty:[1]

Frieda did not impose on her husband, ill though he was, that female bossiness, that stealthy overpowering need to subjugate, which women, crying to themselves that they are doing a man good, can wind round him in oppressive folds. She could leave him alone and was cheerfully alive in her own sunny activity, or she would deftly touch him, flashing out some vain feminine illogicality that stirred him to comic denunciation.

Sitting up in bed, Lawrence would spend the mornings writing those epigrammatic, sarcastic and sometimes frivolous verses which he named *Pansies*, a play on the French word *pensées*. They were to land him eventually in a lot of trouble, to add to the irritations he was already experiencing. The English newspapers had got hold of *Lady Chatterley's Lover* and were subjecting its author to a flood of abuse. The periodical *John Bull*, which had started the hue and cry about *The Rainbow* thirteen years earlier, was again leading the campaign of outraged Philistines: "... the most evil outpouring that has ever besmirched the literature of our country. The sewers of French pornography would be dragged in vain to find a parallel in beastliness. The creations of muddy-minded perverts, peddled in the back-street bookstalls of Paris, are prudish by comparison ..."

These attacks were, as it soon transpired, only the warning signals for yet severer persecutions. It was unfortunate that the Home Secretary at that time was a religious fanatic, Sir William Joynson-Hicks, generally known as Jix. He mobilised his forces to track down all copies of *Lady Chatterley's Lover* which had slipped into England in order to corrupt its innocence. Detectives sniffed around among Lawrence's agents and publishers, policemen called on his friends, and there were even mutterings of a legal prosecution. Two copies of the manuscript of *Pansies*, which Lawrence had sent to his London agents by registered post, were seized. The matter was raised in the House of Commons and caused quite a stir.

Lawrence was furious. "Those dirty *canaille*," he raged, "to be calling *me* obscene!" Visitors came and went, among them Aldous and Maria Huxley, Barbara, and Lawrence's sister Ada, but for one reason or another none of them succeeded in lightening the atmosphere in the Hôtel Beau Rivage. Barbara was suffering from a nervous breakdown and was more in need of receiving than of giving comfort. Ada's visit depressed her brother, and they did not see one another again. Frieda was sick and tired of hotel rooms and the vagabond life; but where could she find a permanent resting-place? If she had anywhere she could call home, it was the Kiowa Ranch, but a return to New Mexico was out of the question as long as Lorenzo was still alive. Italy? France? England? She had no roots there. At the beginning of March 1929 she went once more to visit her mother.

Lawrence felt strong enough to travel to Paris, accompanied by Rhys Davies. He was hoping to arrange for the publication of a cheap private edition of *Lady Chatterley's Lover*, so as to take the wind out of the sails of the American pirates. Frieda joined him later, and they called on Harry Crosby, a rich American publisher,* in the *Moulin du Soleil* in Ermenonville, where Rousseau had once lived and Cagliostro found refuge. One day in April Lawrence went for a walk in the sunshine, while Frieda stayed indoors listening to gramophone records. When he returned, she was still absorbed in the gramophone. In an outburst of rage he seized the records and broke them one by one over her head. In this respect, at any rate, things had not changed between them.

Two weeks later they were in Majorca. Frieda was entranced: it had always been the island of her dreams. The chronicle of their stay there contains no world-shaking events. Lorenzo was bored; Frieda was annoyed because a man had pinched her bottom in the tram; Lorenzo fell ill and his teeth chattered "like castanets"; Frieda, swimming in the sea, noticed that an officer on horseback, dressed in a splendid uniform, was staring at her, and clambering nervously over the rocks to escape him, she sprained an ankle. Officers in splendid uniforms were obviously her undoing.

In spite of her injured foot she went to London to attend the opening of an exhibition of Lawrence's pictures in the Warren Gallery. This time she felt completely in her element in London. She was given a reception worthy of the Queen of Sheba. The gallery arranged a party in her honour, and invited old friends as well as new admirers of Lawrence. Frieda appeared resplendently clad in a brightly coloured evening dress which she had designed herself. In her arms she held a bunch of lilies—a symbol, as she declared, of Lawrence's purity. All the same, she felt some misgivings when she caught sight of her sister-in-law Ada among the champagne-drinking guests. Ready as Lawrence always was to defend his "phallic" philosophy against all the world, he was disturbed by the thought that he might hurt the feelings of his puritanical sister. But to Frieda's great relief Ada did not seem at all shocked.

* Eight months after this Crosby was found shot dead in a studio apartment in New York. Beside him lay the body of the young wife of one of his friends. It had obviously been a suicide pact. Crosby was thirty-two at the time of his death.

The critics were hostile almost to a man. Some of them demanded that the exhibition should be closed under the Obscenities Act of 1857. It was not only the popular weeklies like *John Bull* which this time set themselves up as the mouthpieces of outraged public opinion—the art critic of the *Daily Telegraph* wrote of the exhibition: "Probably no greater insult has ever been offered to the London public."

Three weeks after the exhibition opened, when twelve thousand people had already passed through and a number of pictures had been sold, two detectives and two police constables arrived armed with a warrant. Ignoring the protests of the gallery owner, they removed thirteen of the oil paintings and watercolours from the walls. The raid was interrupted, however, by a ludicrous incident. While it was still going on, the Aga Khan dropped in unexpectedly to view the pictures. All at once police officiousness turned into obsequiousness. The distinguished guest's express wish to view the contested pictures was instantly complied with, the two policemen offering their backs as mobile easels—"Light all right, Your Highness?" The Aga Khan, visibly impressed, talked of the possibility of arranging an exhibition of the pictures in Paris. Lawrence was on this occasion not the only victim of public morality: another picture not painted by him at all—it was *Ecce Homo* by George Grosz—was removed by the police at the same time.[2]

The last visitor to enter the gallery that evening was Frieda. She was completely unaware that a raid had taken place and stared in horror at the empty spaces on the walls.

It soon became known that the raid had been set in motion by the same guardians of public morals who had previously been responsible for the banning of *The Rainbow*. This time, however, there was an organised resistance: a protest petition was signed by many eminent people and apparently made some impact; in the event, the eighty-two-year-old judge refused to grant an order that the pictures be destroyed.

In the following week Frieda received a telegram from Pino Orioli. Lawrence, who had meanwhile left Majorca to join the Huxleys in Forte dei Marmi and had then gone on to Florence, was lying seriously ill in Pino's apartment. The exertions of the journey had proved too much for him, and the recent excitements—the simultaneous attacks against *Lady Chatterley's Lover* and his pictures—had precipitated a nervous breakdown. Frieda's reappearance wrought miracles, and a few days after her arrival he was able to travel with her to Baden-Baden.

It was not the first time that Frieda had had such a remarkable effect on Lawrence's health. Aldous Huxley, in a letter to a friend dated 21 November 1957, wrote:

I think I told you the other day about the miraculous way in which she raised Lawrence almost from death when he was ill with influenza (superimposed upon chronic and deepening TB) in my house. (Incidentally, the miracle was chronic. Thanks to Frieda, Lawrence remained alive for at least five years after he ought, by all the rules of medicine, to have been in the grave).

They stayed only three nights in the Goldener Löwe Hotel, and then Frieda took him to convalesce at the Kurhaus Plättig near Bühl. The old baroness accompanied them. Lawrence was, as Frieda wrote, "as frail as one of those blue bird's eggs." The weather was cold and wet, and they only stayed on because Baroness von Richthofen felt better there than in the town below. For the first time in her life she was beginning to get on Lawrence's nerves. "I have never felt so down," he wrote, "so depressed and ill, as I have here, these ten days: awful! ... Truly old and elderly women are ghastly, ghastly, eating up all life with hoggish greed, to keep themselves alive. They don't mind who else dies. I know my mother-in-law would secretly gloat, if I died at 43 and she lived on at 78."[3]

They returned at last to the Goldener Löwe and celebrated Frieda's fiftieth birthday in the familiar guestroom. Of the nine people who took part in the celebrations no fewer than five, as Lawrence sarcastically observed, were over the age of seventy. They mixed a bowl of peaches and two bottles of champagne and feasted on trout and duck. Nevertheless Frieda was in a highly irritable frame of mind—"but then she always is, in her native land," Lawrence remarked. On this occasion it was scarcely surprising: what woman who still expects something from life finds cause for congratulation in reaching her fiftieth birthday?

Dr Max Mohr invited them to spend some weeks on the Tegernsee and was waiting with a broad smile on the station at Rottach to convey them to a little house very close to his own farm. Here it was pure unspoiled country, such as Frieda loved. The little inn in which they ate their meals smelled of the stables and the meadows were fragrant with hay. Frieda was still limping, and Dr Mohr sent a local bone-setter to treat her: he set her ankle to rights with a single manipulation. Impressed, Lawrence accepted Dr Mohr's advice to consult another friend of his. This man, a former parson, ran a private clinic near Munich, and his cure was based on a special diet of his own invention, starting with preparations of arsenic and phosphorus. After a few days it became apparent that Lawrence could not stand up to so drastic a treatment, and he was put on a raw food diet. Autumn was already in the air, and Lawrence felt that the damp atmosphere of the shady valley might put an end to him even without the help of quacks, and so, at the end of September, they fled back to Bandol.

This time they rented a bungalow at the far end of the little bay. The Villa Beau Soleil had been fitted up by a wealthy man as a love nest for his *femme entretenue*, and there were a large number of gilt-framed mirrors on the heliotrope walls, as well as a marble bath and full central heating.

On fine afternoons Lawrence would sit out on the sunny terrace, a blue flannel jacket draped untidily over his pointed shoulders, his sharp knees threatening to cut through his trousers. He was scarcely more than a living skeleton; his face was grey, and even his beard had lost its red sheen.

He received his visitors sitting up in bed. When his strength allowed, he would accompany them on short walks, moving slowly and tiring swiftly. Max Mohr was often there, kind and helpful as always, even if his advice did not always turn out well. He had booked in at a nearby hotel for a month. Earl and Achsah Brewster spent the whole winter in Bandol. Norman Douglas and Pino Orioli turned up like birds of passage at Christmas, Else Jaffe came from Heidelberg and stayed two weeks, Barbara hastened over from London to help Frieda nurse the sick man.

Everybody realised that his days were now numbered. They came to see him once again while he still lived and secretly to say good-bye. But Frieda would not permit the threat of death to cast a shadow over the house. Her loud laughter, if sometimes rather forced, was designed to keep up the illusion of normality. Friends were encouraged to drop in for afternoon tea. On good days Lawrence would tell amusing or touching stories about his younger days, and sometimes he would sing folksongs, Frieda accompanying him on the piano and the visitors joining in the chorus, until a fit of coughing put a stop to it.

It was tragically clear that he was losing strength daily. The vital flame was now flickering unsteadily. At the end of January 1930 an English doctor, Andrew Morland, visited him. He was holidaying on the Côte d'Azur and Mark Gertler, who had himself suffered from tuberculosis, had begged him to take a look at Lawrence. Dr Morland quickly won his patient's confidence. He recommended an immediate transfer to a little sanatorium in Vence, in the mountains above Nice.

The walls of Lawrence's room in the Ad Astra Sanatorium in Vence were an ugly blue, but the view from the balcony was enchanting, and the air was certainly better than in Bandol. On fine days he would sit with Frieda in the garden, where the almond trees were blossoming and the mimosas gleaming in the February sun. Frieda and Barbara had taken rooms in a cheap hotel nearby. After the last hectic days in the Villa Beau Soleil and the laborious journey it was a relief to Frieda to know he was now receiving proper care.

More visitors came: H. G. Wells, who was spending the winter in his villa in Grasse, appeared looking like the celebrated author he was; the Aga Khan brought his beautiful second wife, Andrée, and again spoke of his intention of exhibiting Lorenzo's pictures in Paris.

But after a fortnight Lawrence was feeling iller than ever. He found the sanatorium atmosphere unbearable. As Dr Morland later observed: "His case illustrates the incompatibility between a certain type of genius and the ordered way of life necessary for recovery from tuberculosis."

So Frieda and Barbara set about finding a villa in which they could all live together. It was a wearisome search, for nobody was willing to have a consumptive patient in the house. Eventually, however, they were successful. The landlord of the Villa Robermond (later renamed the Villa Aurella) was prepared to take them from 1 March.

That was still a week away. Lawrence was impatient and in a tense state of nerves. All he wanted was to get away—from this house of illness, from Europe. He was homesick for Kiowa Ranch on the other side of the ocean, with its views of distant blue mountains and many-coloured forests. He was now quite determined to return to New Mexico as soon as his health permitted. Barbara was despatched to Nice to check that their passports were still in order. Aldous and Maria Huxley came over from London. The sick man's room looked like a flower garden. Frieda was completely exhausted, but scarcely dared to leave his bedside. Lawrence begged her to stay with him during the nights, and she complied, sleeping on a bamboo chair in a corner of the room. She could hear him groaning and coughing, but there was nothing she could do to help him.

One night I thought of the occasion long ago when I knew I loved him, when a tenderness for him rose in me that I had not known before. He had taken my two little girls and me for a walk in

Sherwood Forest, through some field we walked, and the children ran all over the place, and we came to a brook ... it ran rather fast under a small stone bridge. The children were thrilled ... He made them paper boats and put burning matches into them; "this is the Spanish Armada, and you don't know what that was." "Yes, we do," the older girl said promptly. I can see him now, crouching down so intent on the game, so young and quick.

From the neighbouring rooms she could hear the coughing of other patients through the walls, old coughs and young coughs and the tearful voice of a little girl: "Maman, maman, je souffre tant!" She was glad that Lawrence had now become a little deaf.

The Villa Robermond lay above Vence. An Italian, Dominique Matteucci, who lived in a little house in the garden with his common-law wife, Lilli Gallois, performed the duties of a concierge; an English nurse was engaged from Nice. Frieda brought Lawrence from the sanatorium in a taxi, and helped by the driver, he laboriously climbed the few steps up to the verandah. "I am very ill," he said. He was put to bed and a new doctor, a Corsican named Maestracci, examined him. Closing the door of the sick room behind him, the doctor said: "It is very grave. There is not much hope."
Next day was a Sunday. Lawrence begged Frieda not to leave him.

So I sat by his bed and read. He was reading the *Life of Columbus*. After lunch he began to suffer very much and about tea-time he said: "I must have a temperature, I am delirious. Give me the thermometer." This is the only time, seeing his tortured face, that I cried, and he said: "Don't cry," in a quick, compelling voice. So I ceased to cry any more. He called Aldous and Maria Huxley who were there, and for the first time he cried out to them in his agony. "I ought to have some morphine now."

Huxley went to fetch the doctor. Maria sat down beside the bed and held Lawrence's head comfortingly between her hands. "You have my mother's hands," he told her. Then he suddenly raised himself bolt upright and, staring across the room with horrified eyes, cried: "I see my body there on the table."
Dr Maestracci, the young physician from Corsica, was not at home, and Barbara went in search of another doctor. The senior doctor at the Ad Astra Sanatorium at first refused to visit the dying man, but at last

he yielded to Barbara's desperate pleading. He gave an injection which brought Lawrence some relief. He began to breathe more easily, but after a while he muttered: "Hold me, hold me, I don't know where I am, I don't know where my hands are ... where am I?"

Barbara and Aldous Huxley again went off to fetch the Corsican doctor. They got back just before eleven o'clock at night to find Frieda and Maria in the kitchen. "We could not get Dr Maestracci," said Barbara anxiously.

"It doesn't matter," Frieda gently replied.

Lawrence was dead. He had died at ten o'clock. It was 2 March 1930.

"Then we buried him, very simply," Frieda wrote, "like a bird we put him away, a few of us who loved him. We put flowers into his grave and all I said was: 'Good-bye, Lorenzo,' as his friends and I put lots of mimosa on his coffin."

The head of the grave, into which the simple and unadorned oak coffin was lowered, lay against the sunny inner wall of the cemetery. Beyond the cypresses, standing upright like dark candles against the sky, the sea glittered far below. No priest was present: that was Frieda's wish, and certainly as the dead man would have wanted it. She did not wear mourning—a fact that caused a lot of ill-natured gossip in the town.[4]

Not long afterwards a woman dressed in black visited the grave and laid a bunch of flowers on it. It was Louie Bunows, to whom Lawrence had once been engaged. He had broken off with her three weeks before he met Frieda, and in all the ensuing years they had not exchanged a single letter. Now, however, she came once more to demonstrate her loyalty. On her return home she wrote to his sister Ada: "I went to Vence and saw the poor lad's grave."

23

"You will know that Lorenzo is dead," Frieda wrote to Witter Bynner, their friend from former days in Mexico. "He faced the end so splendidly, so like a *man*, and I could help him through, thank God. Dead, he looked proud and at peace and fulfilled."

"Proud and at peace and fulfilled"—it was words like these that had encouraged Frieda's daughter on the day of the burial to cast a glance into the simple coffin. Like Frieda, Barbara had never before in her life seen a dead person. She did as she was bid, and was startled—the expression on Lawrence's face seemed to her less peaceful than mocking.

The coffin was nailed down and Frieda stood beside it for perhaps ten minutes, in utter silence, her head bowed. It was her moment of parting from the man who for eighteen years had been the focal point of her life.

What came after that was confusion and distraction, drama and ritual —but never despair, never apathy. The start of a cult, maybe, but above all an intense effort to find a way through, a passionate resolve not to go under, not to give up, not to stagnate. She was already fifty years old—*only* fifty years old—and her life was not yet done: she had to keep going.

What sort of woman was she as she stood at this watershed in her life? Her personality had so many facets that people who knew her only superficially might have found her inconsistent, erratic and capricious. Inconsistencies there certainly were, particularly in her statements and her judgments, which often, in an endearingly but sometimes irritatingly feminine way, lacked logic: they were usually impulsive and always frank, without any ifs and buts, cautious hedging or ulterior motives (though there were some exceptions in this regard). But fickle she was not. In fact, if one takes the time of her "awakening" by Lawrence as the starting-point, her character, with all its virtues and all its flaws, reveals an over-all stability which remained unaffected by her frequent vacillations. Whatever the outward changes—and obviously with increasing age she became broader, stouter and heavier— the true inner core never changed, was never sublimated or extinguished. The fascination of her personality remained as powerful as in her younger years. She never strove to assert herself or to occupy the centre of the stage, yet nobody who had once met her could ever forget her. When David Garnett saw her for the first time in Bavaria, she reminded him of a lioness: that was in 1912. When Rhys Davies met her in Bandol he had exactly the same impression and used, quite independently, the self-same simile—and that was in 1928. In all the intervening years she had lost none of her astounding vitality. Huxley called her Rabelaisian, since her full-blooded enjoyment of life found frequent expression in uproarious laughter and a hedonistic abandonment to the pleasures of the moment.

This faculty she possessed of living in the present occasionally gave the impression of an almost childlike naiveté. She seemed uncomplicated, but that was only because she cared nothing for the opinion of others and insisted, sometimes to the point of obstinacy, on ignoring social conventions and moral taboos. Presumably Lawrence was aware of her occasional sexual escapades, but he also knew that these left their own fundamental relationship unaffected. When they were not a conscious demonstration against his urge to dominate, her affairs evolved from simple sensual enjoyment, from an exuberant earthbound awareness that was not prepared to yield either to his dictates or to moral dogmas of any kind. Self-confident, generous and kind-hearted, Frieda went her own way according to her laws, radiating warmth and well-being like some pagan goddess of Nature, a mixture of Cybele and Aphrodite Pandemos.

From all the deprivations, disappointments and persecutions of her life with Lawrence a woman of another kind would have emerged neurotic and embittered, but Frieda's happy temperament enabled her to endure such trials with stoic equanimity. "You and I, we have a masochistic streak," she once told Barbara, and that might very well be true, as one realises when one thinks of all the humiliations she tolerated from Lorenzo because she believed unshakeably in his genius and his love.

For all her remarkable reserves of strength, Frieda showed little ability to deal practically with the many problems arising out of Lawrence's death. They were admittedly ticklish matters relating to copyright and to the posthumous publication of his writings. It was not only important to get them settled, but also urgent, since her financial position was precarious. The flow of royalties and fees had increased during the last years of Lawrence's life, and Frieda estimated that his savings amounted to four thousand pounds—a much too optimistic valuation, as it later turned out. But since Lawrence's will, made fifteen years earlier, could not be found, she was by law temporarily denied access to the capital, though she drew the interest on it.

Deciding to return to New Mexico, she wrote to Witter Bynner: "Now I have one desire—to take him to the ranch and make a lovely place for him there. He wanted so much to go." She was considering selling some of Lawrence's manuscripts and pictures and starting a collection among his friends. In this way she hoped to raise sufficient money to exhume his body and convey it to a new grave at the ranch. The project kept her busy, giving her a task to sustain her in the days of aimless drifting. But it also sowed in her the seeds of future idolatry.

In the meantime she instructed Dominique and Nicola, a young stonemason from Calabria, to prepare a headstone for Lorenzo's grave in Vence. It was to contain a mosaic in black, red and white pebbles of a phoenix rising from the ashes—Lawrence's original symbol for Rananim and subsequently for himself.

She spent some days with Ravagli and his family. Angelo had invited her to Savona after reading of Lawrence's death in the *Corriera della Sera*. Frieda knew his wife Ina-Serafina from the days when she and Lorenzo had been living in the Villa Bernarda, and she was godmother to their son who had been born at that time and named Federico after her.

At the end of March she went to London to try, not very successfully, to settle her affairs. Aldous Huxley was on hand to help her, and later he wrote:[1]

> She seemed such a powerful Valkyrie—but as I found out when she came to London after Lawrence's death and had to deal with business and stay by herself in a hotel, she was amazingly incapable and, under her emphatic and sometimes truculent façade, deeply afraid. She had relied *totally* on Lawrence, and felt completely lost until she found another man to support her.

While her mother was in England Barbara stayed on alone at the Villa Robermond, her only company being the farm dog, which slept beside her bed. The events of the past weeks had been a severe strain on the girl's nerves. Lawrence seemed still to be invisibly present in the large empty house, and at night Barbara left the door to his room open, so that his spirit could go in and out unhindered.

Frieda, when she arrived back, was concerned about her daughter's state of health, but her whole attention was taken up for the next two weeks by a new visitor: John Middleton Murry, who had come to Vence to "give advice". The first question he asked was: "Did he say anything about me? If I could have held him in my arms just once!" He had come to Vence to offer Frieda comfort and tenderness, but he also expected to be repaid in the same coin. Unlike Barbara, he did not believe that the spirit of the dead man wandered through the rooms of his last home.

Lawrence, it might be recalled, had imagined just such a situation in his short story *The Border Line*, in which the spirit of the dead husband returns to take revenge on his successor. Morbid fantasies of this sort held no terrors for Murry, and now he was no longer held back by thoughts of loyalty towards a friend. Frieda herself was urgently in need of tenderness and love to rescue her from the vacuum caused by Lorenzo's death. In sharing her bed with Murry she was staking a claim on the future rather than making a break with the past.[2]

It was not of course too late for her to start a new chapter. But can one be surprised that she should have been assailed by vague fears of time running out? In the pressure and confusion of events it is by no means easy to recognise the motives behind her acts at this time.

Hardly had Murry departed when another friend from older and happier days arrived in the Villa Robermond. This was Pino Orioli, the cheerful story-teller from Florence, who never had anything but good to say of Lawrence, unless he happened to be repeating malicious words put in his mouth by the friend who shared his sexual inclinations, Norman Douglas. In Pino's company it was impossible to remain gloomy, and shortly after his arrival Frieda was eagerly suggesting that they should all three go on a trip to Pieve di Teco.

It would be hard to discover a less likely goal for an outing, for Pieve di Teco was a tiny and totally uninteresting village on the Italian side of the border. But Angelo Ravagli happened at the time to be stationed there. Frieda, Barbara and Pino made the somewhat complicated rail journey to Ormea (Pieve di Teco was itself too small and insignificant to boast a railway station), and there they were met by the smart *capitano dei Bersaglieri*, who took them to a little hotel. Forty years later Barbara still shuddered to recall that seedy little hovel.

Ravagli took Pino off to a café, and later Pino told Barbara what they had talked about. Angelo wanted to finish with Frieda, and that was why he had invited Pino to a *tête-à-tête*. Pino told Frieda what

Ravagli had said and urged her to forget him. But she would have none of it. "You don't understand Angelo," she said. "He is like a humming-bird." Pino's reply to that was that he didn't care whether Angelo was like a humming-bird or a parrot: in his opinion she should cast him off. But Frieda persisted in her belief that Pino did not understand Angelo. "I can make a second Lawrence of him," she declared enthusiastically. She subsequently spoke to Ravagli himself and persuaded him to continue their relationship.[3]

Barbara was already in a very unsettled state, and the shock caused by Orioli's story drove her to the verge of hysteria. Frieda was alarmed and eagerly adopted Pino's suggestion that Barbara should go with him to Florence. She returned to Vence alone, while in Florence Pino and Norman Douglas sought for a week to divert Barbara's attention to other things.

After another short visit to London, Frieda again made the pilgrimage to Baden-Baden. She took Barbara with her, thinking the change would do her good. This time they found Nusch, still a strikingly beautiful woman, with the baroness. Soon, at Frieda's suggestion, Norman Douglas and Pino Orioli joined them, and together with Frieda, who was forcedly cheerful, and Nusch, high-spirited as ever, the two men strove to rouse Barbara from her melancholia. The weather was terrible and none of them enjoyed taking walks in the rain. On the other hand, little was gained just sitting in the wine-parlour of the Goldener Löwe Hotel, attempting to restore Barbara's spirits. Then Barbara caught a cold, which developed into bronchitis and made things even worse. Frieda decided to break off her stay in Baden-Baden and to take Barbara back to Vence.

By now it had become abundantly clear that Barbara was seriously ill. She had fits of delirium, in the course of which she gave vent to violent outbursts of hatred against her mother. As a child she had been forced to listen to her father's family condemning Frieda as a woman steeped in unspeakable sin, and the seeds then sown seemed now in her demented fantasy to be bearing poisonous fruits. In her mind Frieda was an enemy to be fought off—but how can a daughter fight against her own mother?

The doctor whom Frieda summoned to the Villa Robermond was highly alarmed and ordered complete rest for the patient. "It is a case of *grande hystérie*," he said. "She must stay in bed and be kept from any form of excitement."

"There's no end to my sorrows," Frieda wrote in a despairing note to Witter Bynner. "My lovely daughter Barby is very ill and the horror of it, it's her brain."

One evening Barbara was lying in bed while Frieda sat in the next room, playing the piano. The muffled sound of her playing was still present in her daughter's mind forty years later. "I felt I was trapped. I had to escape—at once, whatever the cost. I climbed through the window and ran like a mad thing up the hill to the little house in which the cook, Madame Lilli [Gallois], was living. The family was having their supper: Madame Lilli, Dominique and the young Italian Nicola. They looked at me without surprise as if they had expected me. I was trembling with fear, unable to utter a word. Madame Lilli poured me out a glass of wine, then led me into the bedroom and put me into her own bed. I lay awake for hours, my forehead bathed in sweat. During the night I looked out of the window and saw Nicola crouching under a tree in the moonlight, motionless as a statue, looking up at me. When in the morning I stepped out on the balcony I was so weak that I thought I should fall down. I was convinced that I was dying. Madame Lilli gave me a raw egg to drink, and I think that saved me. Soon afterwards my mother came to fetch me. I snatched up a tin can and flung it at her. She led me back to the Villa Robermond, and then I fainted."

Dr Maestracci was away at the time, and the old doctor whom Frieda called was quite unable to deal with the patient's delusions and long periods of unconsciousness. Frieda was desperate, and convinced of the healing, revitalising powers of sex, she encouraged young Nicola to spend the night in Barbara's bed. In some curious way Lawrence's phallic ecstasies seem to have become mixed in Frieda's mind with the theories of Dr Otto Gross. The experiment was repeated a number of times until Dr Maestracci, returning from Corsica, put an abrupt stop to it.*

On the doctor's recommendation a specialist was brought in from Nice for consultation. Frieda sent an urgent summons to Elsa, her elder daughter, and her son, Monty, in England. Barbara's illness dragged on for many months, and Frieda scarcely ever stirred from her side. In October they left the Villa Robermond and went to live with "Aunt Crotch". Martha Gordon-Crotch, who came from Yorkshire, was one

---

* In a letter to the author Mrs Barbara Barr has written: "When Frieda met her two sisters in Germany at her mother's deathbed, she told them about Nicola. They were horrified and both said: 'I would have let my daughter die.'...Ottoline Morrell said to me in London: '...How *could* Frieda? She is obsessed with sex.'"

of the eccentric ladies of the Côte d'Azur, a friend of Emma Goldman, the famous international anarchist, and all the other intellectual nomads who roamed the Riviera. She kept a shop in Vence, where she sold antiques and pottery. It was inevitable that sooner or later Frieda should land up in her house.

A telegram summoned Frieda to Baden-Baden, where her mother lay seriously ill. The baroness died on 21 November, at the age of seventy-nine. She had outlived Lawrence, as he had once cynically prophesied, but his death had broken the curiously close emotional tie between them. It was as if his dying had robbed the baroness of all will to live.

A few days after Frieda's return Barbara set off for England, where, in the unruffled tranquillity of her Uncle Ted's vicarage in Great Maplestead, she soon recovered her strength.

Christmas was always a critical time for Frieda. She had stayed in Vence after Barbara's departure, partly because her money was low: the problems of Lawrence's estate were still not solved, and were not to be settled for some time yet. Since his will could not be produced, the authorities took the view that it did not exist, and so the procedures governing intestacy, complicated in this case by the claims of Lawrence's brother and sisters, had to be followed through their long and weary course. Frieda was feeling lonely, and the thought of spending Christmas among a group of indifferent strangers was unbearable to her. She travelled to Florence in order to be with Pino Orioli, and there she also found Richard Aldington. Together they celebrated Christmas Eve, though their mood was scarcely in keeping with its solemn character, for Pino, as usual on such occasions, had drunk rather too much Chianti. Their intention of attending midnight mass in the Chiesa della Santissima Annunziata was nipped in the bud, for Pino came into conflict at the entrance with a priest collecting alms. After a bibulous trek from church to church they wound up at last in the *Duomo*, where Pino put the patience of the congregation to a severe test.[4]

Episodes such as this reveal the slackness of the ties which now bound Frieda to Europe since the death of Lawrence and of her mother. Her real home was Kiowa Ranch, and she was hoping Barbara would eventually join her there, but meanwhile she persuaded Ravagli to travel to Taos with her. It was an experiment with a time limit attached: Angelo managed to secure six months' unpaid leave from the army, but he had to be back in Italy before the winter.

24

It was, in a real sense, a sentimental journey. Every stage of it conjured up a flood of memories. There was Santa Fe, where they had first met Witter Bynner, grinning broadly as Lawrence furiously dashed that Sicilian cart panel to the ground; there was the "desert" and Mabel in her splendid house at the entry to Taos; and there was the Plaza with Don Fernando's Coffee Shop on the left, and groups of Pueblo Indians, both men and women with bright *ponchos* and black pigtails. They took the winding cart-track up to the ranch, with the majestic panoramic view that Lorenzo had described. Here was the irrigation ditch of Gallina Canyon, which he himself had dug, and before the house the great fir tree on whose trunk Brett had painted a phoenix, his symbol. Deeply moved, Frieda sat down on the chair on which Lorenzo had carved decorations with a penknife, and which was covered in *petit-point* embroidery which she had begun and he had completed.

Angelo Ravagli could not conceal his disappointment over the primitiveness of the house and the loneliness of the ranch. But he was impressed by the beauty and majesty of the landscape, and, being a practical man, he found plenty on the ranch to do. Had not Lorenzo himself once told Frieda, a few days after they had moved into the Villa Bernarda, that he would be a useful man to have at Kiowa?

Lawrence's spirit seemed to be everywhere, and Frieda had the feeling that he was calling on her to defend his memory. Even the newspaper obituaries had, as she bitterly noted, given a wrong impression of him, and some had been maliciously distorting. But the obituary writers had been only the advance guard for the main force of biographers and memoir writers, who were now hastening to snatch their share of plunder from the rich storehouse of his life. Frieda had still been in Vence when Mabel Dodge Luhan sent her the manuscript of her grotesque book, *Lorenzo in Taos*. In spite of her annoyance Frieda had written back in restrained and friendly terms:[1]

> I weep over your *Lorenzo in Taos*. Why was I such a fool and couldn't manage the situation, why did I doubt that he loved me?

How wrong of me. And why were you so bossy, and didn't show him your real understanding and tenderness for him! Lord, what fools we were, and now it's too late, as it always is.

In the same letter she implored Mabel to rewrite her book. The rebuffed millionairess of course had not the slightest intention of doing that, and the resentment she felt against Frieda poisoned their relations for many years.

Even before Mabel Dodge Luhan's neurotic reminiscences John Middleton Murry had appeared on the scene with his biography of Lawrence, *Son of Woman*.

Murry had managed to win the race, but that was all the worse, since his book, unlike Mabel's, could not simply be dismissed as pathological. He had achieved something quite unique: brilliantly written, like most of Murry's work, it concealed beneath a cloak of reverent admiration the sharp dagger of a paid assassin. Aldous Huxley castigated it as "a malignant and vindictive hagiography", and Frieda, receiving a copy at Kiowa Ranch, burned it and sent the ashes to Murry. On the Del Monte Ranch below Kiowa Dorothy Brett was working busily on her own reminiscences, a declaration of love for Lorenzo covering all of three hundred pages. In England Catherine Carswell was writing *The Savage Pilgrimage*, which began to appear as a serial a few months later. This was the first coolly objective biography of Lawrence (if a shade too uncritical), and in it Catherine took Murry severely to task. The battle of Lorenzo's memory had been unleashed.

Aldous Huxley, who had originally planned a memorial volume written by Lawrence's friends, was now, with Frieda's consent, preparing a collection of D.H.L.'s letters, and refused to accept any fee for this time-consuming task. But Frieda was convinced that this was not enough—she felt she must protect Lawrence's memory by showing the world the picture of Lawrence which was locked in her own memory, and so the resolution to write a book about him herself was born.

But she could not begin on it yet. Angelo's leave was at an end, and she was back in Europe. Moving between England and Vence, she was tormented by worry over the outcome of the legal battle regarding Lorenzo's will. His brother George and both his sisters, Emily King and Ada Clarke, were claiming a share of the inheritance, and Frieda's main concern was whether she would be able to convince the court that Lawrence had appointed her his sole heir. She was determined to fight the battle to the end, not only because she wanted Lawrence's last wishes to be respected, but also because she had no doubts about the justice of her claim: after all, she had spent eighteen years of her life with him, sharing in his work, his joys and disappointments, his poverty and his success. So much depended on the result—whether she would be able to live at Kiowa Ranch, indeed whether she would be able to continue her life with Angelo. In common with her other friends, Huxley had urged her not to bring the case to court: he felt that in the absence of any documentary proof her claim would not be upheld. Two weeks before the hearing he wrote in a letter:[2]

> The stupid woman is embarking on enormously expensive legal proceedings against Lawrence's brother now ... Her diplomatic methods consist in calling everyone a liar, a swine and a lousy swindler, and then in the next letter being charming—then she's surprised that people don't succumb to her charm. Since Lawrence is no longer there to keep her in order, she plunges about in the most hopeless way. I like her very much; but she's in many ways quite impossible.

The hearing took place on 3 November 1932. Called as a witness, John Middleton Murry confirmed that he and Lawrence had drawn up their wills on the same day, 9 November 1914. He himself had left everything to Katherine Mansfield, while Lawrence had appointed Frieda his sole heir. Katherine Mansfield and he had signed Lawrence's will as witnesses. Murry's testimony made a strong impression, particularly since he was able to lay before the court his own will, which, apart from the names, had been identical. The judge, Lord Merrivale, decided the case in Frieda's favour.* Before the hearing Frieda's lawyer had proposed a settlement whereby Lawrence's brother and two sisters should each receive five hundred pounds. The judge described this proposal as uncommonly generous. After the hearing, however, Ada waived her claim to a share of the settlement.

Frieda was now at last her own mistress, and, better still, she was

* Witter Bynner declares that in his final address Frieda's counsel painted a moving picture of a married life between Lawrence and Frieda untouched by any discord, whereupon Frieda impulsively cried out: "Oh, but no! That's not true! We fought like hell!" This intervention caused loud laughter, and even the judge could not repress a smile. This dramatic account is not, unfortunately, quite true. All that happened was that Frieda spoke in her evidence of the deep understanding that existed between Lawrence and herself and then added that they did of course quarrel now and again—an admission that was greeted with mild amusement.

able to clear up the position *vis-à-vis* Angelo. He was willing to leave the army and to live permanently with her in New Mexico, on condition that the financial position of his family was assured. Frieda agreed to pay out of her own pocket the share of his officer's pay which he had previously allocated to his wife. In April 1933 they returned together to Taos.

The primitive log cabin depressed Ravagli anew. Like most Italians, he had had a mental picture of America as a land full of modern creature comforts, and here he was having to put up with conditions that he would not have tolerated in any Italian barracks. In the evenings he would sit with Frieda in the tiny living-room lit by two candles, with the wind whistling eerily across the low corrugated-iron roof. They bathed in a tub in front of the fire, and Angelo had to fetch the water from the irrigation ditch outside. After brooding in silence for two or three weeks, he suddenly declared: "I will build a house, a house fit to live in, not an old cowshed like this one."

He flung himself eagerly into the work, measuring out the site Frieda chose below the old log cabin, engaging a number of Mexican labourers, chopping down trees, levelling the ground and sinking the foundations. On 30 May they ceremoniously laid the foundation stone. Beneath it they placed a bottle containing photographs of themselves, some American, French and German coins and two of Angelo's back teeth. And now Angelo was able to show the stuff of which he was made. With his practical intelligence he would undoubtedly have won Lawrence's full respect: he knew how to get the best from his labourers and he kept the account books strictly in order. He worked uninterruptedly from early morning till darkness fell, and all day long Frieda could hear him contentedly singing Italian songs.

She was happy. During the first weeks she had been tormented by the fear that she might lose him. He obviously missed the companionship of army life, and his loneliness was intensified by the fact that he could speak neither English nor Spanish; he did not share her intellectual interests, and she began to wonder whether she had not made a terrible mistake in bringing him here, but now her confidence was restored—the house rising before her eyes would bind him to America.

By the late summer the building was finished and they could move in. There was running water in the kitchen and bathroom, the curtains were fixed and in the living-room stood a piano. Frieda was in the habit of rising early, and her first steps took her to the window. She was always fascinated by the sight of approaching day: the mountain peaks gradually lost their morning glow, the sun pushed the misty shadows down the slopes and at last reached the ranch, while nearby the horses stood among the lucern and Anita, the cow, waited patiently to be milked. Softly, in order not to awaken Angelo, Frieda would go down to the kitchen and, while she made the coffee, she could hear him getting up, singing one of his soldiers' songs as he dressed. He was still in love with military life. His father had been a peasant and he, as one of a large family, had had a hard and impoverished childhood—as a small boy, he told Frieda, he had sold vegetables at the roadside and was grateful to the army for giving him a position and bolstering his self-respect. During the First World War he had been wounded twice and decorated three times. He had been taken prisoner by the Germans and had been well treated, though he was not given enough to eat. True comradeship, he would say, exists only among soldiers.

Ravagli had a brother and sister, living in Buenos Aires, whom they decided to visit during the winter. Preparations for the journey took up a lot of time: a peasant's son like Ravagli did not need to be told that one could not simply lock the door and leave the ranch to its own devices when setting off on a winter journey. The pigs had to be slaughtered and the hams smoked, the horses must have their shoes removed and their saddles hung up out of reach of the rats, the water tanks had to be emptied. An unpleasant experience disturbed their preparations: Ravagli had met an Italian who made a good impression on him, and desirous of helping a fellow countryman in a foreign land, he had suggested making him a loan to start up a business of his own. Frieda, always generous with money, gave him a thousand dollars, but unfortunately the man turned out to be a swindler. Worse still, he spread slanders around which brought Frieda and Angelo into conflict with the police. Ravagli had to make a quick getaway across the border into Colorado in order to avoid arrest. Frieda joined him the following day in Alamosa and they drove to New Orleans in their La Salle—the first car she had ever possessed. In New Orleans they took ship for South America. Angelo's brother and married sister lived in a slum district of Buenos Aires, and the dreariness of life in their self-imposed exile had embittered them and destroyed their souls.[3]

Frieda and Angelo were glad when they at last got back to Taos. Here they were at home. As Frieda wrote:[4]

This country suits my very soul. I love my Taos and Santa Fe friends, I am at home with them. Not that I see so much of them, sitting on my mountainside an hour's motor-drive away from Taos and nearly three from Santa, and often the road is so bad that when the snow is melting in the mountains and comes down in torrents of fierce, rushing streams, we are inaccessible prisoners, but cheerful ones.

Friendly shouts greeted them as they drove into the Plaza in Taos, bathed in spring sunshine. Don Fernando's Coffee Shop had been burnt down. They stopped in front of the printing works of the little local paper, *El Crepusculo de la Libertad*, whose editor was now "Spud" Johnson, Witter Bynner's friend and with him their erstwhile travelling companion in Mexico. Spud was able to tell them all the latest news. Mabel was at the moment in New York, as full of energy and crazy ideas as ever; during the winter she had thrown one party after another in her large house, and a lot more guests were expected for the summer. Dorothy Brett was back again in her log cabin on the Del Monte Ranch below Kiowa, luxuriating in her memories of Lorenzo—her book *Lawrence and Brett* had appeared the previous year—and she had become deafer and stranger than ever. One would meet her sometimes striding through the countryside with her easel under her arm. Hardened as Taos was to curious sights, Brett's clothing could still cause wonder: an enormous Texan hat, a filthy, paint-flecked pullover, her long legs encased in bright-coloured breeches and a large Indian knife stuck into one of her cowboy boots.

They drove up into the mountains, past the Del Monte Ranch, the trees still silver-grey and wintry, and there they found their new house awaiting them, cold and with all the signs of being unlived in.

Mabel soon returned to Taos, radiating her curious mixture of hostility and friendship.

She was a feminine dynamo in whom the polarity of her qualities seemed to generate inexhaustible supplies of energy. Her many faceted personality combined high intelligence and psychopathic qualities, strength of will and capriciousness, kindness and cruelty, occultism and psycho-analysis, the cynicism that springs from the possession of great riches and the boredom to which a combination of wealth and cynicism leads. "Mabel was born bored," Dorothy Brett later declared.[5] "She had an insatiable appetite for tasting life in all its aspects. She tasted and spat it out."

A lust for power combined with boredom can produce dangerous urges: in Mabel they aroused a passionate desire to manipulate human lives like puppets on a string. She could be munificent and helpful—among other things, she had presented Taos with a fully equipped hospital, and many artists could provide testimony to the generosity of her patronage—but she could also be moved by mere caprice to destroy friendships, marriages or even lives by treacherous intrigues.

She was completely unpredictable. Even people who had known her for many years were unable to gauge in advance how she would respond to any given situation. When she "discovered" Taos in the winter of 1916, everyone thought she would lose interest in her new toy within a few months. In fact, she continued to live there right up to her death—a period of forty-six years in all—and became fully identified with the place on which she had impressed her bizarre personality. She believed implicitly in the native Indian soul of America. Her friends and enemies —it is impossible to separate the two categories—might have regarded her marriage to the dignified, silent and rather mysterious Indian, Antonio Luhan, as just another instance of her appetite for new experience, but it is a remarkable fact that, whereas she had previously changed husbands with the same facility as she changed her gloves, her marriage with Tony lasted a full forty years and was brought to an end only by her death.

She found a deep sense of satisfaction in her role as "Empress of Mabeltown". But the Pueblo Indians, whose welfare she considered to be her life's work, were not prepared on that account to let her have her own way in everything. Now and again the authorities were obliged to intervene to protect her protégés from the ambitious plans of their "benefactress". There were times when Mabel seemed to want to be more Indian than the Indians themselves. When at the end of the war a number of young Indians put off their uniforms and returned to their *pueblo* near Taos, they had been so infected by the temptations of Western civilisation that they decided they must have electric light, refrigerators, washing machines and TV sets in their mud huts. Mabel considered it her duty to protect the traditional Indian way of life from such foreign influences, and stated in *El Crepusculo* that the old ways were the best. A member of the rebellious younger generation replied to her that in this case perhaps Mrs Luhan would like to try them: he would himself be glad to give her the opportunity and trade houses with her. He would live in her home with its electric lights, refrigerator and warm inside-bathroom, and she might live at the *pueblo*, fetching water in pails from the Rio Pueblo and carrying it up the steep ladder. It was not Mabel who decided the issue in the end, but the wise elders of the *pueblo*, who, like older generations everywhere in the world, came down on the side of tradition.[6]

Still, it was an effective use of irony on the part of the young letter writer from the *pueblo*. Thanks to her many parties, everyone living in Taos knew all about Mabel's *hacienda*-like house, where she lived in feudal style surrounded by numerous servants. Her outward appearance was apt, however, to surprise anyone meeting her for the first time, for she was small and had lovely eyes, set in a not unpretty face, and a gentle and melodious voice. Like Ottoline Morrell, she loved to appear at parties dressed in flowing and fluttering gowns. At the beginning she modelled herself on Isadora Duncan, but later she chose garments designed by Adrian in Hollywood.

Mabel had not forgiven Frieda for criticising her book *Lorenzo in Taos*. For a time she showed her resentment by inviting Frieda alone to her parties, ignoring Ravagli, with the result that Frieda also did not go. But since no one else in Taos was interested in boycottings of this sort, Mabel eventually yielded magnanimously, and Angelo was accepted into the circle of the elite. However, Mabel soon found another way of demonstrating her hostile brand of friendship.

In this year—1934—Frieda's book appeared. Its title, *Not I, But the Wind* ..., is taken from a poem that Lawrence wrote in 1913 or 1914, in the first stormy years of their life together:

> Not I, not I but the wind that blows through me!
> A fine wind is blowing the new direction of Time.
> If only I let it bear me, carry me, if only it carry me!
> If only I am sensitive, subtle, oh, delicate, a winged gift!
> If only, most lovely of all, I yield myself and am borrowed
> By the fine, fine wind that takes its course through the chaos
> of the world ...

The book is a somewhat too hastily written, but loving account of their shared life, though it reveals more about Frieda than about Lawrence himself. Some months after its appearance Frieda received a letter from Alice Dax, the chemist's wife in Eastwood, who had initiated Lawrence into sex and whom he had enshrined in *Sons and Lovers*. She wrote:[7]

266

I had always been glad that he met you, even from the day after the event, when he told me about you, and I knew that he would leave me ... I loved him. But now I think you will understand why I was glad that you loved him too—you who could give him so much, but my cup was bitter when he wrote from Garda in the richness of fulfilment. How bitterly I envied you that day! How I resented his snobbery and his happiness whilst I was suffering in body and sick in soul, carrying an unwanted child which would never have been conceived but for an unendurable passion which only *he* had roused and my husband had slaked. So—life! And with its irony that same unwanted child is the most enduring and precious joy of all my years.

In the autumn of that year Angelo built the little chapel on the Kiowa Ranch. Frieda had decided to have Lawrence's body cremated and the ashes brought to New Mexico. She felt that this was what he would have wanted, and it was also in keeping with his symbol of the phoenix rising reborn from the ashes. Though friends had collected a sum of money to defray costs, she regarded it as her sacred duty to pay them out of her own income. She chose the spot on which the simple little building should be erected, on a hill which Lawrence had loved. Covered with young cypresses, sunflowers and cactuses, it lay on a level above the new house, some hundred and fifty yards away. "Chapel" is perhaps not the right word to use, for the building that gradually arose bore no Christian symbols: the gable above the entrance was adorned with a phoenix, not a cross. Ravagli undertook to travel to Vence and arrange for the cremation—the journey would give him a welcome opportunity to visit his wife and family in Savona.

Frieda gratefully accepted Mabel's invitation to live in her house in Taos during Angelo's absence, rather than spend the winter alone on Kiowa Ranch. Unfortunately she contracted pneumonia and had to be removed to the hospital in Albuquerque, where for several days she lay dangerously ill. Six weeks elapsed before she could leave the hospital, and even then the doctors advised her against spending the long weeks of convalescence in the frosty mountain air of Taos. The writer Raymond Otis and his wife invited her to stay with them in their house in Santa Fe, and there under their loving care she gradually regained her strength.

For this admirable young married couple the idea of Christian charity was not simply an empty phrase. Frieda had occasionally come across them in the execution of their humanitarian acts, and now she herself was the grateful object of their sympathy. Every morning Otis would sit down beside her bed and read to her passages from his new novel, which dealt with the special problems of Americans of Spanish-Mexican origin: it was the great ambition of his life to find a solution for these. As soon as Frieda was strong enough she went every afternoon with her new friends to visit the Indian *pueblos* in the neighbourhood: in Truchas, Los Alamos and Chimayo. For Frieda, Raymond and Frances Otis represented the old pioneer spirit and idealism of America.[8] She had herself begun to write a new book, in which she planned to describe the whole of her life. In the course of the next twenty years she was continually writing down disconnected fragments based on memories and experiences, and it was one of her aims with this book to show that she now identified herself wholeheartedly with America.

Early in April 1935, Angelo returned from Europe. After a number of bureaucratic tussles he had at last succeeded in carrying out Frieda's instructions. Lorenzo's body had been exhumed and reduced to ashes in the crematorium of the St Pierre cemetery in Marseilles. On his arrival in New York, however, Angelo found himself confronted with an unexpected obstacle: the American immigration officials seemed intent on continuing their feud against Lawrence even after his death, and refused to allow his ashes to enter the United States. Lengthy negotiations and an intervention from above were necessary before Ravagli was at last permitted to bring the precious urn on shore. He arrived hours late in Lamy, the railway station from which there was a bus connection to Santa Fe, and here what had been designed as an act of piety was transformed into a macabre farce.

Frieda and a number of friends drove to Lamy to meet Angelo. As he climbed off the train with all his luggage he was given an enthusiastic welcome and showered from all sides with questions, with which, with his scanty knowledge of English, he found it difficult enough to cope. Amid such confusion he laboured to convey how, after long battles both in Vence and in New York, he had finally managed to triumph over the authorities. Still animatedly chatting, they piled into the car and began the long journey back to Taos. They had gone some twenty miles before Frieda and Angelo discovered to their dismay that in all the excitement of the moment they had left the urn standing on the station platform. Panic-stricken, they turned round and raced back to Lamy, where to their great relief they found it still standing where they had left it. So off they went again towards Taos. During the journey Frieda suggested they should drop in on a painter friend. It was not until they were back at Kiowa Ranch that they realised they had left the urn behind in his studio. The next day they went to fetch the ill-starred receptacle, and this time brought it back safely to the ranch. All this was, however, only the prologue to the main drama.

Frieda had planned a dignified ceremony to accompany the placing of the urn in the chapel. It was to take place at sunset, so that the beauties of Nature could provide an impressive setting. All her friends from Taos and Santa Fe were invited, and Barbara had also arrived from England. She was now married to a Scottish journalist, Stuart Barr, and had come to America both to take part in the ceremony and to introduce her husband to her mother.

Is it to be wondered at that the "Empress of Mabeltown" grew increasingly chagrined as she watched all these preparations? For some time she had had her suspicions that Frieda, thanks to her prestige as Lawrence's widow, might break her own hitherto undisputed monopoly of Taos, and now, in the erection of this shrine and the approaching opening ceremony, she divined a clever move on the part of her "rival" to snatch Lorenzo right out of her hands.

Ever inclined to intrigue, she drew Barbara to one side and whispered a horrible secret in her ear: she had discovered that Angelo was intending to poison Frieda! Barbara should for Heaven's sake warn her mother of the danger in which she stood. Then, some days before the ceremony, Frieda heard of an elaborate plan to steal Lawrence's ashes.

The story of this plot has been told in several different ways. Frieda's own version was that a girl whom she had never met before came to her and remorsefully begged forgiveness for the part she had played in the conspiracy. In the course of their conversation Frieda, learned of the plot devised, of course, by Mabel, who intended that Brett, who was doing some glass painting in the chapel, should steal the urn; and the ashes would then be scattered over the ranch. This, so Mabel had declared, had been Lorenzo's own express wish, and it was clearly this argument that persuaded others to join the conspiracy.

Throwing down the gauntlet to Frieda was always a sure way of ensuring a battle. Frieda not only put a permanent watch on the urn, but she also let Mabel know that her dark plan was known. The "Empress", however, had other weapons up her sleeve. Frieda had arranged with the Indians on the *pueblo* to take part in the opening ceremony with a ritual dance. A few days before it was due they suddenly notified their withdrawal. It later got about that Tony Luhan, obviously egged on by Mabel, had started a rumour among the Indians that a curse lay on the ashes, since they were the remains of a great man whose rest in the grave had been disturbed. There was nothing else Frieda could do except hastily engage another group of dancers from a distant *pueblo*.

In spite of all these difficulties the ceremony passed off impressively. The judge from Taos who was to have delivered the memorial address did, it is true, cry off at the last moment (more of Mabel's work), but Barbara's husband stepped into the breach. The last rays of the setting sun were illuminating the chapel as the hotly disputed urn was solemnly placed on the appointed spot. On the small plateau beneath the hill a pyre blazed, and round it the Indians performed their ritual dance. Immediately afterwards a violent thunderstorm broke, and the darkening landscape was rent by vivid flashes of lightning.

Mabel Dodge Luhan was not present. Instead, she sent flowers, and with them a note addressed to Frieda. In this Mabel declared that she would have her way when Frieda herself was dead, and she would see to it that the ashes were scattered.

But she had underestimated her rival. At Frieda's request, Angelo mixed Lawrence's ashes with a great quantity of sand and cement. The resulting block, a ton in weight, became the altar in the chapel, and there it still stands today.[9]

Such goings-on were scarcely designed to improve the atmosphere in Taos. When, two years later, Aldous Huxley was at Kiowa, he reported that Frieda and Dorothy Brett were still not on speaking terms.

The Huxleys spent the whole of the summer of 1937 with Frieda. It was the first of many subsequent visits, for they had now turned their backs on England and Europe and were in the process of settling down in California. Aldous Huxley had come a long way since his visit to Lawrence in the Villa Mirenda. The super-intellectual, whose learning encompassed almost the entire spectrum of human knowledge, and who had done his best to demolish the standard of values of the pre-war world, had now laid the frivolous cynicism of his early years aside. He had come to believe that mankind in its search for truth and the meaning of life had wandered into a blind alley. For a time he had hoped that Lawrence's philosophy of "blood-consciousness" would help him find the answers to the questions that tormented him, but he gradually came to feel that this too was an illusion. He had travelled all over the world—to India and Hong Kong, to the West Indies, Venezuela and Mexico—in an attempt to find his way out of the labyrinth of his ideas. At last, like Faust, he came to the conclusion that the solution could not be found through the intellect alone. Increasingly his spirit began to stray from the well-worn paths of rational thought into the nebulous regions of occultism. Maria, who had long had leanings towards mysticism, strengthened him in this resolve. While still in England he had already begun to take an interest in parapsychological phenomena, and his first steps in America led him straight to Duke University in Durham, North Carolina, where Professor J. B. Rhine had become well-known through his experiments in this controversial field.

Aldous Huxley was entranced by the beauty of the country around Taos, but he declared that he would never choose Kiowa Ranch as a permanent home. "I've never been in any place, except parts of Mexico, which gave such an impression of being alien, even hostile to man," he wrote to his brother Julian.[10] It is perhaps somewhat of a mystery how he could make such comparisons: his eyes were now so weak—the right eye in fact, with its milk-coloured cornea, was completely useless—that he had to feel for his knife and fork at table, and Maria had to help him find his wineglass or the salt-cellar. In the same letter he wrote:

> Frieda is well, cheerful and a great deal calmer than she used to be. Later middle age is suiting her. The Capitano turns out to be a very decent sort of middle-class Italian—rather naif, at the same time intelligent and active. As far as one can judge he doesn't exploit Frieda, on the contrary, manages her affairs very efficiently.

Frieda was delighted to have the Huxleys as guests during these four months. She had always got on particularly well with Maria, who was lively and sensitive, and the stimulating presence of her famous husband raised Frieda's spirits. Huxley was an excellent conversationalist: ideas poured out of him in bewildering profusion. He could be talking one moment about the basic dualism in religious schools of thought—Ormuzd versus Ahriman, Jehovah and Satan, Nirvana in contrast to Samsara—and in the next considering the connections between the frescoes of Mantegna and the policies of Lodovico Gonzaga in defending Mantua's independence against Venice in the middle of the fifteenth century. Such encyclopaedic knowledge might easily have proved embarrassing to less highly educated mortals, but Huxley had a wonderful gift of conveying that he was only trying to remind his companion of something he of course knew but had momentarily forgotten. He might for instance say in his soft and musical voice: "As you know, Frieda, Patanjali was already, three centuries before Christ, voicing in his Yoga principles thoughts which are fully compatible with modern psychological thinking ..."

But these nightly conversations were by no means entirely one-sided. Huxley's feelings towards Frieda were not simply a matter of vague loyalty towards the widow of a dead friend: in fact, his admiration for her childlike wisdom and her warm personality, so devoid of all artificiality or neurosis, was so great that fifteen years later he used her as a model for the heroine in one of his few plays. In the invigorating and liberating atmosphere of Kiowa Ranch he made rapid progress with his new book, *Ends and Means*. The novel that preceded that, *Eyeless in Gaza* (1936) had shown something of Frieda's direct influence: the philologist, John Beavis, like the vicar in D. H. Lawrence's short novel *The Virgin and the Gipsy* (in which the main theme of *Lady Chatterley's Lover* is to some extent anticipated), owed his origin to her accounts of her first husband, Ernest Weekley.

Some weeks after the Huxleys left for Los Angeles, Angelo made another journey to Italy. Earlier in the year his wife had sent on Lawrence's pictures—some of them were now hanging in the new house at Kiowa Ranch—and now he went to fetch the manuscript of *Lady Chatterley's Lover*. He stayed in Savona with his wife and children, put things in order in the Villa Bernarda and visited his family in Tredozzio, his birthplace. Frieda moved to Albuquerque for the time he was away, and from there she wrote him cosy domesticated letters:[11]

> I get up at seven and make coffee and go to bed again to have it. Then I have a bath, and tidy, and write. I write with pleasure, this book will be better than *Not I, But the Wind* ... I am making some Christmas presents. I took some whisky bottles and dressed them as ladies. I made their faces with a piece of white cotton and painted the hair with black shoe polish and rouged their faces. They look very pretty, you wouldn't believe it.

Only a small part of the new book was to be devoted to Lawrence. She wanted in it to describe her new life in America, to record the journey to South America she had made with Angelo and, above all, to recall her childhood, her youthful years and her first marriage.

Since Kiowa Ranch was so remote as to be practically unreachable and uninhabitable during the cold season, Frieda bought a house in the valley outside Taos in which she could spend the winters. The house, Los Pinos, was in El Prado, a little cluster of villas on the road to Questa. It had belonged to Baron von Maltzahn, a young Austrian who had left New Mexico with a heavy heart to return to his native land. A few days after his departure Hitler marched into Austria, and Frieda wrote: "I fear that instead of having done him a good turn by buying his place, I may have done him a bad one. I wouldn't put my head in the Nazi noose."[12]

The rhythmic pattern which was to persist, interrupted by occasional pleasant interludes, for the rest of her life had by now been established. Summer was spent at the Kiowa Ranch, where there was always plenty of variety to be had. Old friends never had any difficulty in gaining access: Witter Bynner and Spud Johnson were welcome guests whenever she wanted to recall former days in Mexico; even Monty came for a visit in the following summer; and Else Jaffe's son, Friedel, turned up with his wife and children. Kiowa Ranch was also gradually developing into a Mecca for Lawrence's admirers. Most of them were Americans of whom Frieda knew nothing until they arrived unannounced at her door. "Have had thousands of people," she wrote to Monty in July 1939 after he had returned to England, exaggerating a little in her enthusiasm, no doubt. "They must want to come pretty badly to come up this rotten road." For Angelo there was always plenty to do in the house and the fields. He had also built himself a workshop and a kiln to make pottery and threw himself eagerly into his new hobby, at which he was very adept.

As soon as the frosts came, they moved down to the house in El Prado, and Dorothy Brett followed them. Frieda, never one to bear a grudge for long, had generously forgiven her, and Brett, who had also had enough of long winter months up in the mountains, built herself a house and studio close to Los Pinos, on a piece of land that Frieda gave her. To her ear-trumpet she now added a pair of field-glasses, with which she could keep an attentive eye on the road from Taos to Questa. As soon as she spotted visitors heading for Frieda's house and thought it might be worth her while making their acquaintance, she would drop her paint brushes and wander across to Los Pinos without waiting for an invitation.

Frieda and Angelo often spent part of the winter in the more hospitable climate of the West Coast and, especiallly after the war, on the Gulf of Mexico. Frieda had a number of close friends in California. In Carmel, south of San Francisco, there was the writer Henry Miller, who admired Lawrence (whether Lawrence would in exchange have cared for the moral nihilism of the *Tropics* novels is highly doubtful). Even before the Huxleys settled down near Los Angeles, Frieda had enjoyed visiting Dudley and Esta Nichols in Hollywood. Dudley, a man of unusual artistic integrity, was one of Hollywood's most gifted scriptwriters during its great period of film making.*

Once film producers had begun to take an interest in Lawrence's work, Frieda's circle of acquaintances—thanks also to Aldous and Maria Huxley—widened to include stars such as Charlie Chaplin and film directors such as William Dieterle. Frieda also became friends with Igor Stravinsky and his wife, who were the Huxleys' immediate neighbours.[13]

Lawrence had now been dead nine years. An event which a woman of weaker nature might have considered the end of all her hopes had become for Frieda the beginning of a new and happier life. This had been her avowed intention, and she moved towards her goal with a somnambulistic sure-footedness. Her life together with Ravagli may have turned out so successfully for the very reason that comparisons with her earlier life could not possibly be drawn: nobody could replace Lawrence and nobody could again grant her the inestimable boon of sharing a creative partnership with a genius. Admittedly she had had to pay a high price for the privilege, and it is unlikely that she would have been prepared to pay it again: she was past the age at which one is willing to regard humiliations and privations as a fair exchange for ecstatic stimulus. What Angelo could offer her was the contentment of uncomplicated companionship.

On her sixtieth birthday she could look back with satisfaction on the past years of her life. She celebrated it, as she did every year, at Kiowa together with Witter Bynner, whose birthday fell on the previous day. On this occasion lights were burning in all the rooms and the house was surrounded by a ring of flickering lamps. There was *vino*, beer and cider in plenty, the two large rooms were filled with lively dancers and out in the garden a whole side of beef was roasting on a spit.

* Among other films, Dudley Nichols was responsible for the film scenarios of *The Informer, Stagecoach, For Whom the Bell Tolls, Sister Kenny* and *The Fugitive*.

But all the same a dark shadow lay over the festivities. Two or three weeks earlier an immigration officer had come to the ranch. Politely but inexorably he had questioned her about the nature of her relationship with Angelo, which she cheerfully described as "intimate". But gradually it became clear to her that more was at stake than simply the question of her unmarried status. The authorities were seeking evidence that Frieda was immorally "keeping" Angelo, so that they might have an excuse to bring him before the courts on a charge of "moral turpitude". If he were to be found guilty, deportation would be the inevitable result.[14] The enquiries had begun in El Paso and, from a remark made by the officer, Frieda gathered that the immigration authorities there had not yet forgotten the difficulties Lawrence had once caused them. It was at El Paso, it will be recalled, that Lorenzo had been stopped when, more dead than alive, he was returning to Taos after his visit to Mexico. Only after two days of protests, threats, appeals and desperate telephone calls had the decision not to admit him been reversed through the intervention of the American Ambassador in Mexico City. That had been fourteen years ago, but the immigration people in El Paso, endowed through the nature of their work with good memories and an efficient filing system, still recalled the episode with marked displeasure. Frieda could expect no mercy from them. Whoever it was who had laid the complaint had touched her on her most vulnerable spot. This time it was certainly not Mabel. On the contrary, impelled by eccentric philosophical notions of her own, Mabel moved heaven and earth to save Angelo from a criminal charge.

Fortunately the unsavoury visit was not followed up. It is doubtful whether this was due to Mabel's good offices so much as to the intervention of world history, which brought the authorities face to face with problems of a far weightier kind. Hitler invaded Poland, and it now required forces much stronger than immigration officials to keep— or try to keep—borders intact. Although there was still some time to go before America was also dragged into the war, both Frieda and Angelo were keenly aware of the insecurity of their position. She was of course, in spite of her German birth, protected by her British nationality, but Angelo was still an out and out Italian—which meant, from December 1941 onwards, an enemy alien. "We don't know yet if it is better to stay here where people know us," wrote Frieda a few days after Pearl Harbor. "It is just on the cards that all aliens are interned." This time there could be no doubt where her sympathies lay. She loathed Hitler.

"I feel very American," she wrote. "I think, so does Angelino, his poor Italy has been a victim."

They were neither interned nor persecuted. Hardly sixty miles away in Los Alamos, unknown to them, an army of physicists and engineers was working on a bomb which, for better or worse, was to change the course of history.

25

"I am 71, but well," Frieda wrote to Lady Cynthia Asquith in October 1950. "I have the life I want."

She was now an "old girl", as she called it. Her white hair with its ragged parting still had a golden sheen, and her deep guttural voice betrayed the effects of constant cigarette smoking. But age had not dimmed her *joie de vivre*. The wrinkles in her face came from laughter, her fine clear eyes twinkled humorously and her cheerfulness was as infectious as it had ever been in earlier days.

She now spent less of her time at Kiowa Ranch. It was more comfortable and better for her heart to stay down in the valley below. Whenever she was in El Prado, Dorothy Brett would come over daily from her house nearby, and even Mabel, indestructible as ever, had stopped treating her as a rival and regarded her rather as a sort of honorary president of the artists' colony in Taos. More and more Frieda and Angelo tended to spend the winter months on the Gulf of Mexico. After the war she had bought a small and simple house on the coast at Port Isabel, the southernmost point of the United States. Here the weeks passed in an atmosphere of idyllic tranquillity. Frieda enjoyed watching the Mexican fishermen in their sailing boats, and was fascinated by the sight of ships, loaded with bananas or pineapples, steaming into the canal which connected the sea with Brownsville, the great cotton city on the banks of the Rio Grande. At evening the ships seemed to be gliding directly across the flat land until they disappeared into the golden mists of the setting sun. Angelo amused himself sailing out to sea with the fishermen or sitting in the shadow of the house, painting. Frequently they would go for a walk together on Padre Island, an endless sand dune separating the lagoon from the open sea and populated by pelicans, seagulls and cranes.

"You can't imagine how rich and full my life is. For an old woman, amazing," wrote Frieda to her son Monty. Her younger sister, Nusch, came to visit her in Port Isabel. They had not seen each other for fifteen years, but, as Frieda admiringly noted, Johanna was still the elegant *grande dame* she remembered. Among Frieda's other visitors was

277

the poet Stephen Spender who, when he called on her in Taos, bought with him a young American musician, Leonard Bernstein, then on the threshold of the career that was to carry him to world fame. Tennessee Williams settled down on Kiowa Ranch to write a play, but fled after three days because he found Lawrence's ghost too overpowering in the little log cabin. Travelling backwards and forwards between Santa Fe and Mexico, Witter Bynner visited Frieda wherever she happened to be. He had now, rather belatedly, completed his own book about Lawrence, *Journey with Genius*, which was full of pinpricks against the genius and admiration for Frieda. It was only one of several books about D. H. Lawrence which came out in the space of a few months. After a number of years they were to fill whole shelves in the public libraries.

The war years had played a significant part in arousing interest in and understanding for Lawrence's books. New editions were brought out both in England and America, and translations began to appear in other countries. Such recognition filled Frieda with deep pride, and the knowledge that she had been justified in her unshakeable belief in his genius brought her no less satisfaction than the material benefits she was now reaping from his belated success. Her interests were being well looked after by Laurence Pollinger, Lawrence's London agent. Frieda never mentioned his name without adding to it an expression of trust and praise.

Her thoughts were now turning with increasing frequency to the past. In the happy tranquillity of old age she set about ordering her life and gathering up once again the torn strands of old friendships. True, the world of her early years had long disappeared, war had swept over the Metz of her childhood, the Berlin of her youth, the Silesia of the Richthofen family. In a letter to an English friend she wrote:[1]

> I had a document from a Richthofen cousin, trying to account for the members of the family. A sad story: 25 estate houses & all destroyed by the Russians, people turned out, old women burned out, dying—3 young ones committed suicide & were "verschleppt" by the Russians. I never saw Silesia & always wanted to! I loved the family, great "individualists", with a strain of mysticism. This is a tale of woe—there are lots of them.

Even before the war she had begun an exchange of letters with Karl von Marbahr, who had idolised her when she was still a young girl in Metz and he a smart lieutenant. How willingly would he have married her then! His nostalgic letters revealed that he still clung to the vanished dream. And she too thought of him with love. When, during the war, she started on a new version of her memoirs—one of many autobiographical fragments—she decided to dedicate the projected book to him. Her draft introduction reads almost like a love letter written by an old woman who has remained eternally young at heart:[2]

> And now I have not heard from you for more than three years. But it is always the same: I don't hear from you, I go on with my living all those years since I was seventeen and you were twenty-four and we never met again and I forget you. Then suddenly you are there and nearer than anything else in the world and I hear your unforgettable voice right in my ears ...

When the war was over she conjured up another figure from the shadows of the past: John Middleton Murry. She had long forgiven him for his biography of Lorenzo—that "malignant and vindictive hagiography"—which he had later followed up with his apologetic *Reminiscences*. Following the death of his second wife, Murry had made a disastrous third marriage, which led to a nervous breakdown. It had needed yet another woman, Mary Gamble, to rescue him from his own privately created hell. Now he was living with Mary, who was to become his fourth wife, and farming in Norfolk, and he wrote to Frieda: "You know I am not trying to flatter you, my dear, when I say that she reminds me of you more than any other woman."

But there was one matter in Frieda's own life that still needed tidying up. The intervention of the immigration authorities in El Paso had revealed both to her and to Ravagli the insecurity of their life together. Since that embarrassing episode neither of them had dared to leave the United States for fear they would not be permitted to return. Frieda was additionally worried by the feeling that she had placed Angelo in an equivocal position, and she decided that their relationship must be normalised.

Ravagli's Italian wife was still living in Savona. He obtained her consent to a formal dissolution of the marriage, and a divorce was granted by the District Court at Taos on 17 August 1950.[3] All legal obstacles having now been removed, Frieda and Angelo were married at the Taos County Courthouse on 31 October 1950.*

"Of course nothing is really changed," Frieda wrote to Monty,

---

* Neither the divorce nor Ravagli's marriage to Frieda were legally recognised in Italy. Following Frieda's death six years later, Angelo returned to Italy and resumed life with his first wife in the Villa Bernarda.

"except that we can now both become American citizens and he can go to Italy without danger of not being able to return, and I could come to England."

It was not until June 1952 that she in fact made the journey to England. Frieda was now seventy-two, and it was her last chance of seeing her children and grandchildren. She also wrote to Ida Wilhelmy, the devoted nanny of her Nottingham years, whom Ernest Weekley dismissed when Frieda eloped with Lawrence. She invited Ida, who now lived in Germany, to stay with her at the Kingsley Hotel, Frieda's usual place of abode when she was in London.

Monty, however, insisted that this time his mother should spend at least a few days in his house. He was now curator of the Bethnal Green Museum in the East End of London, and he lived in a fine old house, built by one of Oliver Cromwell's ancestors, which went with the job. It was a happy time: Frieda was filled with matriarchal pride at her first sight of her five grandchildren, and the youngsters were fascinated by the lively old lady, exotically dressed and overloaded with turquoise bracelets and necklaces, of whose existence they had up till then had only dark hints.

One afternoon Elsa's husband, Edward Seaman, a naval commander, called for Frieda in his car and took her to Putney to see his house. He drove past it at a snail's pace, for she was not to be invited inside. "I am quite willing to talk to him," Frieda declared, but her son-in-law shook his head: "No, it would not be advisable." In his study on the first floor, completely unaware of her proximity, Ernest Weekley sat immersed in his books.

He was now eighty-seven and he had never married again. A year previously Nottingham University had bestowed an honorary doctorate on him, and in his speech of thanks the old professor recalled with emotion that it was now fifty-three years since he had given his first lecture at University College. Surely as his mind wandered back over the past, he must have remembered the woman to whom he had then been married? But he had never forgiven Frieda. He did not talk about her, even to his children, and nobody would have dared mention her name in his presence. When Monty returned from Taos, the professor, who knew where he had been, did not by so much as a word show any desire to know how she was, and Monty was himself reluctant to volunteer the information.

Implacable and irreconcilable to the end, Ernest Weekley died on 7 May 1954, two years after Frieda's visit to London. In a drawer of his writing desk several photographs of Frieda were discovered, taken at the time of their wedding.[4]

During her visit to London Frieda met only one of her old English friends. She let John Middleton Murry know that she was there, and he came up from his farm in Norfolk to see her. They met in the lounge of the Kingsley Hotel, and Mary Gamble, who was with him, wrote: "She greeted John as if they had only met last week and was immediately friendly to me."

It was, as she herself surely knew, Frieda's last visit to London. Back in Taos she received an endless stream of visitors: admirers of Lawrence's work, journalists, sensation-seekers and students preparing theses on subjects such as "Lawrence's Influence on American Literature", "Lawrence and his Use of Topography", "A Comparison between Lawrence and Proust". When Angelo was away, Brett would come to keep her company. Herself now over sixty, she had become a landmark in her own right in Taos. She was busy painting pictures of Indian ritual dances. Though she had lost her former shyness, she was still as eccentric as ever. She had a new idol, whom she worshipped as selflessly as she had once worshipped Lorenzo. This was the conductor Leopold Stokowski, whom she had got to know in Mabel's house.

At the beginning of 1951 Maria Huxley had undergone an operation for cancer of the breast. Frieda had visited her in Los Angeles, and later, Angelo brought her home from the hospital in his car. Maria knew that she had not long to live, but she remained remarkably composed, sustained by her occult beliefs. "To me," she declared, "dying is no more than going from one room to another."

For a short time Aldous pursued an incongruous double life, dividing his time between the harsh realities of the dream factory in Hollywood and the "ultimate reality" of mystical experience. But his film work, with which he had some success, was gradually pushed aside, and his last writings reflected his growing desire to experience what he, as an agnostic, considered unknowable. The great builder of bridges between the various disciplines of knowledge was now attempting to span the gap between intellect and intuition, and was experimenting somewhat uncritically with hypnosis and the mysteries of personal magnetism.

In his early years he had attempted to penetrate the regions of darkness with the sharp rays of his intellect: now he was exploring darkness in search of colour and form. Not long after Maria's incurable cancer had been diagnosed, he began to see a possibility of perceiving God, without believing in him, in the hallucinations induced by mescalin, LSD and psilocybin. He attempted to describe such hallucinatory experiences in his book *The Doors of Perception*, and together with Dr Humphrey Osmond, a London psychiatrist, he coined the word which was to become part of the vocabulary of the hippy subculture: "psychedelic". In this phase of his bitter odyssey he was using mescalin as a means of gaining entry to the realms of the occult. As a result he unwittingly lent the authority of his renowned name to the taking of drugs.

In his desperation he snatched at any chance, however remote, that might help to relieve Maria's sufferings and postpone the inevitable. Hypnosis, acupuncture, the latest psycho-pharmacological theories on methods of extending consciousness—he even flew with her to the Lebanon to visit a faith-healer. But it was all to no avail: Maria died on 12 February 1955. Aldous sat beside her death-bed, trying with one hand on the crown of her head and the other on her solar plexus to ease her "going from one room to another" by the power of his personal magnetism.

Frieda was in Port Isabel when the news came through. Aldous Huxley gave her a detailed description of Maria's death in a letter covering several pages, and added:[5]

> I thought very often of that spring night in Vence, twenty-five years ago, while I was sitting beside Maria's bed ... It's so difficult to know what one can do for someone who is dying—what one can do, incidentally, for oneself. What I did seemed to be of some help for her, as well as for me. The men of the middle ages used to talk of the *ars moriandi*—the art of dying.

Two months later he travelled right across the American continent to visit Frieda on the Gulf of Mexico. He stayed two days in Port Isabel and then journeyed up the east coast to Washington and New York to discuss the production of his new play, *The Genius and the Goddess*. The goddess is named Katy, but in reality she is none other than Frieda herself.

She had been able to see her elder sister again. Else Jaffe came to America in the spring of 1954 to visit her son, Friedel, in New York, and afterwards she came to stay with Frieda. Else's heart was not what it used to be (although she was to survive Frieda by many years), and she felt unable to face the journey to Taos high up in the mountains.

So the two sisters met in Albuquerque. The significance of this meeting after so many years was heightened by the feeling they both had that it would almost certainly be their last.

For Frieda, whose vigour had astounded her friends only a short while before, was now beginning to show signs of her age. She had diabetes and was increasingly plagued by asthma. However, needless to say, her vitality remained unbroken and she took no notice of the warning signs.

In April 1956 she and Angelo were returning to Taos from their winter sojourn in Port Isabel when, high up in the mountains, Angelo took a wrong turning. To their great surprise they found themselves in Las Vegas instead of Santa Fe, and they had to drive through several snow-covered mountain passes to regain the right road. The excitements and exertions of the journey had obviously put a great strain on Frieda, and that night she collapsed in the bathroom. "Funny," she said to Angelo when he came to help her, "I can't get up." Alarmed, he sent for a doctor, and she was taken by ambulance to the hospital in Santa Fe. She had to spend the next two weeks in bed. According to the diagnosis she was suffering from a virus infection, but presumably she had in fact had a slight stroke.[6]

Soon afterwards Barbara arrived from England. She found her mother still weak but in excellent spirits. There was so much to talk about—"We have a quiet female time," wrote Frieda to Middleton Murry. Koteliansky had died in the previous year, Mabel was unwell, Aldous Huxley had married again.* The film rights of *Sons and Lovers* had been sold and *Lady Chatterley's Lover* was being made into a film in France, with Danielle Darrieux in the title role. Frieda had made her will: one half of her estate and all future copyright receipts were to go to Angelo, while the other half was to be divided up between her three children. Kiowa Ranch, however, together with the little memorial

---

* Aldous Huxley married Laura Archera in March 1956 in a drive-in-wedding chapel in Yuma, Arizona. Laura, who had started out as a solo violinist, had been a film cutter at the time she met the Huxleys, and their common interest in occultism forged a strong bond between them. After 1956 Huxley tried out a new method of improving the sight which had been developed by Dr W. H. Bates, though it was frowned on by orthodox ophthalmologists. Nevertheless, Huxley managed to improve his sight considerably. He died on 22 November 1963, like Maria, of cancer. At his express wish his body was cremated entirely without ceremony. As Laura declared: "The entire cost was $328.50, the minimum. Aldous wanted no money spent on this sort of thing." In her books of reminiscences, dedicated to "the Flower Children of all times", she claims to have received definite proof of Huxley's existence in the after-life.

chapel, was to go to the University of New Mexico as a Lawrence Foundation.

Barby left on 17 July, and on the same day Angelo, who had been on a visit to England and Italy, returned to El Prado. On Wednesday, 8 August, at about 11 p.m., Frieda had a severe stroke. Angelo, startled by a noise, found her lying on the floor beside her bed, unable to rise or to speak. She was paralysed all down the right side. A woman doctor, Dr Howe, arrived within ten minutes and remained with Frieda the rest of the night. The whole of the next day Frieda was in a state of semi-consciousness, and the doctors thought it inadvisable to move her to the hospital. Rachel Hawk, her neighbour from the Del Monte Ranch, came to lend a hand, and two nurses were engaged. Her condition improved up to the morning of Friday, but in the afternoon she had a relapse and sank into a deep coma. She died at seven in the morning on Saturday, 11 August 1956. It was her seventy-seventh birthday.

Frieda had wanted a simple unadorned coffin and a primitive wooden cross over her grave. But here Angelo betrayed his Italian peasant origins : fearing that such simplicity might lead people to think him mean, he ordered a richly decorated coffin and an expensive granite headstone.

The coffin was laid out in the mortuary chapel at Taos, surrounded by a mass of flowers. "When we saw her Sunday she was completely at peace and noble and the aristocrat she was," wrote Joe Glasco to Barbara. (Glasco and the writer Bill Goyen were two young Americans who had been Frieda's neighbours ever since, after the war, she had given them a piece of land on her ranch as a token of friendship.) "On Monday all day her friends came to see her then in the Chapel with all the flowers. There was no music, just Frieda and the flowers."

In the afternoon the funeral procession set off along the steep road up to the ranch. Among the inhabitants of Taos who followed the coffin were some over eighty years old. The funeral ceremony at the ranch was short and simple. Bill Goyen spoke a few words of farewell and read the poem by Lawrence that Frieda had so much loved: "Not I, not I but the wind that blows through me ..." After that a tape recording was played of Frieda herself reciting Psalm 121: "I will lift up mine eyes unto the hills ..."[7]

The grave lies in a place chosen by Frieda, a few paces from Lawrence's memorial chapel.

26

Would Shakespeare have become a wool merchant if he had not been caught poaching? Would the French Revolution have taken a different course if years of vagabond life had not instilled in Rousseau, its great precursor, a contempt for social conventions? Would Russia have become a communist state if the German government had not permitted Lenin, exiled in Switzerland, to cross Germany in a sealed railway compartment? Would the sexual revolt of the sixties have been less radical if fifty years earlier D. H. Lawrence had not happened to meet Frieda Weekley?

Such armchair speculations are hardly necessary to demonstrate the truism that history is not made by prominent personalities or social and economic forces alone, but owes something to mere chance. However, one might without fear of contradiction assert that, while Lawrence, even without Frieda, would undoubtedly have been one of the most significant writers of our century, he would almost certainly never have written *Lady Chatterley's Lover*.

On 30 April 1959 Robert K. Christenberry, Postmaster of the City of New York, issued an order for the temporary seizure of twenty-four cartons sent by the Grove Press, at that time a small but reputable firm of publishers. The parcels contained copies of *Lady Chatterley's Lover* in an edition designed for public sale in America. Christenberry was able to order the interception under existing regulations, for the postal distribution of *Lady Chatterley's Lover* had already been forbidden in the United States thirty years previously, when Lawrence brought out his private edition in co-operation with Pino Orioli. The Post Office Department in the United States is vested with judicial powers, and in accordance with established procedure a trial was required to review the decision. The hearing took place in Washington two weeks later, and the case for the Post Office was presented by their lawyer, Saul J. Mindel. Starting with an assurance that the Post Office did not presume to act as censor and that he was not disputing the novel's literary value, Mindel nevertheless went on to declare that this was submerged and outweighed by the obscenity contained in it. This charge, he averred,[1]

> is made with regard to the effect of the book on the average member of the community, and not upon a particular class, much more sophisticated than the average, which may become so immersed in its admiration of the author's technical skill in this book and his other works that it overlooks the end to which that skill is applied, that is, the extremely graphic and detailed portrayal of a woman's sex experiences with a variety of men before and during her marriage. A literary critic, a book reviewer, may enter his plea that *Lady Chatterley's Lover* should not be barred, but in doing so he merely expresses his personal opinion in the matter. He can speak only for himself and not for the community at large.

This view was a fair reflection of the line then generally taken in American courts, which was that, in deciding whether a book was obscene or not, the question of its literary value was of only subsidiary importance. It was this argument that had led in 1930 to Theodore Dreiser's novel *An American Tragedy* being banned as obscene and indecent, a decision which today seems quite incomprehensible. Four years later, however, an important breakthrough occurred: the federal courts in New York decided that James Joyce's *Ulysses* was *not* obscene —the "obscenity" of the critical last chapter did *not* "outbalance" the work as a whole.

In spite of this, the Postmaster General upheld the seizure of copies of *Lady Chatterley's Lover*. Barney Rosset, head of the Grove Press, decided to appeal against his ruling. On 21 July 1959 the Federal Court, sitting in New York, decided that *Lady Chatterley's Lover* could not be considered an obscene book. The government entered an appeal against this reversal, but in the upper courts the decision in favour of *Lady Chatterley's Lover* was upheld.

The publishers' lawyer, Charles Rembar, based his defence on the argument that the postal authorities, in imposing their ban, had gone against the American Constitution, which in its First Amendment states: "Congress shall make no law ... abridging the freedom of speech, or of the press." It had never of course been the intention of the First Amendment to extend protection to pornographic rubbish, but up till then the courts had hardly even considered the question of literary value. When they did, some judges inclined to the view that the higher the quality, the worse the offence, since the effect of a well-written book was greater and more dangerous than that of a badly written one. The *Lady Chatterley* trial put an end to this approach. Since then American courts have always taken the opposite view: they have declared that no book of true literary merit can be suppressed on the grounds of obscenity. The term "literary merit" is obviously a very elastic one which cannot be measured by any absolute standard, and the tendency now is to interpret it very liberally. Rembar's argument did more than just win the case for *Lady Chatterley*: it established the principle that sex is a legitimate subject for literary treatment.

The consequences of this soon became apparent in Great Britain. How could the work of a prominent British author continue to be banned in his native land when it was now freely accessible in the United States? With the deliberate intention of forcing the issue, Penguin Books decided to bring out a paperback edition of *Lady Chatterley's Lover*. The challenge was swiftly taken up. The Director of Public Prosecutions brought a charge against the publishers under the new Obscene Publications Act, which had become law only in the previous year. In contrast to the sober one-day hearing in America, in which only two literary critics were invited to give evidence, the trial at the Old Bailey deployed all the traditional pomp of English law. Starting on 20 October 1960, it lasted five full days, and the defence called no fewer than thirty-five witnesses.[2] It was an all-star cast, with high church dignitaries such as the Bishop of Woolwich, and famous authors such as E. M. Forster, Rebecca West and Cecil Day Lewis. Yet for all the imposing names and the lavish expenditure of time and money, the trial in London was far less concerned with fundamental issues than its counterpart in America had been. Here was no battle for basic democratic freedoms, but just a matter of two simple questions —firstly, whether the book tended to "deprave and corrupt"; and secondly, whether its publication would be for the good of the community as a whole (by virtue, for instance, of being good literature). One after another the witnesses stood up to testify to Lawrence's literary greatness and to the morality of his purpose.

It was a very imposing parade, and it might have been expected that Mervyn Griffith-Jones, the prosecuting counsel, who was no less passionately convinced of the importance and justice of his cause than his opponent, would have called up an equally impressive army of experts to crush the defending forces. But nothing of that sort occurred. Surprisingly, Griffith-Jones elected to produce no expert witnesses, though he would have had no difficulty in finding churchmen, teachers and writers prepared to point with complete sincerity to the dangers of permissiveness and to draw alarming parallels with the fall of the Roman Empire.

Poor Lady Chatterley! Prosecuting counsel let no opportunity go by of attacking her. He seemed to forget that adultery had been one of the basic themes of world literature ever since the *Iliad* and the Bible. Not only that, but, as the trial reached its third, fourth and fifth days, he directed his attack less and less against the book and more and more against Lady Chatterley herself, and he left no doubt that he saw her as a fictional version of Frieda.

Poor Frieda, brought to trial four years after her death! And even the judge, Mr Justice Byrne, seemed to hint, as far as his judicial impartiality would allow him, that he would have found her guilty.

The jurors, a collection of ordinary middle-aged men and women conforming in every way to the statistical conception of "average citizens", took three hours to reach their verdict, which had, according to the law, to be unanimous. Their verdict was "Not Guilty", which meant that the publishers were acquitted, Lady Chatterley exonerated and the book cleared for publication.

Before the applause had died away in the courtroom Sir Allen Lane, head of Penguin Books, was on the telephone to his office, giving the signal to start at once with the distribution of the two hundred thousand copies that had been printed. Within six weeks two million copies of the English paperback edition of *Lady Chatterley's Lover* had been sold, and in the following six months this number rose by a further 1,300,000. In the United States sales amounted, two years after the book had been released, to six million copies.

Did all these millions of people buy the book because prominent critics had proclaimed its literary value? No, of course not. They wanted to read it because it had long been banned, because they were curious about it and, above all, because they hoped that, even if the court had decided otherwise, it might prove after all to be obscene. Both its release and its huge success can be seen as expressions of the change in the moral climate which had been building up during the previous decade. At the same time this build-up was given an unparalleled boost.

Since in the United States literary value had become the criterion by which books could be protected from the law, other works were not slow in reaping the benefit. It was no longer necessary, having bought copies of Henry Miller's *Tropics* novels in Paris, to smuggle them past the American customs officials hidden in suitcases among the underwear—they could be bought now at every drugstore. Writers suddenly found themselves free to explore a new territory which one might, if the word were not so obviously out of place in this context, describe as virgin. In the theatre and cinema too, obscurantism and evasiveness had been dealt a decisive blow. Nevertheless, the boundaries between pornography and "literary value" are ill-defined, and it is a sobering thought that our hard-won liberation from the fetters of Victorian prudery can so swiftly be taken as a green light for voyeurism. This new development cannot be confined within the bounds of a single country. In Britain as in America, the authorities have, since the *Lady Chatterley* trial, been chary of giving extra publicity to other books by staging trials of which the outcome must be so uncertain, and, because the world has shrunk in the past hundred years to the size of a wasps' nest, an act of copulation in New York can soon become a talking point in London, Berlin and Tokyo.

It would be absurd to maintain that *Lady Chatterley's Lover* alone has been responsible for all this: no seed takes root unless it is sown on fruitful soil. But certainly no other single factor contributed more strikingly to the loosening of the moral code than the two law trials concerning Lawrence's novel. What a magnificent stroke of irony that history should have presented the twentieth century with a puritan as its phallic messiah! At the time he was working on *Lady Chatterley's Lover* Lawrence read the memoirs of Casanova and was disgusted by their rakish frivolity. His intention in making use in this novel of four-letter words offensive to "decent society" was to cleanse these expressions of their impure associations. Yet when Maria Huxley, who typed a part of the manuscript, herself used one or two of them in conversation, Lawrence was profoundly shocked and reproached her vehemently.[3]

He would surely have had one of his famous outbursts of rage if anyone had ventured to prophesy that the novel he had written to proclaim the sacredness of physical love and to condemn the evil of commercialisation would become an instrument in the commercialisation of sex. Certainly he would not have been at all amused by the irony of the situation. Frieda—his model and his inspiration—perhaps would: in fact, she would probably have broken out into one of her characteristic outbursts of loud laughter, if she had lived to see it all happen.

Notes

CHAPTER 1

Extracts from the official records of the trial, October 1960.

CHAPTER 2

1 The details concerning Frieda von Richthofen's ancestry are largely based on the jubilee publication *Praetorius von Richthofen 1561–1961* (Dr Hartmann Freiherr von Richthofen). Other information was kindly provided by Professor Dr Bolko Freiherr von Richthofen

2 *Ferdinand Freiherr von Richthofen*, a memorial address delivered by Erich von Drygalski in 1906 at a meeting of the Gesellschaft für Erdkunde in Berlin. Ferdinand Freiherr von Richthofen: *Tagebücher aus China*, Volume 2

3 Dr Joseph Portsch: *Schlesien. Eine Landeskunde für das deutsche Volk* (Breslau, 1911)

4 Both Frieda von Richthofen and her sister Else Jaffe used to speak of their grandmother as *Gräfin* (Countess) Laszowska. Genealogical researches carried out at the request of the author failed to find any confirmation that Amalie Luise von Laszowska (1811–60) in fact had a claim to that title. Her father was Karl von Laszowska auf Stein und Leschczin, and her mother's maiden name was Skrebensky. This gave Lawrence the name for his hero in *The Rainbow*

CHAPTER 3

1 The account of Frieda's early years is based to a large extent on her own fragmentary writings, edited by Professor E. W. Tedlock and published under the title *The Memoirs and Correspondence*

2 Mrs Barbara Barr, Frieda's younger daughter, in a BBC broadcast on 14 November 1961

3 Georg Lang: *Metz und seine Umgebungen* (Metz, 1875), *Meyers Grosses Konversationslexikon*, 6th edition, Volume 13, 1909

4 Frieda Lawrence: *The Memoirs and Correspondence*. The undated letter must have been written in 1938 or 1939 and not, as its position in Tedlock's book suggests, in the autumn of 1944

5 For information concerning the girls' school run by the Blass sisters the author is indebted to Dr Marianne von Eckardt and Mr C. Montague Weekley

6 Details of Oswald Freiherr von Richthofen's household in Berlin were kindly supplied to the author by his grandson of the same name, at present German Ambassador in Singapore

CHAPTER 4

1 Ernest Weekley: *An Etymological Dictionary of Modern English* (Dover Publications Inc., New York, 1967) contains a biographical essay on Ernest Weekley, written by Montague Weekley

2 Frieda Lawrence: *The Memoirs and Correspondence*

3 Both E. W. Tedlock and E. Nehls state that the wedding took place "in September 1899". The date recorded in the *Genealogisches Handbuch des Adels* is, however, 29 August 1899. The *Evangelische Kirchengemeinde-Amt*, the office of the Evangelical Church in Freiburg, has confirmed this latter date to the author. Adding, however, that there is no reference in the records of the individual

churches in Freiburg to a marriage, the office remarks: "Perhaps it took place in the English Church, Turnseestrasse 59."

4 Frieda Lawrence: *The Memoirs and Correspondence*

CHAPTER 5

1 The Weekleys moved twice during the years in Nottingham, each time to a nicer house in a better residential district. The addresses were: 9 Goldswong Terrace, 8 Vickers Road and Cowley, Private Road, Mapperley

2 Elsa was born on 13 September 1903, Barbara on 20 October 1904

3 In his *Flowers of the Forest* David Garnett records that Max von Schreibershofen was adjutant to the German Crown Prince. In a letter to the author, however, Dr Else Jaffe declares most emphatically that her brother-in-law was never adjutant to any prince

4 Quotations taken from *The Memoirs and Correspondence*

5 In her memoirs Frieda only hints at this friendship and does not mention Dowson by name. For purposes of concealment she turned the lace manufacturer into a barrister. The author is greatly indebted to Frieda's daughter, Mrs Barbara Barr, for this information

6 In *The Memoirs and Correspondence* Dr Otto Gross is concealed behind the name Octavio. The author is indebted to Dr Else Jaffe and her daughter Dr Marianne von Eckardt for the identification as well as for details of Gross's life and for drawing his attention to Leonhard Frank's description

CHAPTER 6

1 D. H. Lawrence: *Nottingham and the Mining Countryside*. This chapter, as well as the two following chapters, are based, apart from Lawrence's own writings, mainly on Moore's *The Intelligent Heart* and extracts in Nehl's *D. H. Lawrence: A Composite Biography*, Volume 1

2 *Nottingham and the Mining Countryside*

3 E.T. (Jessie Chambers): *D. H. Lawrence: A Personal Record*

4 From a BBC broadcast in 1948. Printed in Nehls' *D. H. Lawrence: A Composite Biography*, Volume 1

5 Quoted in the *Cambridge Quarterly*, May 1969

6 Moore: *The Intelligent Heart*

CHAPTER 7

1 From a personal report by Philip F. T. Smith, published in Moore's *The Intelligent Heart*

2 Lawrence: *Lilies in the Fire*

3 MacShane: *The Life and Work of Ford Madox Ford*

4 The author here follows Hueffer's account. Jessie Chambers maintains that she sent only some of Lawrence's poems to the *English Review* without his knowledge

5 Ford Madox Ford: *Return to Yesterday*, and Violet Hunt: *I Have This to Say*

6 Lawrence: letter to A. W. McLeod, 5 December 1910

7 E.T. (Jessie Chambers): *D. H. Lawrence*

8 Ernest Rhys: *Everyman Remembers*, London, 1931

9 Heilbrun: *The Garnett Family*

CHAPTER 8

1 Dated "Tuesday": presumably 7 May 1912

2 Dated by Ernest Weekley in error "13 April 1912"; presumably written on 13 May

3 Frieda Lawrence: *Not I, But the Wind* . . .

4 Letter from Icking, 3 July 1912

5 David Garnett: *The Golden Echo*

CHAPTER 9

1 Information supplied by Mrs Barbara Barr
2 E.T. (Jessie Chambers): *D. H. Lawrence*
3 Letter from Fiascherino, undated (presumably February 1914)
4 Undated letter from Fiascherino (presumably February 1914)

CHAPTER 10

1 David Garnett: *The Golden Echo*
2 Murry: *Between Two Worlds*. Lea: *The Life of John Middleton Murry*
3 C. Asquith: *Remember and Be Glad*

CHAPTER 11

1 Letter from Lerici, 22 April 1914
2 Murry: *Between Two Worlds*
3 Lawrence: *Kangaroo*
4 Aldous Huxley: Introduction to *The Letters of D. H. Lawrence*
5 Carswell: *The Savage Pilgrimage*
6 Aldington: *Life for Life's Sake*

CHAPTER 12

1 Lawrence: letter to Amy Lowell, 18 December 1914
2 Compton Mackenzie: *The Four Winds of Love: The South Wind*. Also: *My Life and Times, Octave IV*
3 Ottoline: *The Early Memoirs of Lady Ottoline Morrell*. Leonard Woolf: *Beginning Again*. C. M. Bowra: *Memoirs*. Julian Huxley: *Memoirs*
4 Russell: *Autobiography*
5 Russell: *Autobiography*
6 Letter of 8 December 1915. Quoted in Russell's article in *Harper's Magazine*, February 1953
7 Russell: *Autobiography*
8 Huxley: *The Letters of D. H. Lawrence*. See also Daleski: *The Forked Flame*
9 Lawrence: *The Rainbow*
10 Leavis: *D. H. Lawrence, Novelist*
11 See also Perkin: *The Origins of Modern English Society 1780–1880*
12 Marcus: *The Other Victorians*. Cecil: *Life in Edwardian England*

CHAPTER 13

1 *Collected Letters*, date uncertain (presumably 21 November 1918), ed.Moore
2 Aldous Huxley: Introduction to *The Letters of D. H. Lawrence*
3 Margot Asquith: *Autobiography*
4 Lawrence in a letter to Lady Ottoline Morrell, 9 September 1915. See also *Kangaroo*
5 Cecil Gray: *Musical Chairs*, 1948. Lawrence: *Kangaroo*
6 Record of a BBC broadcast interview with the Hocking family, Lawrence's neighbours, quoted by Nehls, Volume 1
7 Adolf Wasner: *Rittmeister Manfred Freiherr v. Richthofen, Deutschlands grösster Fliegerheld*. Floyd Gibbons: *The Red Knight of Germany*. Colin Ross: *The Red Baron* (in *The Observer* Colour Supplement, 21 April 1968)
8 Reminiscences of Cecily Lambert Minchin, published in Nehls, Volume 1

CHAPTER 14

1 David Garnett: *Flowers of the Forest*
2 Rainer Maria Rilke: *Briefe aus den Jahren 1914–1921*, 1938

3 William Manchester: *The Arms of Krupp 1587–1968*, 1969
4 Aldington: *Pinorman*
5 The original copy of this letter has been destroyed. Moore gives the probable date as 6 February 1920
6 Mackenzie: *My Life and Times, Octave V*
7 Nehls, Volume 2
8 Lawrence: Foreword to *Memoirs of the Foreign Legion* by M. M. (Maurice Magnus), 1925
9 West: *D. H. Lawrence, an Elegy*, 1930

CHAPTER 15

1 Nehls, Volume 2
2 Luhan: *Lorenzo in Taos*
3 Earl and Achsah Brewster: *D. H. Lawrence: Reminiscences and Correspondence*
4 Letter from Thirroul, 28 May 1922
5 Lawrence: *Aaron's Rod*
6 Lawrence: *Kangaroo*

CHAPTER 16

1 Luhan: *Lorenzo in Taos*
2 Luhan: *Lorenzo in Taos*
3 Frieda Lawrence: *Not I, But the Wind* . . .
4 Lawrence: *New Mexico* in *Selected Essays*
5 Moore: *The Intelligent Heart*

CHAPTER 17

1 Frieda Lawrence: *Not I, But the Wind* . . .
2 See also Jean Franco: *The Modern Culture of Latin America*
3 Lawrence: *Phoenix*

CHAPTER 18

1 Lea: *The Life of John Middleton Murry*
2 Frieda Lawrence: *The Memoirs and Correspondence*
3 Carswell: *The Savage Pilgrimage*. Mrs Carswell draws attention to the short story *The Border Line* in connection with this
4 Letter of 21 November 1957 to the actress Nancy Kelly. Miss Kelly played the main character, based on Frieda, in Huxley's play, *The Genius and the Goddess*
5 *A Letter from Germany*, 1924
6 Brooke: *Queen of the Headhunters*

CHAPTER 19

1 Luhan: *Lorenzo in Taos*
2 Brett: *Lawrence and Brett*
3 Brett: *Lawrence and Brett*
4 Frieda Lawrence: *Not I, But the Wind* . . .
5 Nehls, Volume 3
6 Murry: *Reminiscences of D. H. Lawrence*

CHAPTER 20

1 Frieda Lawrence: *Not I, But the Wind* . . .
2 Nehls, Volume 3

3 Letter to Baroness von Richthofen, 4 April 1926
4 Aldington: *Pinorman*
5 Letter to E. D. McDonald, 16 July 1926

CHAPTER 21

1 Huxley: *Two or Three Graces*
2 Information supplied to the author by Mrs Barbara Barr
3 Schoenberner: *Confessions of a European Intellectual*
4 Frieda Lawrence: *The Memoirs and Correspondence.* The letter, undated, was probably written before the outbreak of war

CHAPTER 22

1 *Horizon* II (No. 10, October 1940)
2 See the detailed account by Philip Trotter, part-owner of the Warren Gallery, published in Nehls, Volume 3
3 Letter to Orioli, 2 August 1929
4 Frieda Lawrence: *Not I, But the Wind* ... Information supplied to the author by Mrs Barbara Barr

CHAPTER 23

1 Aldous Huxley in a letter to E. W. Tedlock, 24 September 1959 (*The Memoirs and Correspondence*)
2 The author is indebted to Mrs Barbara Barr for this information
3 This account of the visit to Pieve di Teco, the ensuing stay in Baden-Baden and Barbara's illness is based on information very kindly supplied to the author by Mrs Barbara Barr
4 Aldington: *Pinorman*

CHAPTER 24

1 Letter from Vence, 28 April 1930, published in part in *The Memoirs and Correspondence*
2 Letter to Mrs Flora Strousse, 15 October 1932
3 Frieda Lawrence: *The Memoirs and Correspondence*
4 Frieda Lawrence: *The Memoirs and Correspondence*
5 Brett: *My Long and Beautiful Journey*, published in *South Dakota Review*, Summer 1967, vol. 5, No. 2
6 Claire Morrill: *Three Women of Taos*, published in *South Dakota Review*, vol. 2, No. 2
7 Frieda Lawrence: *The Memoirs and Correspondence*
8 See Frieda's obituary of Raymond Otis in *The Memoirs and Correspondence*
9 This account of the transfer of Lawrence's ashes is based on information supplied by Mrs Barbara Barr, as well as on Frieda's description of it (*The Memoirs and Correspondence*) and on Moore's *The Intelligent Heart*
10 Letter to Sir Julian Huxley, 3 June 1937
11 Undated letter in *The Memoirs and Correspondence*
12 Letter to Witter Bynner, 28 March 1938
13 See also Robert Craft: *With Aldous Huxley* in *Encounter*, November 1965
14 Letter to Witter Bynner, 25 July 1939

CHAPTER 25

1 Unpublished letter to Rolf Gardiner. 21 June 1947
2 Frieda Lawrence: *The Memoirs and Correspondence*
3 Angelo Nunzio Gaspero Ravagli vs. Ina Serafina Astengo Ravagli, Taos County Cause No. 4754
4 Information supplied by Montague Weekley and Mrs Barbara Barr. Also Ian Weekley: *Frieda Lawrence, a Memoir*, published privately in 1962

5 *Letters of Aldous Huxley*
6 Information supplied to the author by Mrs Barbara Barr. See also Barbara Barr: *I Look Back* in *The Twentieth Century*, London, March 1959
7 Nehls, Volume 3

CHAPTER 26

1 Rembar: *The End of Obscenity*
2 *Lady Chatterley's Lover*, Regina *v.* Penguin Books, 1960 (record of the trial at the Central Criminal Court)
3 Aldous Huxley in an interview with George Wickers and Ray Frazer in the series *Writers at Work* (*The Paris Review Interviews*, Secker & Warburg, London, 1963)

Bibliography

In the writing of this book the undermentioned provided essential information:

Frieda Lawrence: *Not I, But the Wind* ... , The Viking Press, New York, 1934; Heinemann, London, 1935
——: *The Memoirs and Correspondence*, edited by E. W. Tedlock, Heinemann, London, 1961; Knopf, New York, 1964
Heinemann, London, 1932; *The Letters of D. H. Lawrence*, edited by Aldous Huxley, The Viking Press, New York, 1932
D. H. Lawrence: *Collected Letters*, edited by Harry T. Moore, Heinemann, London, 1962; The Viking Press, New York, 1962
Harry T. Moore: *The Intelligent Heart*, Heinemann, London, 1955; Farrar, Straus, New York, 1955
Edward Nehls: *D. H. Lawrence: A Composite Biography*, 3 volumes, Wisconsin University Press, Madison, 1957–59
Warren Roberts: *A Bibliography of D. H. Lawrence*, Hart-Davis, London, 1963
D. H. Lawrence: All works by him cited in this book

Acknowledgment is also made to the following:

Richard Aldington: *D. H. Lawrence: Portrait of a Genius But* ... , Heinemann, London, 1950; Duell, Sloan and Pearce, New York, 1950
——: *Pinorman*, Heinemann, London, 1954
A. Alvarez: *Beyond All This Fiddle*, Allen Lane, The Penguin Press, London, 1968
Cynthia Asquith: *Remember and Be Glad*, Barrie, London, 1952; Scribners, New York, 1952
——: *Diaries 1915–1918*, Hutchinson, London, 1968; Knopf, New York, 1969
Margot Asquith (Countess of Oxford and Asquith): *Autobiography*, Eyre & Spottiswoode, London, 1962; Houghton Mifflin, Boston, 1963
Dorothy Brett: *Lawrence and Brett: A Friendship*, Lippincott, Philadelphia, 1933
Earl and Achsah Brewster: *D. H. Lawrence: Reminiscences and Correspondence*, Martin Secker, London, 1934
Sylvia Brooke: *Queen of the Headhunters*, Sidgwick & Jackson, London, 1970
Witter Bynner: *Journey with Genius*, John Day, New York, 1951
Catherine Carswell: *The Savage Pilgrimage*, Secker & Warburg, London, 1932
Robert Cecil: *Life in Edwardian England*, Batsford, London, 1969; Putnam, New York, 1969
H. M. Daleski: *The Forked Flame*, Chatto & Windus, London, 1965; Northwestern University Press, Evanston, Illinois, 1965
Emile Delavenay: *D. H. Lawrence, l'homme et la genèse de son oeuvre*, C. Klincksieck, Paris, 1969
Loval Dickson: *H. G. Wells, His Turbulent Life and Times*, Macmillan, London, 1969
E. T. (Jessie Chambers): *D. H. Lawrence: A Personal Record*, Cape, London, 1935
Jean Franco: *The Modern Culture of Latin America. Society and the Artist*. Penguin, Harmondsworth, 1970; Praeger, New York, 1967.
Leonhard Frank: *Links wo das Herz ist*, Nymphenburger Verlag, Munich, 1952; *Heart on the Left*, Barker, London, 1954

David Garnett: *The Golden Echo*, Chatto & Windus, London, 1953; Harcourt Brace, New York, 1954

——: *The Flowers of the Forest*, Chatto & Windus, London, 1955; Harcourt Brace, New York, 1956

Genealogisches Handbuch des Adels: Freiherrliche Häuser B, Band 3, 1963

Carolyn G. Heilbrun: *The Garnett Family*, Allen & Unwin, London, 1961; Macmillan, New York, 1961

Letters of Aldous Huxley, edited by Grover Smith, Chatto & Windus, London, 1969; Harper and Row, New York, 1970

Laura Archera Huxley: *This Timeless Moment*, Chatto & Windus, London, 1969; Farrar, Straus and Giroux, New York, 1968

D. H. Lawrence: *Lawrence in Love, Letters to Louie Burrows*, edited by J. T. Boulton, University of Nottingham, 1968

——: *Letters to Martin Secker 1911–1930*, privately published, London, 1970

F. A. Lea: *The Life of John Middleton Murry*, Methuen, London, 1959; Oxford University Press, New York, 1960

F. R. Leavis: *D. H. Lawrence, Novelist*, Chatto & Windus, London, 1957

M. D. Luhan: *Lorenzo in Taos*, Knopf, New York, 1932

Compton Mackenzie: *My Life and Times, Octaves IV and V*, Chatto & Windus, London, 1965

Frank MacShane: *The Life and Work of Ford Madox Ford*, Routledge, London, 1966; Horizon Press, New York, 1965

Steven Marcus: *The Other Victorians: A Study of Sexuality and Pornography in Mid-Nineteenth Century England*, Weidenfeld & Nicolson, London, 1969

C. A. Marsden: *Nottinghamshire*, Hale, London, 1953

Knud Merrild: *A Poet and Two Painters*, Routledge, London, 1938; The Viking Press, New York, 1939

J. Middleton Murry: *Son of Woman*, Cape, London, 1931

——: *Reminiscences of D. H. Lawrence*, Cape, London, 1933; Henry Holt, New York, 1933

——: *Between Two Worlds*, Cape, London, 1935; Messner, New York, 1936

Mary Middleton Murry: *To Keep Faith*, Constable, London, 1959

Morrell: *Ottoline, The Early Memoirs of Lady Ottoline Morrell*, ed. Hardy, Faber & Faber, London, 1963

Harold Perkin: *The Origins of Modern English Society 1780–1880*, Routledge & Kegan Paul, London, 1969

Charles Rembar: *The End of Obscenity*, Deutsch, London, 1969; Random House, New York, 1968

C. H. Rolph: *The Trial of Lady Chatterley*, Penguin Books, Harmondsworth, 1961

Bertrand Russell: *Autobiography, 1st and 2nd vol.*, Allen & Unwin, London, 1967, 1968; Little Brown, Boston, 1968

Franz Schoenberner: *Confessions of a European Intellectual*, Macmillan, New York, 1946

Rebecca West: *Ending in Earnest: A Literary Log*, Doubleday, Doran, New York, 1931

Index

Bynner, Witter (1881–1968), 183, 191, 192, 193, 194, 195, 203, 252, 254, 258, 259, 261n, 264, 273, 274, 278

Byrne, Sir Laurence (1896–1965), 288

Byron, Lord George Gordon (1788–1824), 32–3, 107n

Campbell, Gordon (*afterwards* Lord Glenavy) (1885–1963), 109

Cannan, Gilbert (1884–1955), 120, 165–6

Cannan, Mary (Mary Ansell, Mrs J. Barrie), 120, 165–6, 170, 204, 221

Carlyle, Thomas (1795–1881), 58, 62

Carossa, Hans (1878–1956), 233–4

Carswell, Catherine (*née* MacFarlane; Mrs H. P. M. Jackson, Mrs D. Carswell) (1879–1946), 112, 119, 139–40, 146, 199, 200, 204, 216, 226, 240, 260

Carswell, Donald (1882–1940), 199, 216

Carswell, John Patrick (1918–), 199

Cavendish-Bentinck, Lady Ottoline. *See* Morrell, Lady Ottoline

Chambers, Alan (1882–1946), 49–50

Chambers, Edmund (1863–1946), 47

Chambers, J. David (1898–1970), 47, 48

Chambers, Jessie (Mrs J. R. Wood) (1887–1944), 47–9, 50–2, 53, 55, 58, 60, 61, 62, 64, 65, 66, 68–9, 71–2, 75, 90, 91–2, 93, 226

Chambers, May (Mrs W. Holbrook) (1883–1955), 75

Chaplin, Charlie (1889–), 88, 274

Chaworth, Mary, 33, 43

Chaworth, William, 32–3

Chekhov, Anton (1860–1904), 70, 102

Chesterton, Gilbert Keith (1874–1936), 60, 95

Christenberry, Robert K. (1899–), 285

Churchill, (Sir) Winston Spencer (1874–1965), 104

Clarke, Ada. *See* Lawrence, Ada

Conrad, Joseph (Korzeniowski) (1856–1924), 59

Corke, Helen (1882–), 56–7, 67, 68, 71, 87

Cortez, Fernando (1485–1547), 192

Crippen, Henry Hawley (1861–1910), 224

Crosby, Harry Grew (1898–1929), 245

Cyriax, Antonia (Anjuta), 95, 97

Darrieux, Danielle, 283

Darwin, Charles (1809–82), 135, 227

Davies, Rhys (1903–), 243–4, 245, 253

Dax, Alice, 53–4, 141, 266

Day Lewis, Cecil (1904–72), 287

Diaghilev, Sergei (1872–1929), 156

Dieterle, William (1893–), 274

Dodge, Mabel. *See* Luhan, Mabel Dodge Sterne

Doolittle, Hilda ("H.D.", Mrs R. Aldington) (1886–1961), 113

Dostoevsky, Fyodor Mikhailovich (1821–81), 69, 70, 84, 104

Douglas, Lord Alfred (1870–1945), 163

Douglas, Norman (1868–1952), 161, 163, 164–5, 167, 169, 172–3, 224, 248, 255, 256

Dowson, Will, 33, 77, 90

Draper, Albert, 133

Dreiser, Theodore (1871–1945), 286

Duckworth, Gerald (1871–1937), 88

Duncan, Isadora (1878–1927), 161, 176, 266

Eastman, Max (1883–1969), 176

Eder, Dr David (1866–1936), 111–12, 136, 181–2

Edward VII, King (1841–1910), 18, 136, 165

Edward VIII, King. *See* Wales, Prince of

Eichendorff, Joseph von (1788–1857), 22
Eisner, Kurt (1867–1919), 159
Elbe, Anna von, 17–18
Eliot, George (Mary Ann Evans) (1819–80), 30
Eliot, Thomas Stearns (1888–1965), 61, 200
Eliot, Vivien (*née* Vivienne Haigh-Wood) (1888–1947), 200
Esher, Viscount (1852–1930), 130, 206
Evans, John, 189

Farr, Florence, 66–7
Feltrelline, Signora, 90
Flaubert, Gustave (1821–80), 53
Ford, Madox Ford. *See* Hueffer, Ford Madox
Forster, Edward Morgan (1879–1970), 287
Francis, Joseph I (1830–1916), 192
Frank, Leonard (1882–1961), 34, 36
Freeman, Bessie, 186
Freud, Sigmund (1856–1939), 36, 39, 75, 99, 111, 112, 136, 190
Friedrich III (1831–88), 172
Friedrich, Wilhelm IV (1795–1861), 17

Gallois, Lilli, 250, 257
Galsworthy, John (1867–1933), 58, 69, 151
Ganson, Charles, 176
Ganson, Mabel. *See* Luhan, Mabel
Gardiner, Gerald (*afterwards* Lord Gardiner) (1900–), 2
Garnett, Constance (1862–1946), 69–70, 84, 95, 107
Garnett, David ("Bunny") (1892–), 70, 84–5, 87, 88, 99–100, 117, 156–7, 241, 253
Garnett, Edward (1868–1937), 69, 70, 77, 83, 84, 87, 88–9, 90, 93, 94, 95, 97, 98, 99, 109, 117, 136
Garnett, Richard (1835–1906), 69
Gaudier-Brzeska, Henri (1891–1915), 103

Geldern, Count, 192
George VI, King (1895–1952), 206
Gertler, Mark (1892–1939), 124, 146, 151, 156, 216, 248
Glasco, Joe, 284
Goethe, Johann Wolfgang von (1749–1832), 32
Gogol, Nikolay (1809–52), 70
Goldman, Emma (1869–1940), 258
Goncharov, Ivan (1812–91), 70
Gonzaga, Lodovico, 271
Gordon-Crotch, Martha, 257–8
Gorki, Maxim (1868–1936), 169
Goyen, Bill, 284
Grant, Duncan (1885–), 123, 156
Gray, Cecil (1895–1951), 149, 150, 151
Greene, Graham (1904–), 169
Griffith-Jones, Mervyn (1909–), 1–3, 287
Gross, Dr Otto, 34, 35–8, 39, 77, 257
Grosz, George (1893–1959), 246

Haeckel, Ernst (1834–1919), 53
Hardy, Thomas (1840–1928), 59
Harrison, Austin (1873–1928), 63
Hauptmann, Gerhart (1862–1946), 19
Hawk, Michael, 209
Hawk, Rachel, 209, 284
Hedin, Sven (1865–1952), 5
Heinemann, William (1863–1920), 63, 84
Hemingway, Ernest (1898–1961), 59
Herzen, Aleksandr (1812–70), 70
Heseltine, Philip ("Peter Warlock") (1894–1930), 130, 149, 175
Hitler, Adolf (1889–1945), 127, 145, 159n, 233, 273, 275
Holbrook, William (1884–), 75
Hopkin, William E. (1862–1951), 226
Howe, Dr, 284
Hueffer, Ford Madox (Ford Madox Ford) (1873–1939), 58–61, 62, 63, 66, 67, 69, 122, 143
Hueffer, Francis (Franz Hüffer) (1845–88), 58

Richthofen, Freiin Frieda von—*cont.*
sixtieth birthday, 274; interrogated by immigration officer, 275; despises Hitler, 275–6; spends winters in Port Isabel, 277; reunion with Johanna, 277; exchange of letters with Karl von Marbahr, 278–9; correspondence with Murry, 279; marries Ravagli, 279; last trip to England, 280–1; with Maria Huxley in Los Angeles, 281; portrayed as "Katy" in Huxley's *The Genius and the Goddess*, 282; meets Else Jaffe in Albuquerque, 283; temporarily paralysed, 283; visited by Barbara, 283; death, 284

Richthofen, Ferdinand von (1833–1905), 5

Richthofen, Friedrich von (1845–1915), 7–8, 9–12, 81, 160

Richthofen, Johann Ludwig von (1800–80), 7

Richthofen, Johanna von ("Nusch", *later* Frau v. Schreibershofen, Frau E. Krug) (1882–1971), 9, 10, 12–13, 14, 15, 17, 19, 30, 31, 78–9, 175, 225, 232, 277

Richthofen, Kurt von, 14–16, 17, 23

Richthofen, Ludwig Praetorius von (1770–1850), 6–7

Richthofen, Manfred von (1892–1918), 148, 151–2, 214

Richthofen, Oswald von (1847–1906), 5, 17, 19–20

Rilke, Rainer Maria (1875–1926), 158, 169

Rivera, Diego (1886–1957), 193

Robbins, Catherine ("Jane", Mrs H. G. Wells) (*d.* 1927), 115, 116

Robertson, Stewart A. (1866–1933), 63

Rosset, Barney (1922–), 286

Rousseau, Jean-Baptiste (1671–1741), 245

Russell, Bertrand (Earl Russell) (1872–1970), 123, 124, 125–7, 128, 129, 130, 180, 207

Sand, George (Dupin) (1804–76), 135

Sassoon, Siegfried (1886–1967), 123

Schiller, Friedrich (1759–1805), 13

Schloffer, Friedel (Frau Gross), 34, 35, 38

Schmidt (Faber), Samuel (*later* Praetorius) (1543–1605), 4

Schnitzler, Arthur (1862–1931), 190

Schoenberner, Franz (1892–1970), 232–4

Schopenhauer, Arthur (1788–1860), 53, 58

Schreibershofen, Max von (1864–), 30, 175

Schultheiss, Paul (*alias* Schulze, *later* Scultetus, *afterwards* Praetorius), (1521–?), 4

Seaman, Edward, 280

Seaman, Elsa. *See* Weekley, Elsa

Secker, Martin (1882–), 171, 174, 218

Seidel, Frau, 10, 13, 18

Seltzer, Thomas (1873–1943), 190

Serena, Federico, 163

Shaw, George Bernard (1856–1950), 66, 115, 116, 206

Shearman, Sir Montague (1857–1930), 156

Shelley, Percy Bysshe (1792–1822), 139

Simpson, George W., 190

Siqueiros, David Alfaro (1898–), 193

Sitwell, Sir Osbert (1892–1969), 123, 156

Sitwell, Sacheverell (1897–), 156

Smith, Philip F. T., 56

Smith, Sydney (1771–1845), 134

Snowden, Philip (1864–1937), 53, 115

Sombart, Werner, 34

Spencer, Stanley, 124

Spender, Stephen (1909–), 123, 277

Splingaert, Paul, 5

Sterne, Mabel. *See* Luhan, Mabel

Sterne, Maurice, 176

Stokowski, Leopold (1882–), 281

Strachey, Lytton (1880–1932), 124